Akira Segami

TRANSLATED BY
Satsuki Yamashita

ADAPTED BY
Nunzio DeFilippis & Christina Weir

LETTERED BY
North Market Street Graphics

BALLANTINE BOOKS · NEW YORK

A Del Rey Manga/Kodansha Trade Paperback Original

Kagetora, volume 8 copyright © 2005 by Akira Segami
English translation copyright © 2008 by Akira Segami

Published in the United States by Del Rey Books, an imprint of The Random House Publishing Group, a division of Random House, Inc., New York.

DEL REY is a registered trademark and the Del Rey colophon is a trademark of Random House, Inc.

Publication rights arranged through Kodansha Ltd.

First published in Japan in 2005 by Kodansha Ltd., Tokyo.

ISBN 978-0-345-49617-1

Printed in the United States of America

www.delreymanga.com

9 8 7 6 5 4 3 2 1

Translator—Satsuki Yamashita
Adaptor—Nunzio DeFilippis and Christina Weir
Lettering—North Market Street Graphics

Contents

Featured in Magazine Special 2005 No. 6 – No. 8
& Weekly Shonen Magazine 2005 No. 8 – No. 11

Zzzz...

KAGE

A Note from the Author

There is a theory
that Basho was a ninja.
I guess it's possible,
because he traveled really
fast. I would like to travel too,
though not that fast.
Like hot springs. Maybe I can
be a wanderer or a hermit.
But not a ninja. (laugh)

Segami

Honorifics Explained

Throughout the Del Rey Manga books, you will find Japanese honorifics left intact in the translations. For those not familiar with how the Japanese use honorifics and, more important, how they differ from American honorifics, we present this brief overview.

Politeness has always been a critical facet of Japanese culture. Ever since the feudal era, when Japan was a highly stratified society, use of honorifics—which can be defined as polite speech that indicates relationship or status—has played an essential role in the Japanese language. When addressing someone in Japanese, an honorific usually takes the form of a suffix attached to one's name (example: "Asuna-san"), is used as a title at the end of one's name, or appears in place of the name itself (example: "Negi-sensei," or simply "Sensei!").

Honorifics can be expressions of respect or endearment. In the context of manga and anime, honorifics give insight into the nature of the relationship between characters. Many English translations leave out these important honorifics, and therefore distort the feel of the original Japanese. Because Japanese honorifics contain nuances that English honorifics lack, it is our policy at Del Rey not to translate them. Here, instead, is a guide to some of the honorifics you may encounter in Del Rey Manga.

-san: This is the most common honorific and is equivalent to Mr., Miss, Ms., or Mrs. It is the all-purpose honorific and can be used in any situation where politeness is required.

-sama: This is one level higher than "-san," and it is used to confer great respect.

-dono: This comes from the word "tono," which means "lord." It is an even higher level than "-sama" and confers utmost respect.

-kun: This suffix is used at the end of boys' names to express familiarity or endearment. It is also sometimes used by men among friends, or when addressing someone younger or of a lower station.

-chan: This is used to express endearment, mostly toward girls. It is also used for little boys, pets, and even among lovers. It gives a sense of childish cuteness.

Bozu: This is an informal way to refer to a boy, similar to the English terms "kid" and "squirt."

**Sempai/
Senpai:** This title suggests that the addressee is one's senior in a group or organization. It is most often used in a school setting, where underclassmen refer to their upperclassmen as "sempai." It can also be used in the workplace, such as when a newer employee addresses an employee who has seniority in the company.

Kohai: This is the opposite of "sempai" and is used toward underclassmen in school or newcomers in the workplace. It connotes that the addressee is of a lower station.

Sensei: Literally meaning "one who has come before," this title is used for teachers, doctors, or masters of any profession or art.

[blank]: This is usually forgotten in these lists, but it is perhaps the most significant difference between Japanese and English. The lack of honorific means that the speaker has permission to address the person in a very intimate way. Usually, only family, spouses, or very close friends have this kind of permission. Known as yobisute, it can be gratifying when someone who has earned the intimacy starts to call one by one's name without an honorific. But when that intimacy hasn't been earned, it can be very insulting.

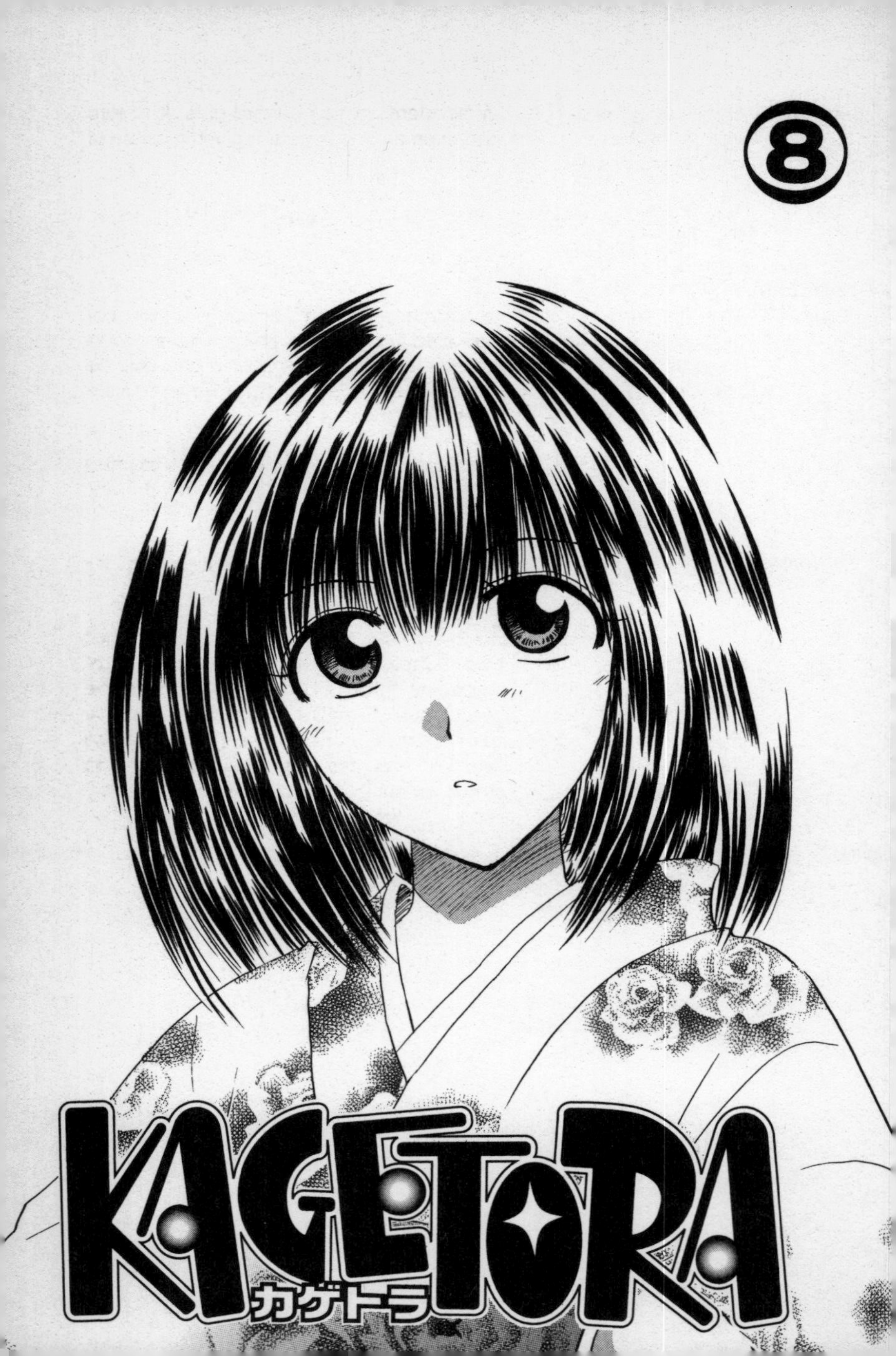
8
KAGETORA
カゲトラ

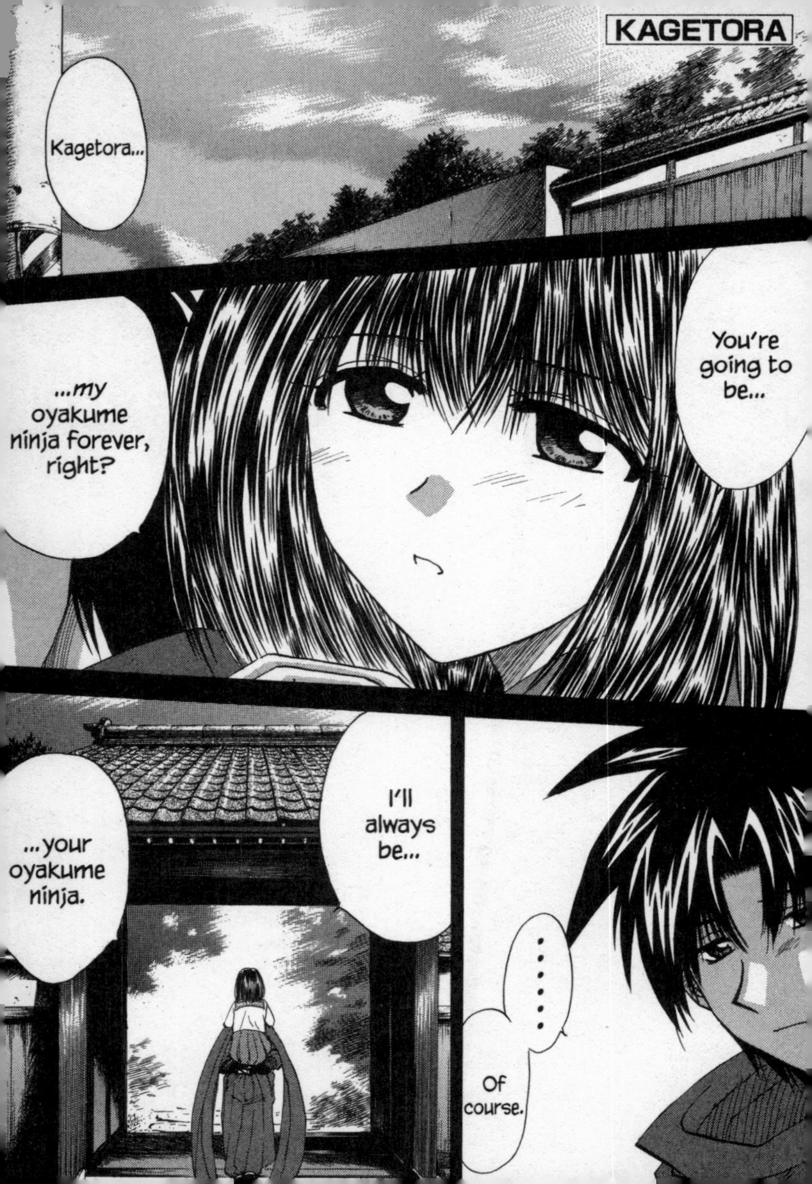
Kagetora...
You're going to be...
...my oyakume ninja forever, right?
......
Of course.
I'll always be...
...your oyakume ninja.

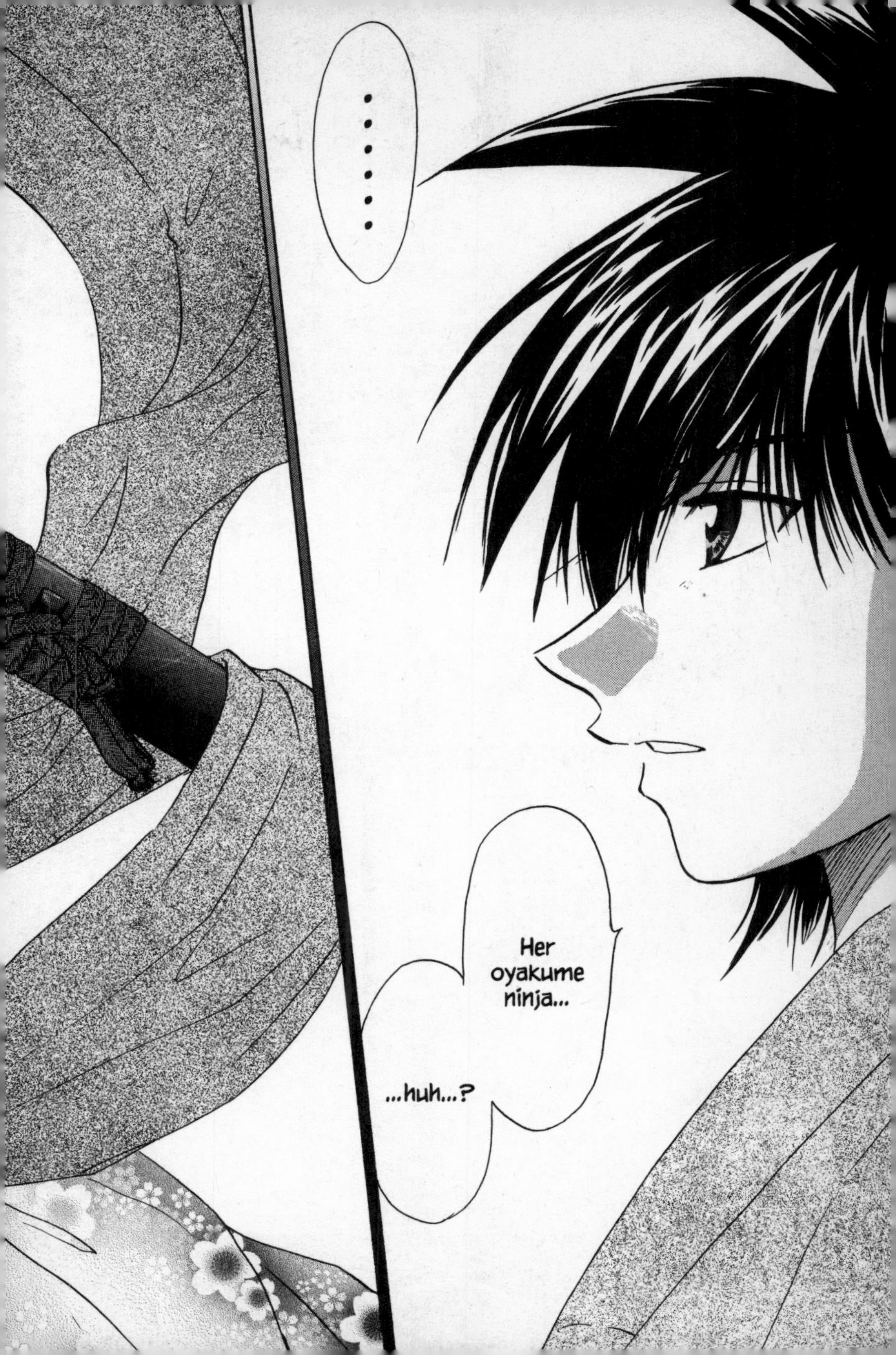
......
Her oyakume ninja...
...huh...?

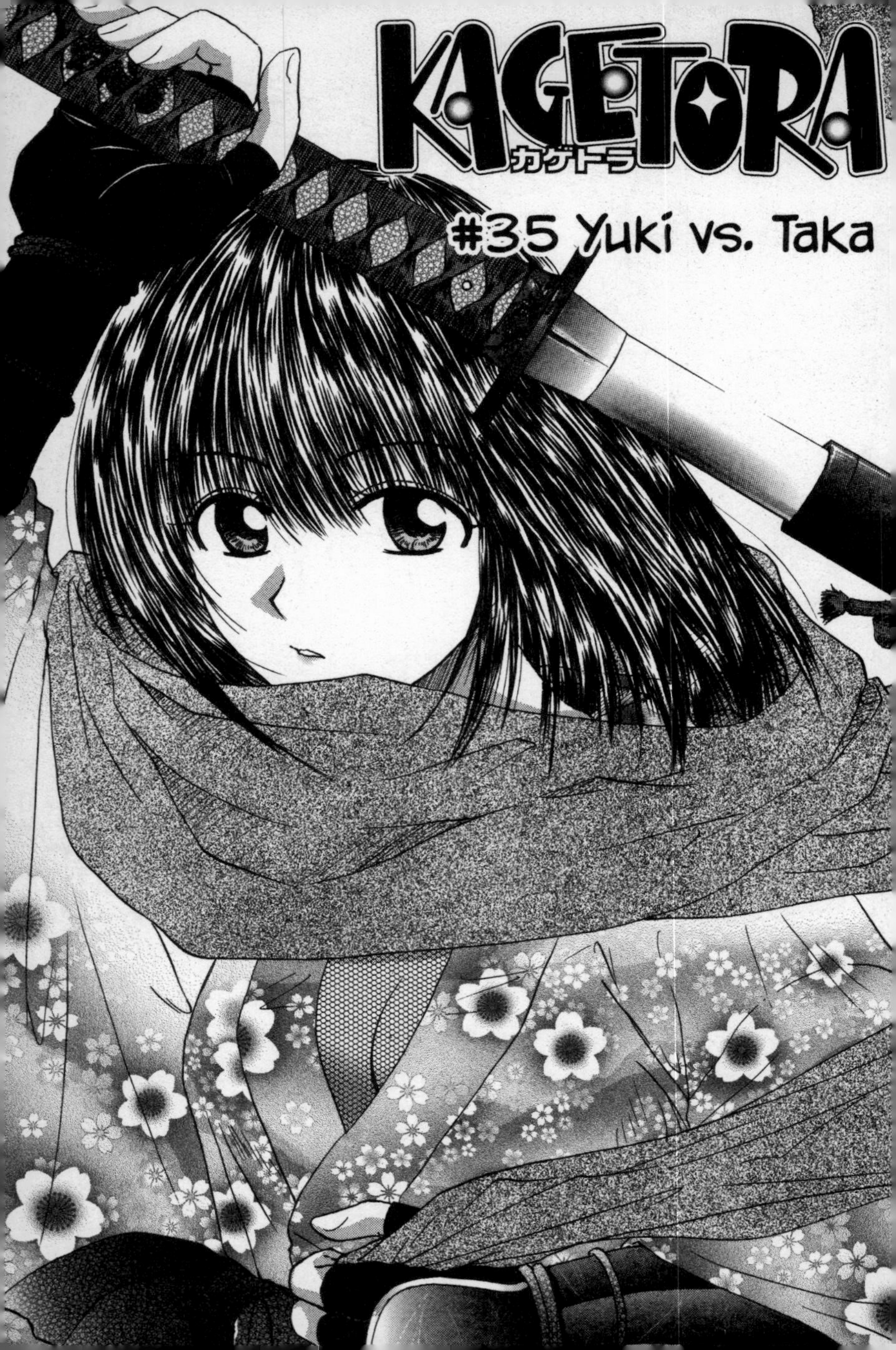
KAGETORA
カゲトラ
#35 Yuki vs. Taka

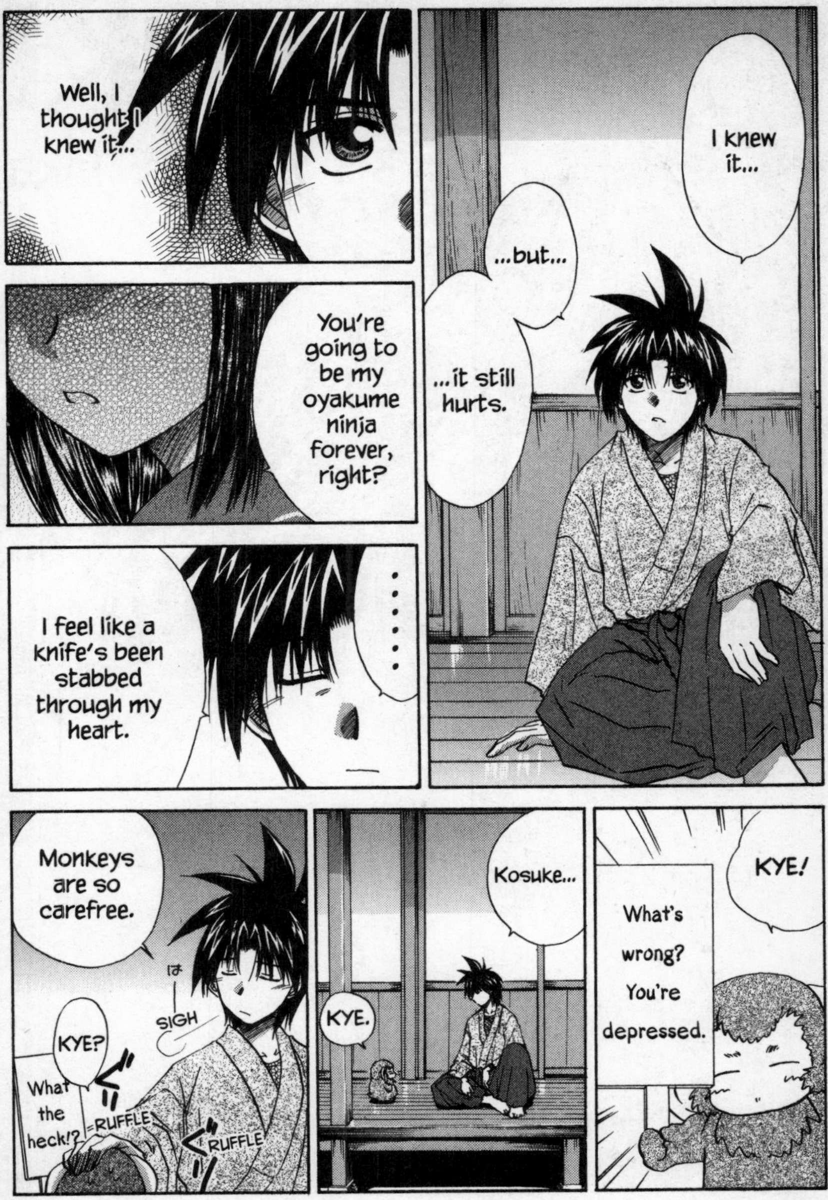
I knew it...
...but...
...it still hurts.
Well, I thought I knew it...
You're going to be my oyakume ninja forever, right?
......
I feel like a knife's been stabbed through my heart.
KYE!
What's wrong? You're depressed.
Kosuke...
KYE.
Monkeys are so carefree.
は
SIGH
KYE?
RUFFLE
RUFFLE
What the heck!?

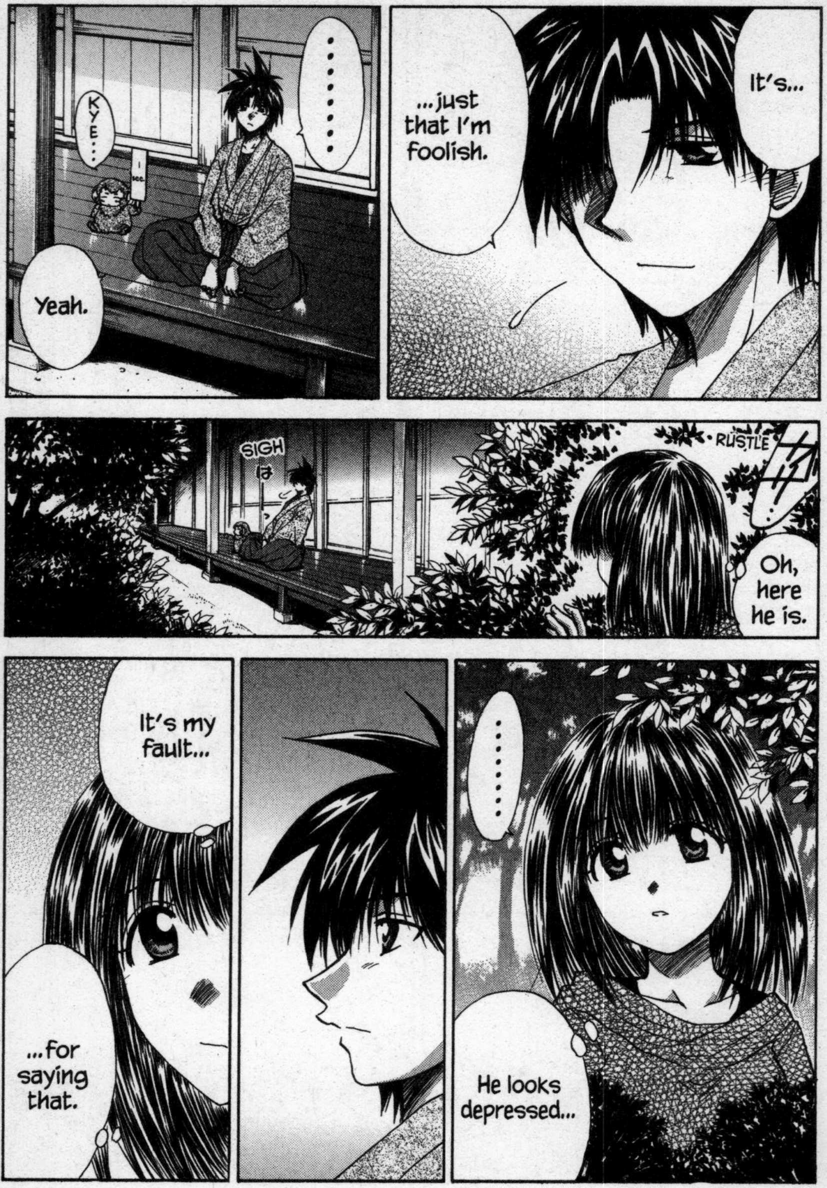
It's...
...just that I'm foolish.
......
KYE...
I see.
Yeah.
RUSTLE
Oh, here he is.
SIGH
は
......
He looks depressed...
It's my fault...
...for saying that.

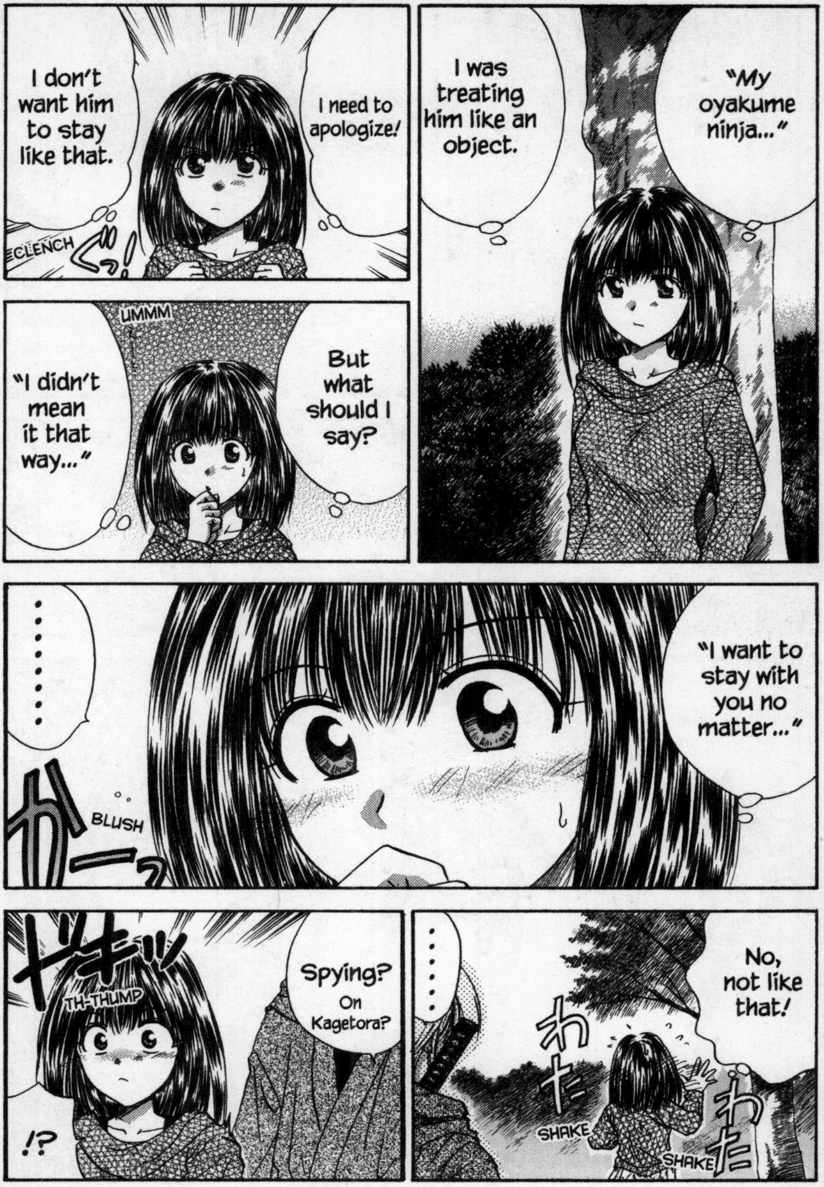
"My oyakume ninja..."
I was treating him like an object.
I need to apologize!
I don't want him to stay like that.
CLENCH
UMMM
But what should I say?
"I didn't mean it that way..."
"I want to stay with you no matter..."
......
BLUSH
No, not like that!
......
SHAKE
SHAKE
Spying? On Kagetora?
TH-THUMP
!?

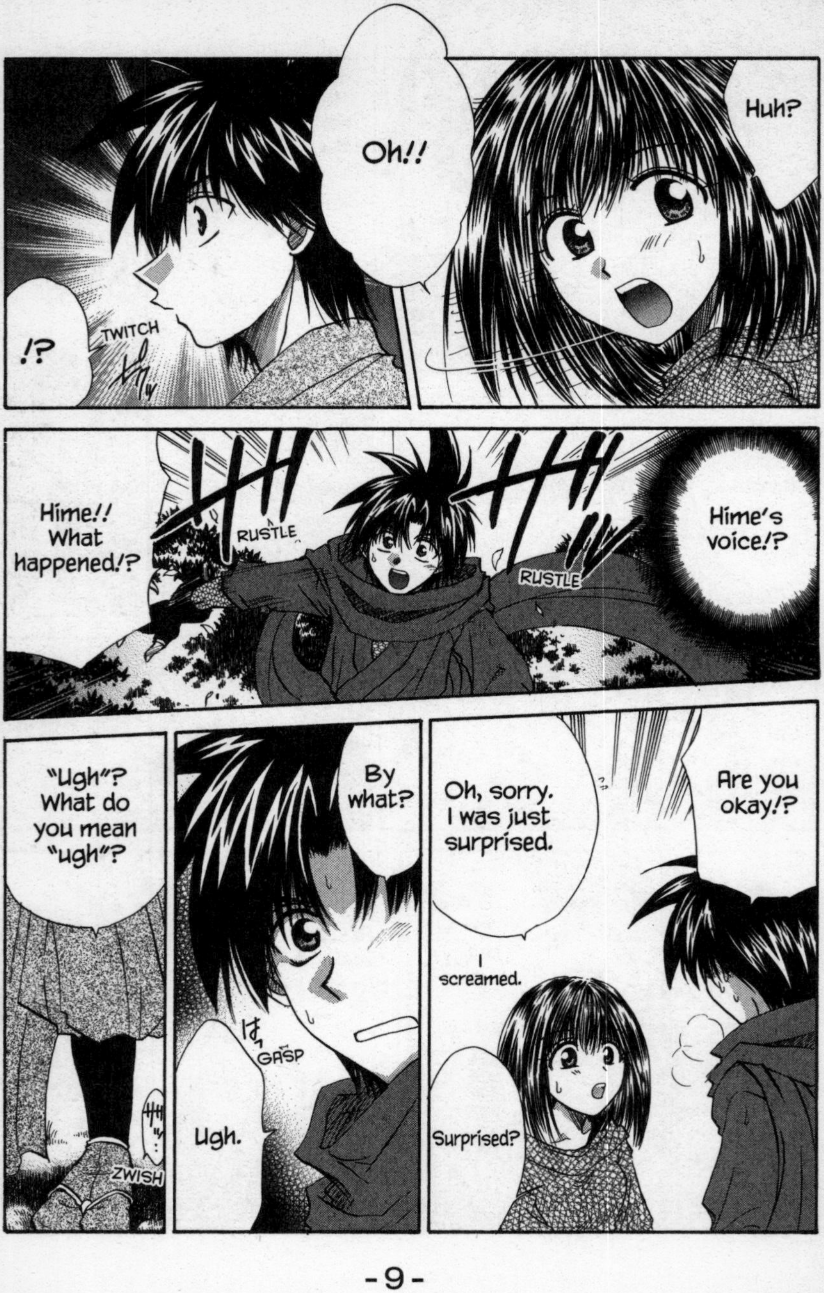

Huh?
Oh!!
TWITCH
!?
Hime's voice!?
RUSTLE
RUSTLE
Hime!! What happened!?
Are you okay!?
Oh, sorry. I was just surprised.
I screamed.
Surprised?
By what?
GASP
Ugh.
"Ugh"? What do you mean "ugh"?
ZWISH

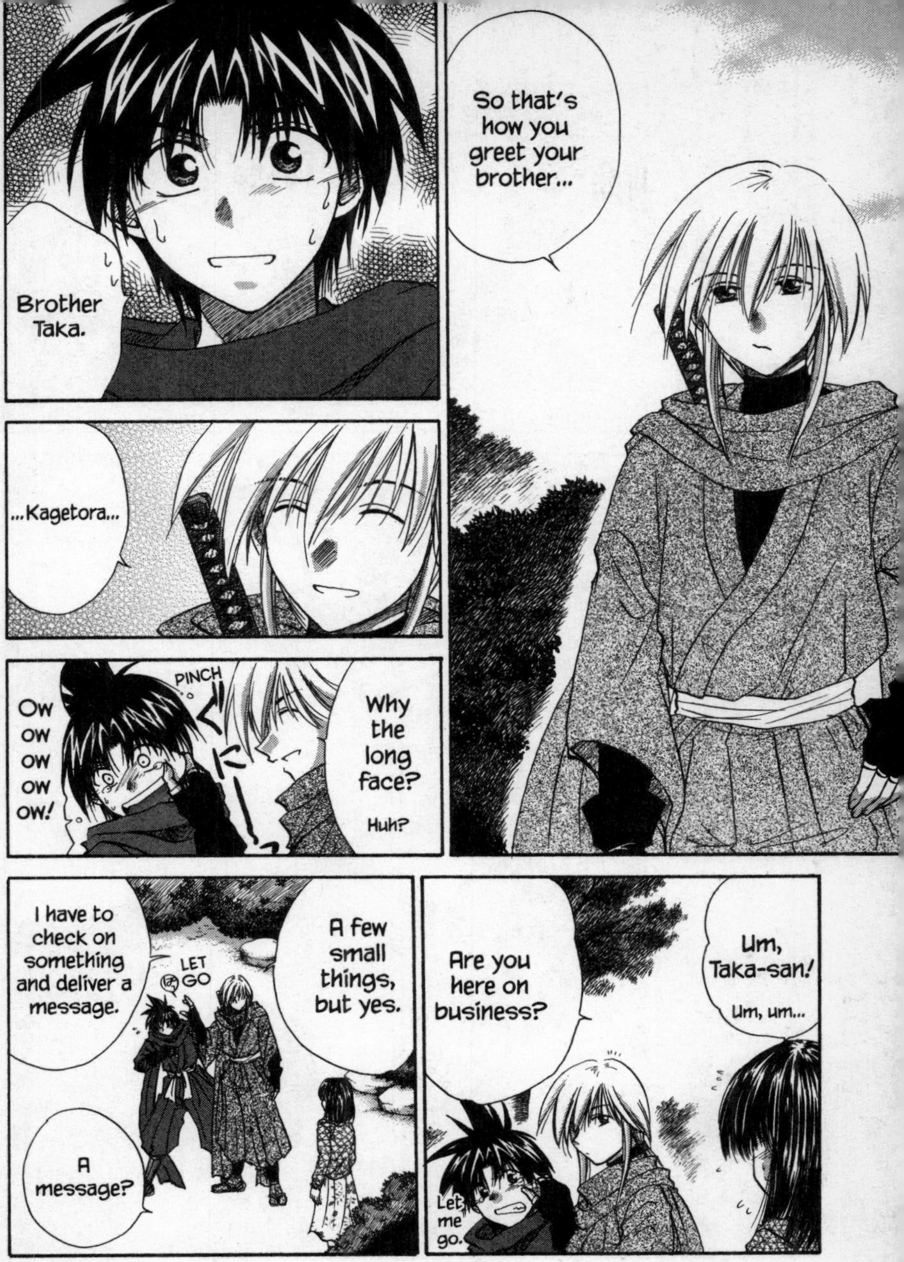
So that's how you greet your brother...
Brother Taka.
...Kagetora...
Why the long face?
Huh?
PINCH
Ow ow ow ow ow!
Um, Taka-san!
Um, um...
Are you here on business?
Let me go.
A few small things, but yes.
I have to check on something and deliver a message.
LET GO
A message?

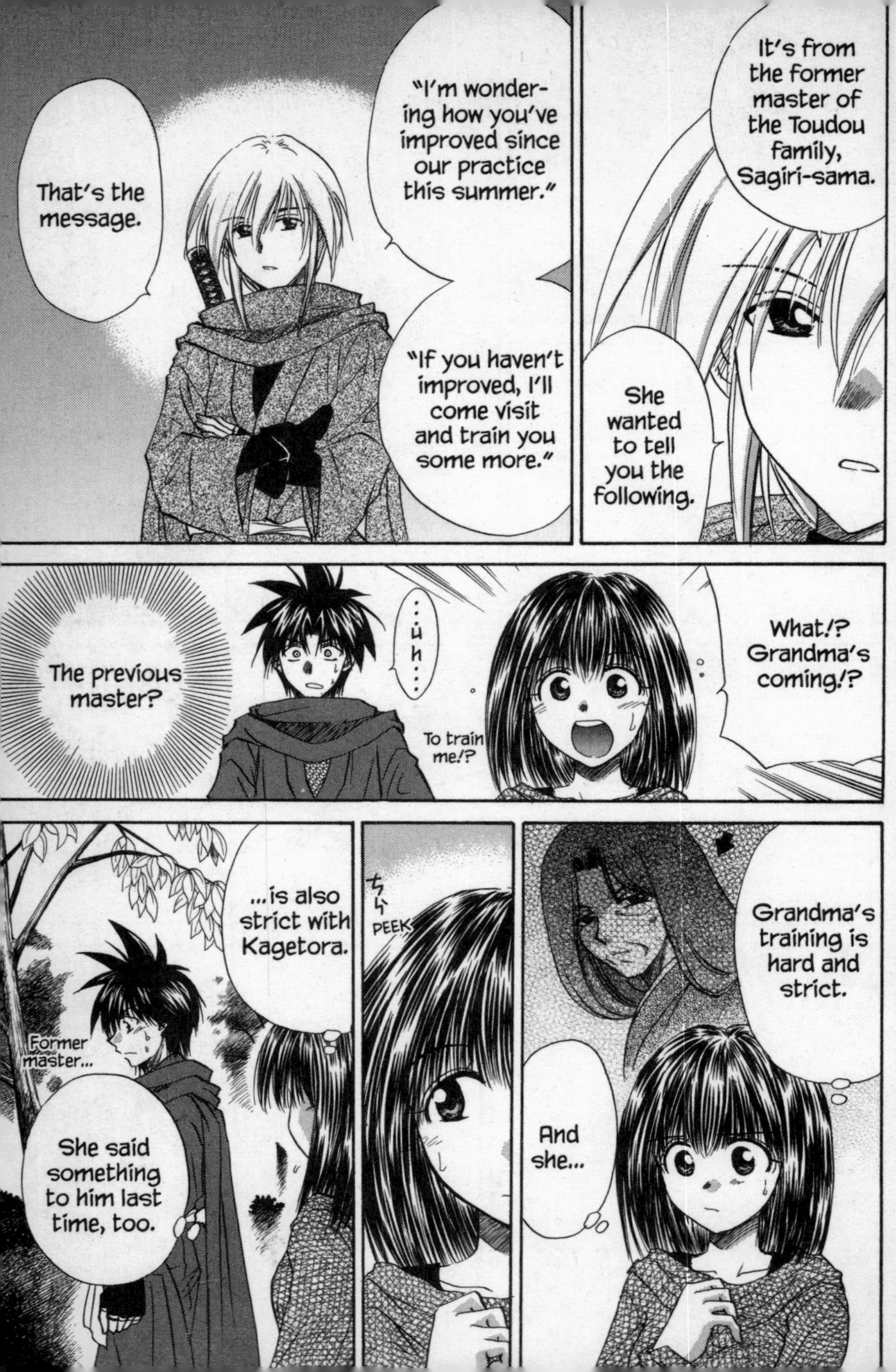
It's from the former master of the Toudou family, Sagiri-sama.
She wanted to tell you the following.
"I'm wondering how you've improved since our practice this summer."
"If you haven't improved, I'll come visit and train you some more."
That's the message.
What!? Grandma's coming!?
...uh...
To train me!?
The previous master?
Grandma's training is hard and strict.
And she...
PEEK
...is also strict with Kagetora.
Former master...
She said something to him last time, too.

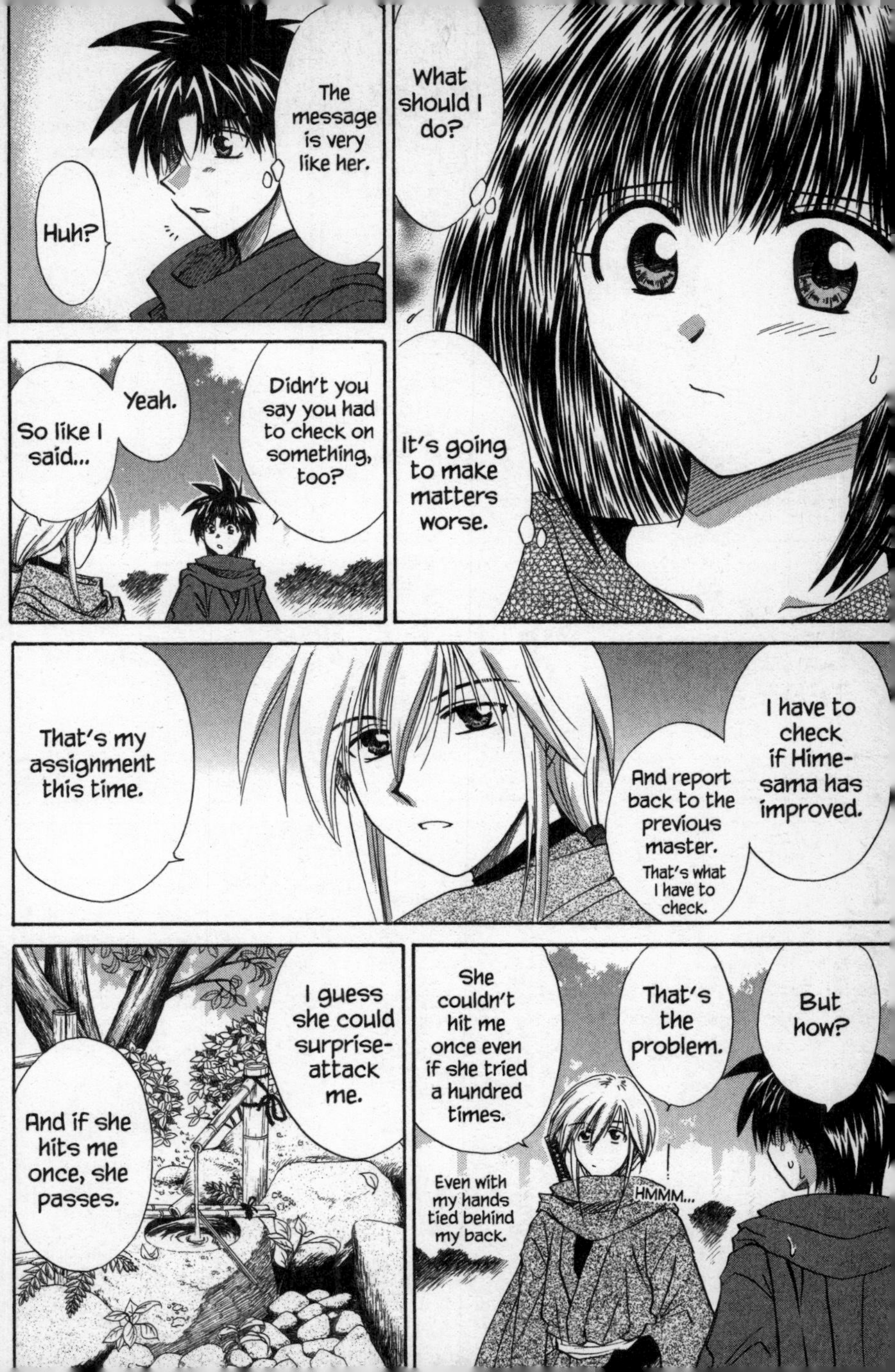
What should I do?
It's going to make matters worse.
The message is very like her.
Huh?
Didn't you say you had to check on something, too?
Yeah.
So like I said...
I have to check if Hime-sama has improved.
And report back to the previous master.
That's what I have to check.
That's my assignment this time.
But how?
That's the problem.
She couldn't hit me once even if she tried a hundred times.
HMMM...
Even with my hands tied behind my back.
I guess she could surprise-attack me.
And if she hits me once, she passes.

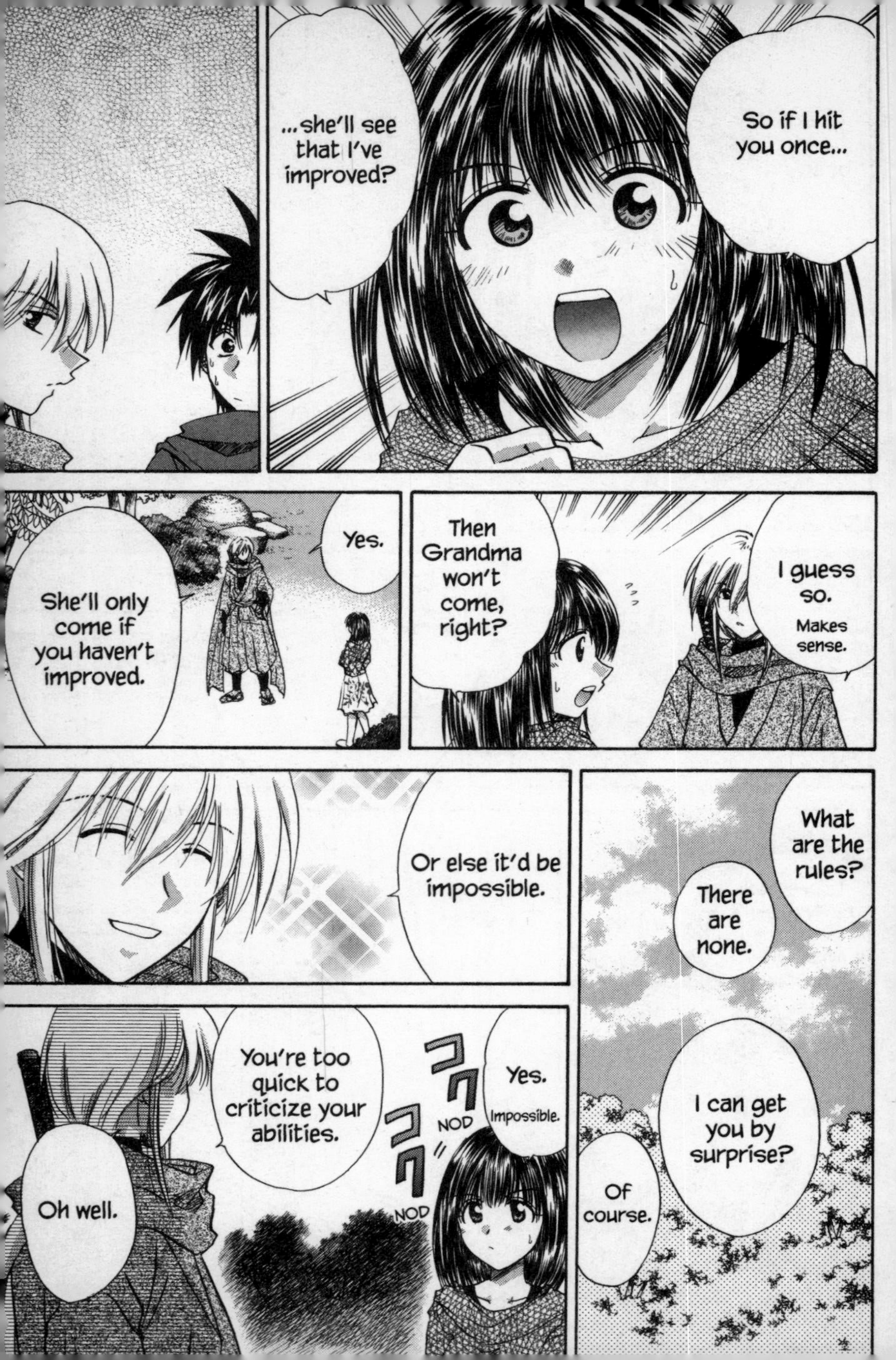
So if I hit you once...
...she'll see that I've improved?
I guess so.
Makes sense.
Then Grandma won't come, right?
Yes.
She'll only come if you haven't improved.
What are the rules?
There are none.
I can get you by surprise?
Of course.
Or else it'd be impossible.
Yes.
Impossible.
NOD
NOD
You're too quick to criticize your abilities.
Oh well.

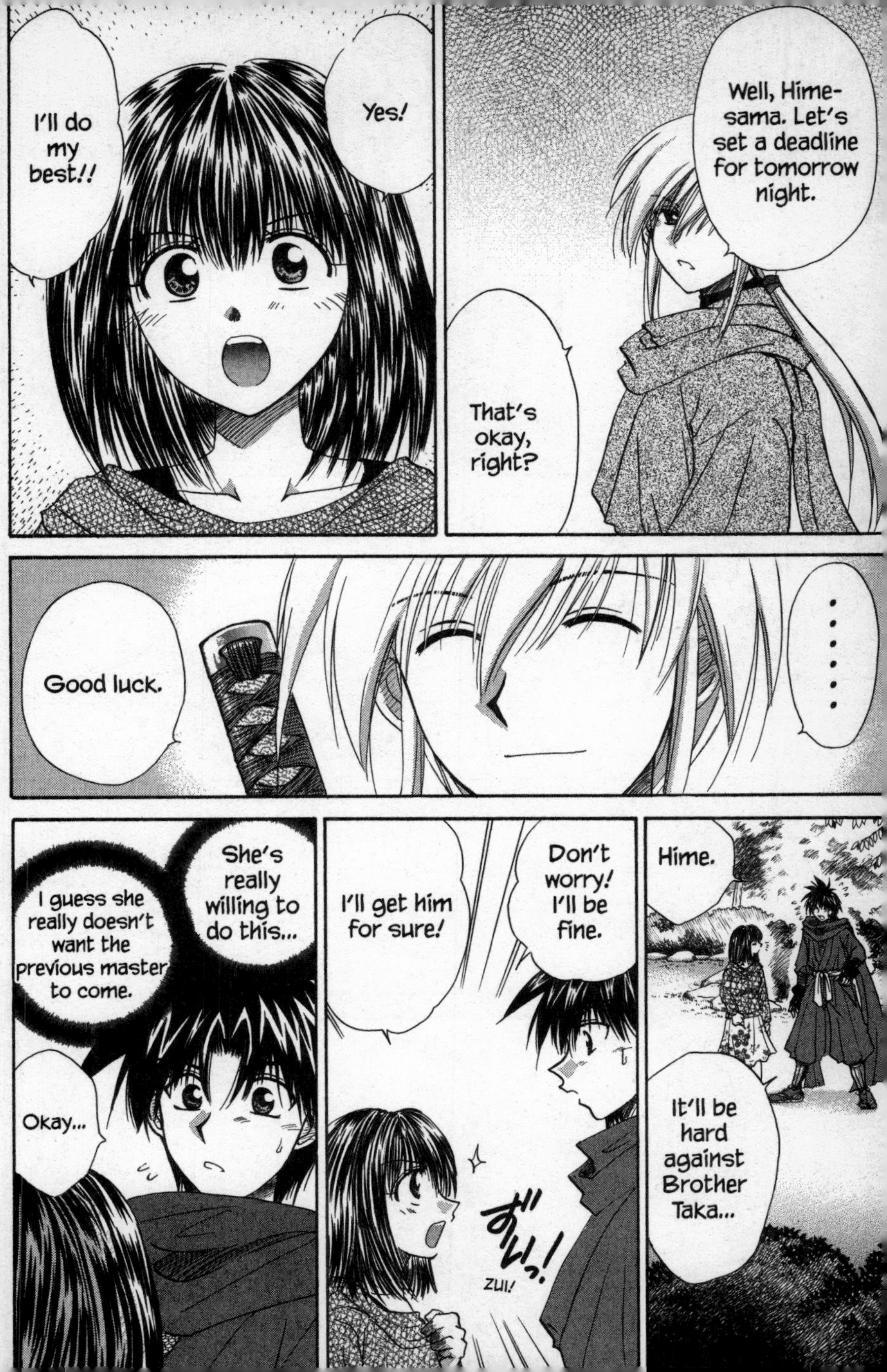
Well, Hime-sama. Let's set a deadline for tomorrow night.
That's okay, right?
Yes!
I'll do my best!!
......
Good luck.
Hime.
It'll be hard against Brother Taka...
Don't worry! I'll be fine.
I'll get him for sure!
ずいっ!
ZUI!
She's really willing to do this...
I guess she really doesn't want the previous master to come.
Okay...

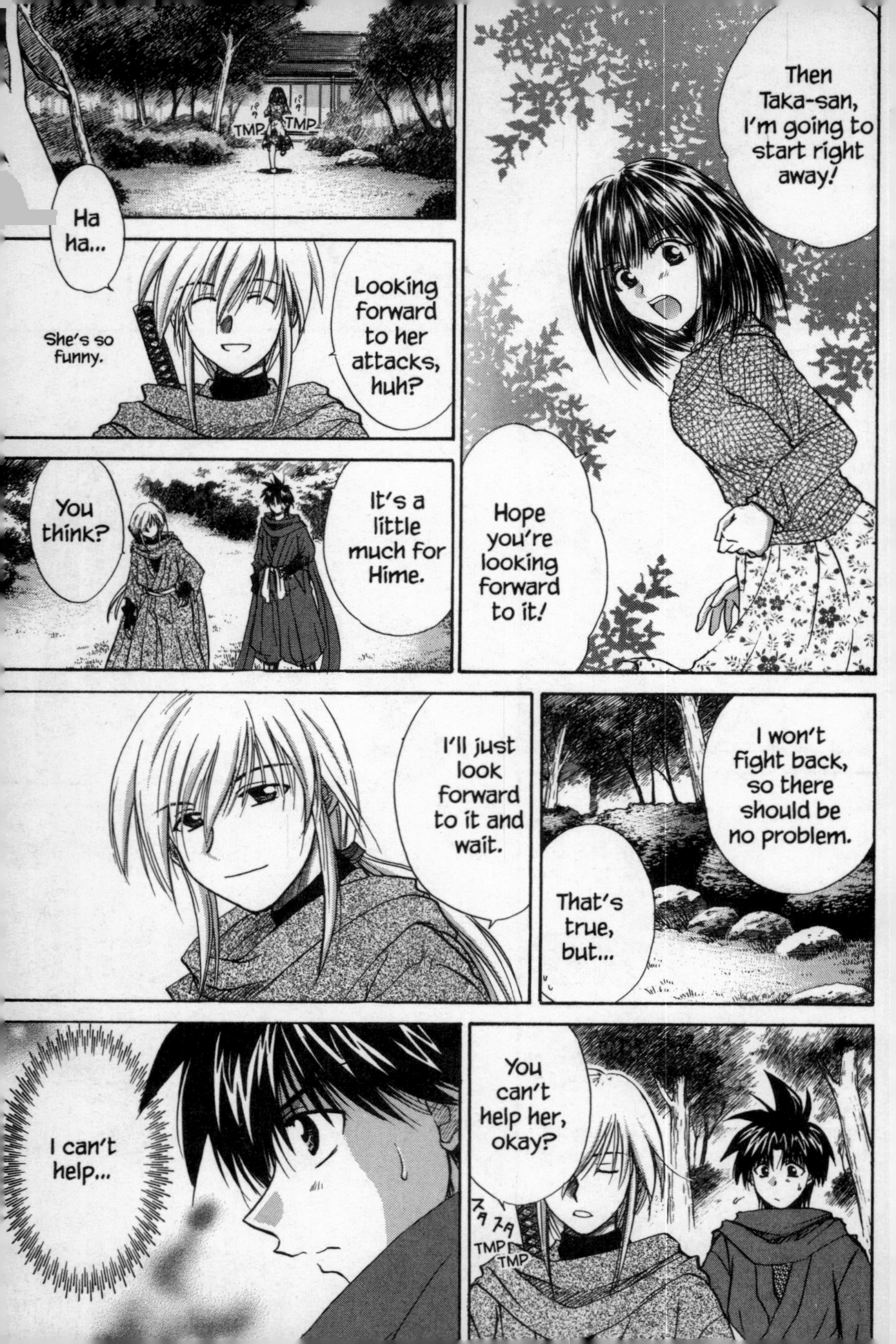
Then Taka-san, I'm going to start right away!
Hope you're looking forward to it!
TMP TMP
Ha ha...
Looking forward to her attacks, huh?
She's so funny.
It's a little much for Hime.
You think?
I won't fight back, so there should be no problem.
That's true, but...
I'll just look forward to it and wait.
You can't help her, okay?
TMP TMP
I can't help...

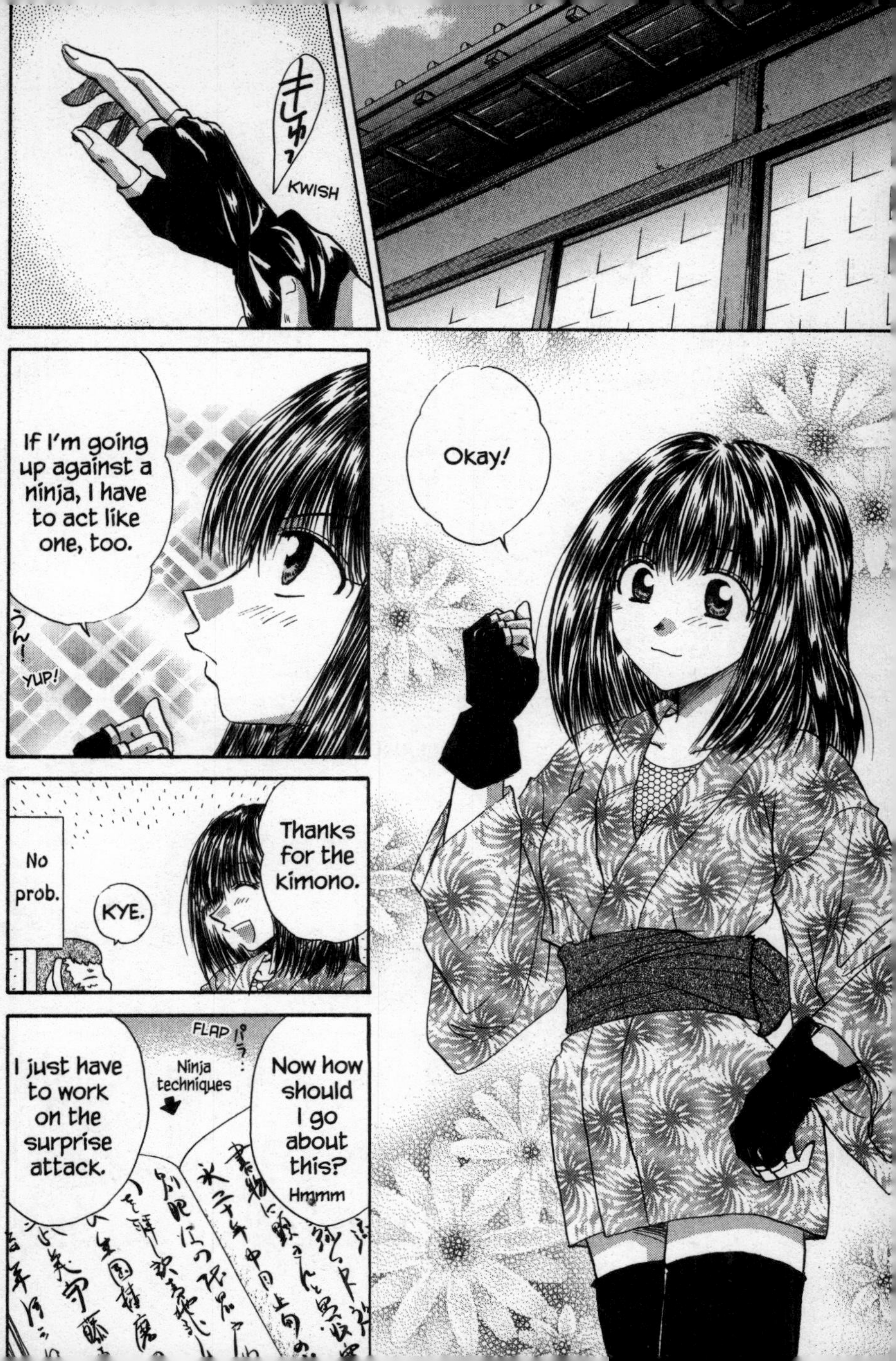

KWISH
Okay!
If I'm going up against a ninja, I have to act like one, too.
うん!
YUP!
Thanks for the kimono.
KYE.
No prob.
Now how should I go about this?
Hmmm
FLAP
Ninja techniques
I just have to work on the surprise attack.

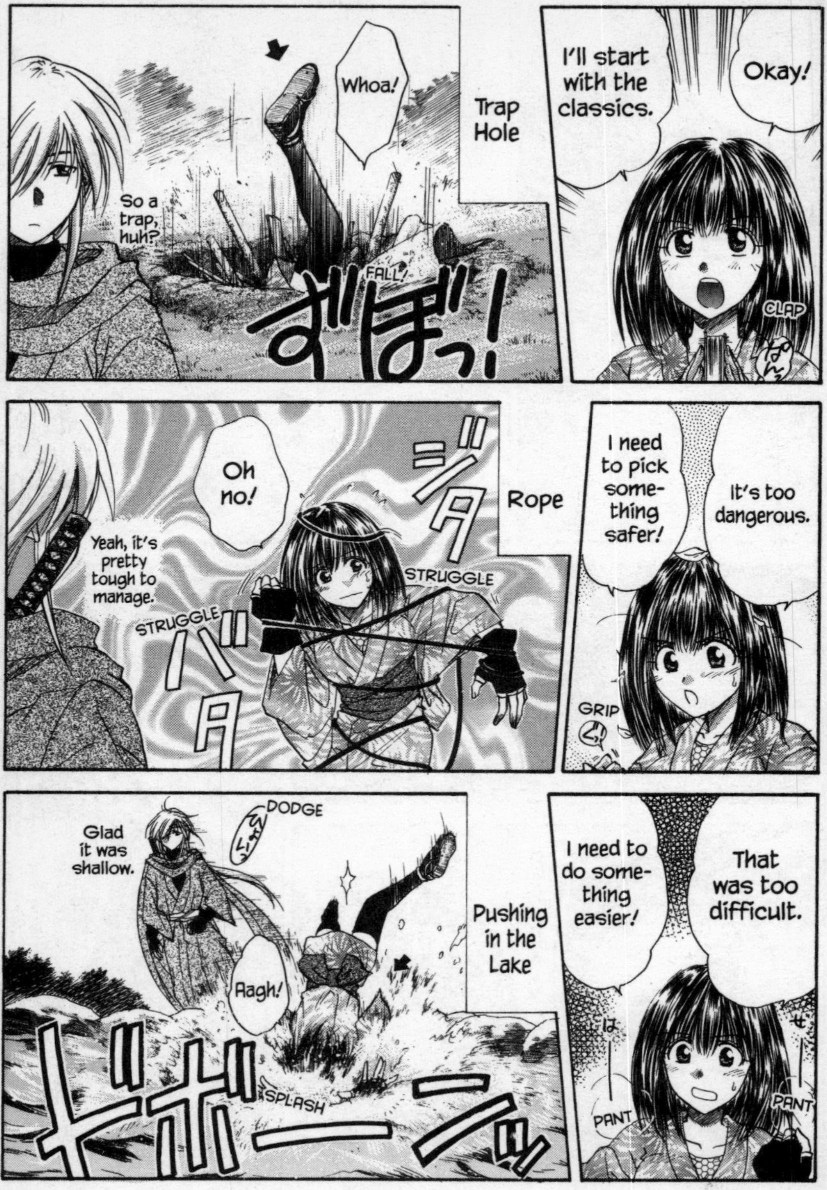
Okay!
I'll start with the classics.
CLAP
Trap Hole
Whoa!
So a trap, huh?
FALL!
ずぼっ!
It's too dangerous.
I need to pick something safer!
GRIP
Rope
Oh no!
STRUGGLE
Yeah, it's pretty tough to manage.
STRUGGLE
ジタバタ
That was too difficult.
I need to do something easier!
PANT
PANT
Pushing in the Lake
DODGE
Glad it was shallow.
Aagh!
SPLASH
ドボーンッ

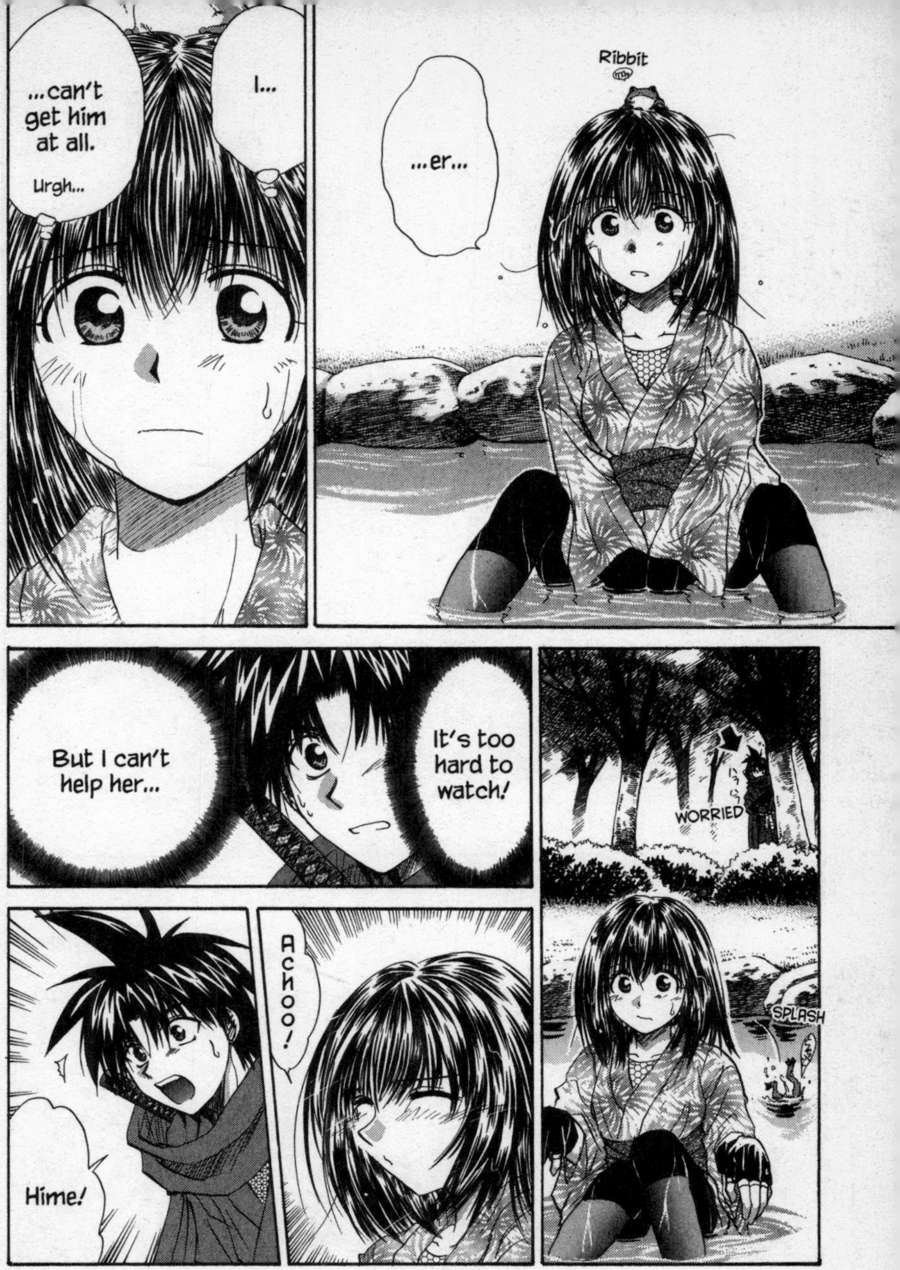
Ribbit
...er...
I...
...can't get him at all.
Urgh...
WORRIED
SPLASH
It's too hard to watch!
But I can't help her...
Achoo!
Hime!

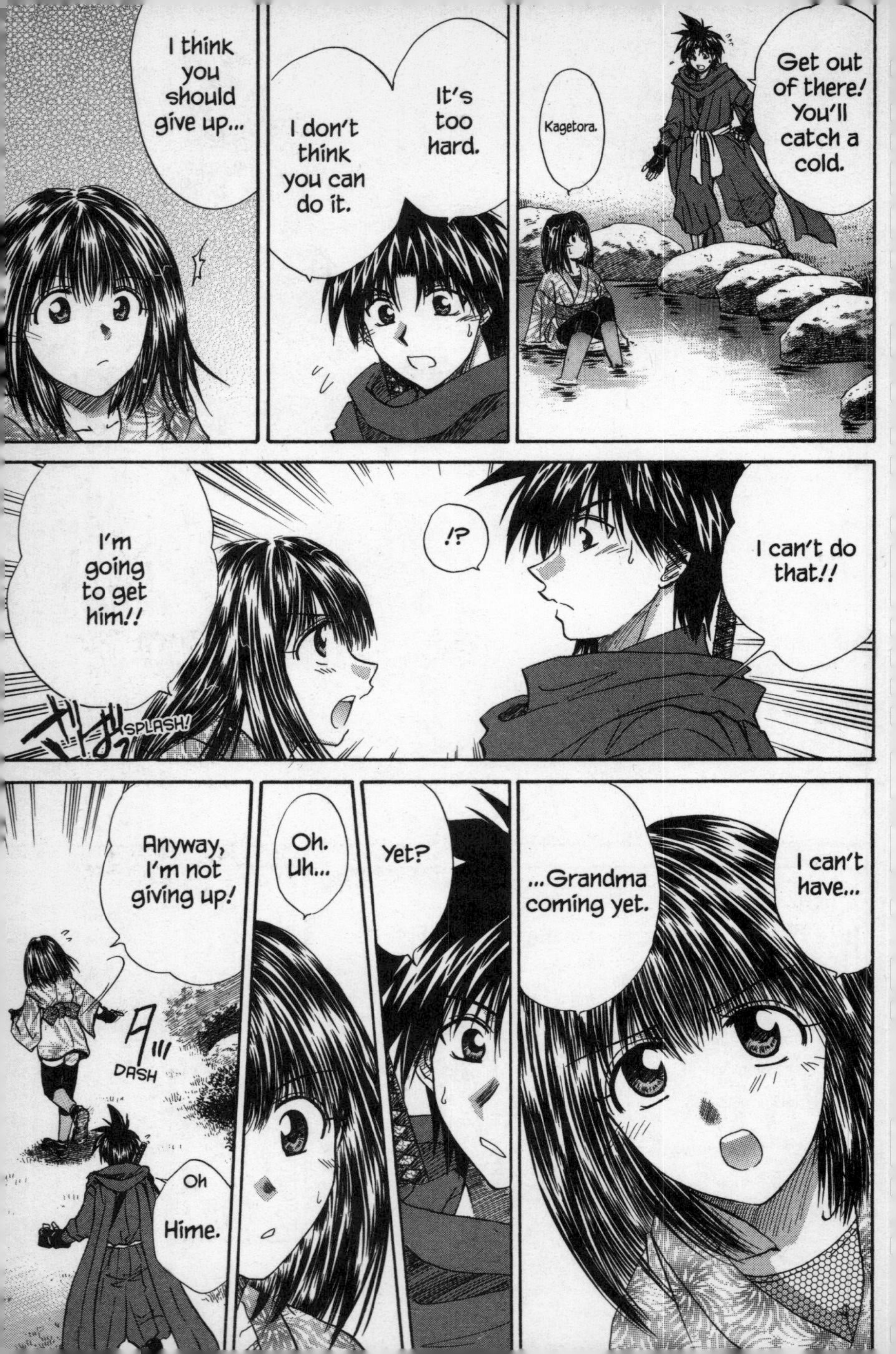
Get out of there! You'll catch a cold.
Kagetora.
It's too hard.
I don't think you can do it.
I think you should give up...
I can't do that!!
!?
I'm going to get him!!
SPLASH!
I can't have...
...Grandma coming yet.
Yet?
Oh. Uh...
Anyway, I'm not giving up!
DASH
Oh
Hime.

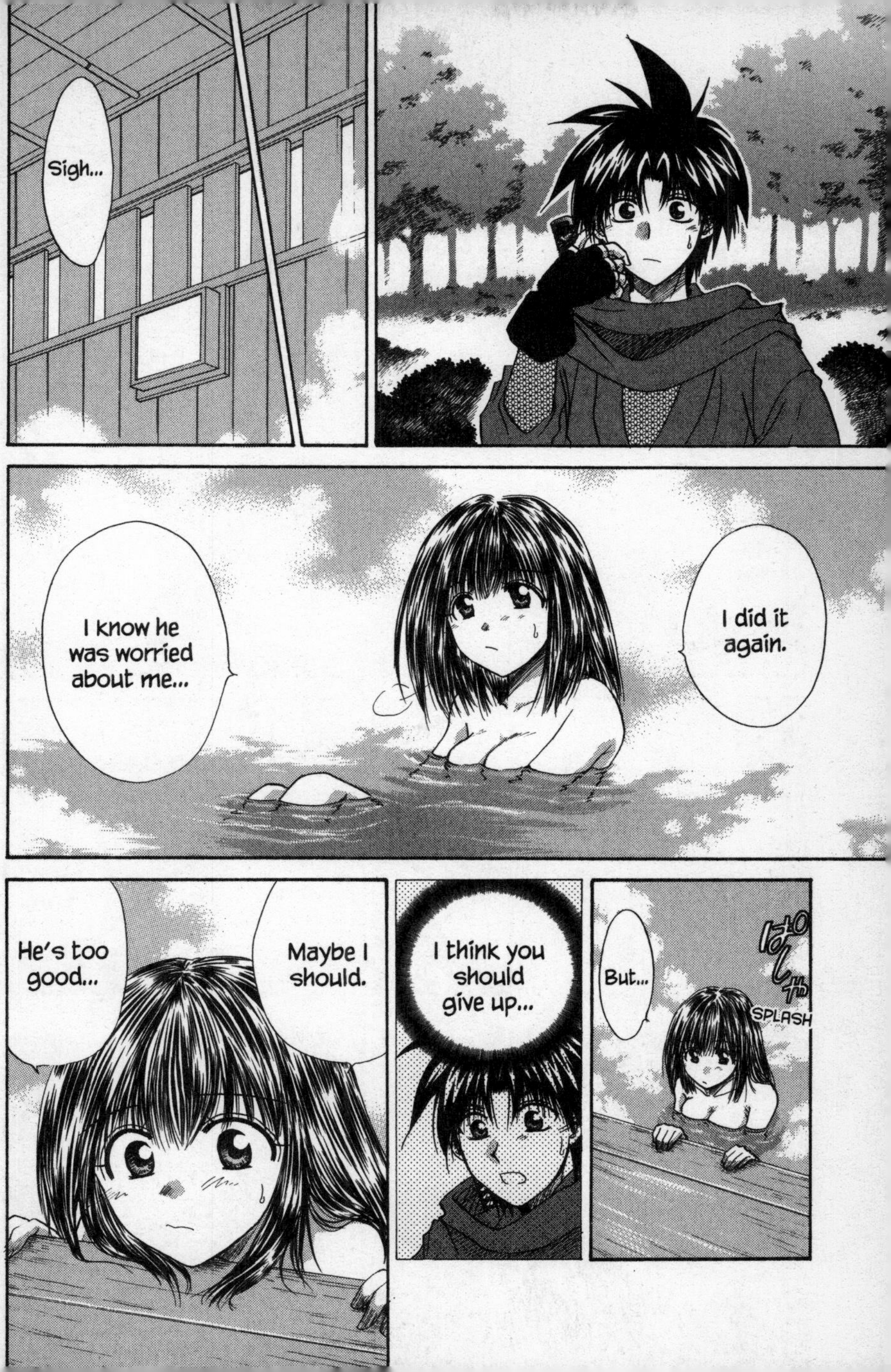
Sigh...
I did it again.
I know he was worried about me...
But...
ぱしゃ
SPLASH
I think you should give up...
Maybe I should.
He's too good...

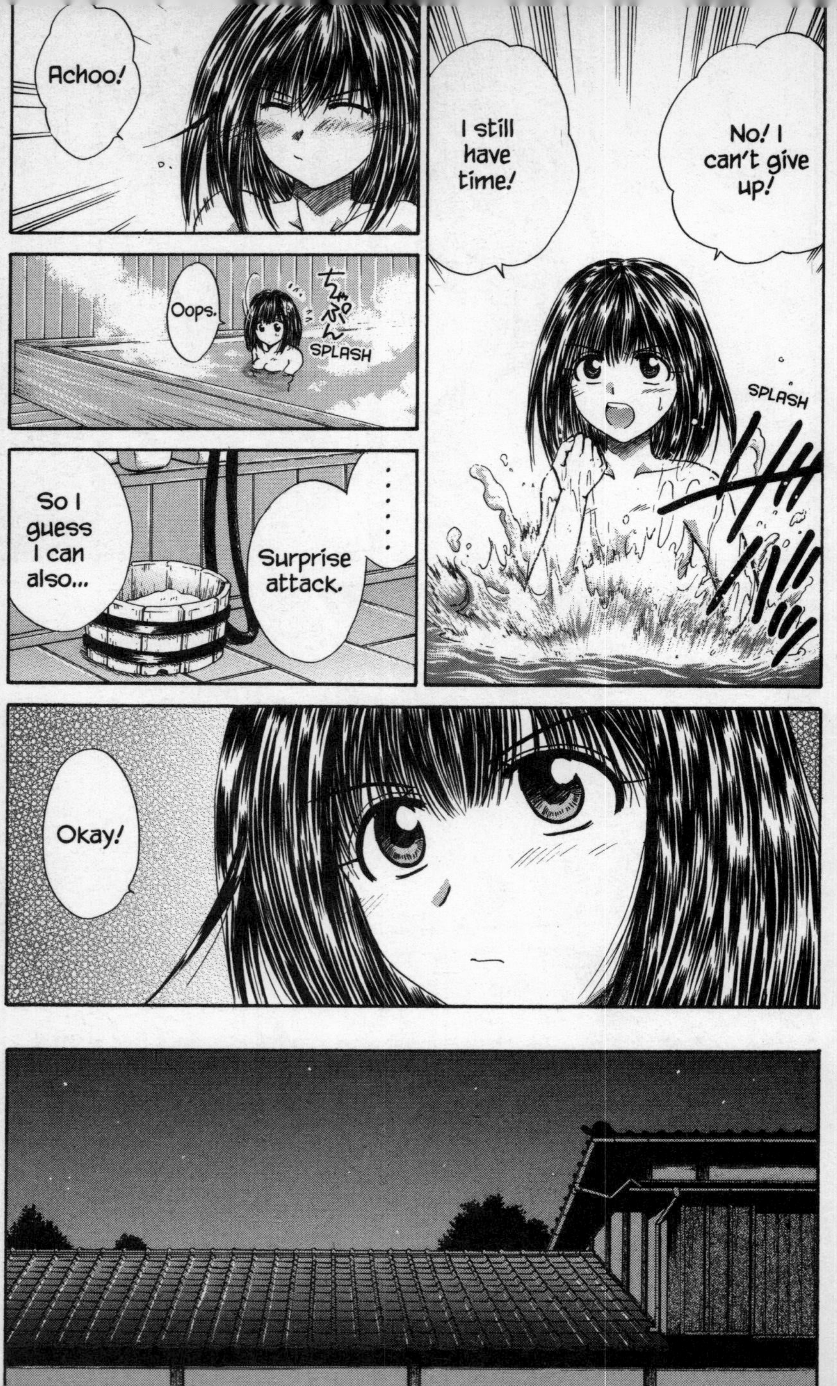
No! I can't give up!
I still have time!
SPLASH
Achoo!
Oops.
ちゃぷん
SPLASH
......
Surprise attack.
So I guess I can also...
Okay!

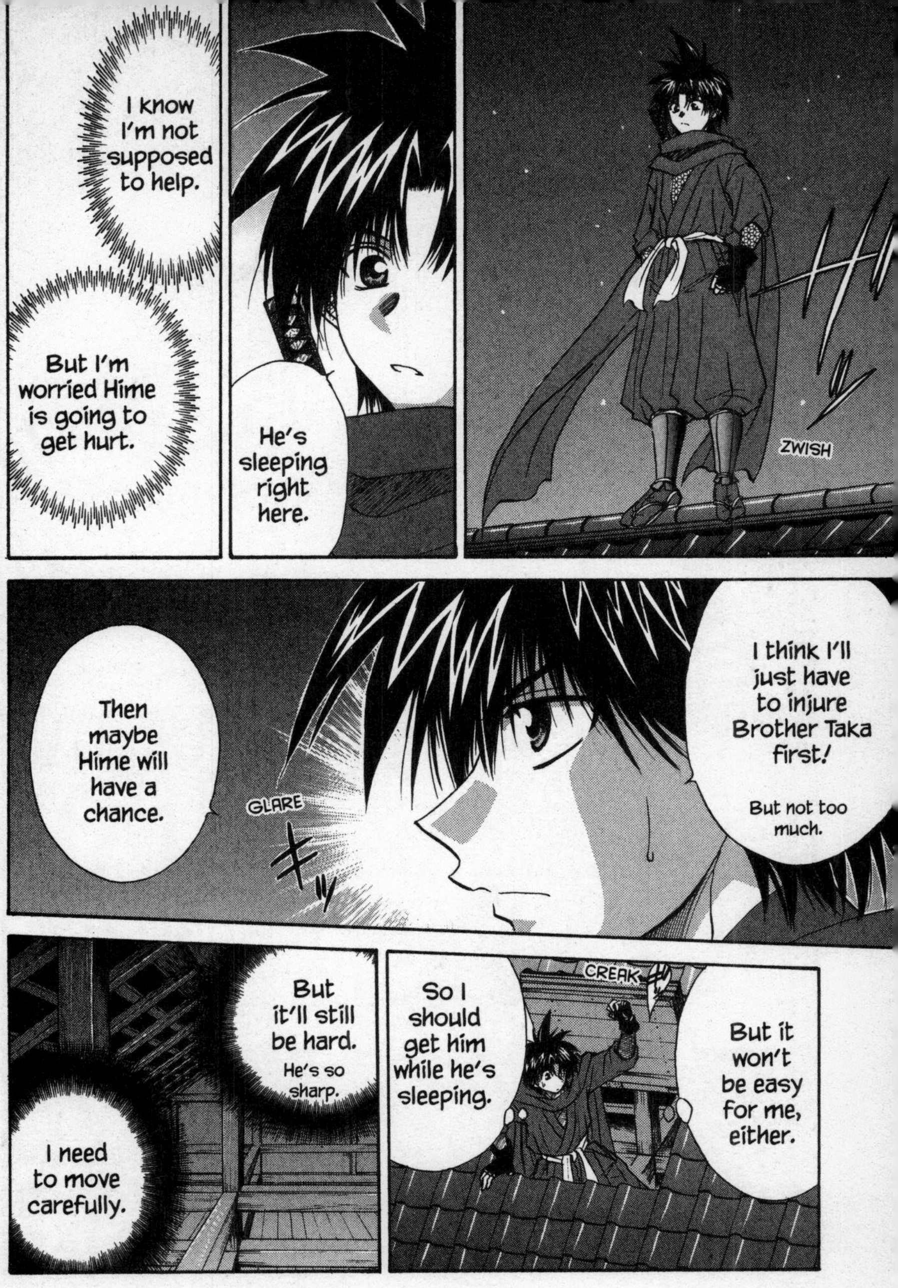
ZWISH
He's sleeping right here.
I know I'm not supposed to help.
But I'm worried Hime is going to get hurt.
I think I'll just have to injure Brother Taka first!
But not too much.
GLARE
Then maybe Hime will have a chance.
CREAK
But it won't be easy for me, either.
So I should get him while he's sleeping.
But it'll still be hard.
He's so sharp.
I need to move carefully.

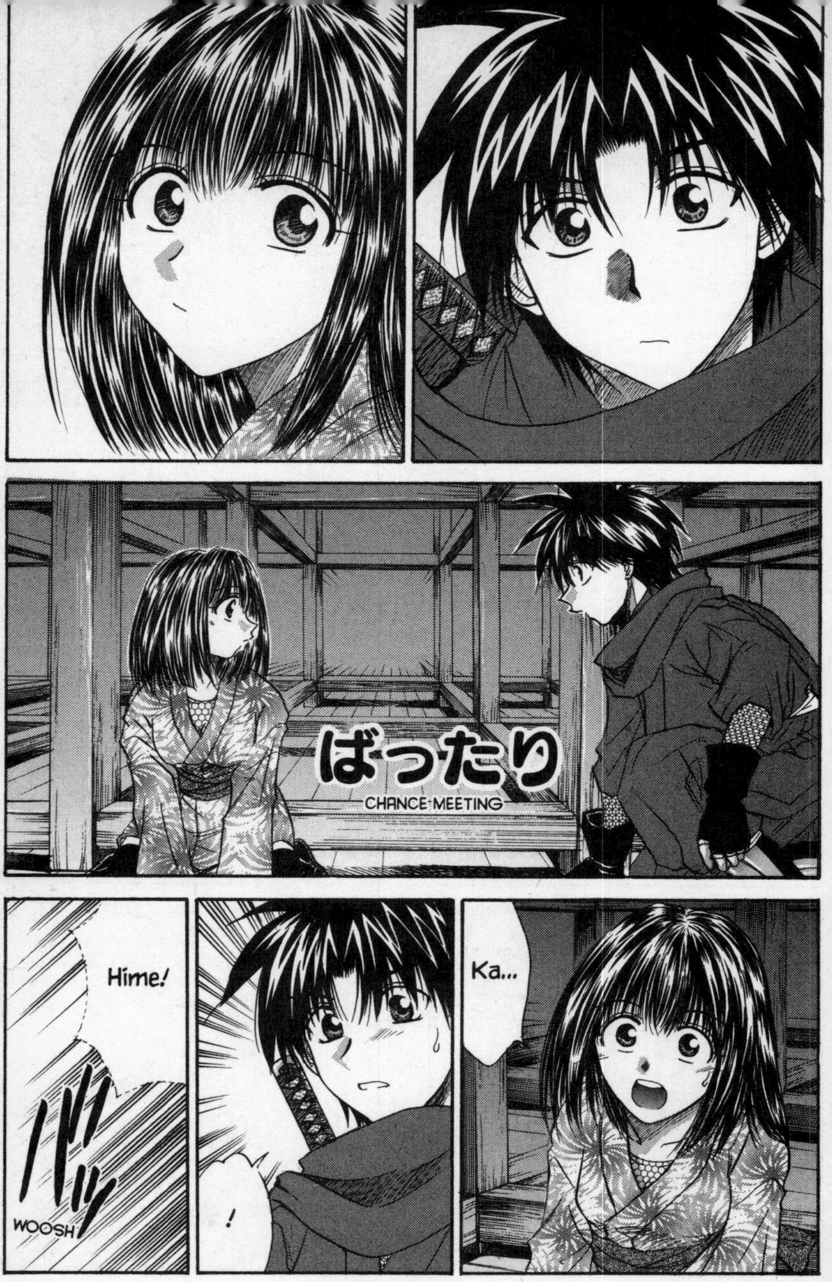
ばったり
CHANCE MEETING
Ka...
!
Hime!
WOOSH

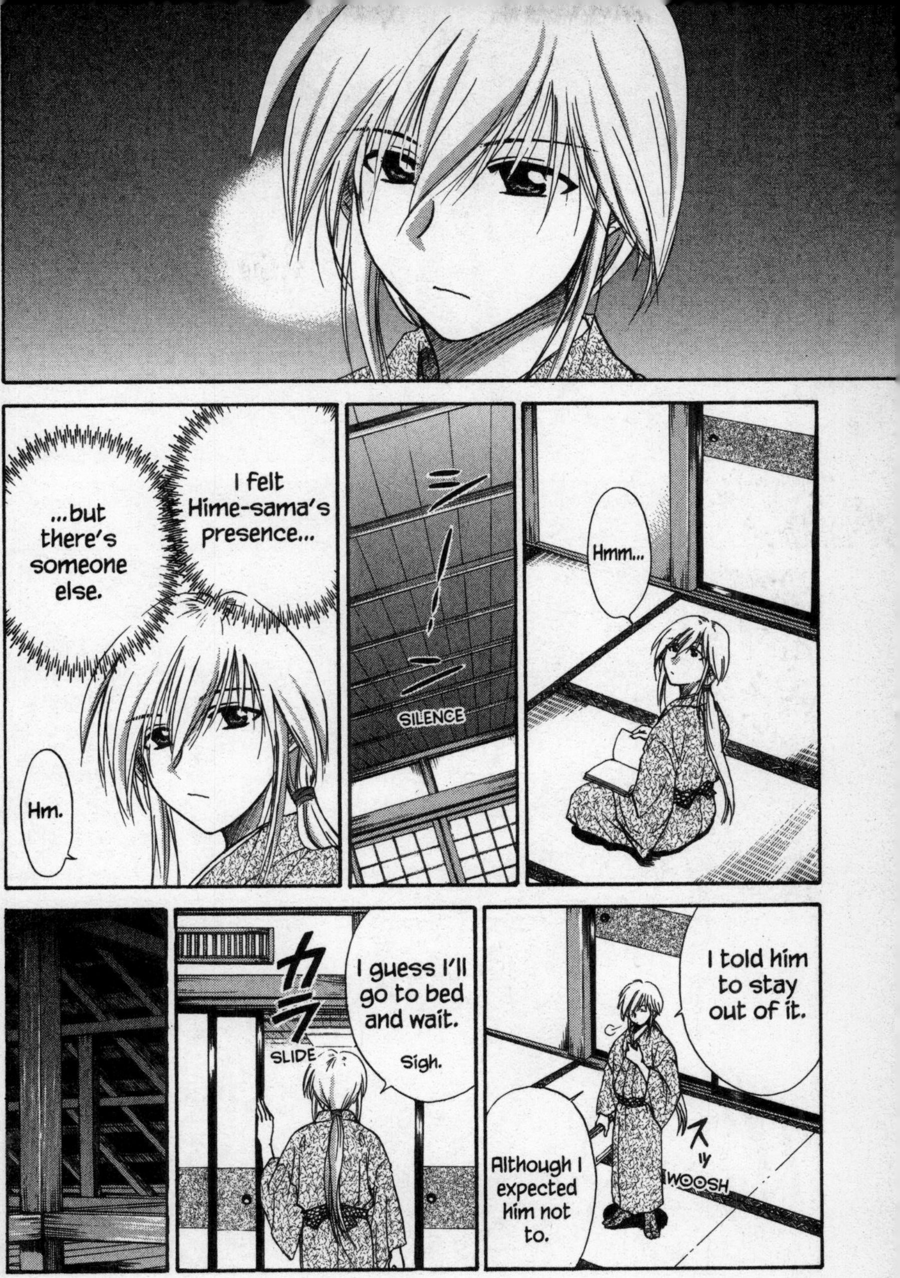
Hmm...
SILENCE
I felt Hime-sama's presence...
...but there's someone else.
Hm.
I told him to stay out of it.
Although I expected him not to.
WOOSH
I guess I'll go to bed and wait.
Sigh.
SLIDE

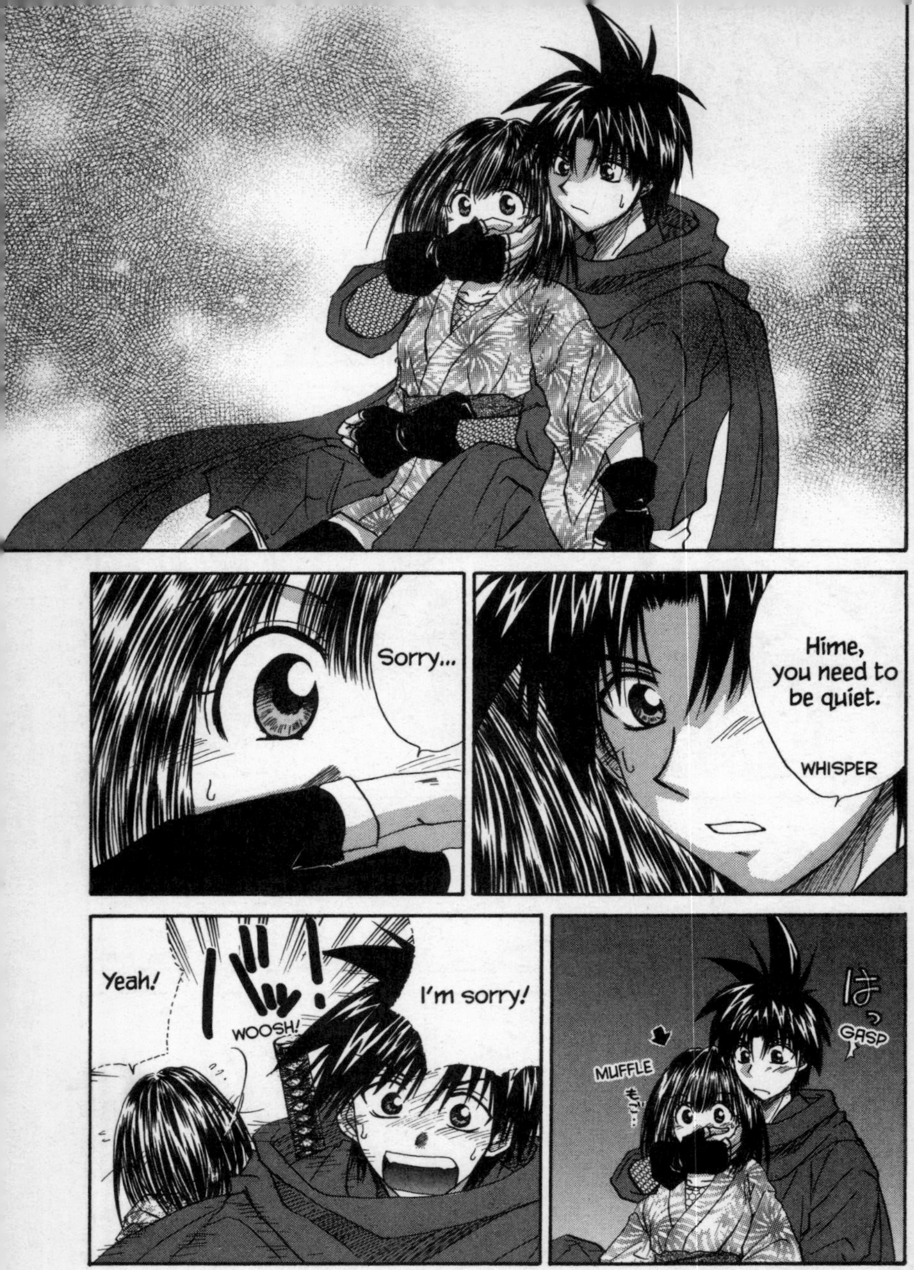
Hime, you need to be quiet.
WHISPER
Sorry...
はっ
GASP
MUFFLE
もご…
I'm sorry!
WOOSH!
Yeah!

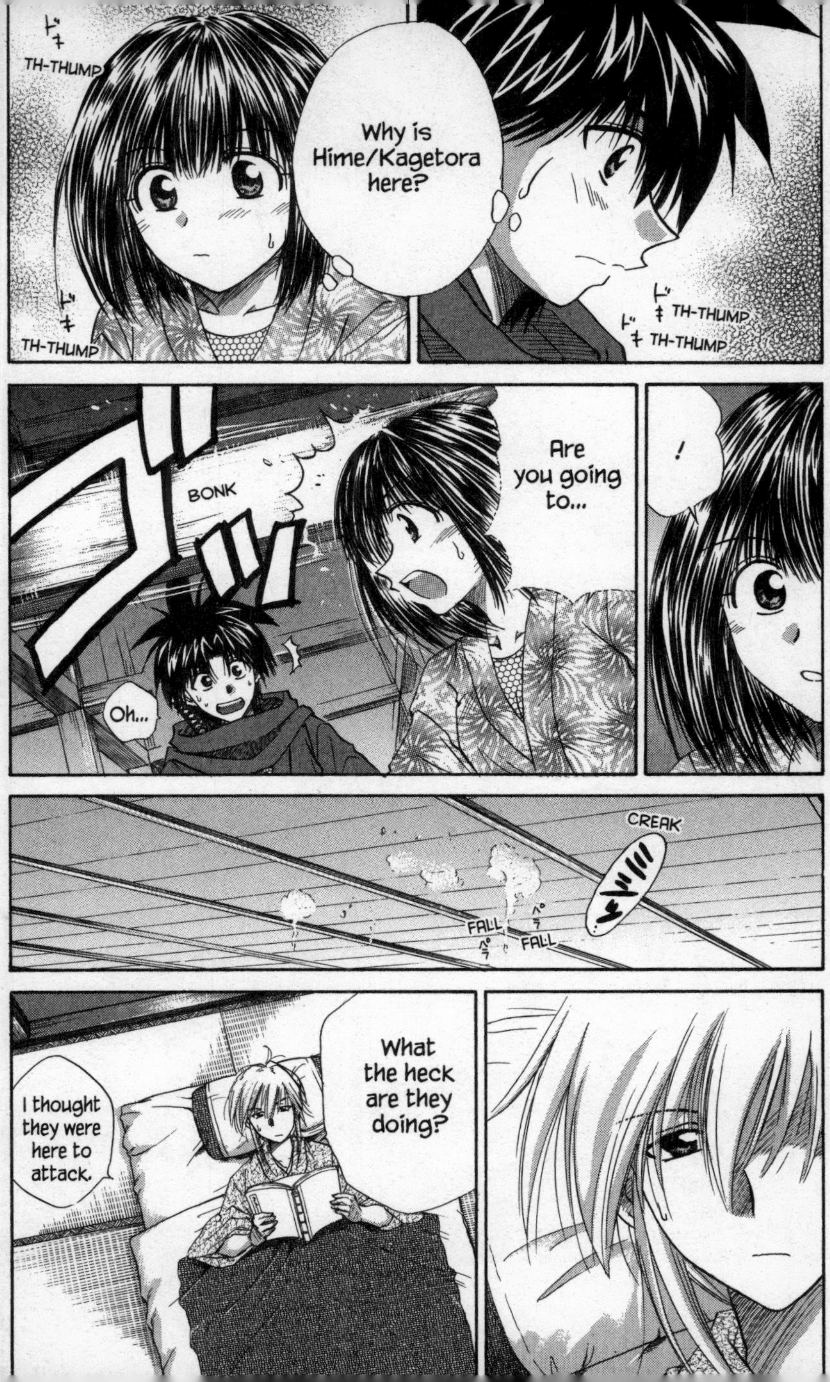
ドキ TH-THUMP
ドキ TH-THUMP
Why is Hime/Kagetora here?
ドキ TH-THUMP
ドキ TH-THUMP
!
Are you going to...
BONK
Oh...
CREAK
FALL FALL
What the heck are they doing?
I thought they were here to attack.

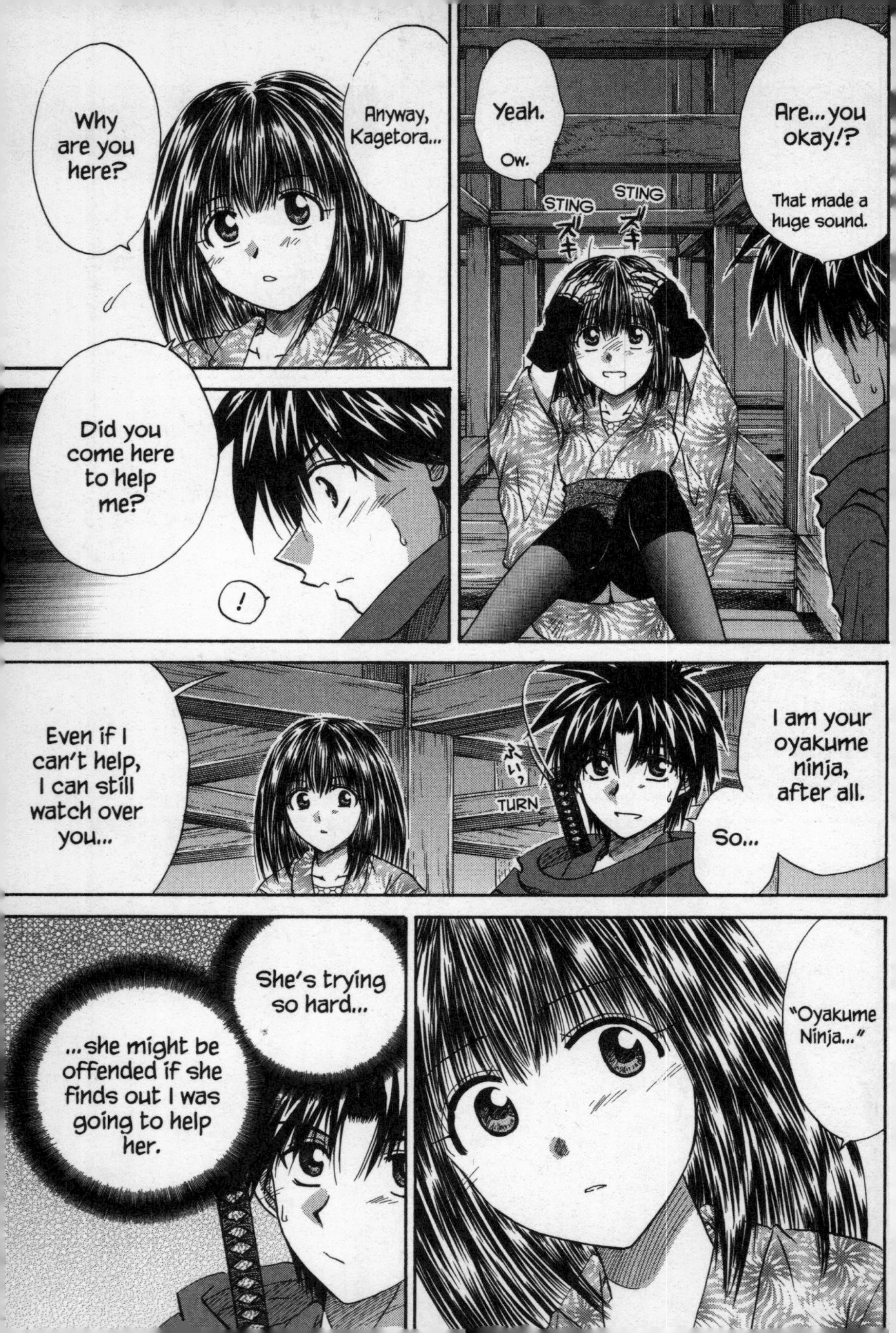
Are...you okay!?
That made a huge sound.
Yeah.
Ow.
STING
STING
Anyway, Kagetora...
Why are you here?
Did you come here to help me?
!
I am your oyakume ninja, after all.
So...
TURN
Even if I can't help, I can still watch over you...
"Oyakume Ninja..."
She's trying so hard...
...she might be offended if she finds out I was going to help her.

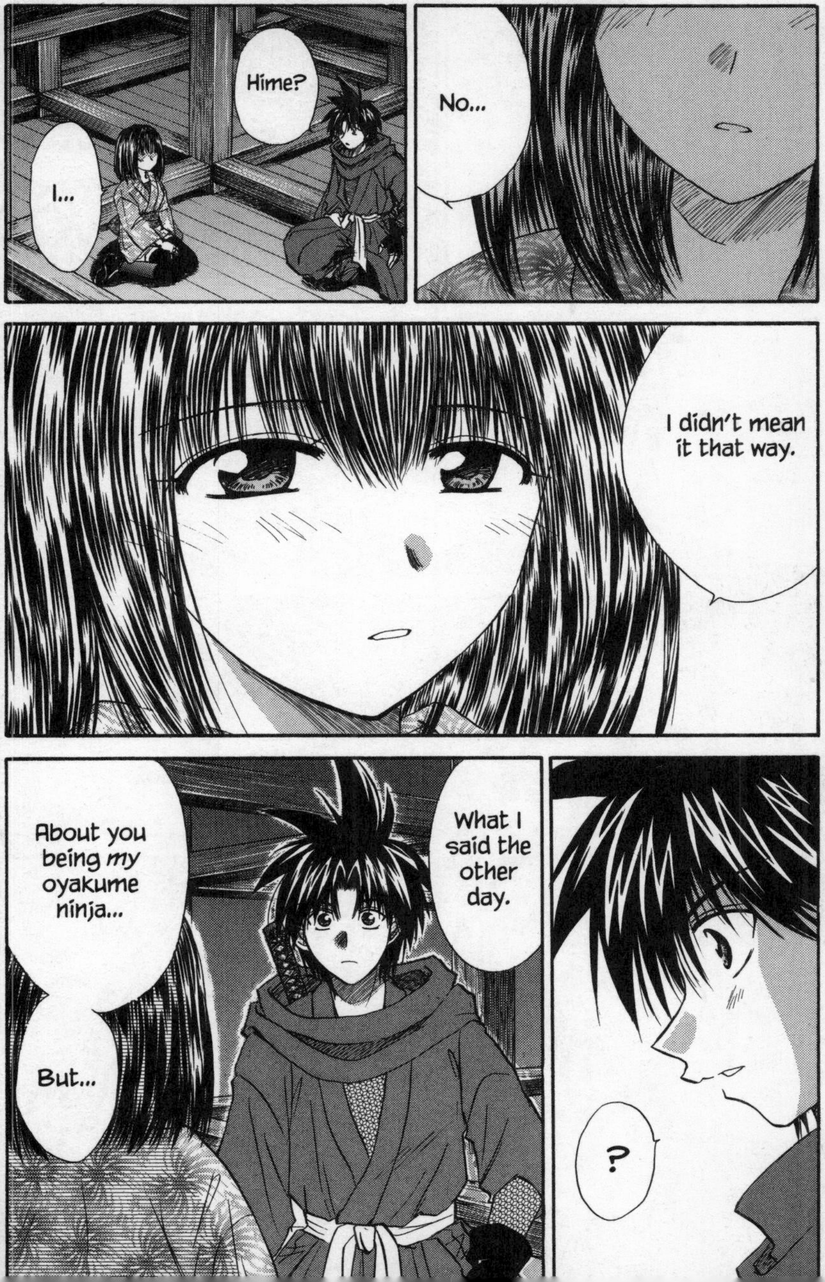
No...
Hime?
I...
I didn't mean it that way.
?
What I said the other day.
About you being *my* oyakume ninja...
But...

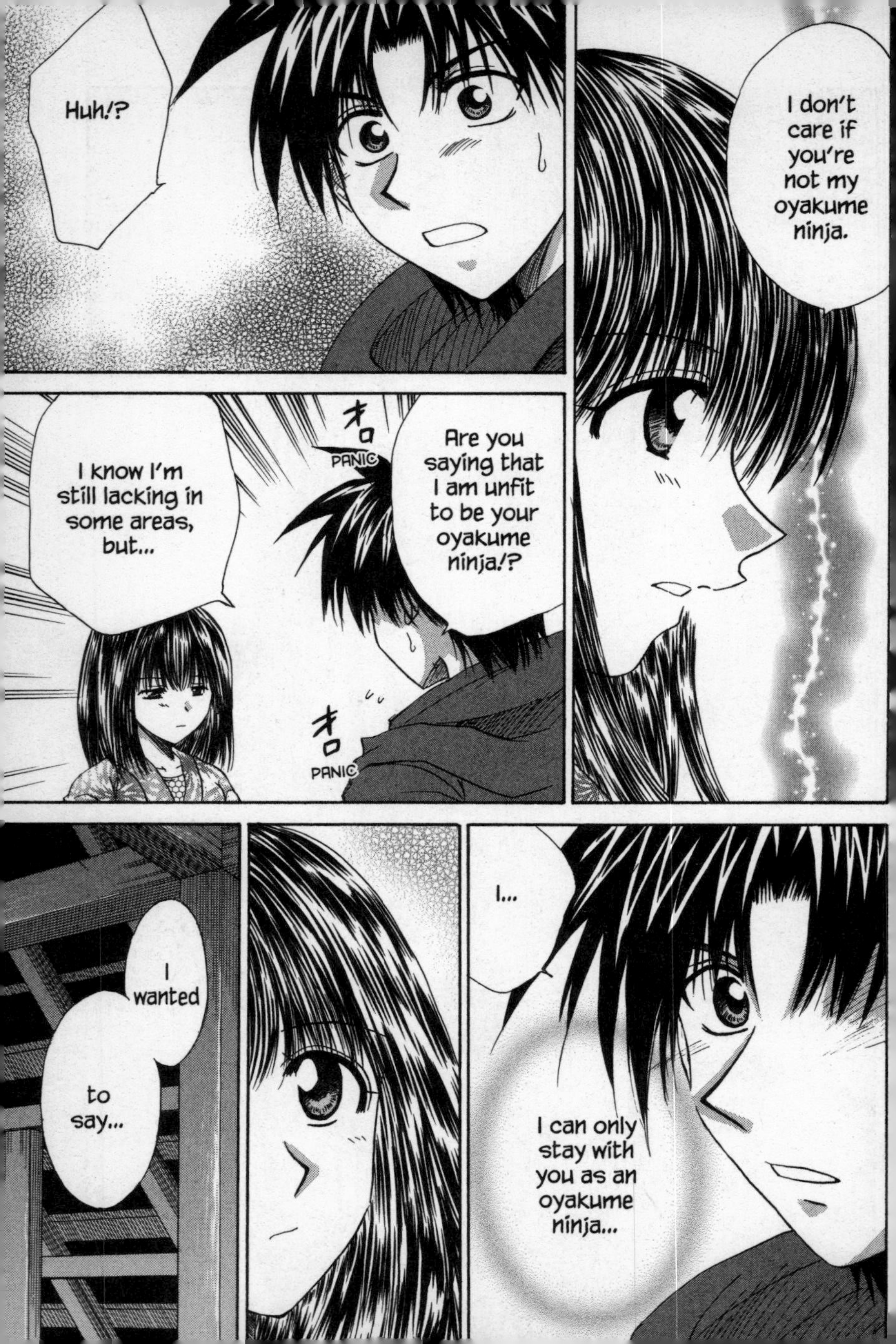
I don't care if you're not my oyakume ninja.
Huh!?
Are you saying that I am unfit to be your oyakume ninja!?
オロ PANIC
オロ PANIC
I know I'm still lacking in some areas, but...
I...
I can only stay with you as an oyakume ninja...
I wanted
to say...

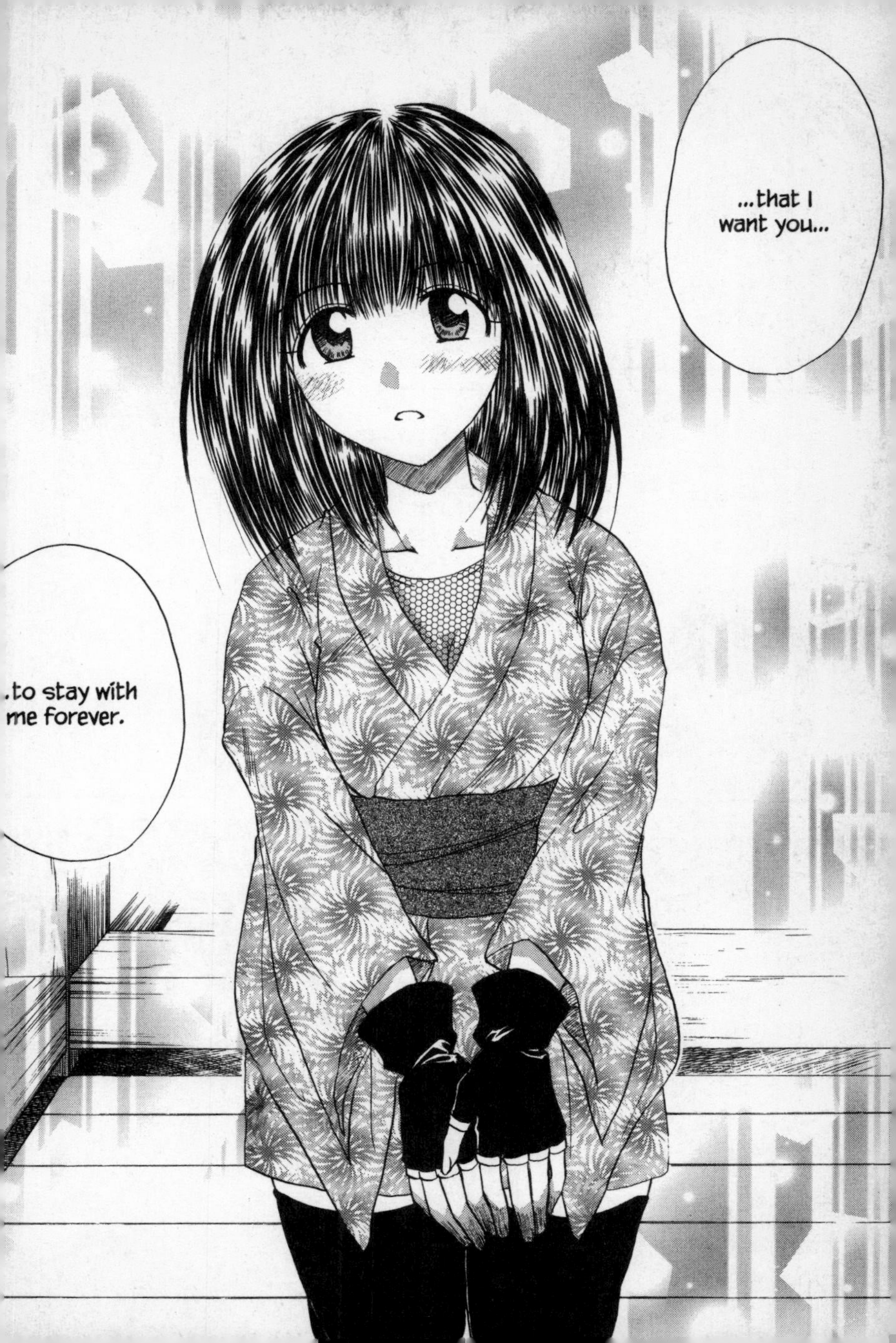
...that I want you...
.to stay with me forever.

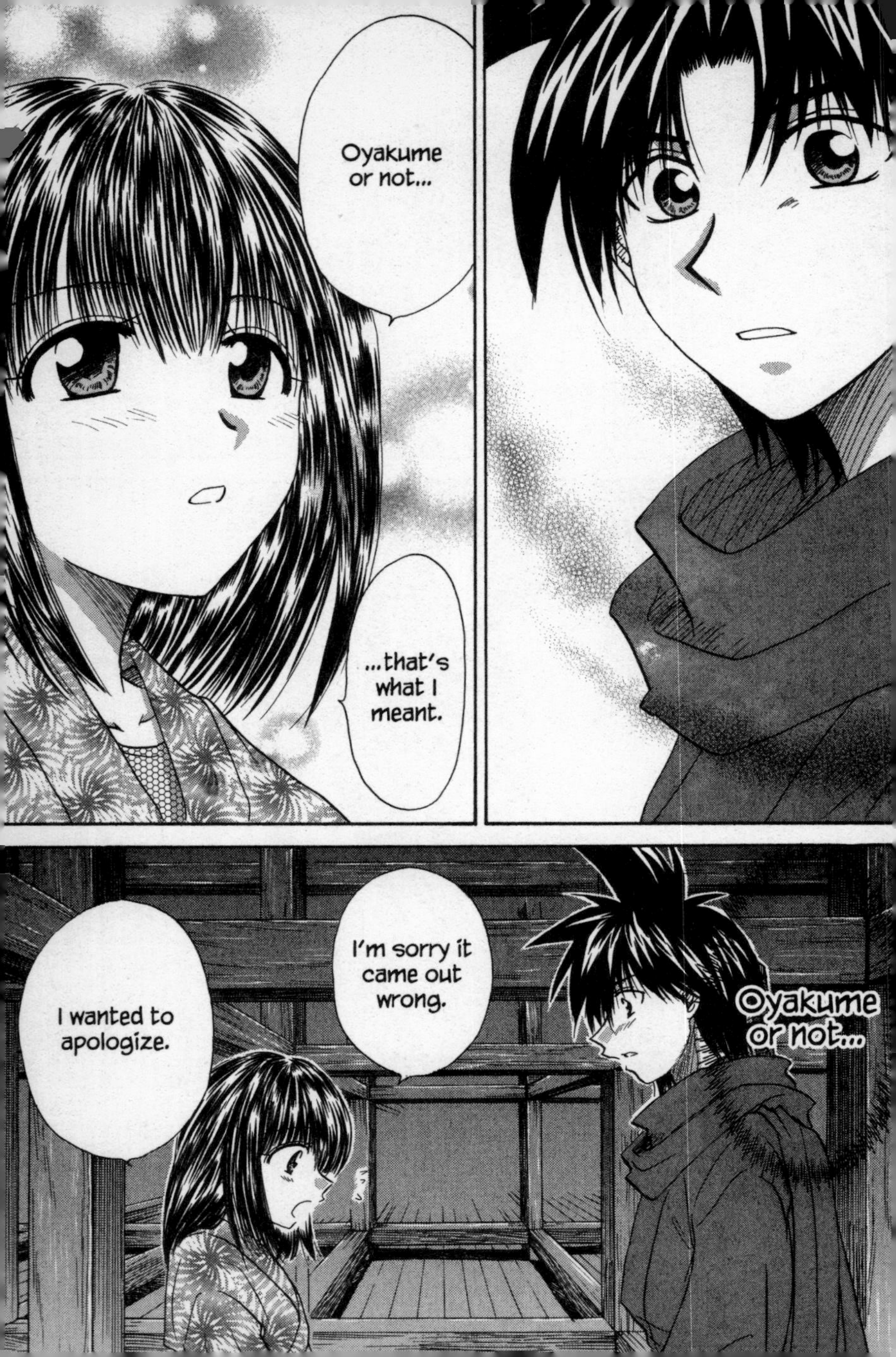
Oyakume or not...
...that's what I meant.
Oyakume or not...
I'm sorry it came out wrong.
I wanted to apologize.

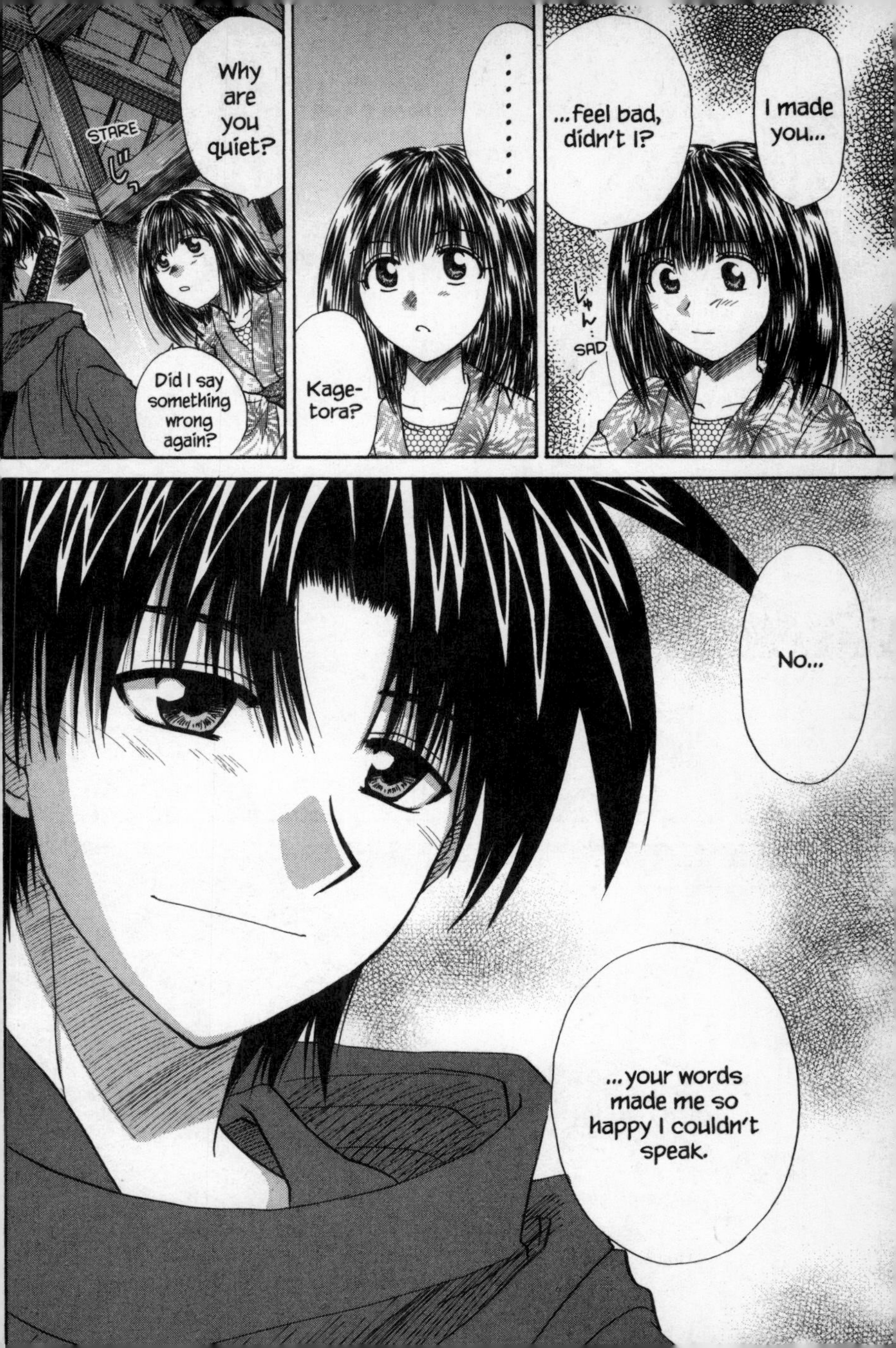
I made you...
...feel bad, didn't I?
SAD
......
Kage-tora?
Why are you quiet?
STARE
じっ
Did I say something wrong again?
No...
...your words made me so happy I couldn't speak.

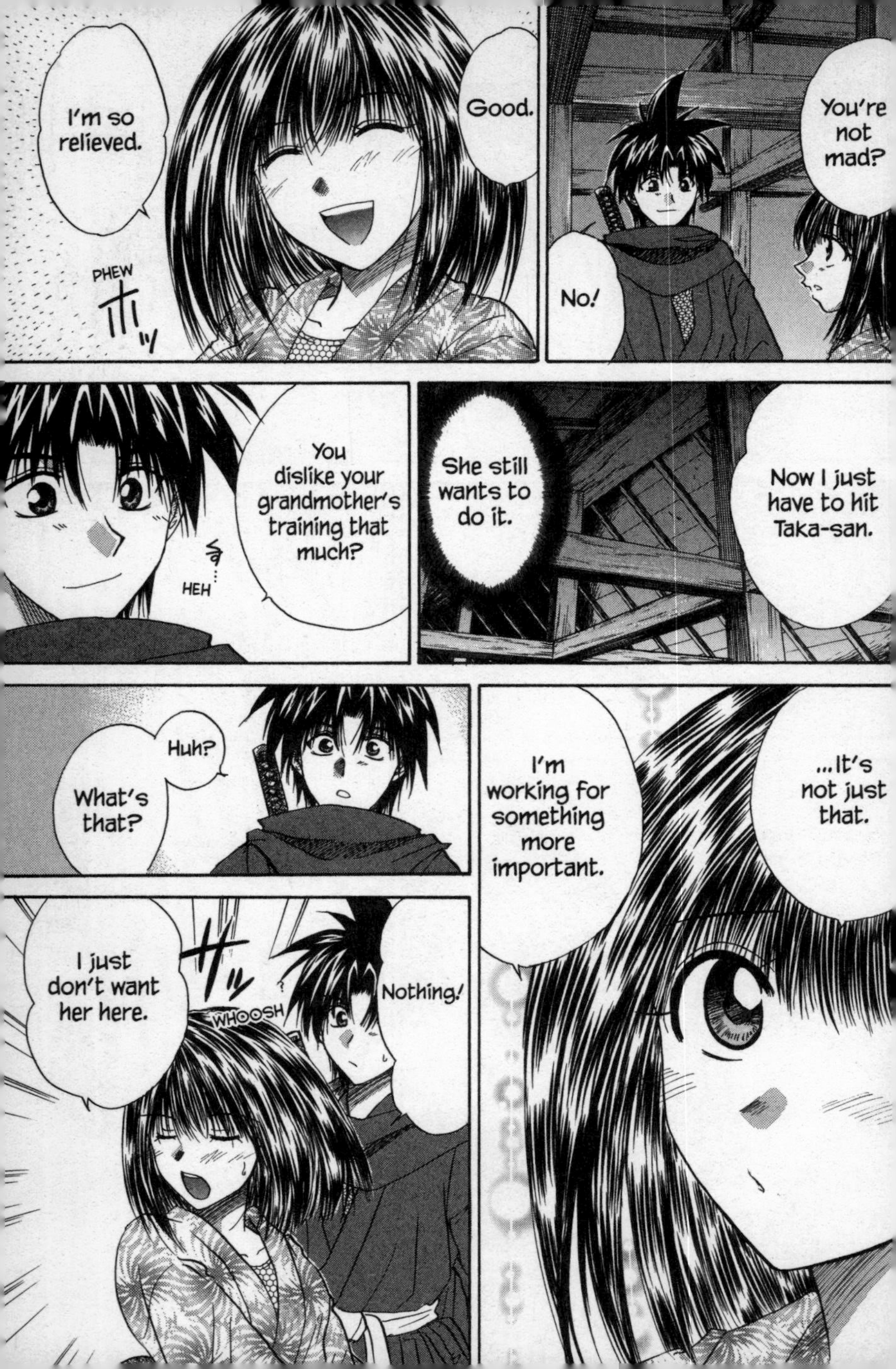
You're not mad?
No!
Good.
I'm so relieved.
PHEW
Now I just have to hit Taka-san.
She still wants to do it.
You dislike your grandmother's training that much?
HEH
...It's not just that.
I'm working for something more important.
Huh?
What's that?
Nothing!
WHOOSH
I just don't want her here.

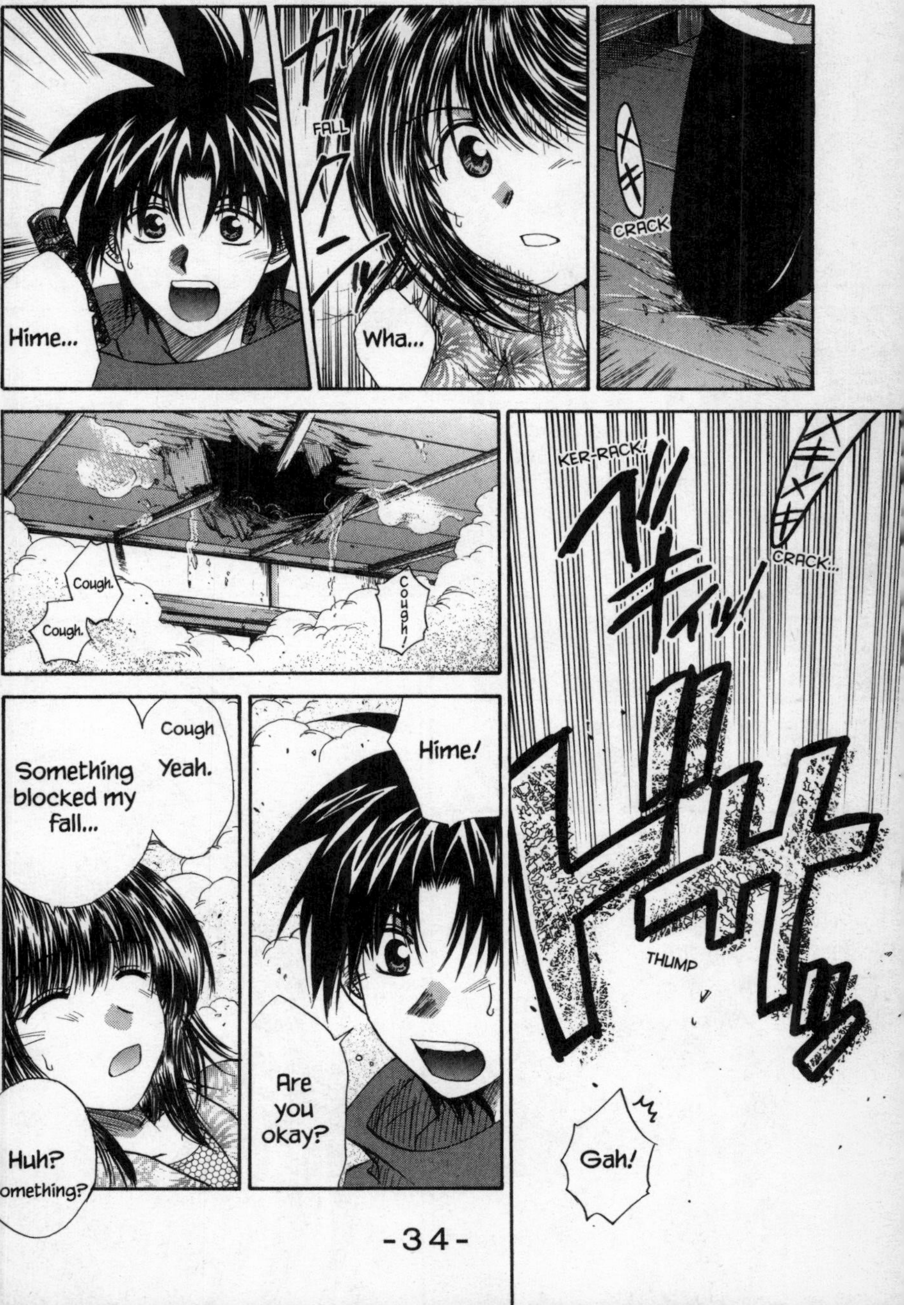
CRACK
FALL
Wha...
Hime...
KER-RACK!
CRACK...
THUMP
Gah!
Cough.
Cough.
Cough!
Hime!
Are you okay?
Cough
Yeah.
Something blocked my fall...
Huh? Something?

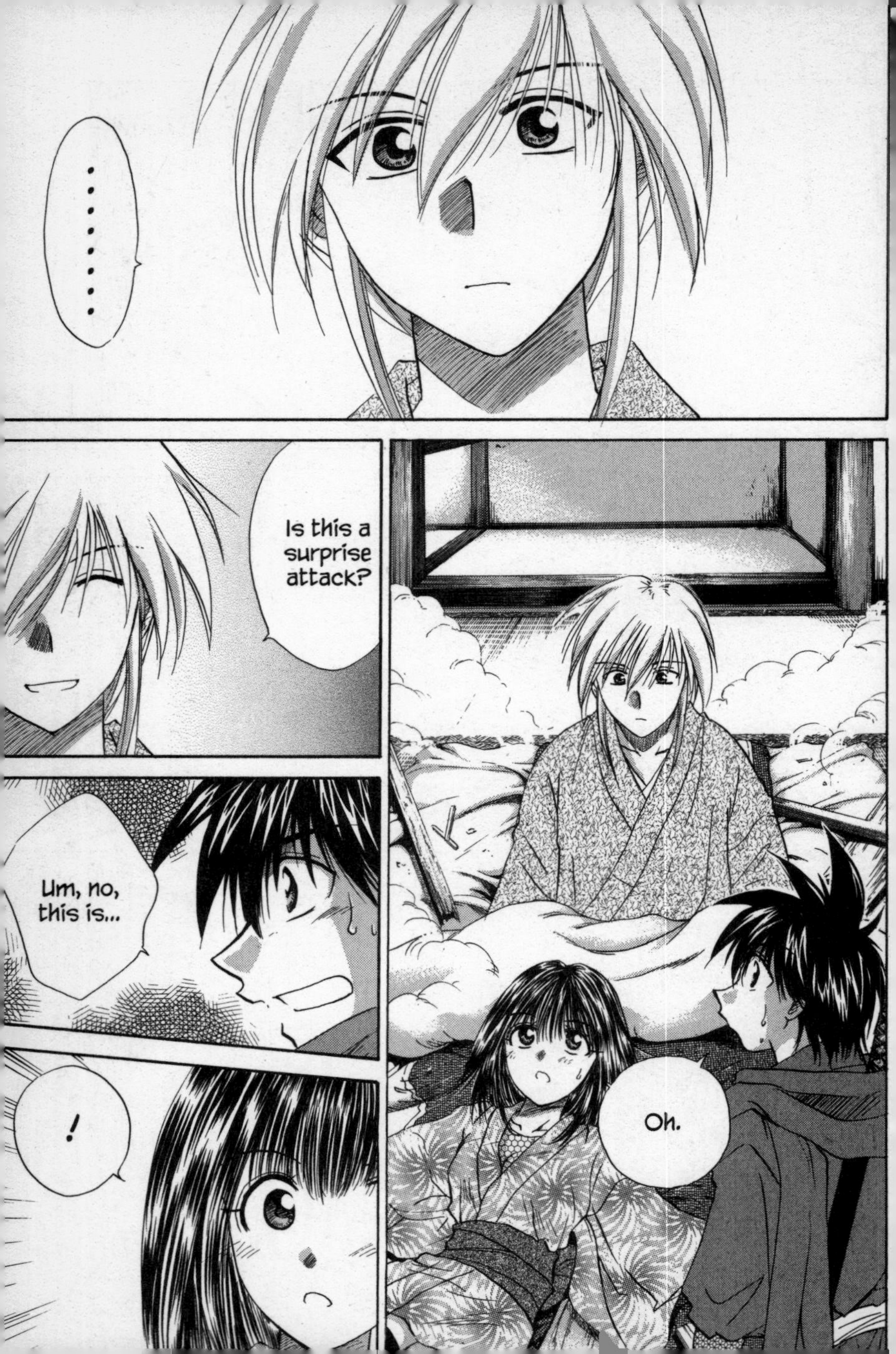
......
Oh.
Is this a surprise attack?
Um, no, this is...
!

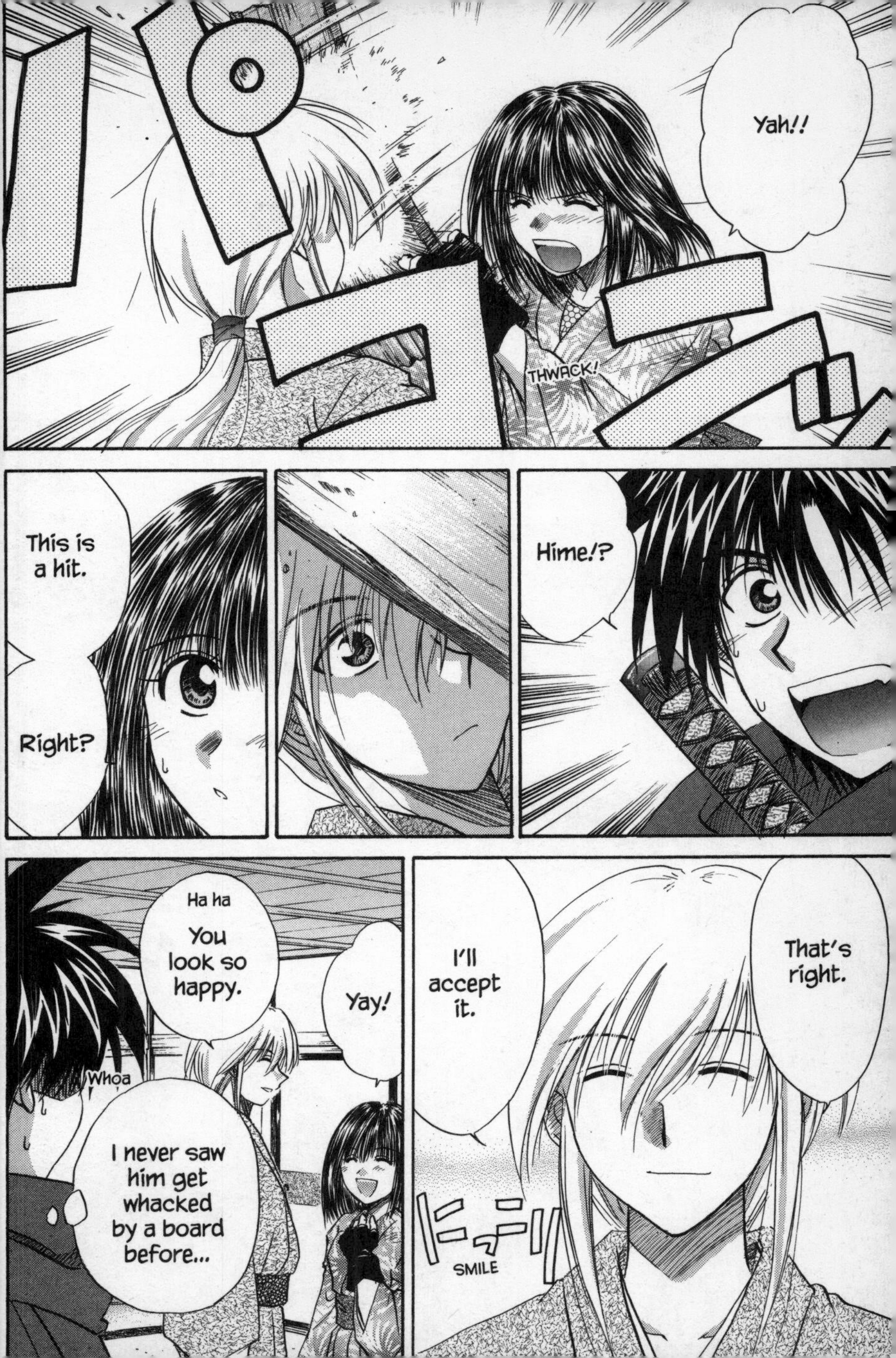
Yah!!
THWACK!
Hime!?
This is a hit.
Right?
That's right.
I'll accept it.
SMILE
Yay!
Ha ha
You look so happy.
Whoa
I never saw him get whacked by a board before...

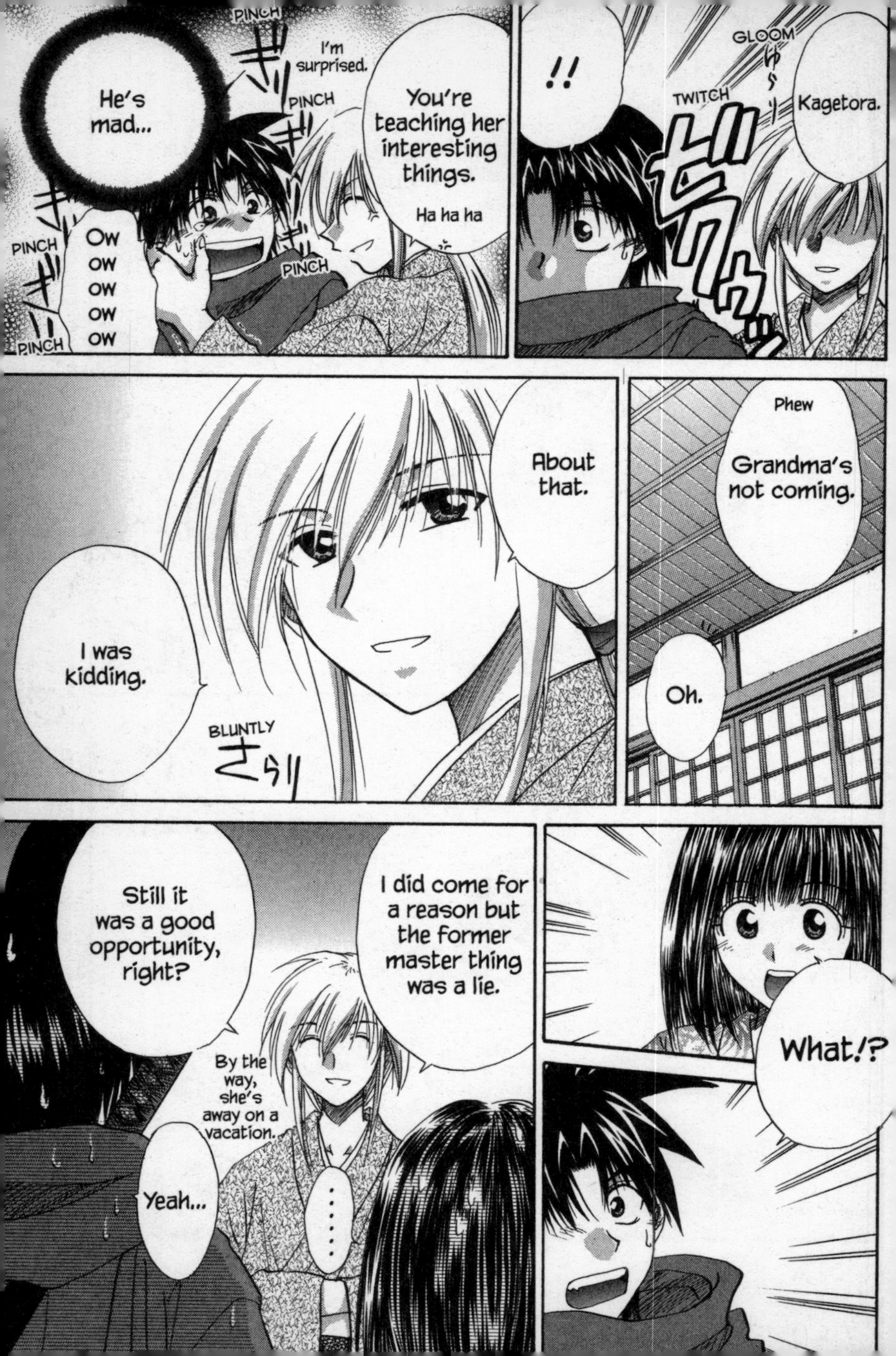
GLOOM
Kagetora.
TWITCH
!!
You're teaching her interesting things.
Ha ha ha
I'm surprised.
PINCH
He's mad...
PINCH
PINCH
Ow ow ow ow ow
PINCH
PINCH
Phew
Grandma's not coming.
Oh.
About that.
I was kidding.
BLUNTLY
What!?
I did come for a reason but the former master thing was a lie.
Still it was a good opportunity, right?
By the way, she's away on a vacation.
......
Yeah...

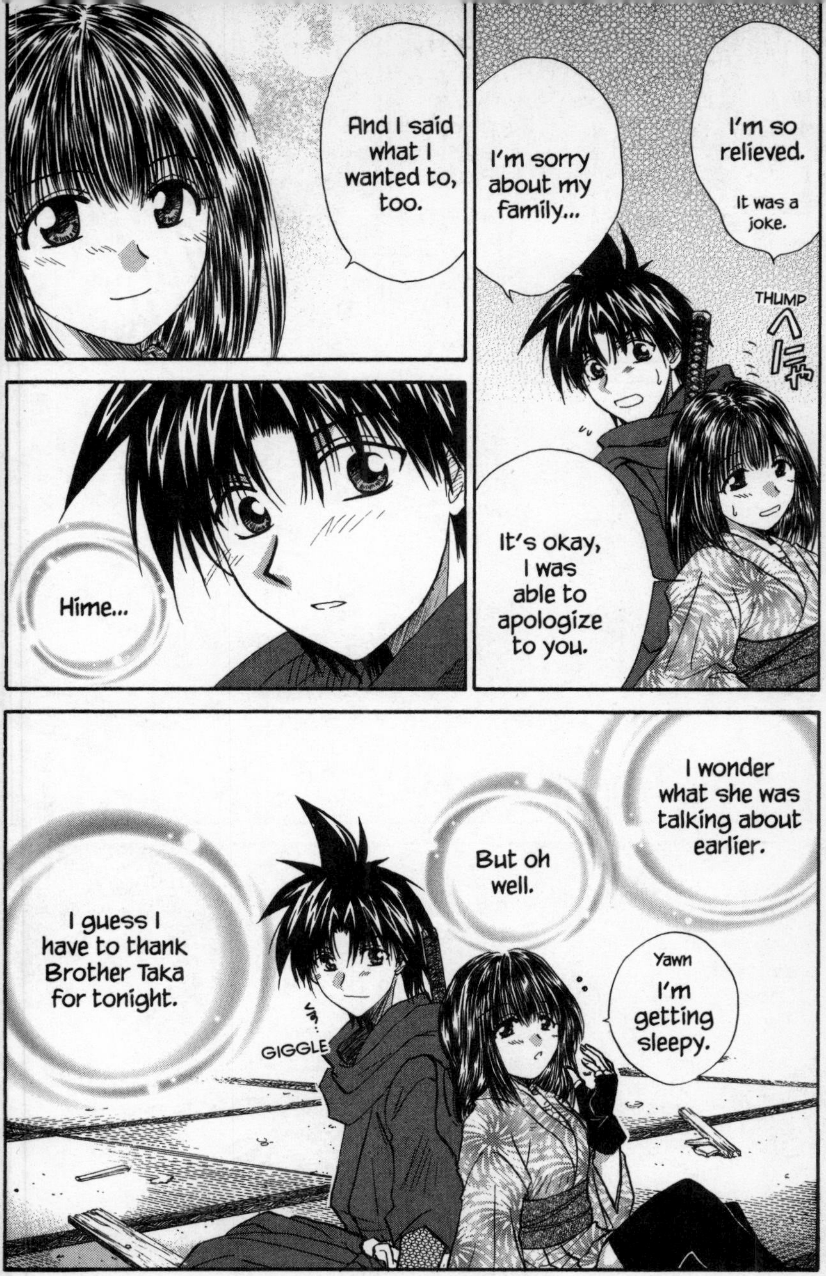
I'm so relieved.
It was a joke.
I'm sorry about my family...
THUMP
It's okay, I was able to apologize to you.
And I said what I wanted to, too.
Hime...
I wonder what she was talking about earlier.
But oh well.
Yawn
I'm getting sleepy.
I guess I have to thank Brother Taka for tonight.
GIGGLE

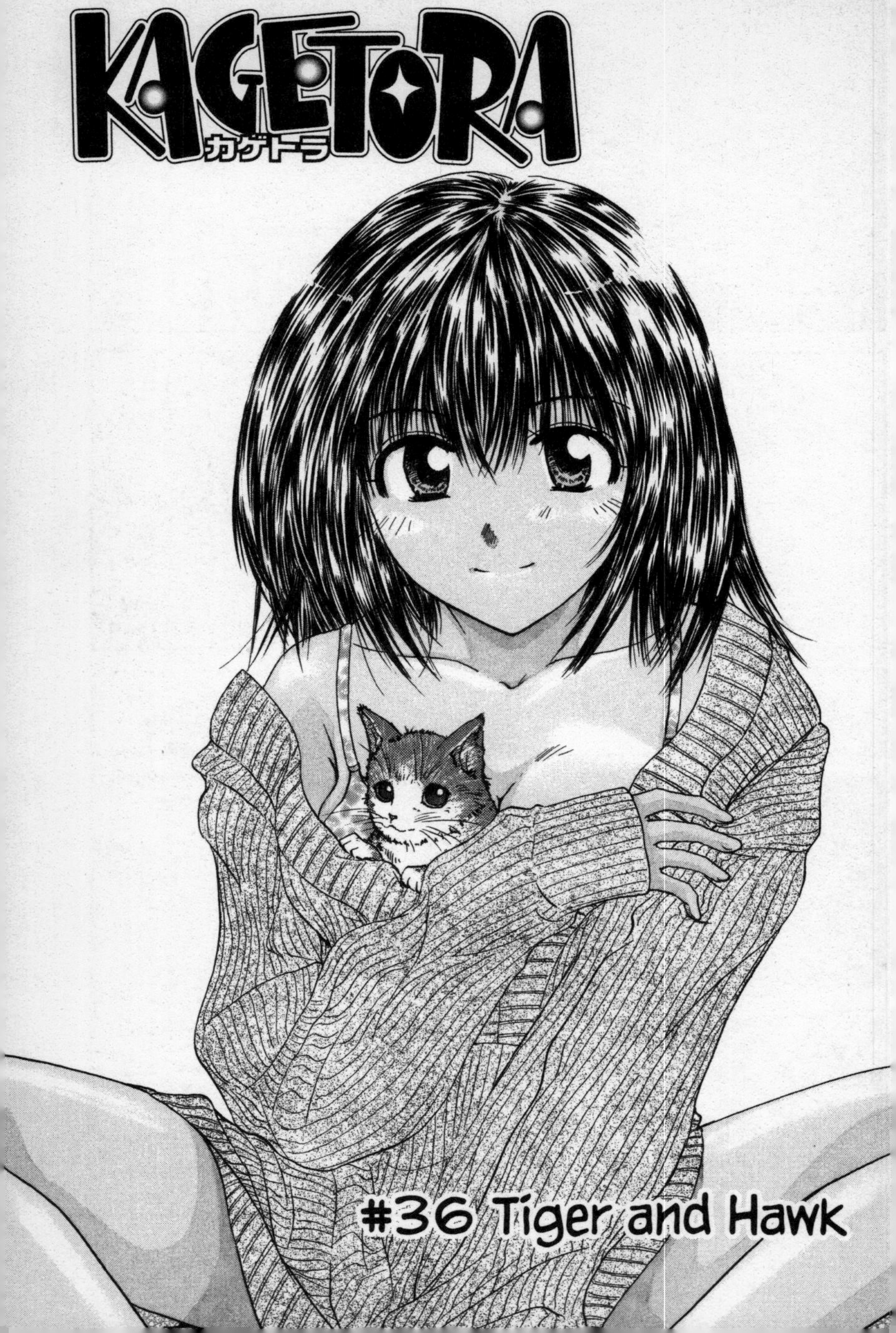
KAGETORA
カゲトラ
#36 Tiger and Hawk

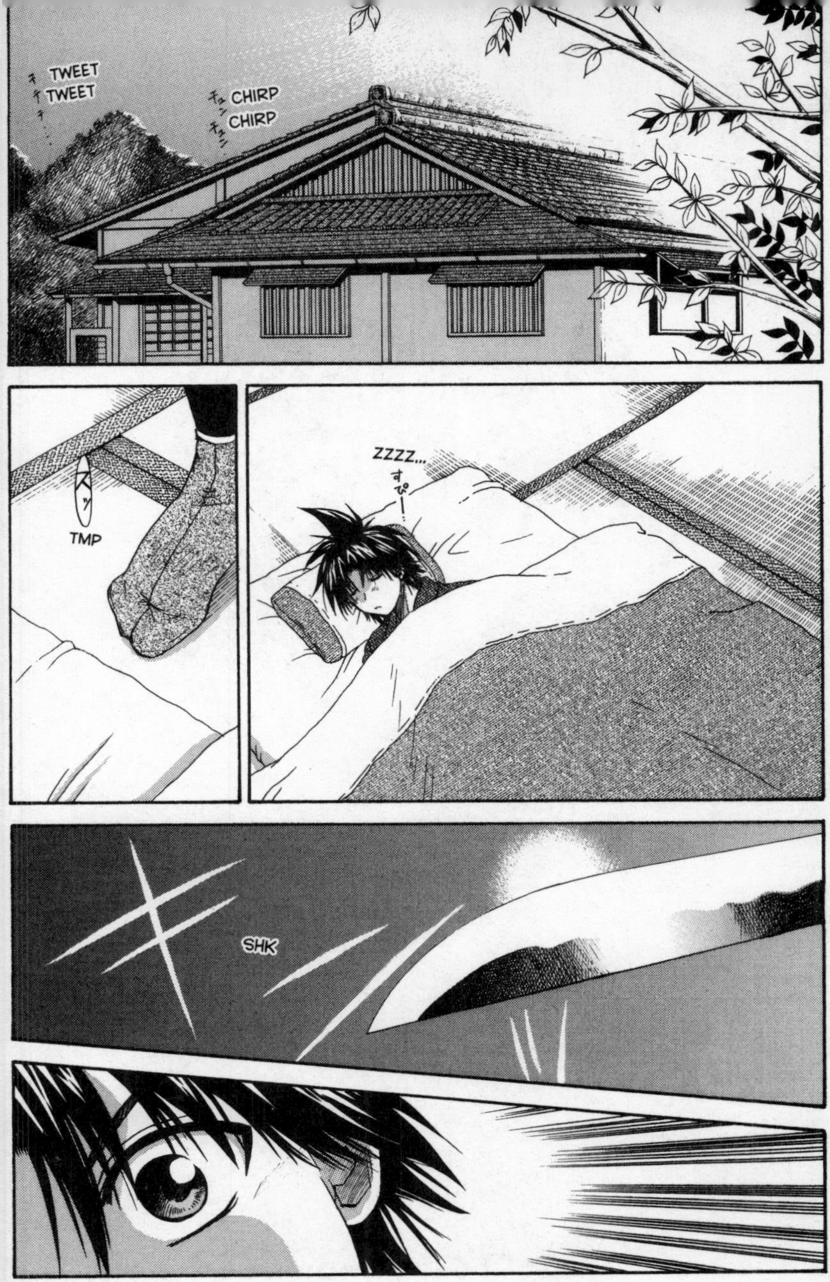
チュンチュン
CHIRP
CHIRP
チチチ
TWEET
TWEET
ZZZZ...
すぴー…
スッ
TMP
SHK

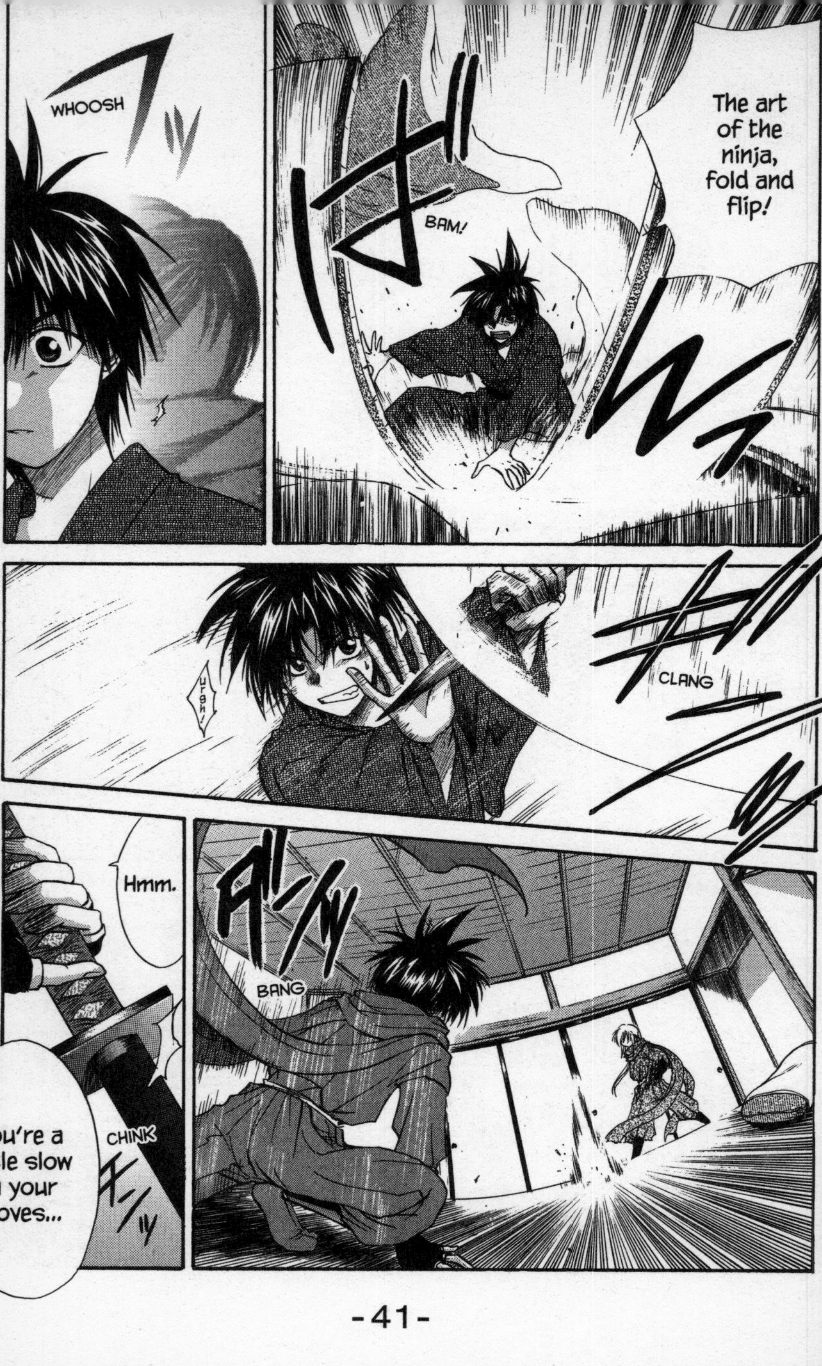

The art of the ninja, fold and flip!
BAM!
WHOOSH
CLANG
Urgh!
BANG
Hmm.
You're a little slow in your moves...
CHINK

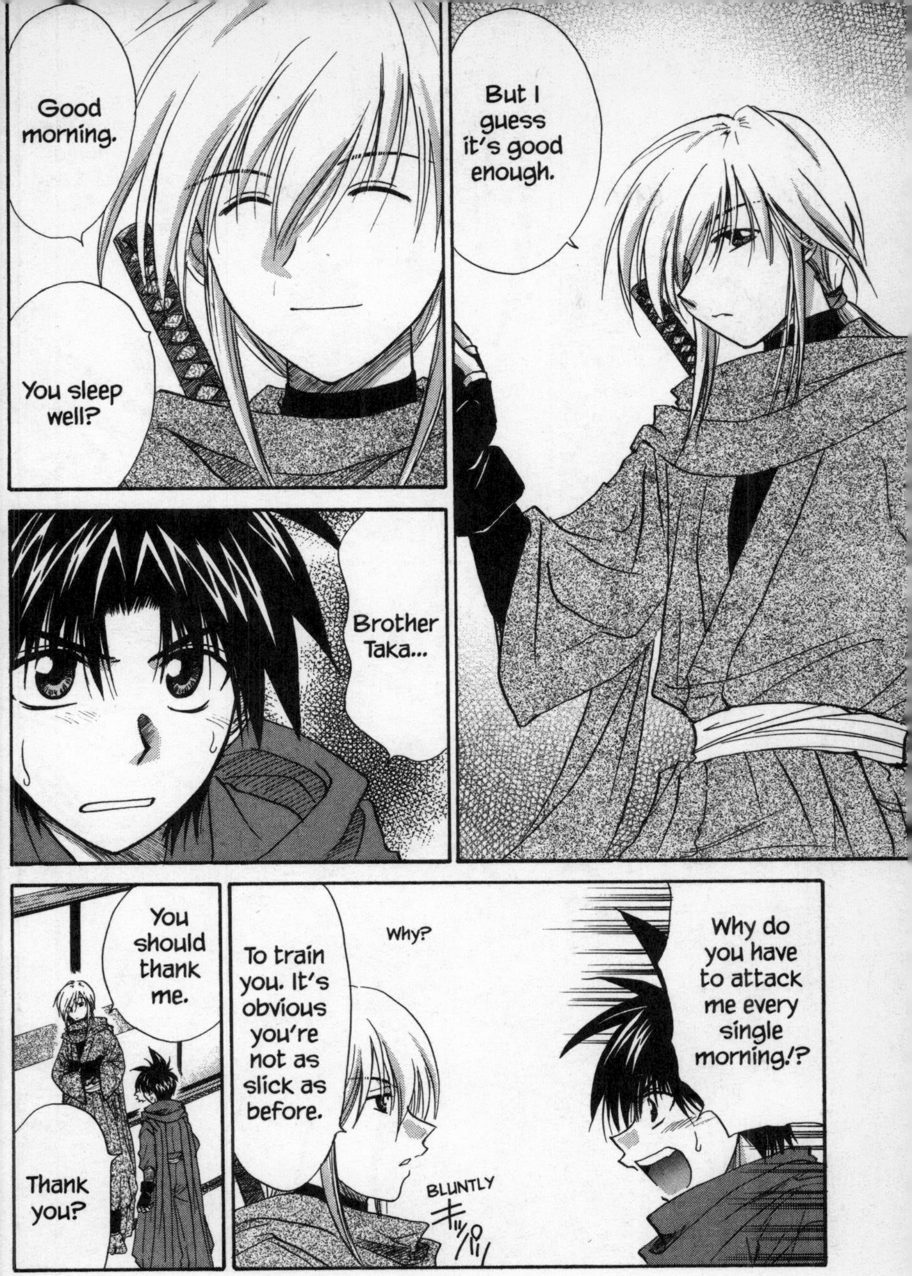
But I guess it's good enough.
Good morning.
You sleep well?
Brother Taka...
Why do you have to attack me every single morning!?
Why?
To train you. It's obvious you're not as slick as before.
BLUNTLY
You should thank me.
Thank you?

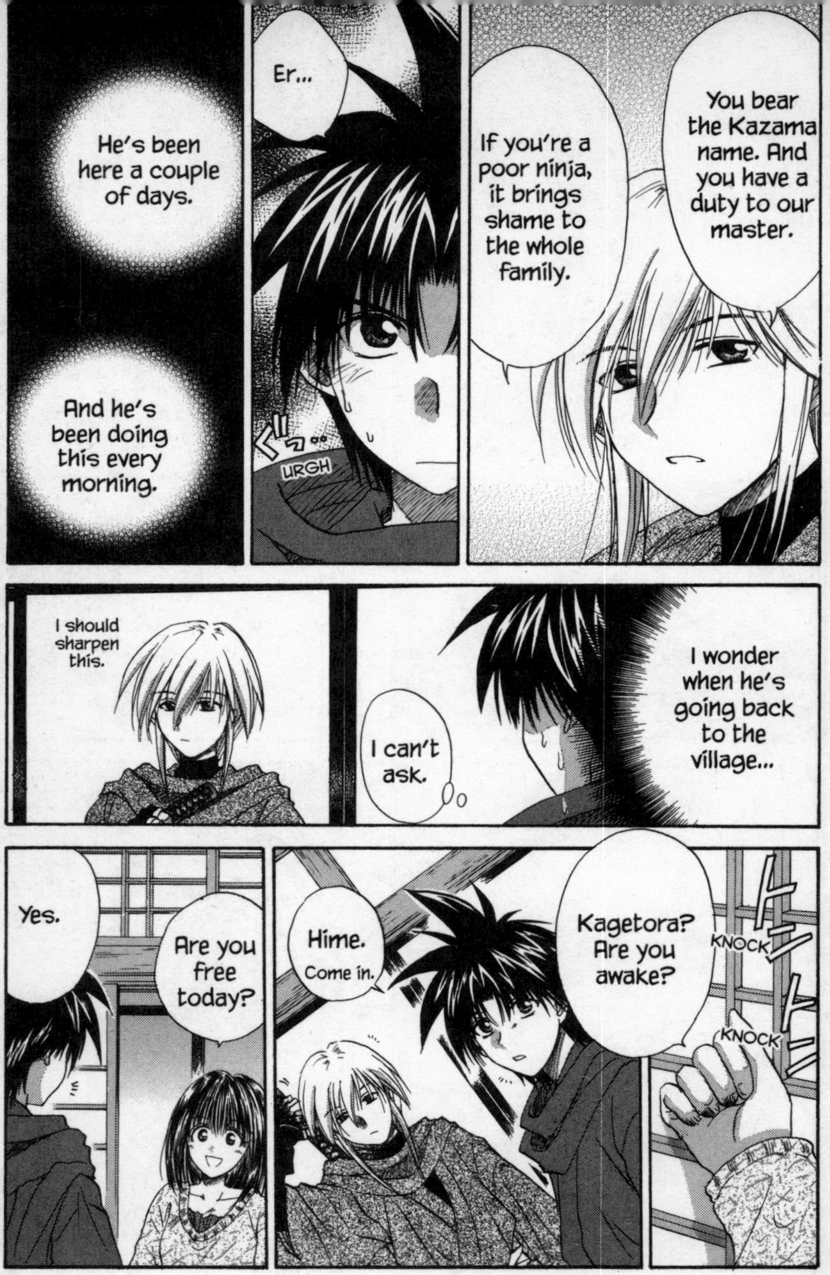
You bear the Kazama name. And you have a duty to our master.
If you're a poor ninja, it brings shame to the whole family.
Er...
URGH
He's been here a couple of days.
And he's been doing this every morning.
I wonder when he's going back to the village...
I can't ask.
I should sharpen this.
KNOCK
KNOCK
Kagetora? Are you awake?
Hime.
Come in.
Are you free today?
Yes.

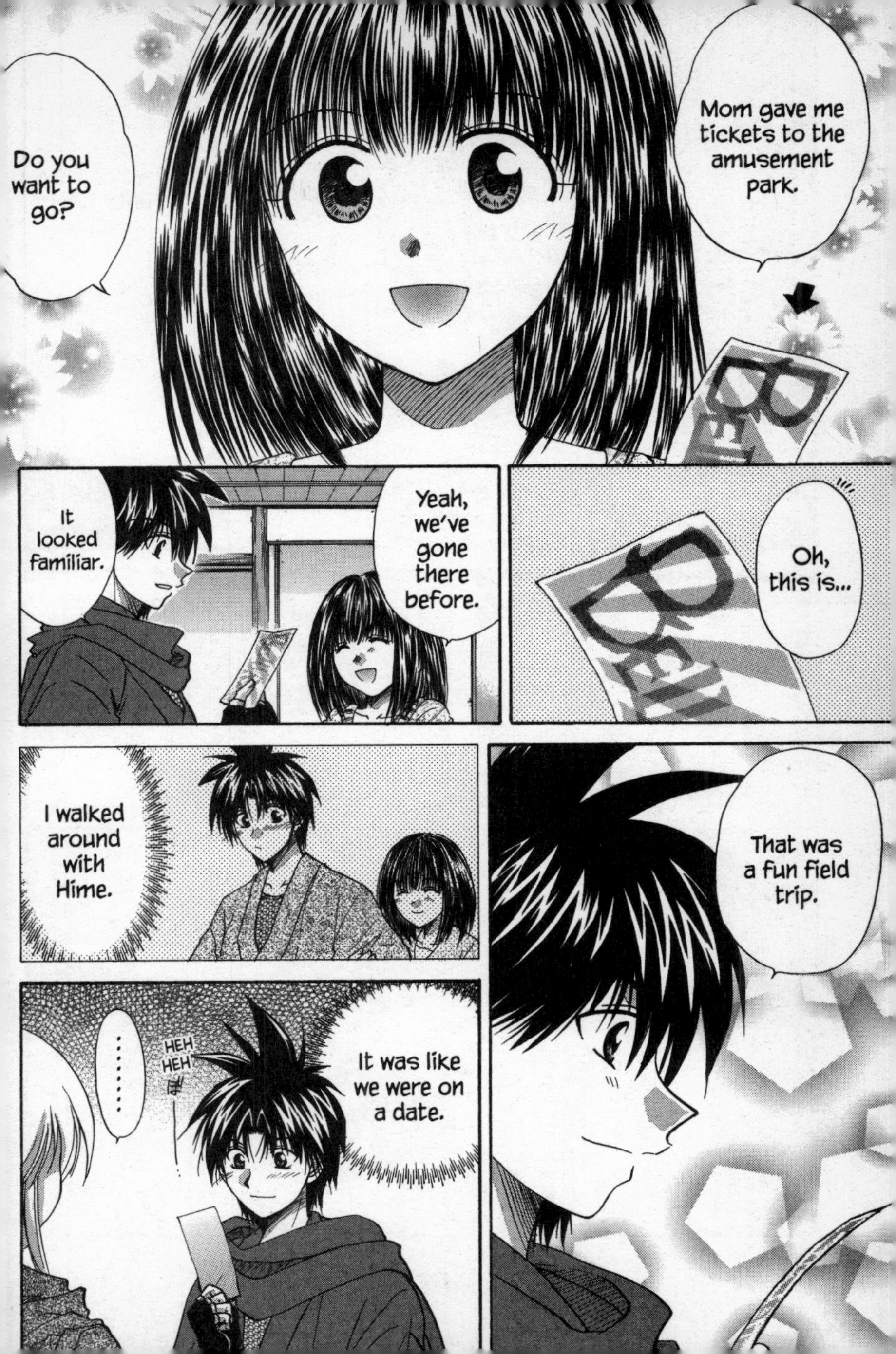
Mom gave me tickets to the amusement park.
Do you want to go?
Oh, this is...
Yeah, we've gone there before.
It looked familiar.
That was a fun field trip.
I walked around with Hime.
It was like we were on a date.
HEH HEH
......

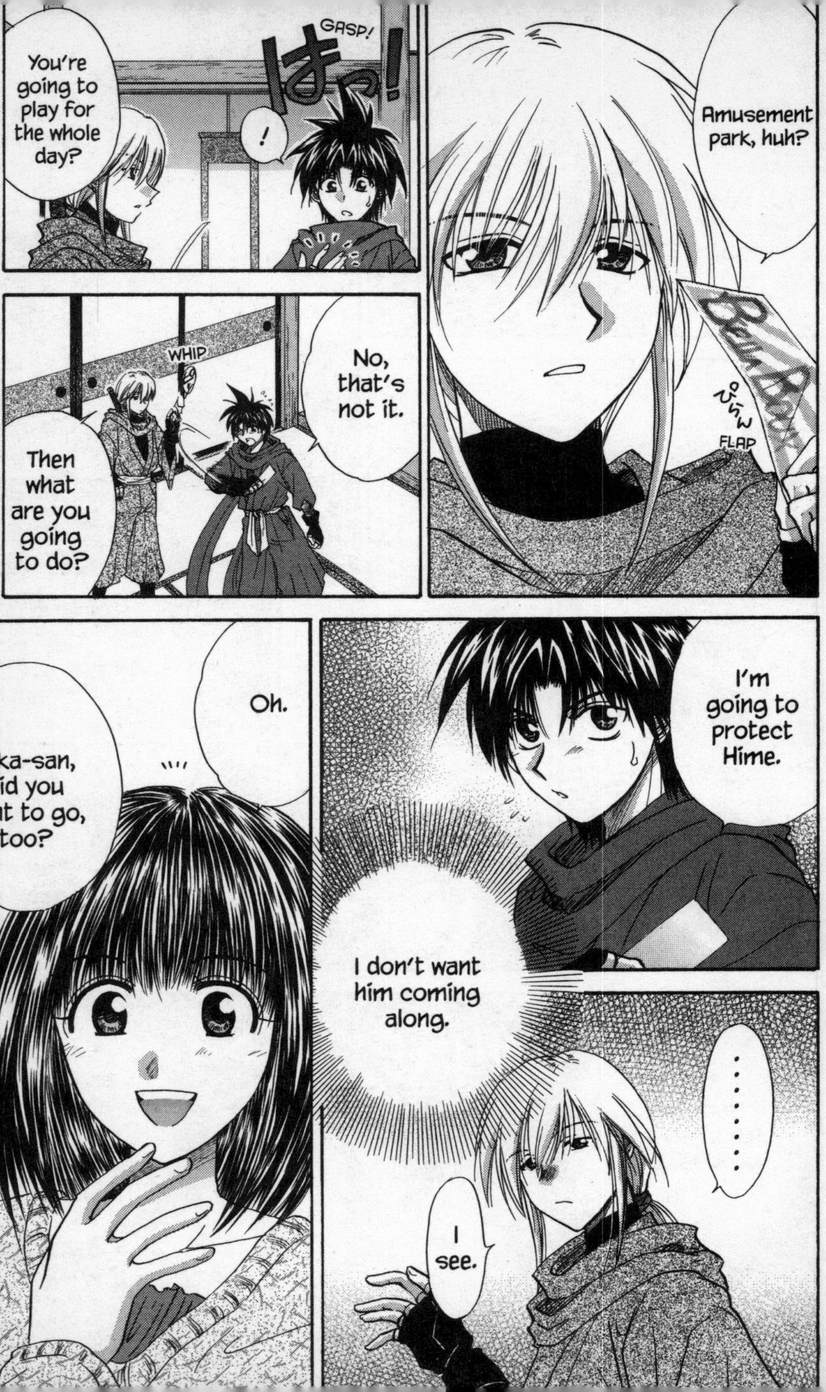

Amusement park, huh?
FLAP
GASP!
はっ!
!
You're going to play for the whole day?
No, that's not it.
WHIP
Then what are you going to do?
I'm going to protect Hime.
I don't want him coming along.
......
I see.
Oh.
Taka-san, did you want to go, too?

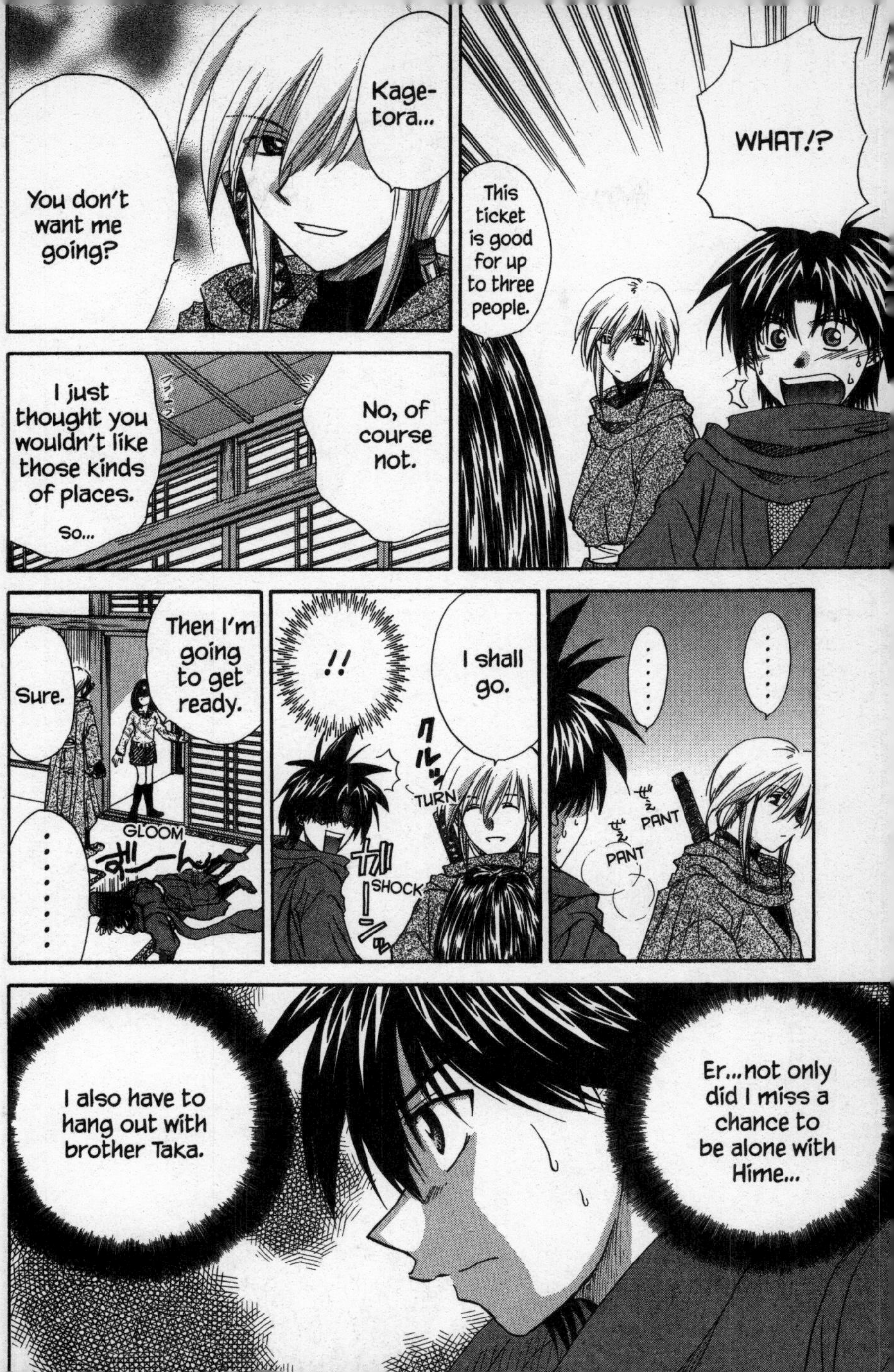
WHAT!?
This ticket is good for up to three people.
Kage-tora...
You don't want me going?
No, of course not.
I just thought you wouldn't like those kinds of places.
So...
......
......
PANT
PANT
I shall go.
!!
TURN
SHOCK
Then I'm going to get ready.
Sure.
......
GLOOM
Er...not only did I miss a chance to be alone with Hime...
I also have to hang out with brother Taka.

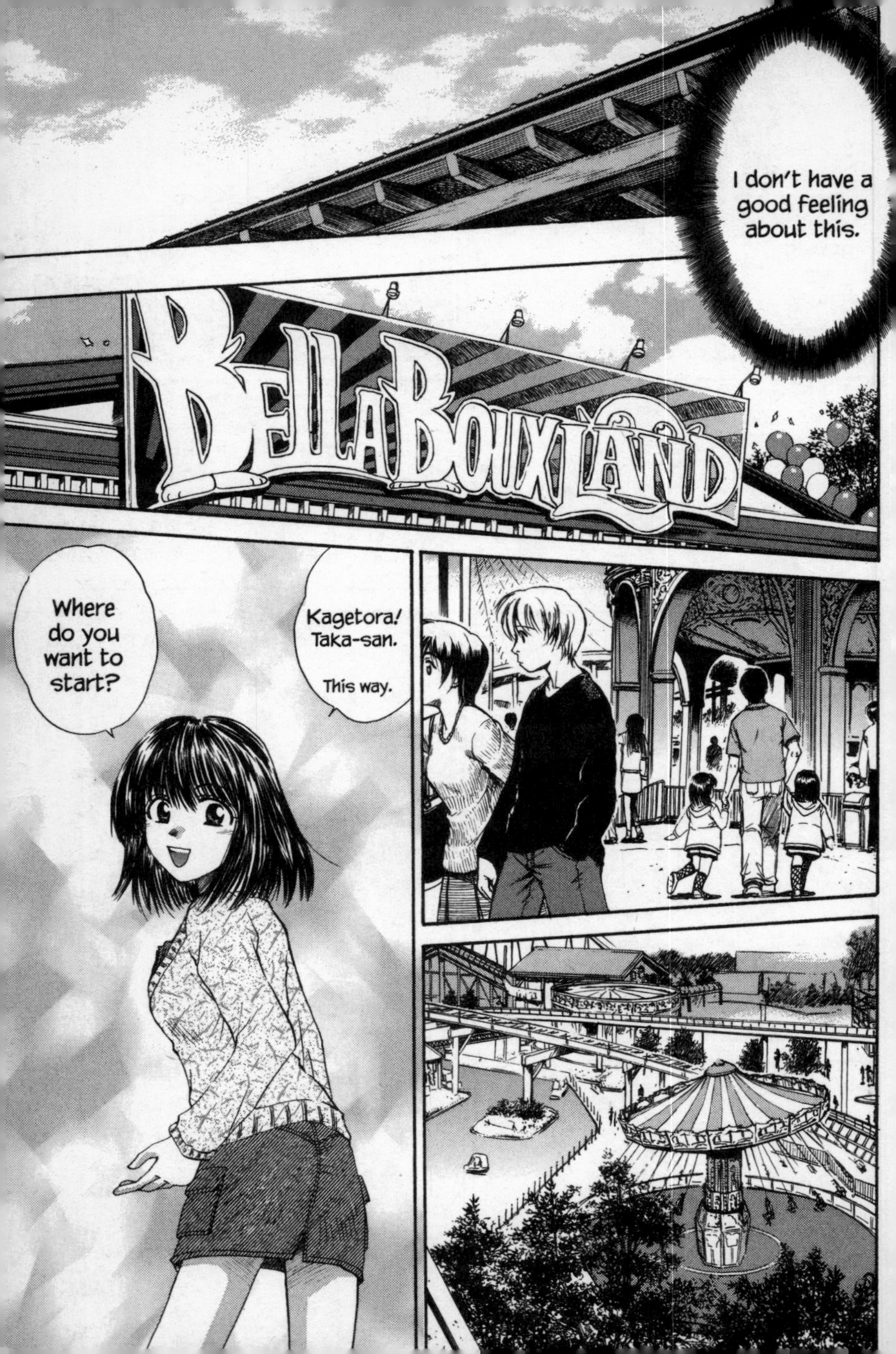
I don't have a good feeling about this.
BELLABOUXLAND
Kagetora! Taka-san.
This way.
Where do you want to start?

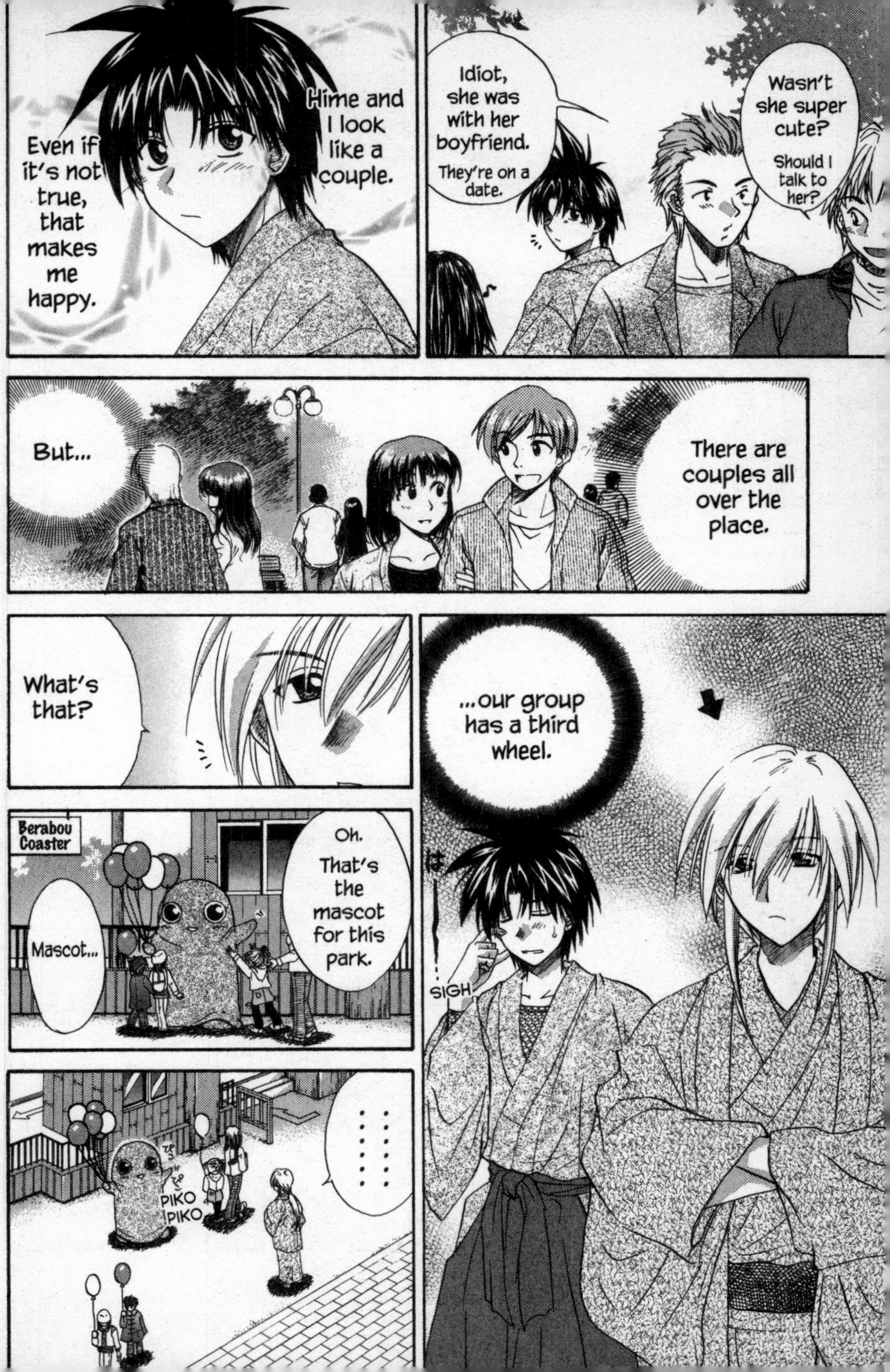
Wasn't she super cute?
Should I talk to her?
Idiot, she was with her boyfriend.
They're on a date.
Hime and I look like a couple.
Even if it's not true, that makes me happy.
There are couples all over the place.
But...
...our group has a third wheel.
SIGH
What's that?
Berabou Coaster
Oh. That's the mascot for this park.
Mascot...
......
PIKO PIKO

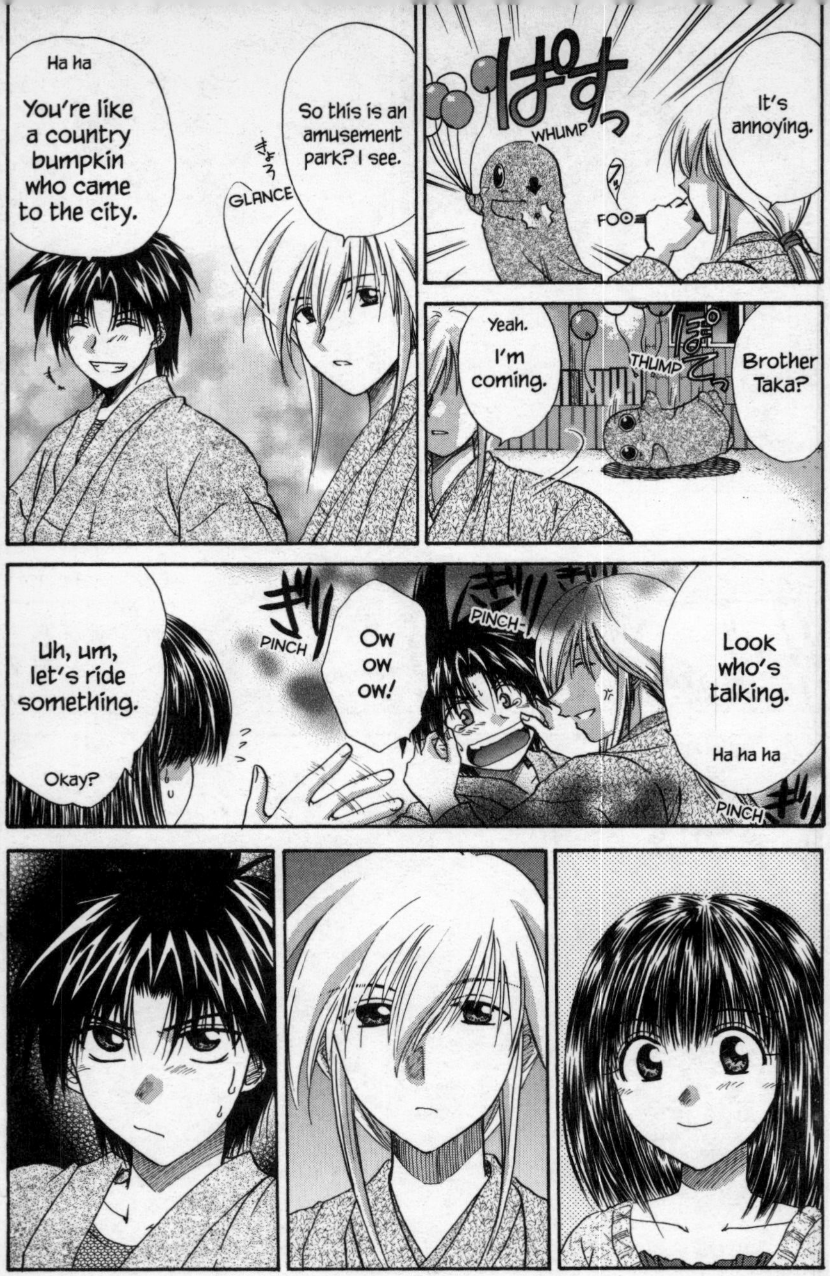

ぱすっ
WHUMP
It's annoying.
フッ
FOO
Brother Taka?
ぽてっ
THUMP
Yeah. I'm coming.
So this is an amusement park? I see.
きょろ
GLANCE
Ha ha
You're like a country bumpkin who came to the city.
Look who's talking.
Ha ha ha
PINCH
PINCH-
Ow ow ow!
PINCH
Uh, um, let's ride something.
Okay?

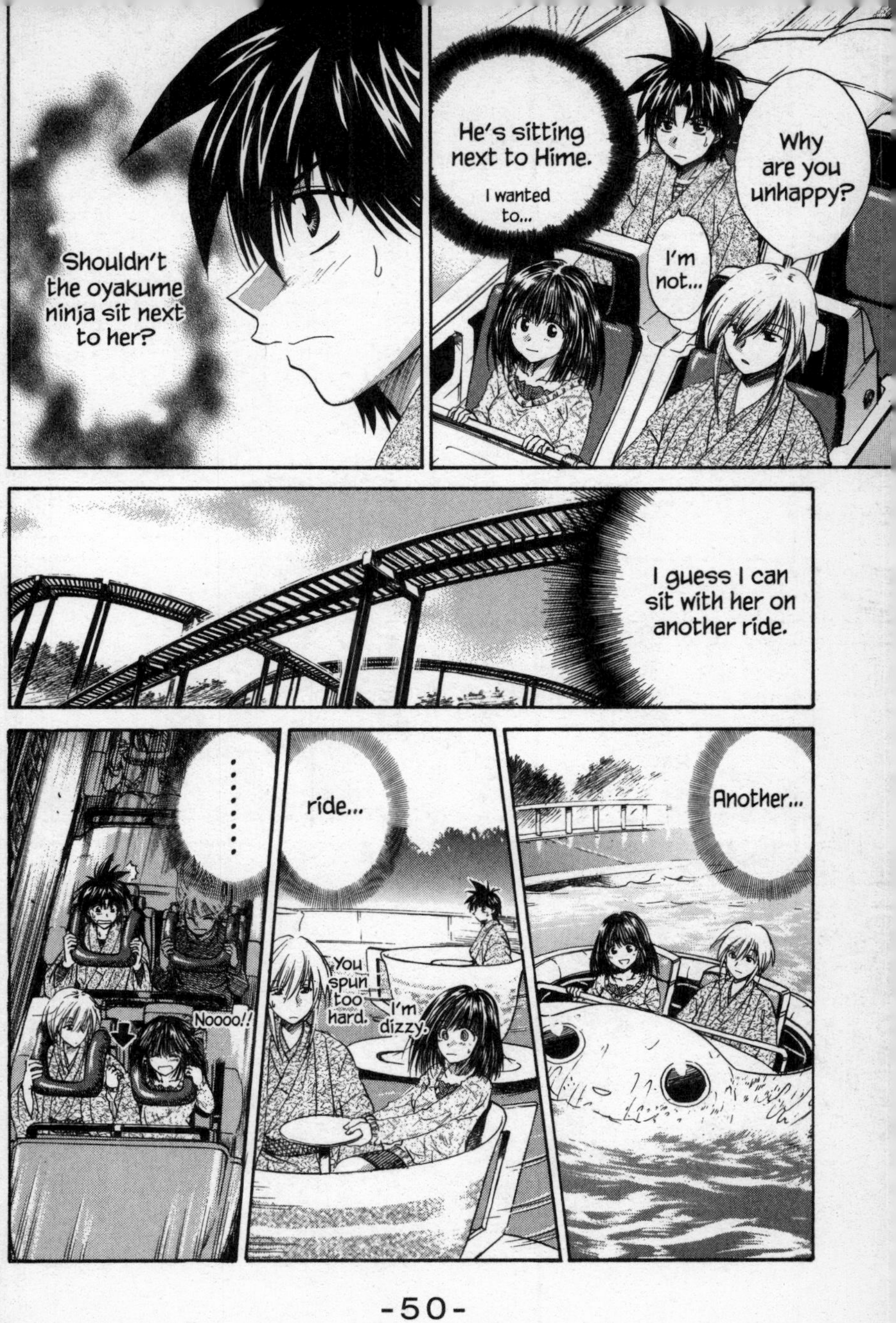
Why are you unhappy?
I'm not...
He's sitting next to Hime.
I wanted to...
Shouldn't the oyakume ninja sit next to her?
I guess I can sit with her on another ride.
Another...
ride...
I'm dizzy.
You spun too hard.
......
Noooo!!

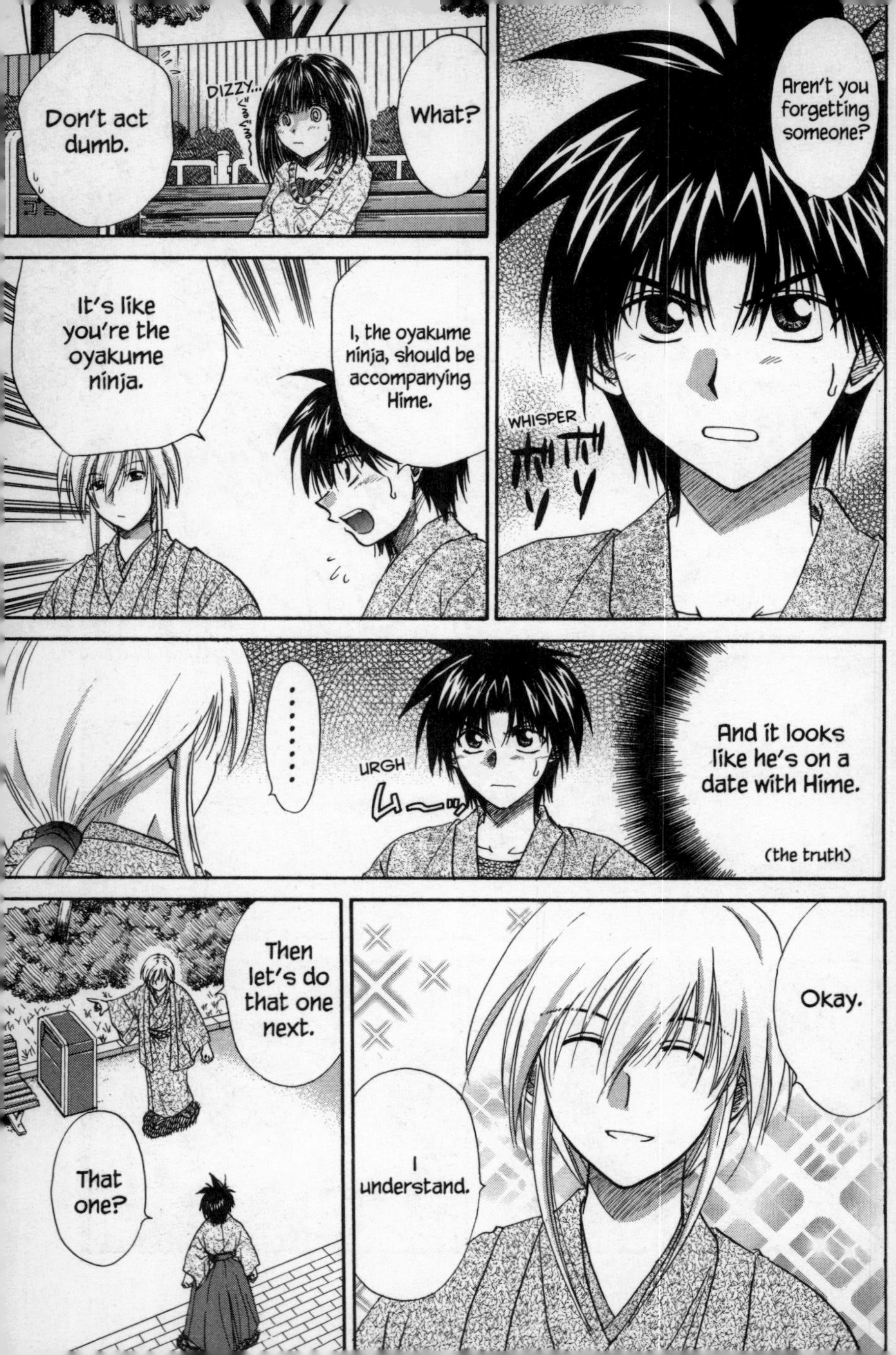

Aren't you forgetting someone?
WHISPER
What?
DIZZY...
Don't act dumb.
I, the oyakume ninja, should be accompanying Hime.
It's like you're the oyakume ninja.
And it looks like he's on a date with Hime.
(the truth)
URGH
....
Okay.
I understand.
Then let's do that one next.
That one?

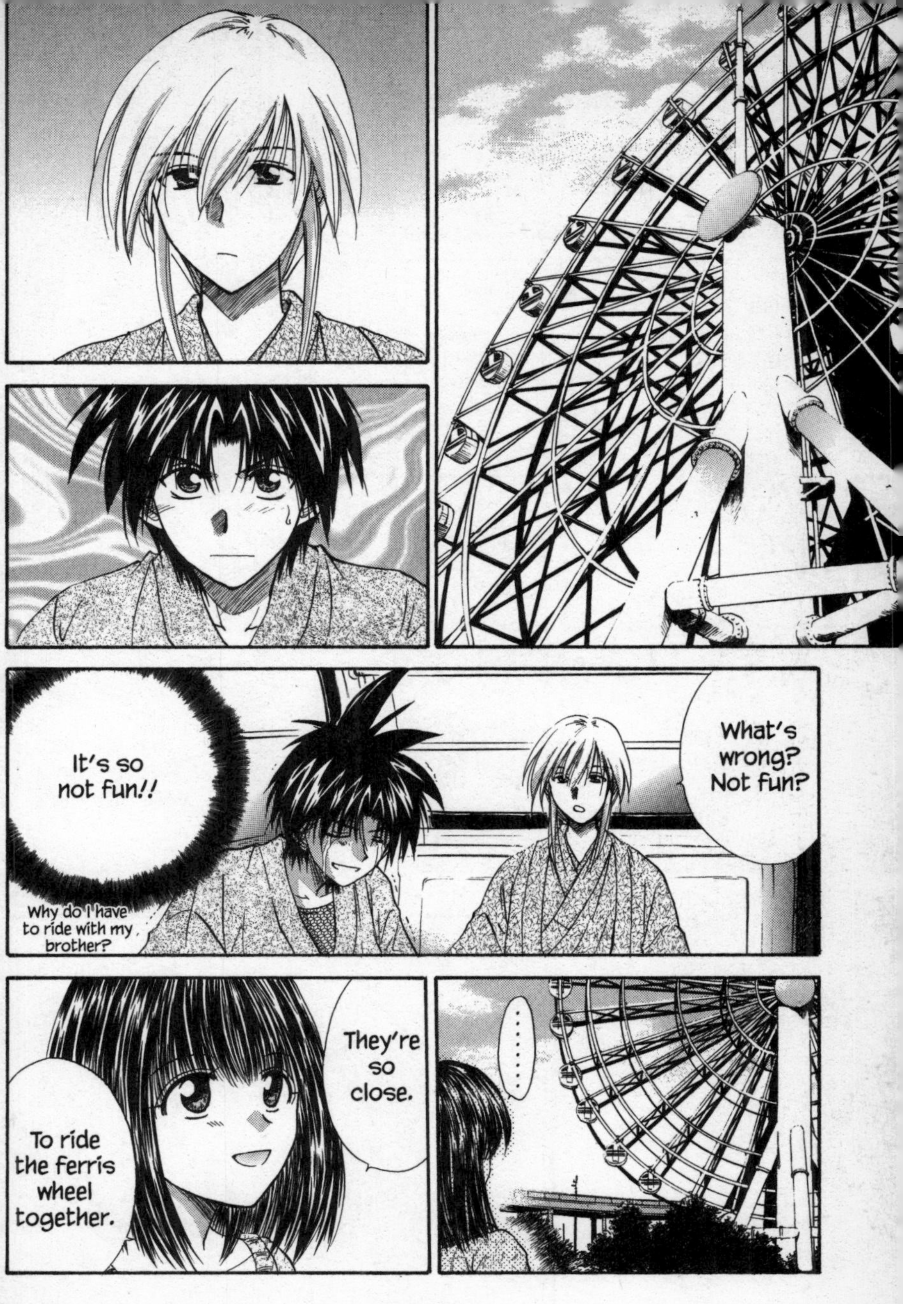
What's wrong? Not fun?
It's so not fun!!
Why do I have to ride with my brother?
……
They're so close.
To ride the ferris wheel together.

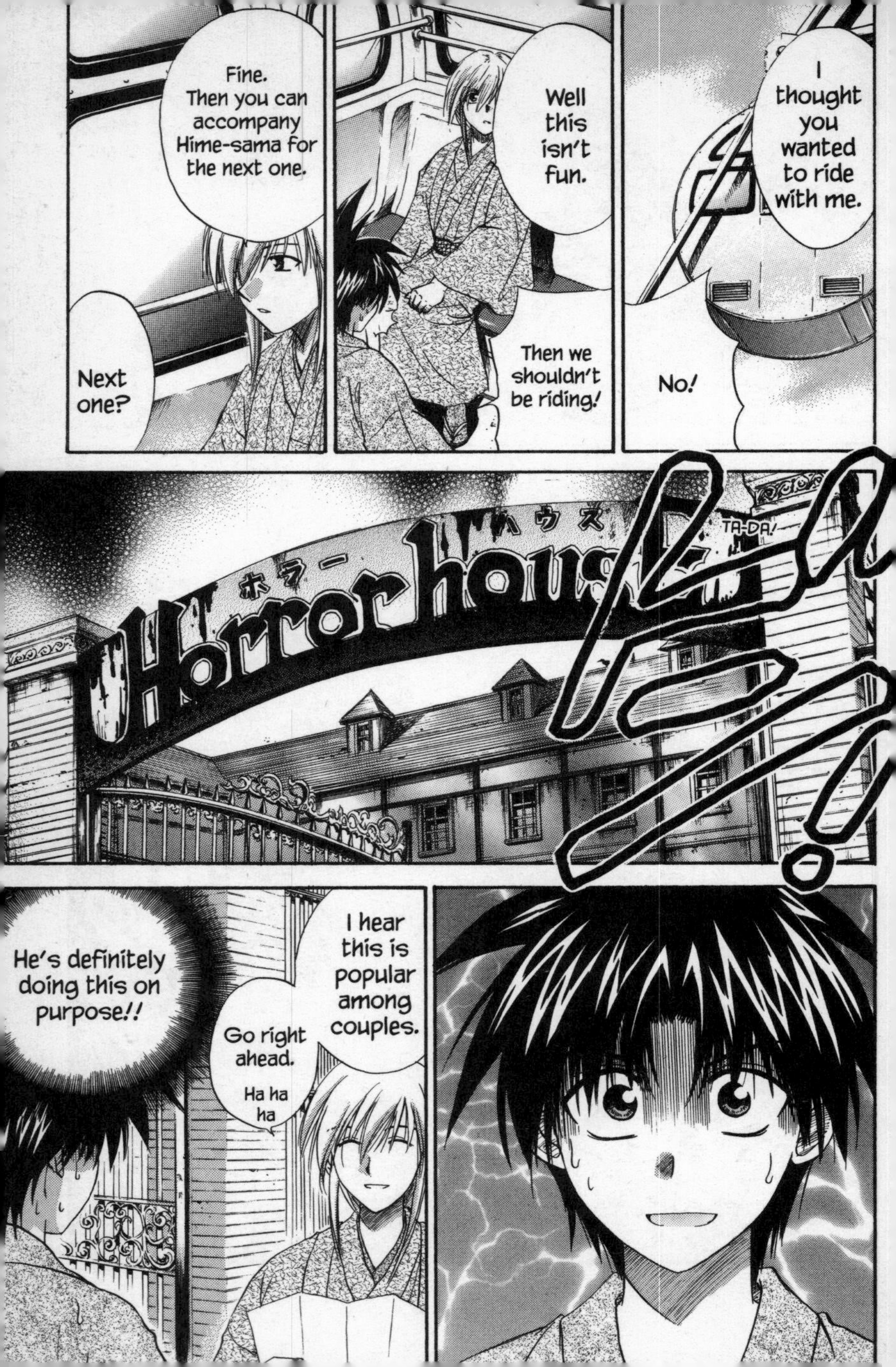
I thought you wanted to ride with me.
No!
Well this isn't fun.
Then we shouldn't be riding!
Fine. Then you can accompany Hime-sama for the next one.
Next one?
ホラーハウス
Horror house
TA-DA!
I hear this is popular among couples.
Go right ahead.
Ha ha ha
He's definitely doing this on purpose!!

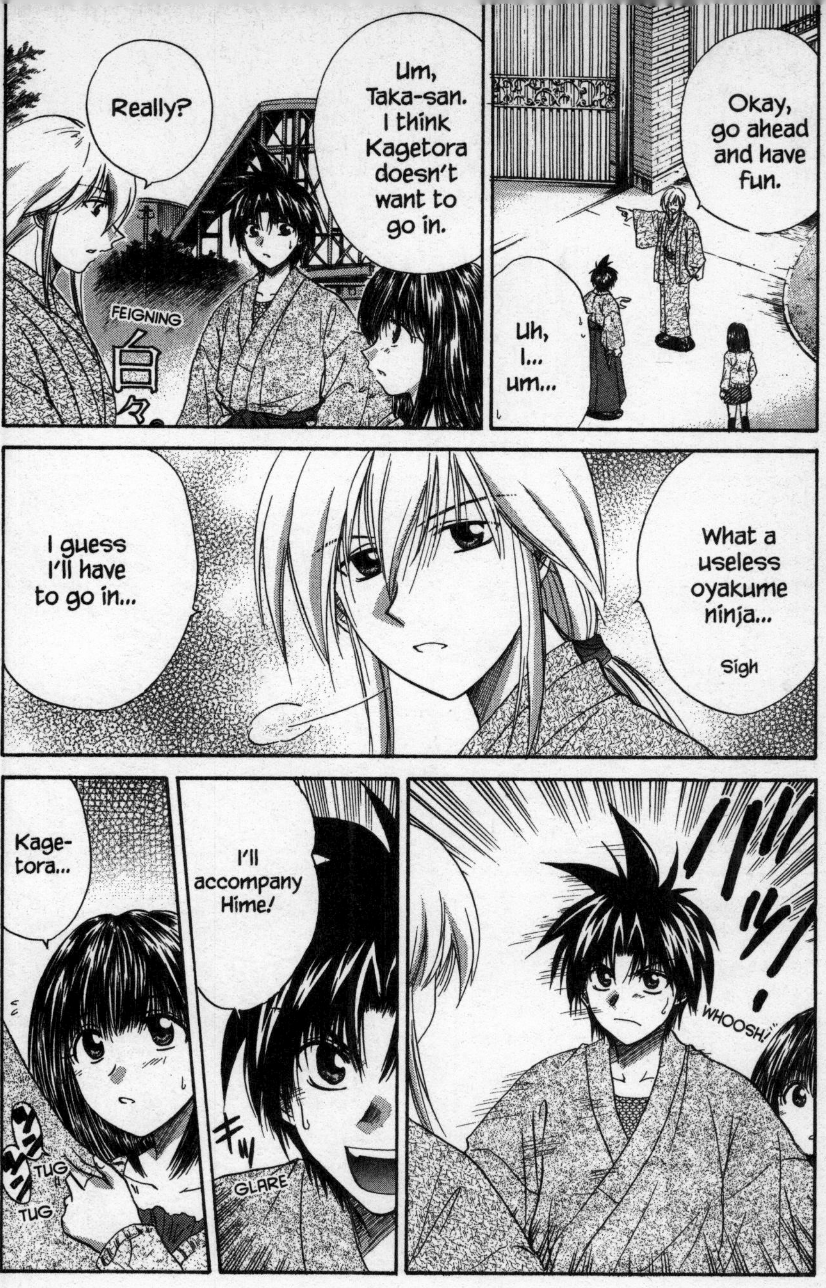
Okay, go ahead and have fun.
Uh, I... um...
Um, Taka-san. I think Kagetora doesn't want to go in.
Really?
FEIGNING
白々
What a useless oyakume ninja... Sigh
I guess I'll have to go in...
WHOOSH!
I'll accompany Hime!
GLARE
Kage-tora...
TUG
TUG

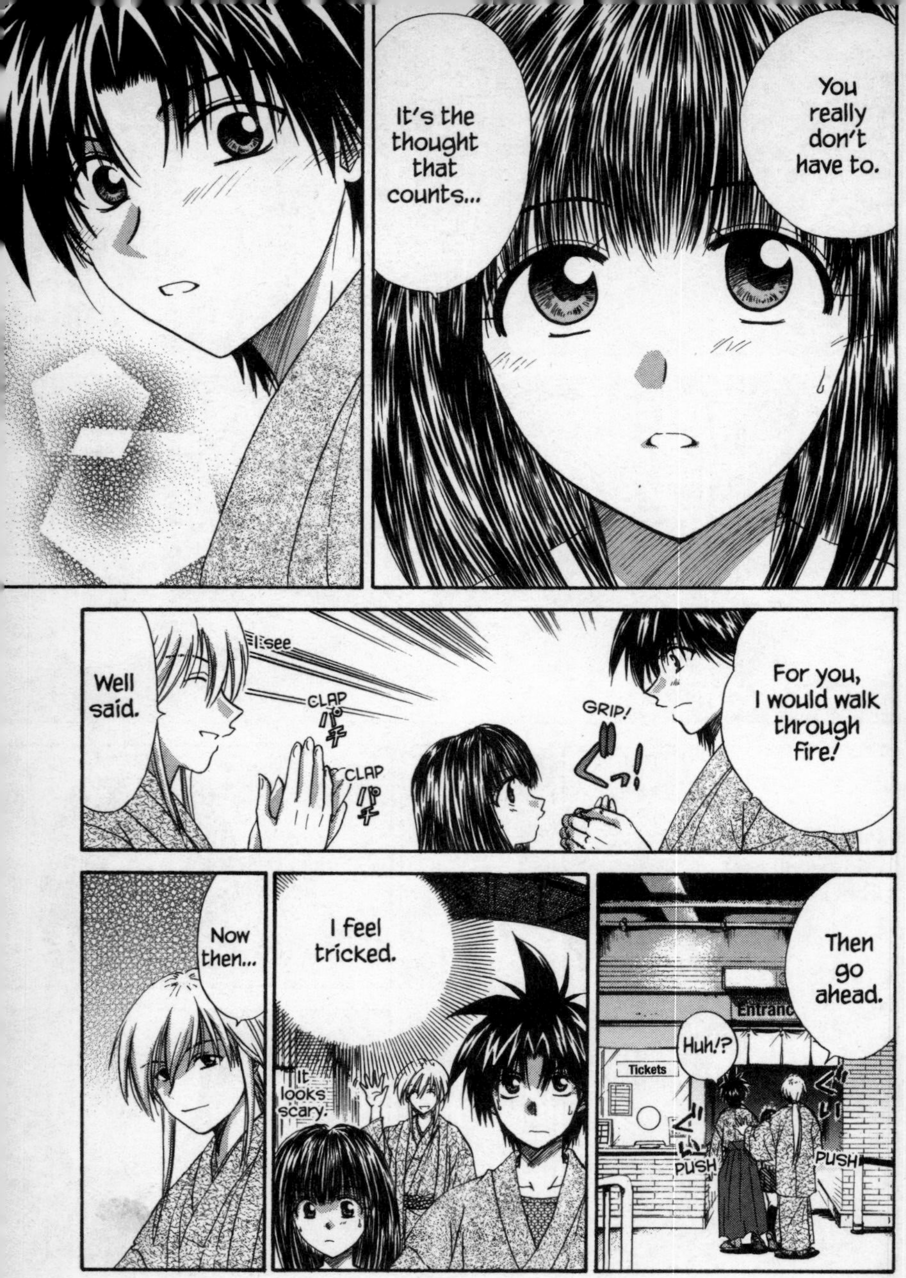
You really don't have to.
It's the thought that counts...
For you, I would walk through fire!
GRIP!
CLAP
CLAP
I see
Well said.
Then go ahead.
Entranc
Huh!?
Tickets
PUSH
PUSH
I feel tricked.
It looks scary.
Now then...

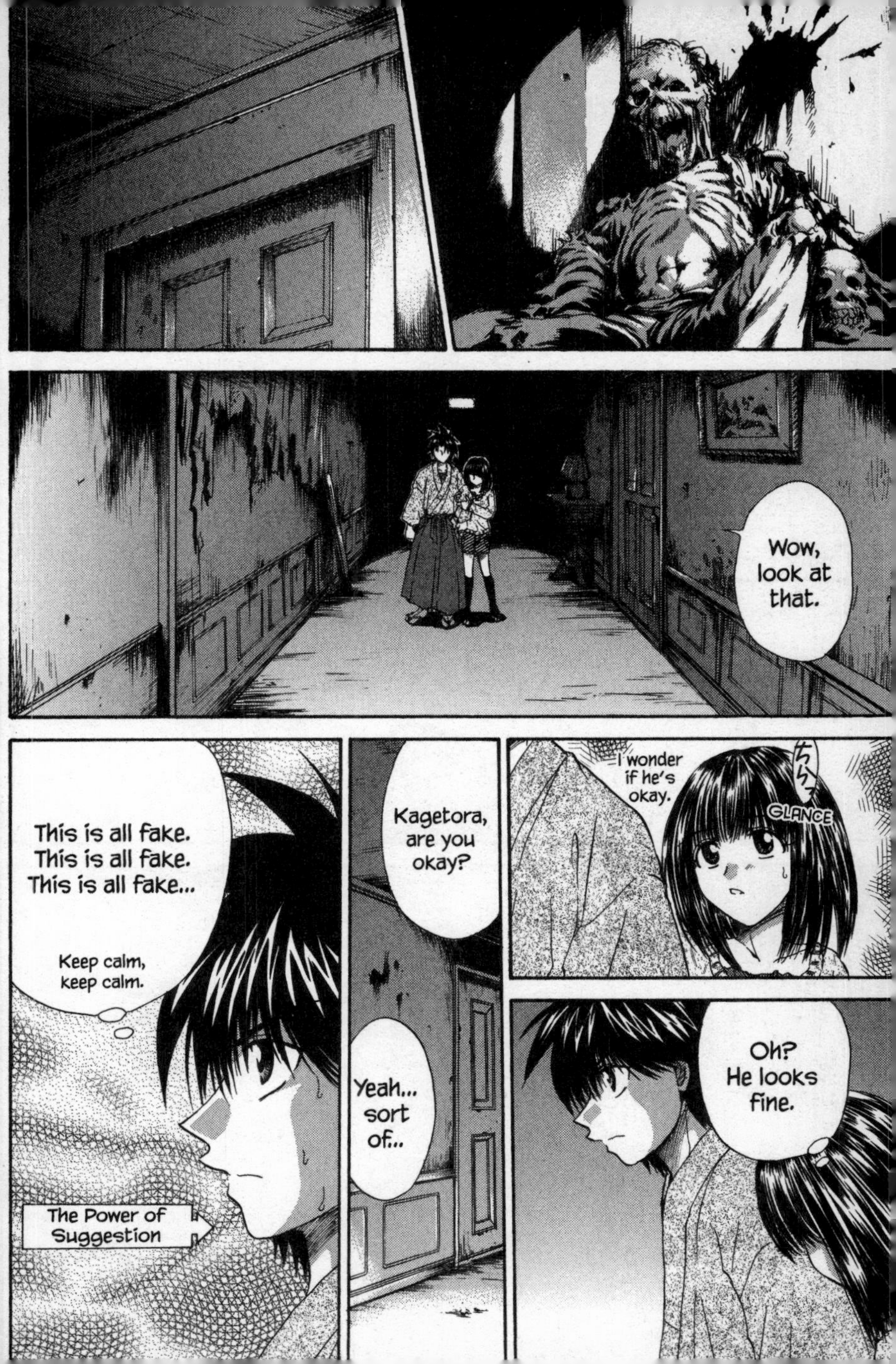
Wow, look at that.
I wonder if he's okay.
ちらっ
GLANCE
Oh? He looks fine.
Kagetora, are you okay?
Yeah... sort of...
This is all fake. This is all fake. This is all fake...
Keep calm, keep calm.
The Power of Suggestion

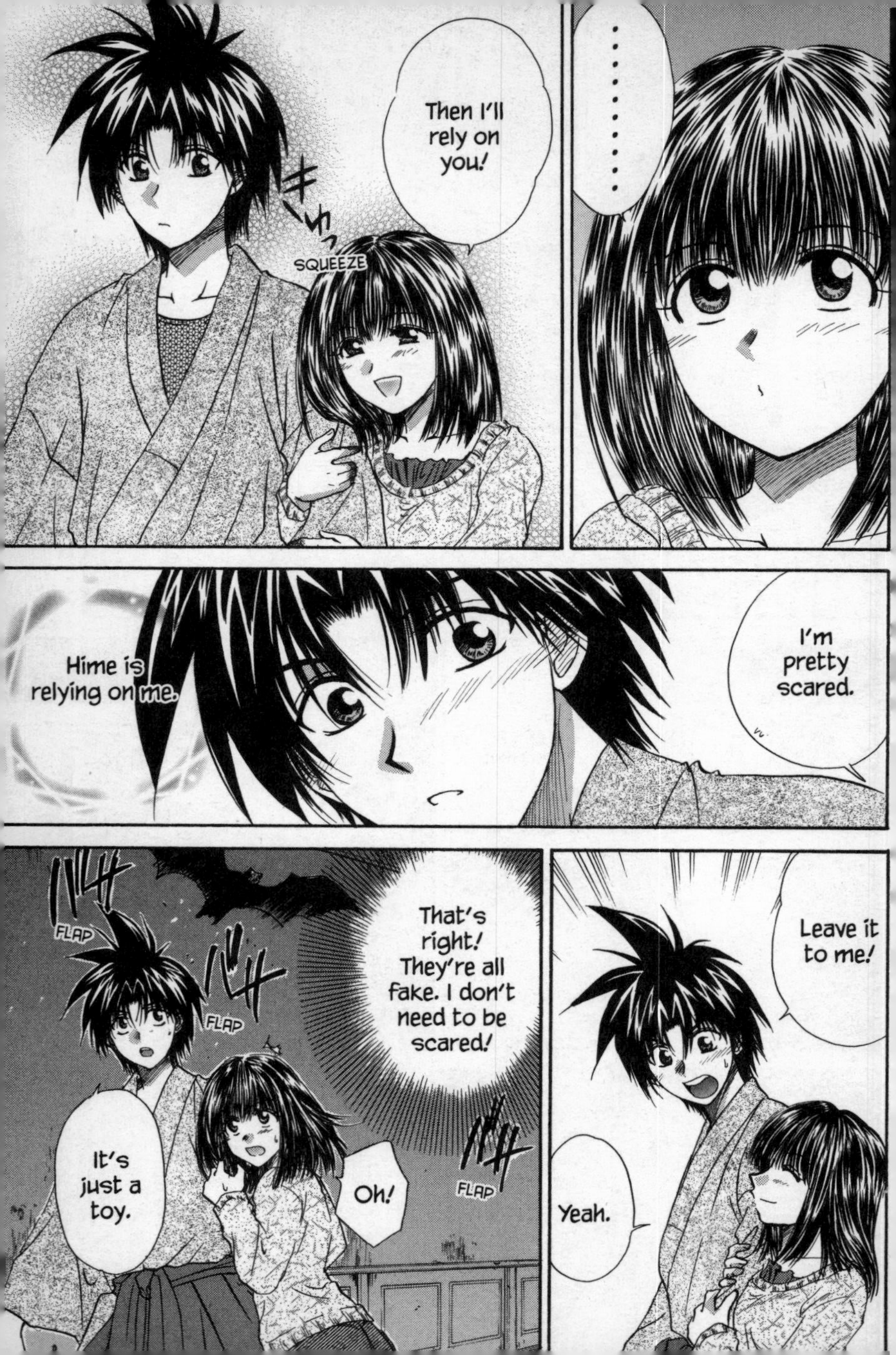

......
Then I'll rely on you!
SQUEEZE
I'm pretty scared.
Hime is relying on me.
Leave it to me!
Yeah.
That's right! They're all fake. I don't need to be scared!
FLAP
FLAP
FLAP
Oh!
It's just a toy.

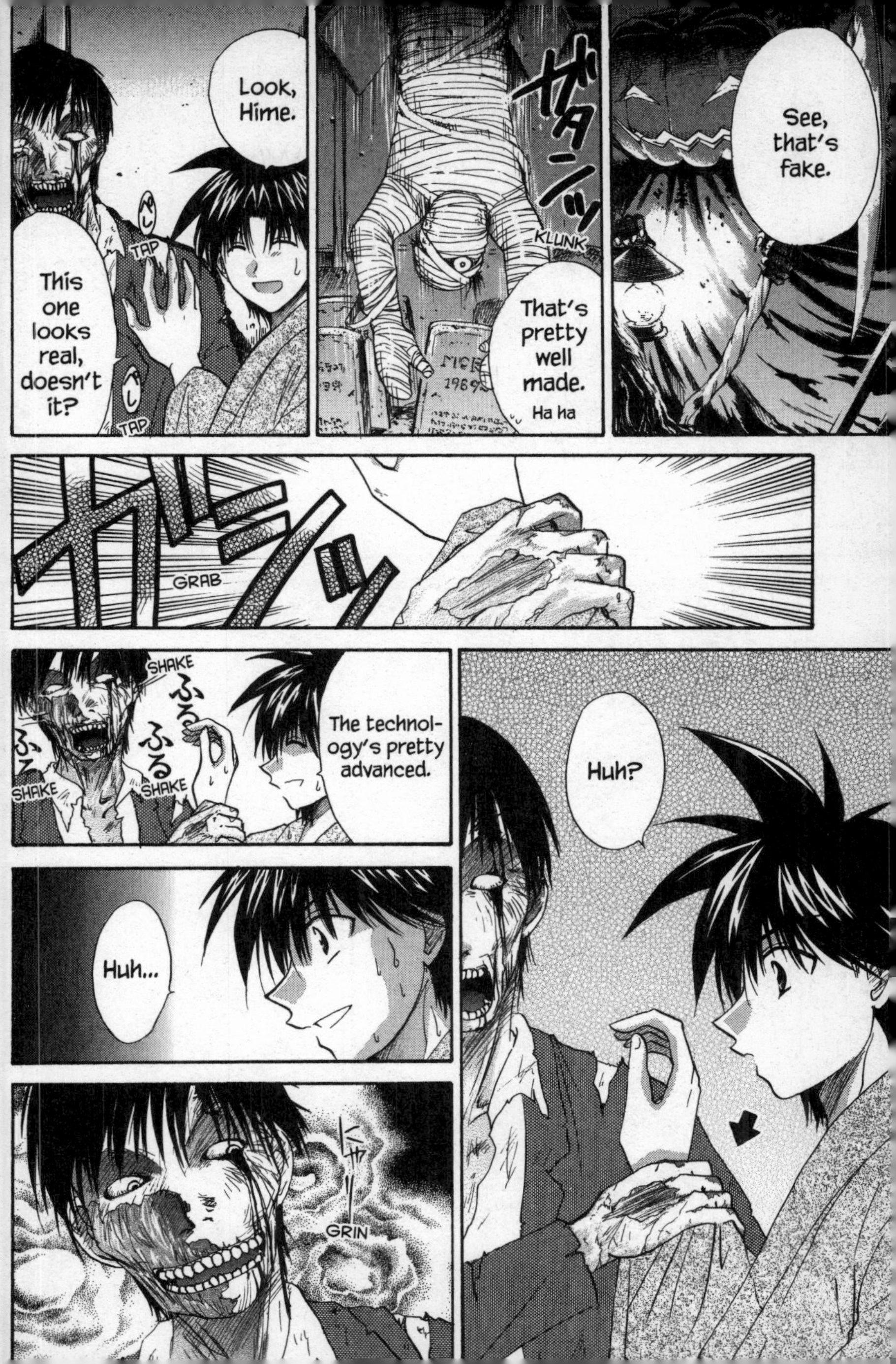
See, that's fake.
KLUNK
That's pretty well made.
Ha ha
Look, Hime.
This one looks real, doesn't it?
TAP
TAP
GRAB
Huh?
The technology's pretty advanced.
SHAKE
SHAKE
SHAKE
Huh...
GRIN

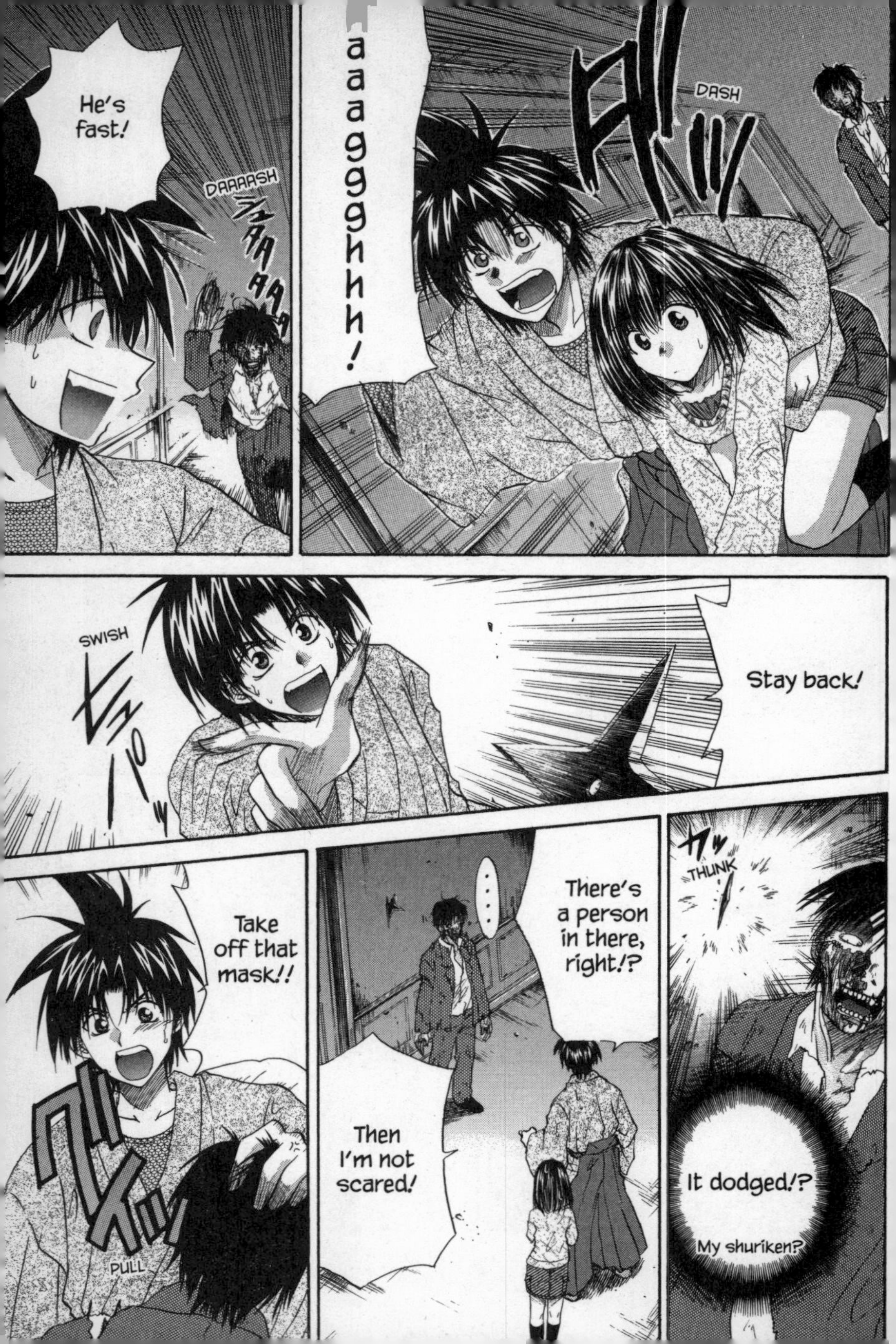
DASH
aaaagghhhh!
He's fast!
DAAAASH
Stay back!
SWISH
THUNK
It dodged!?
My shuriken?
There's a person in there, right!?
...
Then I'm not scared!
Take off that mask!!
PULL

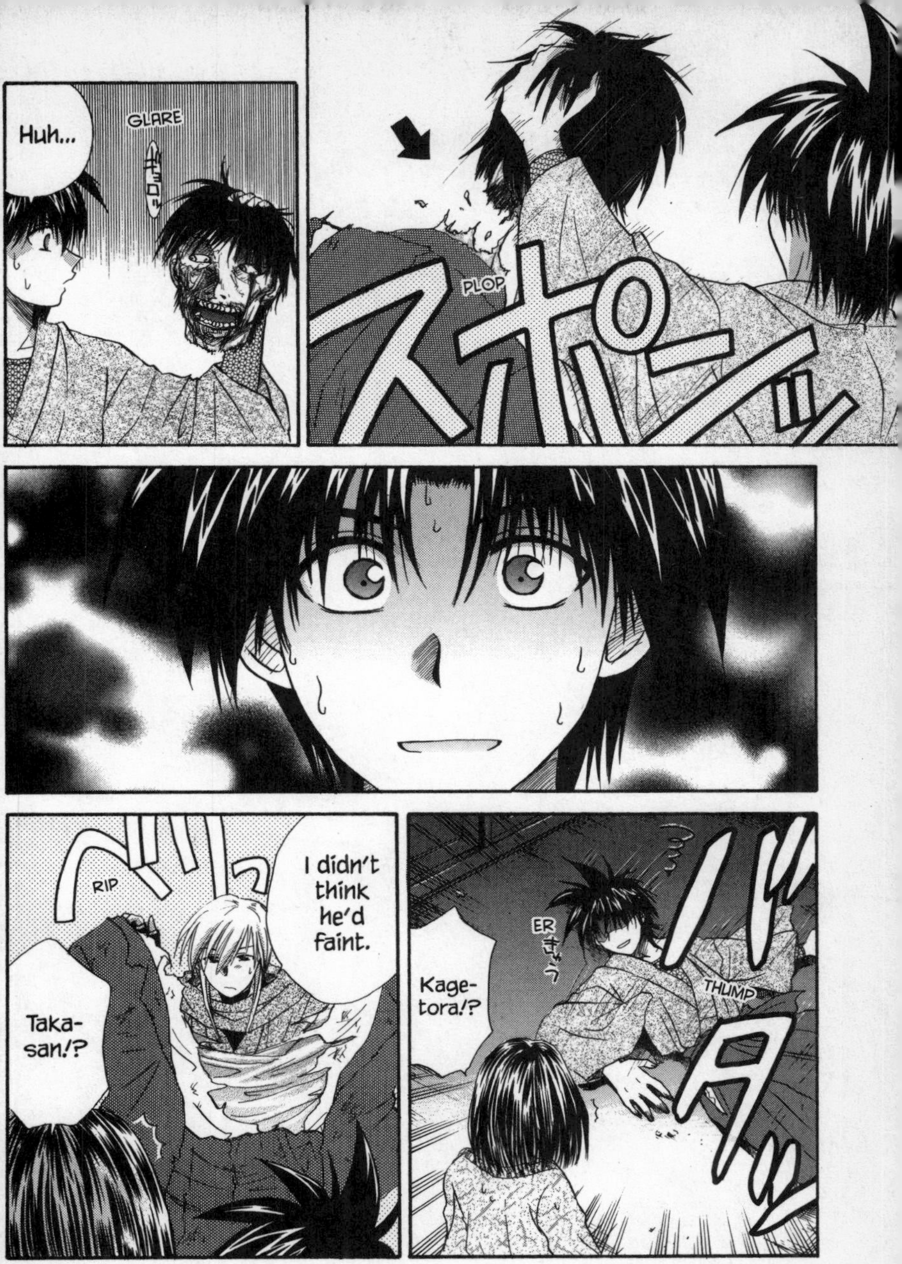
PLOP
Huh...
GLARE
Kage-tora!?
ER
THUMP
I didn't think he'd faint.
RIP
Taka-san!?

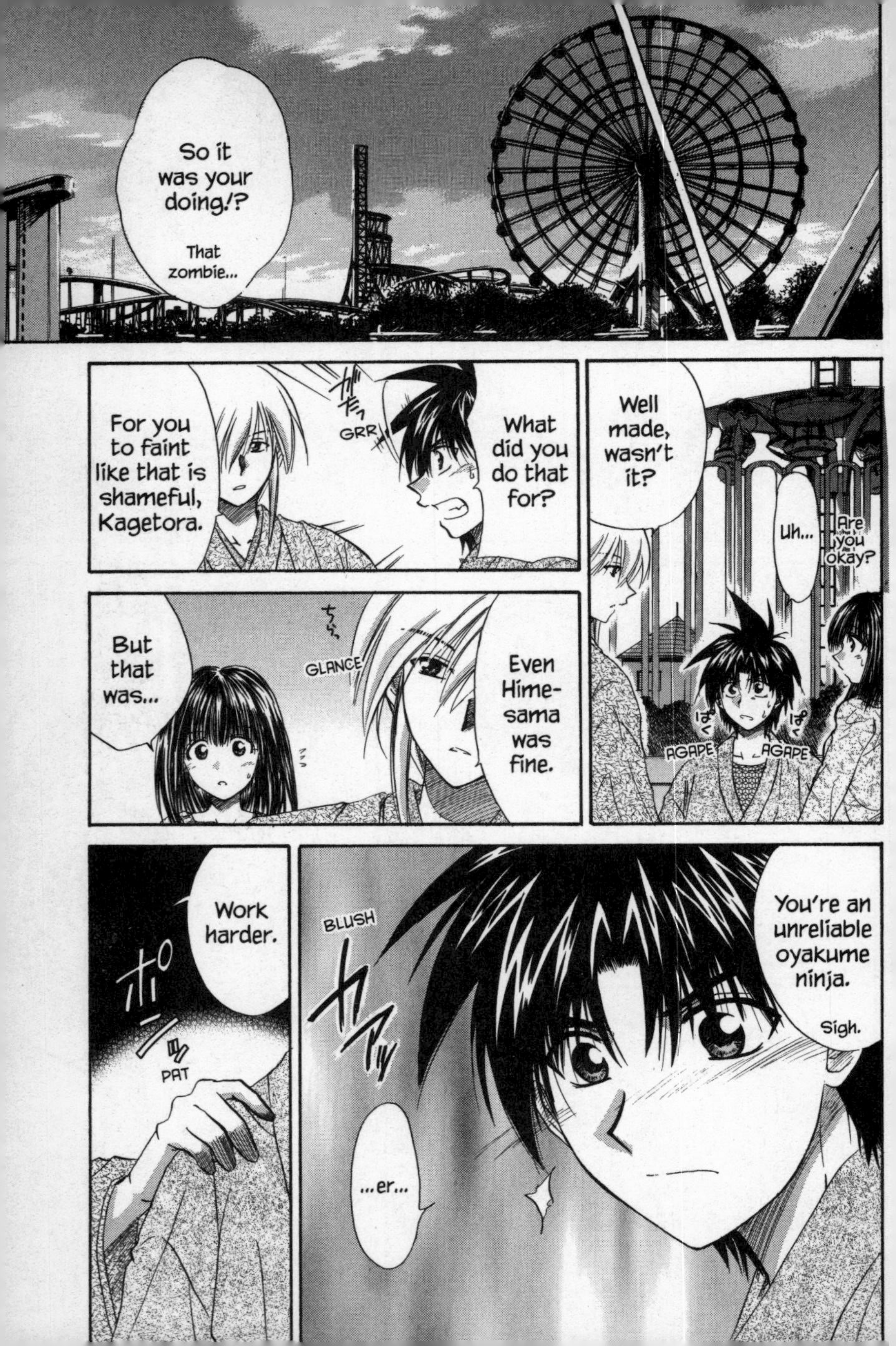
So it was your doing!?
That zombie...
Well made, wasn't it?
Are you okay?
Uh...
AGAPE
AGAPE
What did you do that for?
GRR
For you to faint like that is shameful, Kagetora.
Even Hime-sama was fine.
GLANCE
But that was...
You're an unreliable oyakume ninja.
Sigh.
BLUSH
...er...
Work harder.
PAT

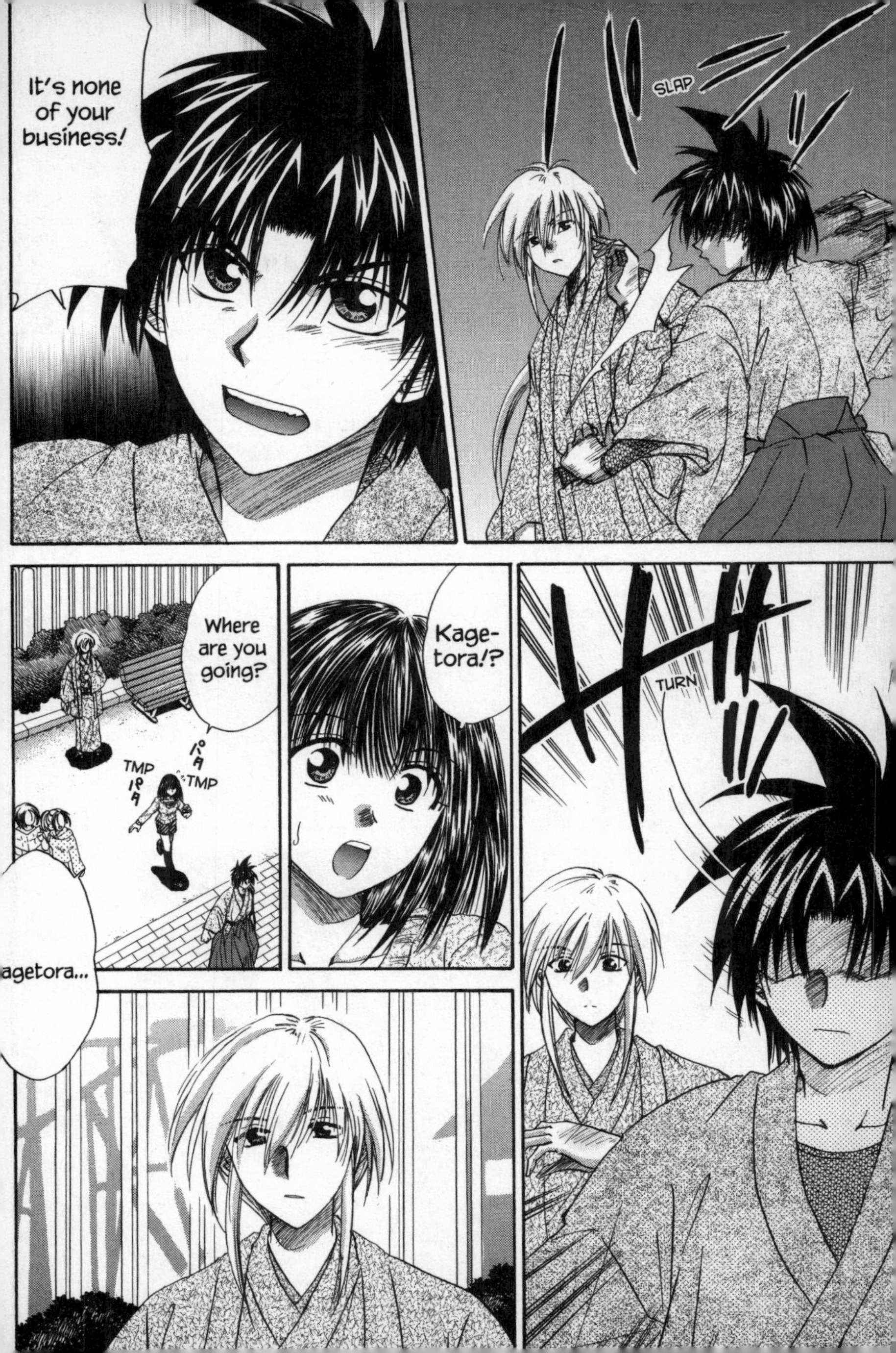
SLAP
It's none of your business!
TURN
Kage-tora!?
Where are you going?
パタ
TMP
パタ
TMP
agetora...

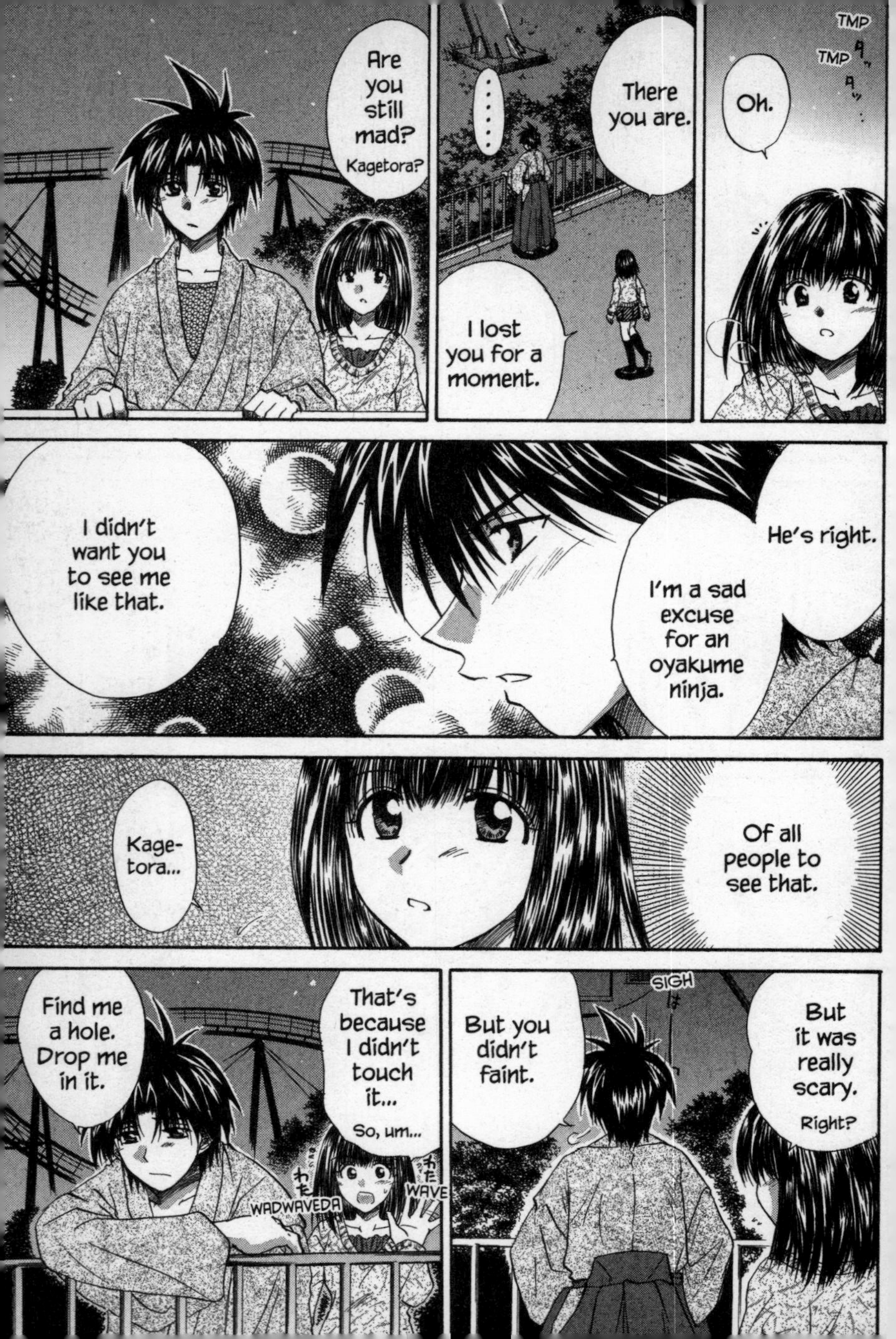
TMP
TMP
Oh.
There you are.
......
I lost you for a moment.
Are you still mad?
Kagetora?
He's right.
I'm a sad excuse for an oyakume ninja.
I didn't want you to see me like that.
Of all people to see that.
Kage-tora...
But it was really scary.
Right?
SIGH
But you didn't faint.
That's because I didn't touch it...
So, um...
WAVE
WADWAVEDA
Find me a hole. Drop me in it.

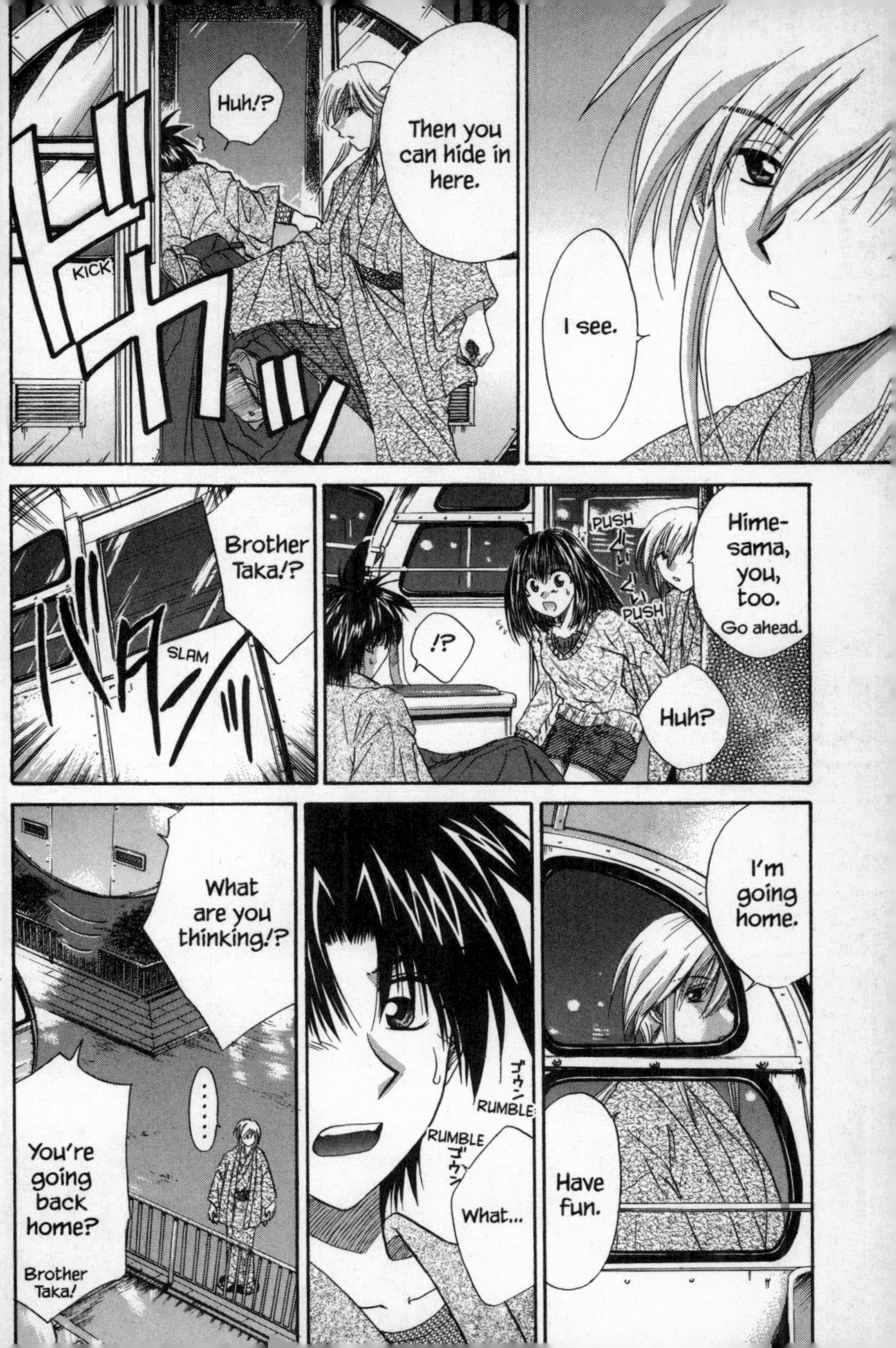
I see.
Then you can hide in here.
Huh!?
KICK
Hime-sama, you, too.
Go ahead.
PUSH
PUSH
Huh?
!?
Brother Taka!?
SLAM
I'm going home.
Have fun.
ゴウン
RUMBLE
RUMBLE
ゴウン
What...
What are you thinking!?
......
You're going back home?
Brother Taka!

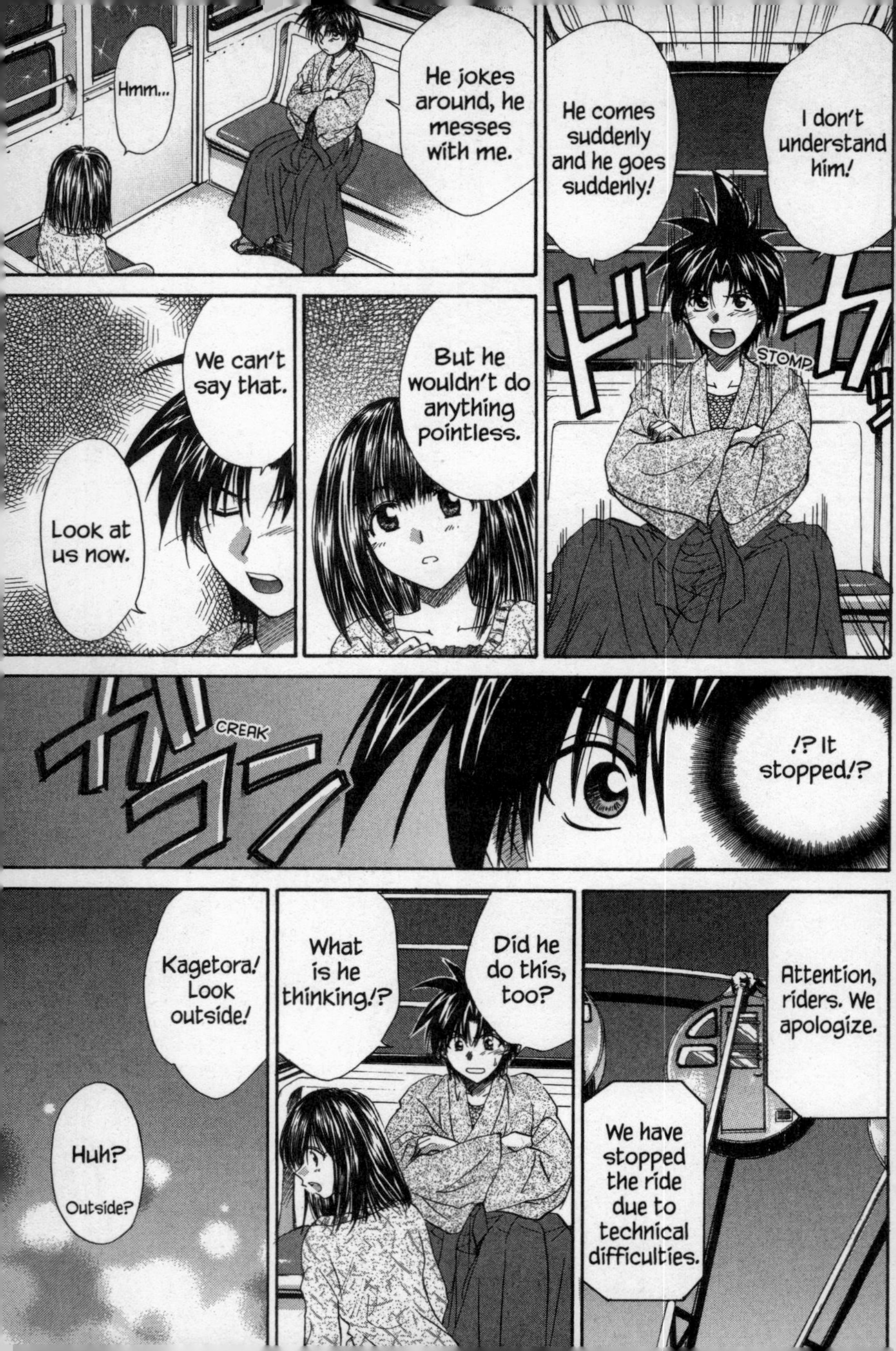
I don't understand him!
He comes suddenly and he goes suddenly!
STOMP
He jokes around, he messes with me.
Hmm...
But he wouldn't do anything pointless.
We can't say that.
Look at us now.
!? It stopped!?
CREAK
Attention, riders. We apologize.
We have stopped the ride due to technical difficulties.
Did he do this, too?
What is he thinking!?
Kagetora! Look outside!
Huh?
Outside?

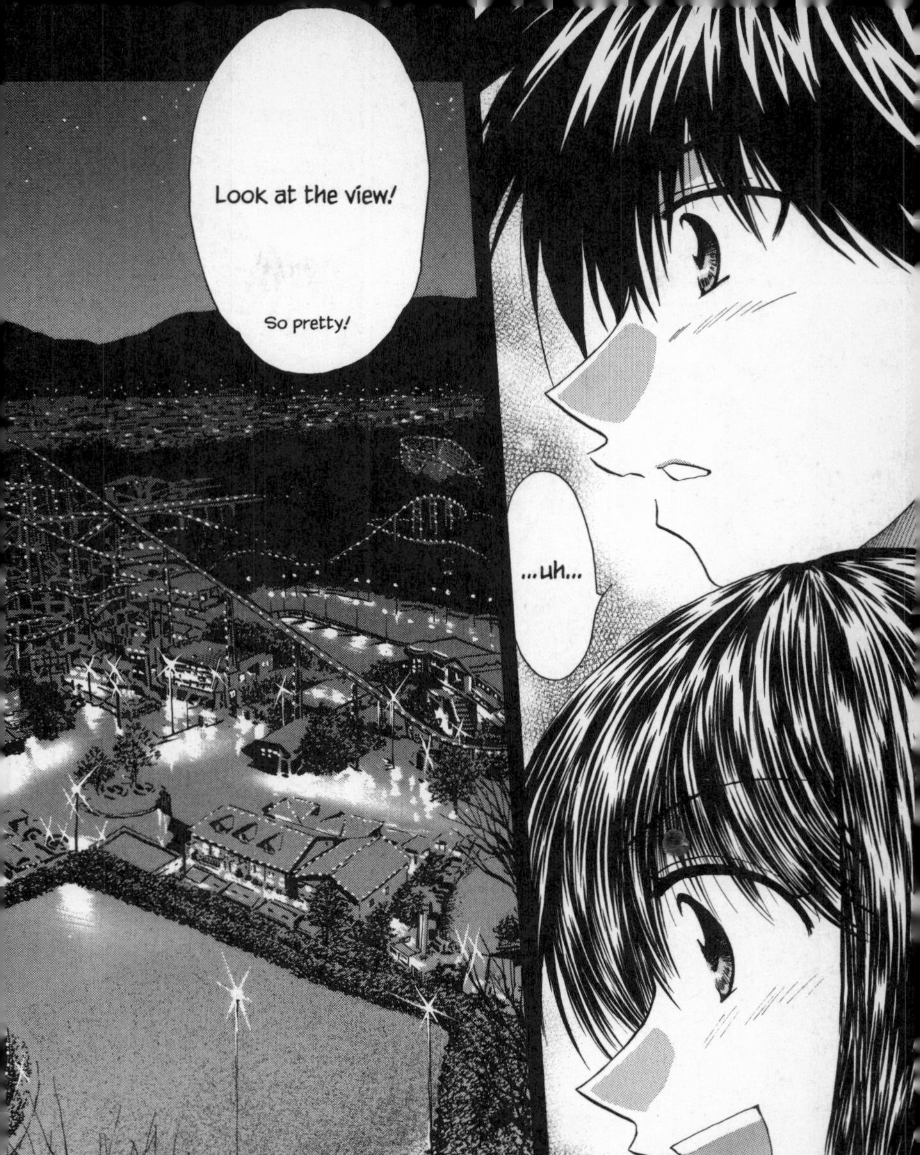
...uh...
See?
Look at the view!
So pretty!

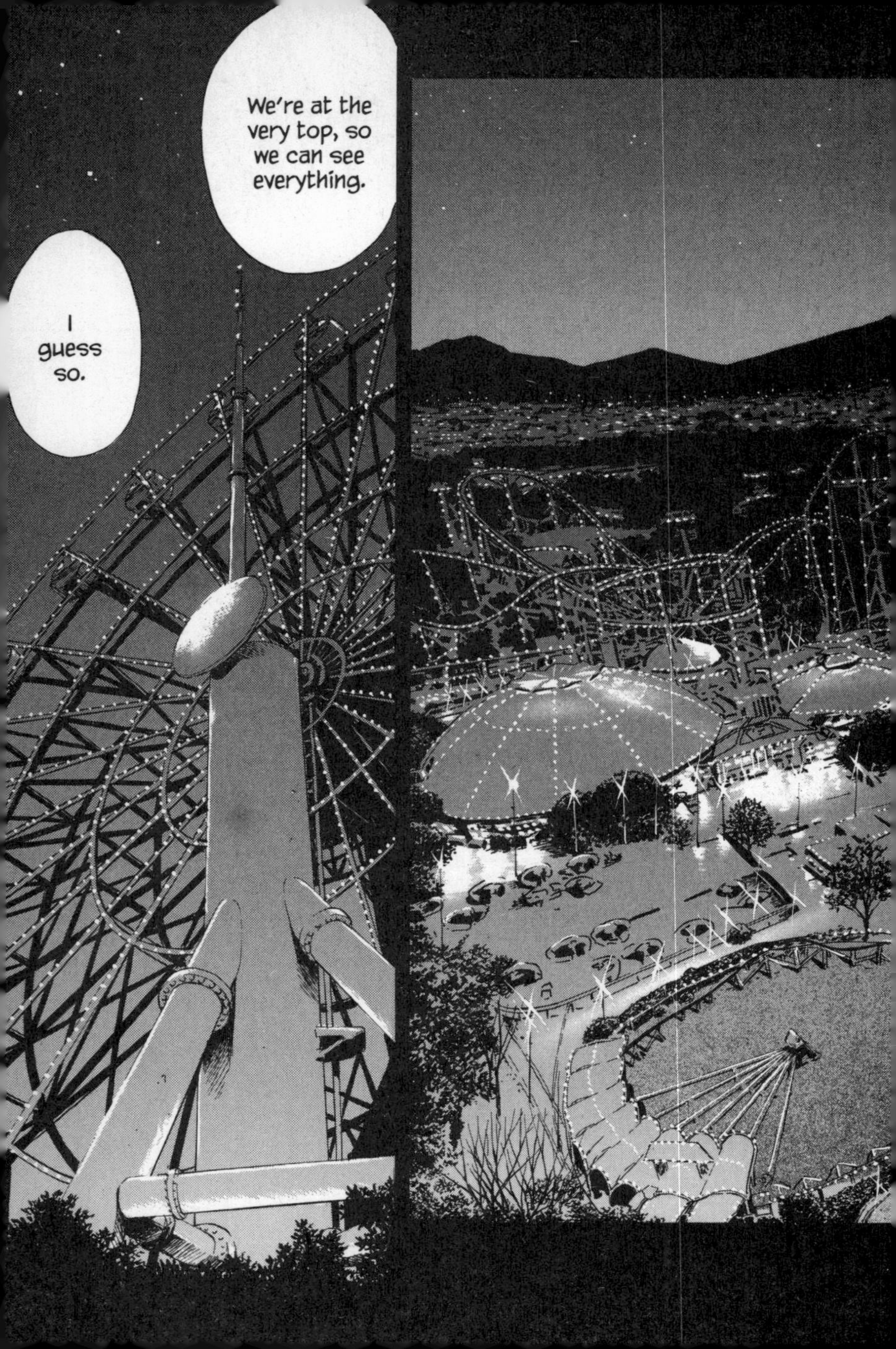
We're at the very top, so we can see everything.
I guess so.

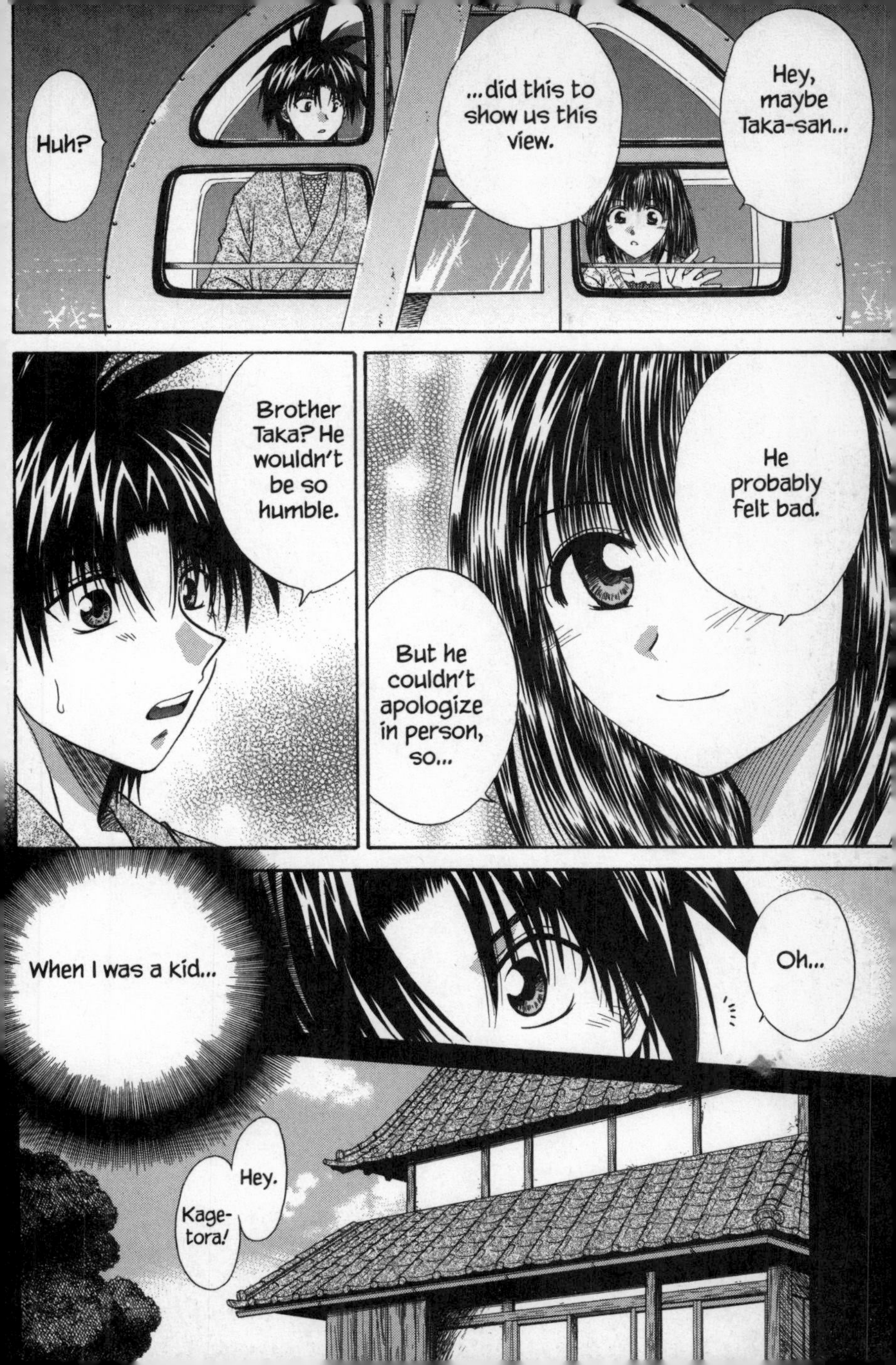
Hey, maybe Taka-san...
...did this to show us this view.
Huh?
He probably felt bad.
But he couldn't apologize in person, so...
Brother Taka? He wouldn't be so humble.
Oh...
When I was a kid...
Hey.
Kage-tora!

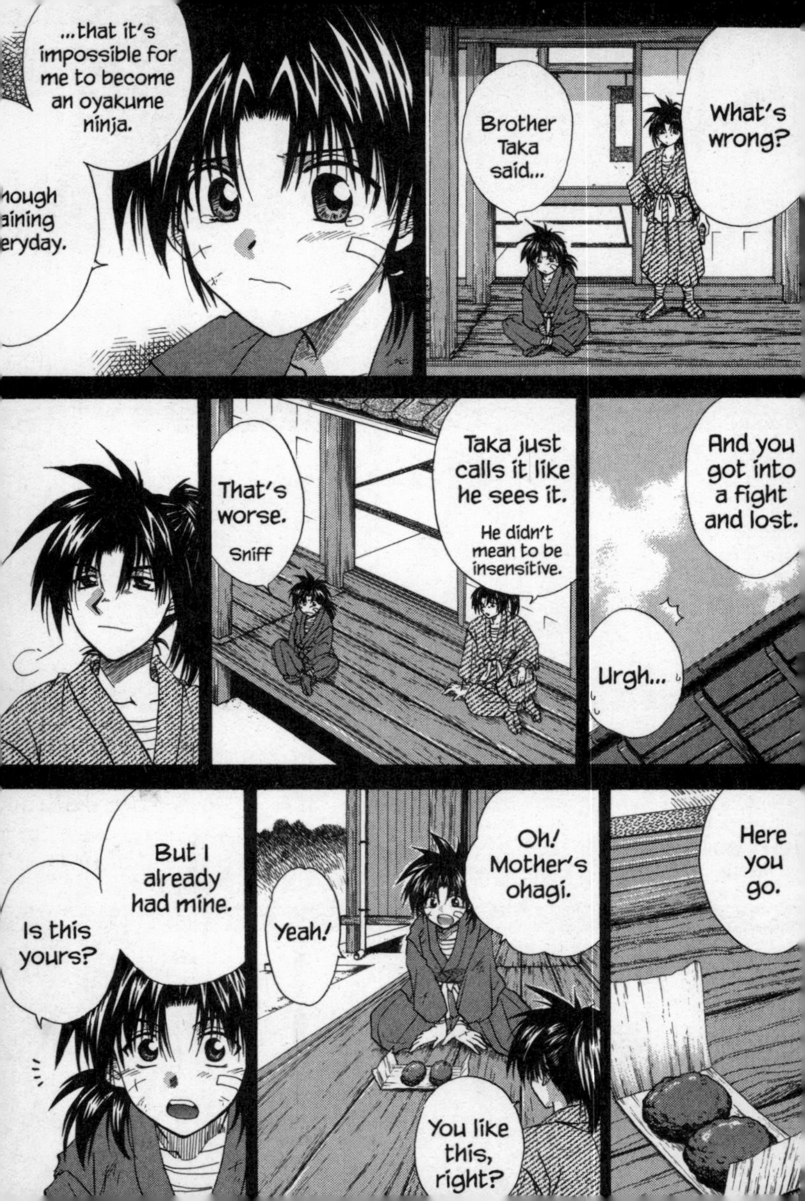

What's wrong?
Brother Taka said...
...that it's impossible for me to become an oyakume ninja.
ough
aining
eryday.
And you got into a fight and lost.
Urgh...
Taka just calls it like he sees it.
He didn't mean to be insensitive.
That's worse.
Sniff
Here you go.
Oh! Mother's ohagi.
You like this, right?
Yeah!
But I already had mine.
Is this yours?

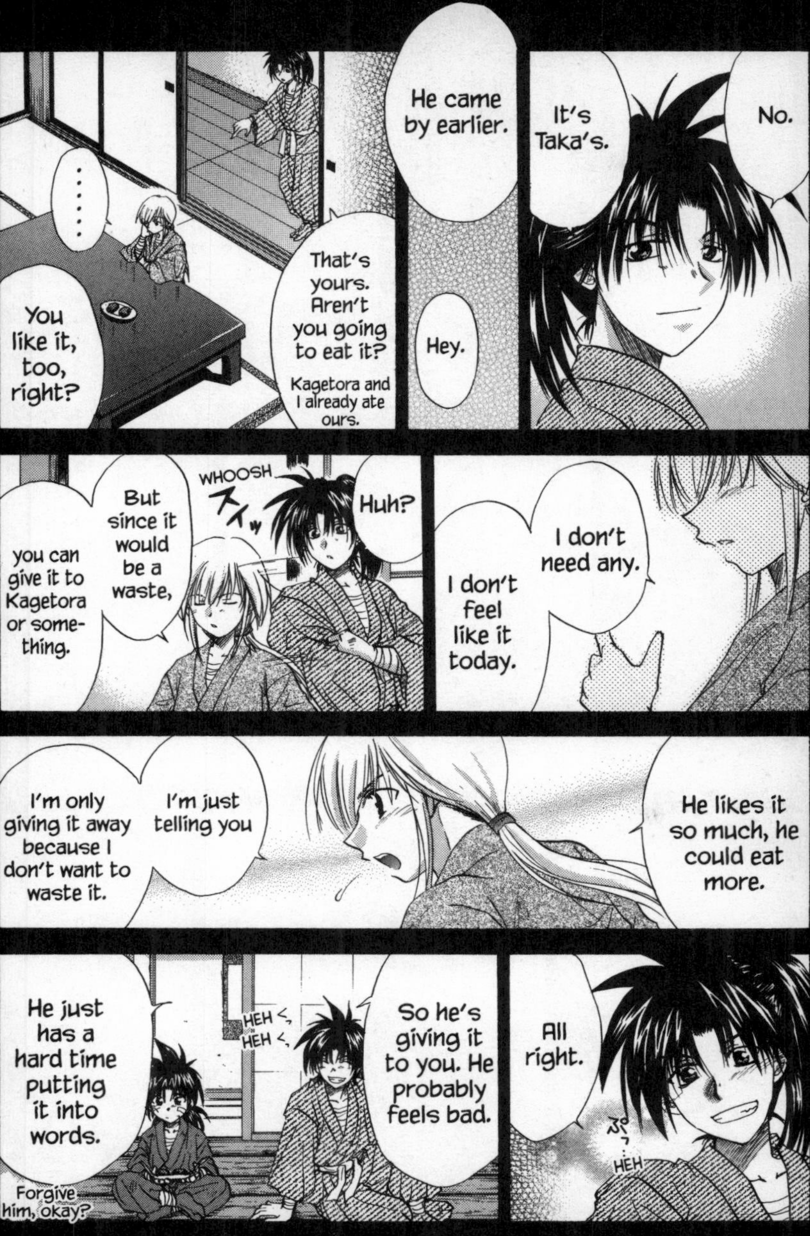
No.
It's Taka's.
He came by earlier.
Hey.
That's yours. Aren't you going to eat it?
Kagetora and I already ate ours.
......
You like it, too, right?
I don't need any.
I don't feel like it today.
Huh?
WHOOSH
But since it would be a waste,
you can give it to Kagetora or something.
He likes it so much, he could eat more.
I'm just telling you
I'm only giving it away because I don't want to waste it.
All right.
HEH
So he's giving it to you. He probably feels bad.
HEH HEH
He just has a hard time putting it into words.
Forgive him, okay?

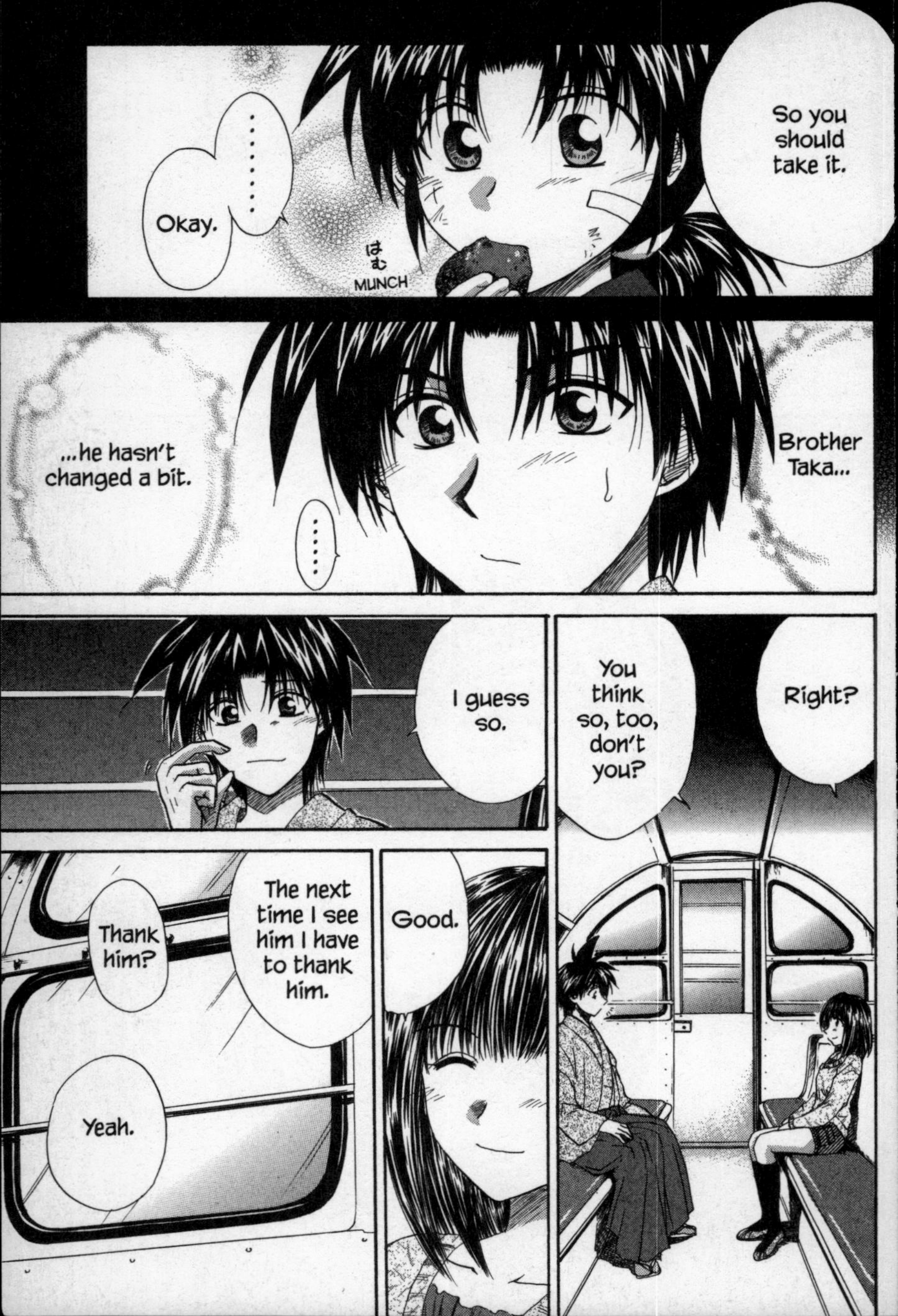

So you should take it.
......
Okay.
はむ
MUNCH
Brother Taka...
......
...he hasn't changed a bit.
Right?
You think so, too, don't you?
I guess so.
Good.
The next time I see him I have to thank him.
Thank him?
Yeah.

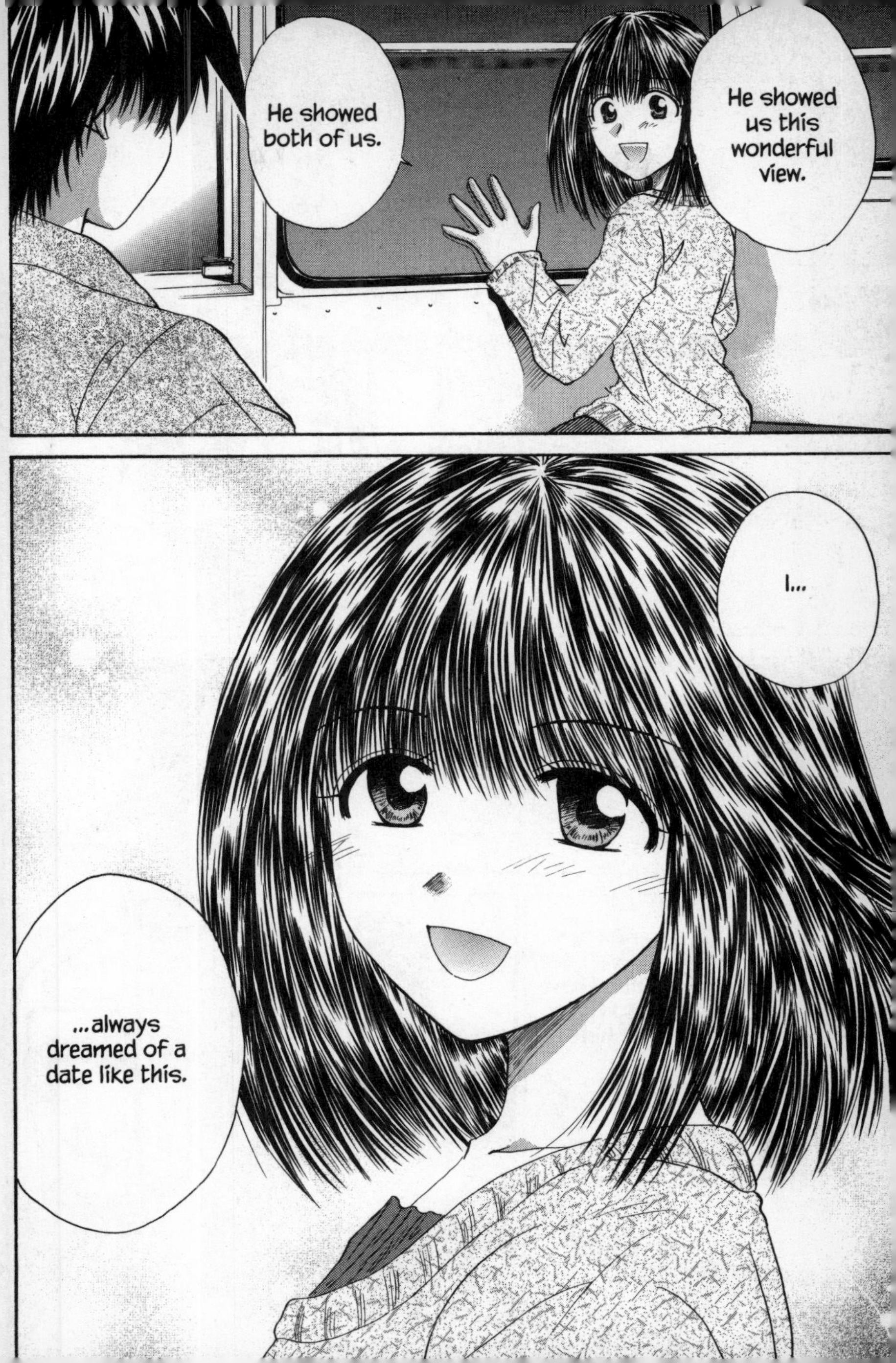
He showed us this wonderful view.
He showed both of us.
I...
...always dreamed of a date like this.

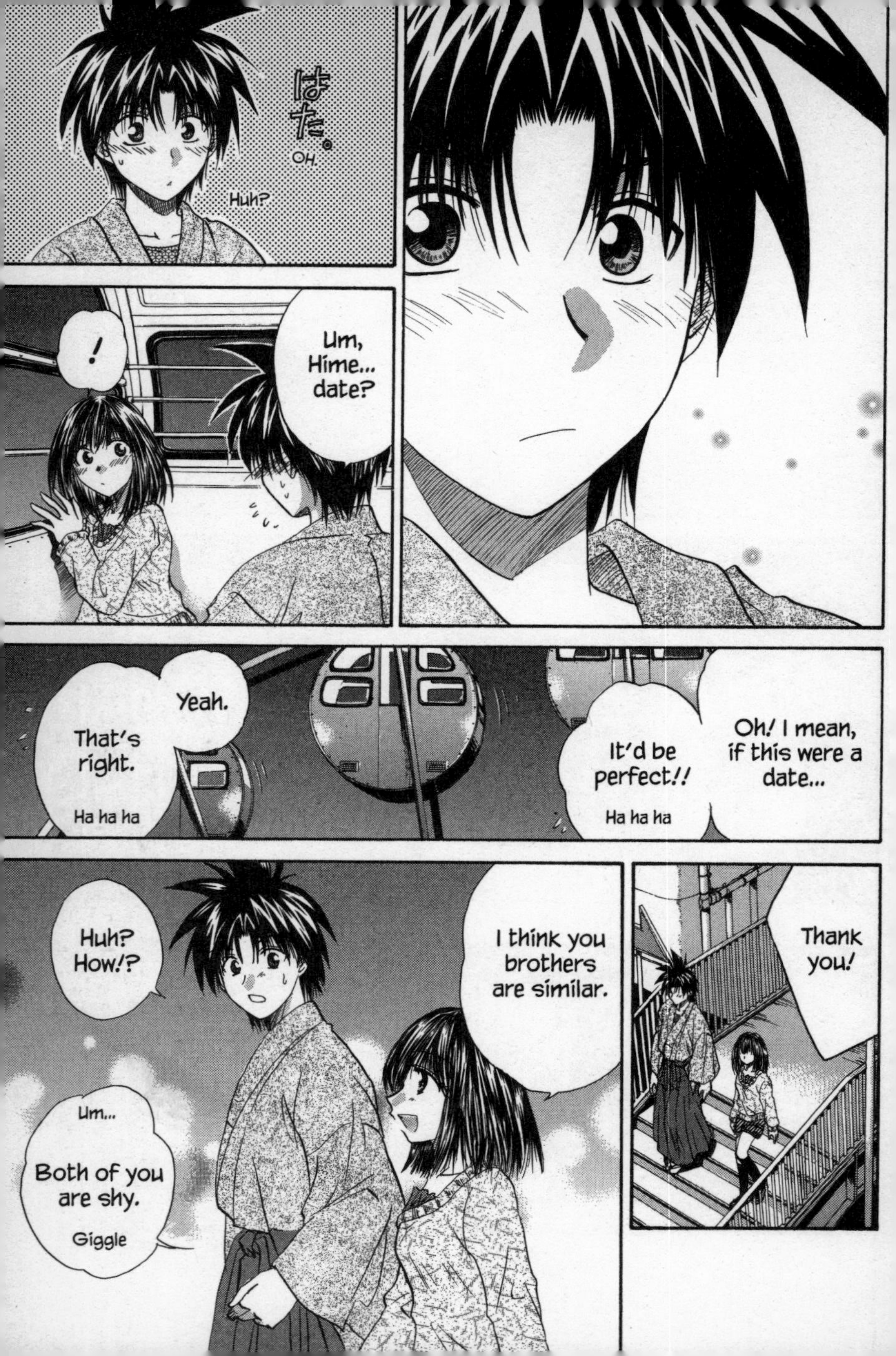
はた。
OH.
Huh?
Um, Hime... date?
!
Oh! I mean, if this were a date...
It'd be perfect!!
Ha ha ha
Yeah.
That's right.
Ha ha ha
Thank you!
I think you brothers are similar.
Huh? How!?
Um...
Both of you are shy.
Giggle

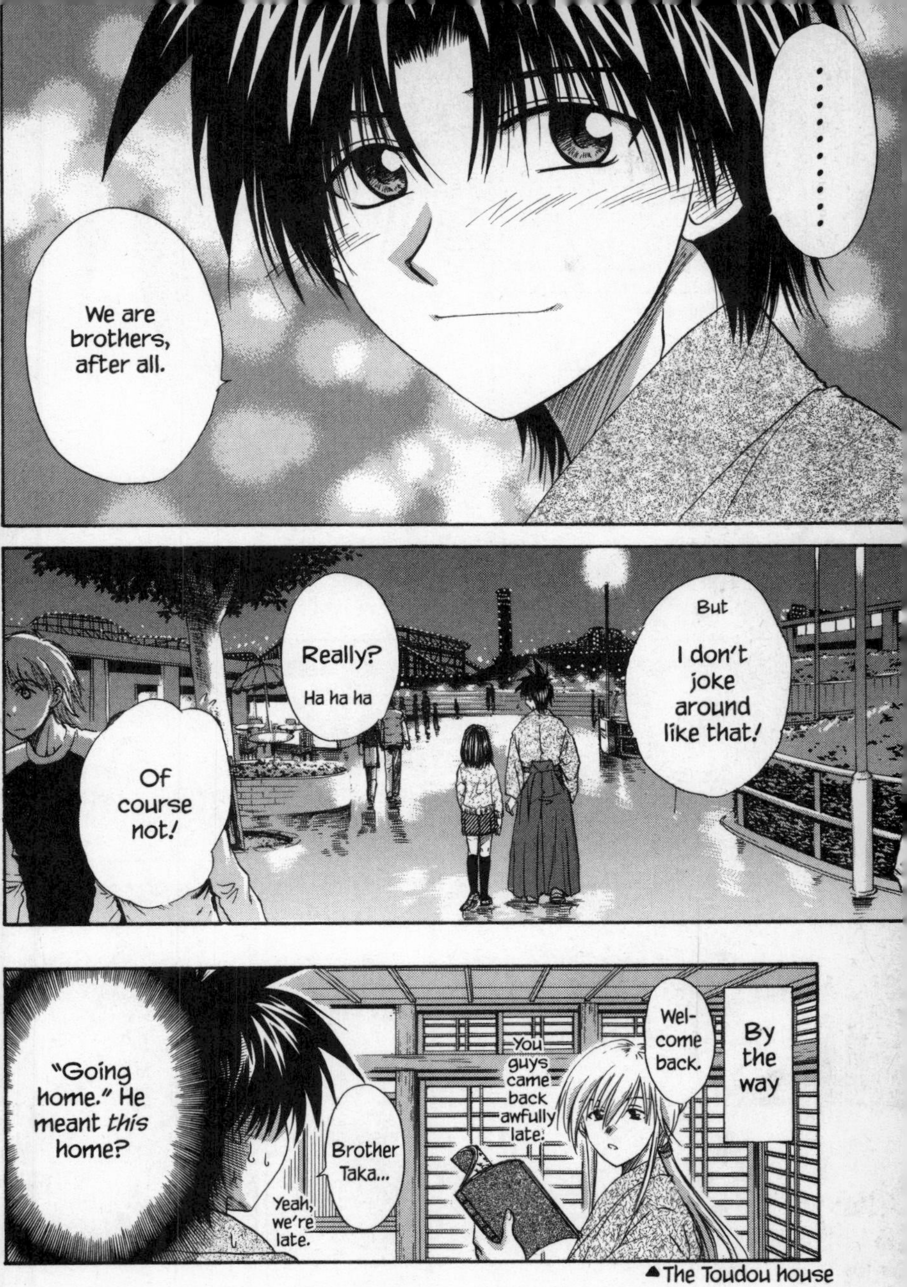

……
We are brothers, after all.
But I don't joke around like that!
Really? Ha ha ha
Of course not!
By the way
Wel-come back.
You guys came back awfully late.
Brother Taka...
Yeah, we're late.
"Going home." He meant *this* home?

▲The Toudou house

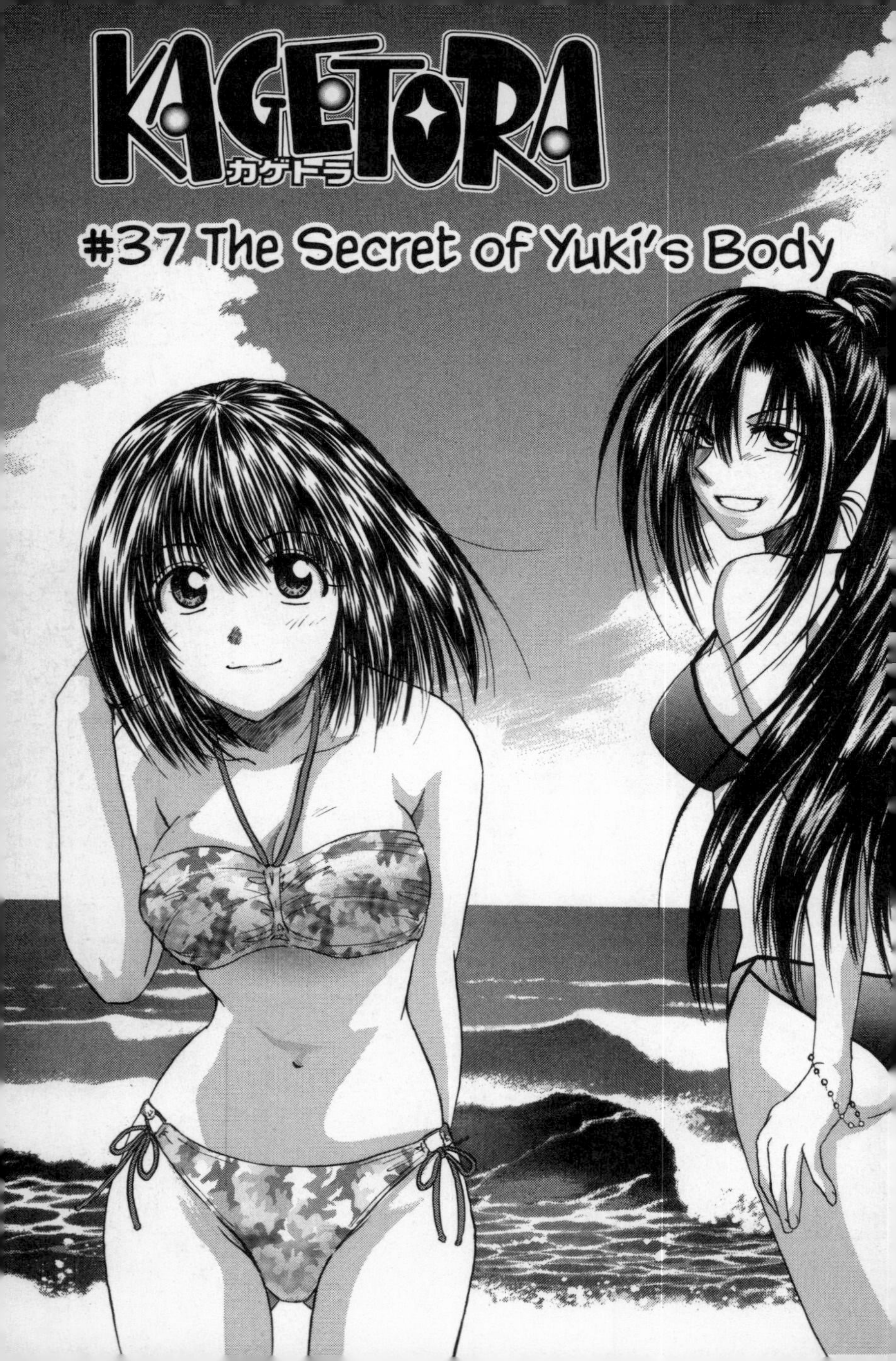
KAGETORA
カゲトラ
#37 The Secret of Yuki's Body

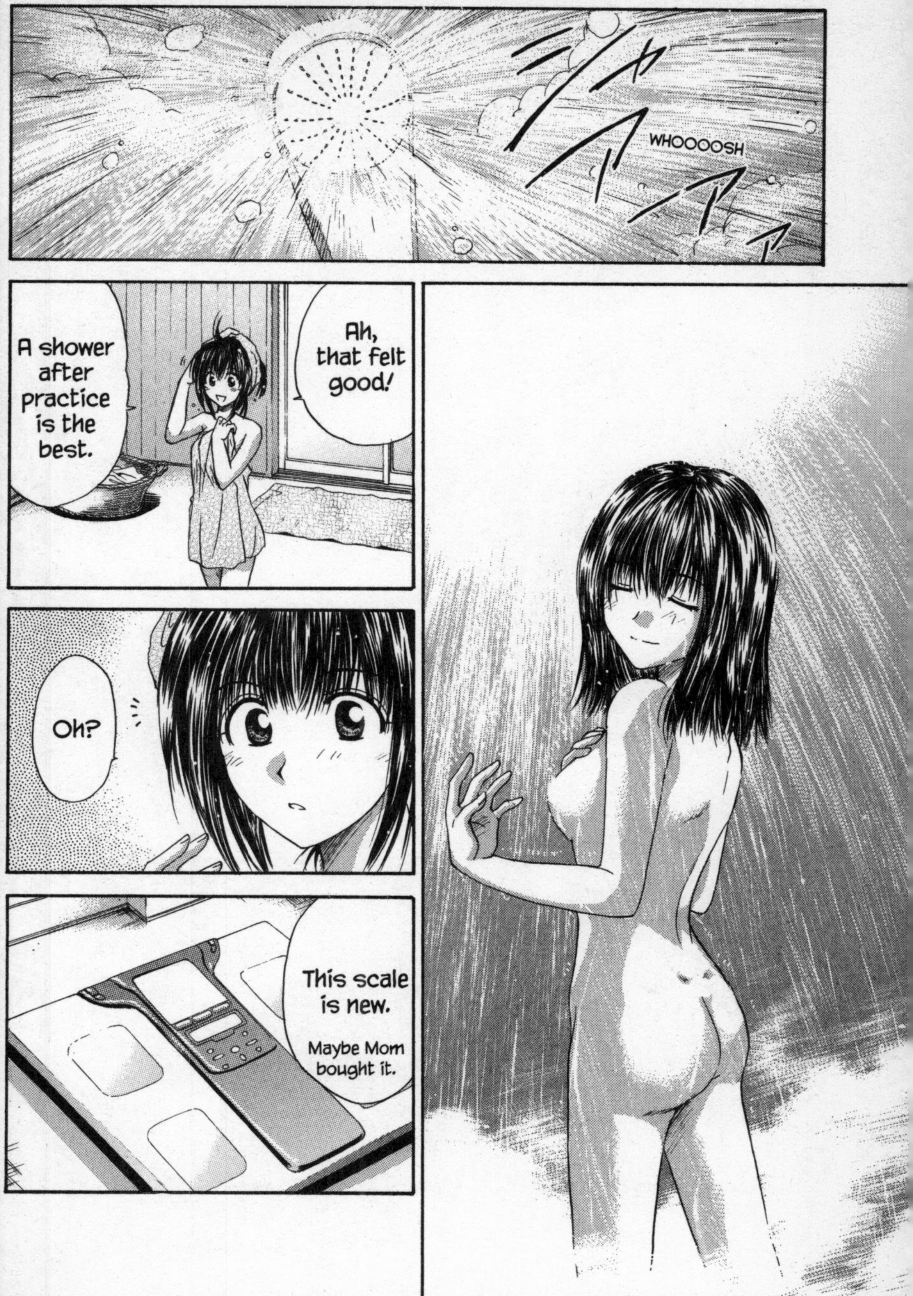
WHOOOOSH
Ah, that felt good!
A shower after practice is the best.
Oh?
This scale is new.
Maybe Mom bought it.

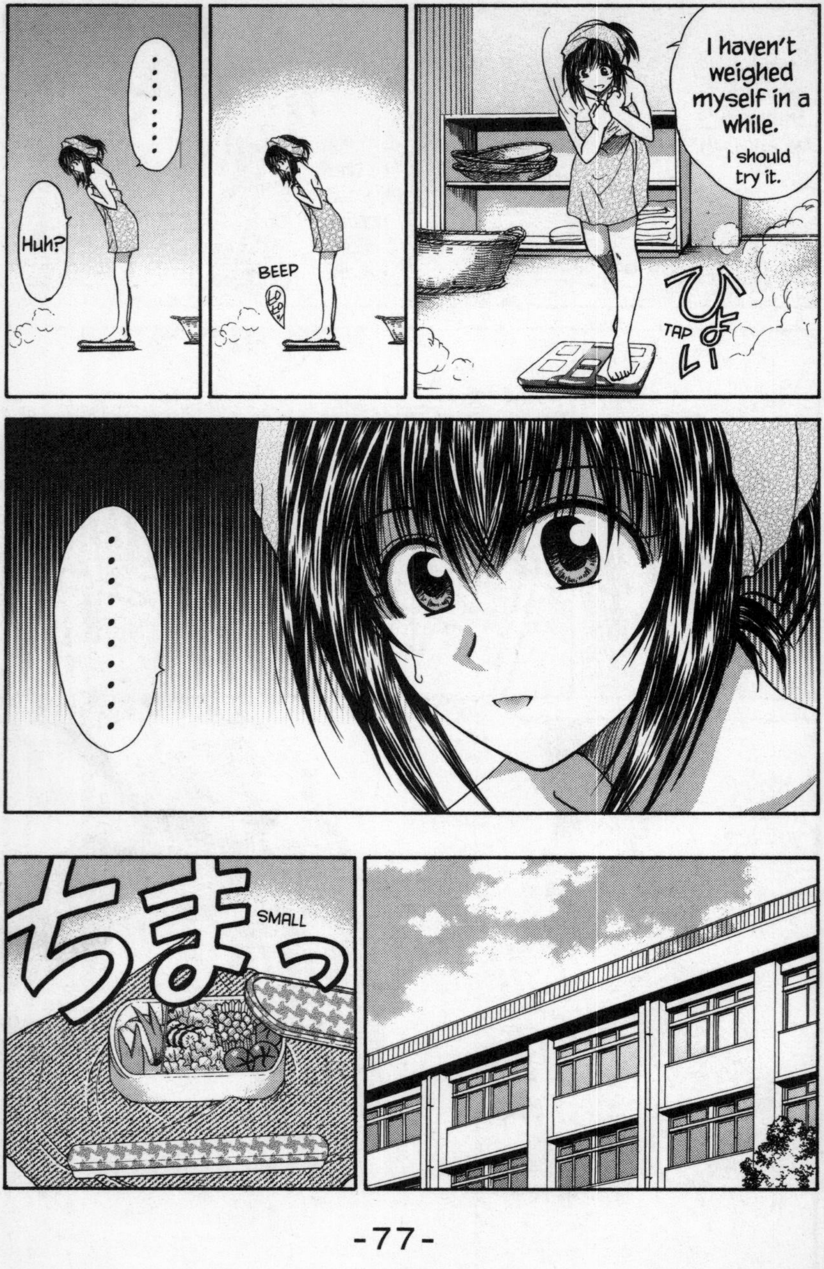

I haven't weighed myself in a while.
I should try it.
ひょい
TAP
BEEP
......
Huh?
......
ちまっ
SMALL

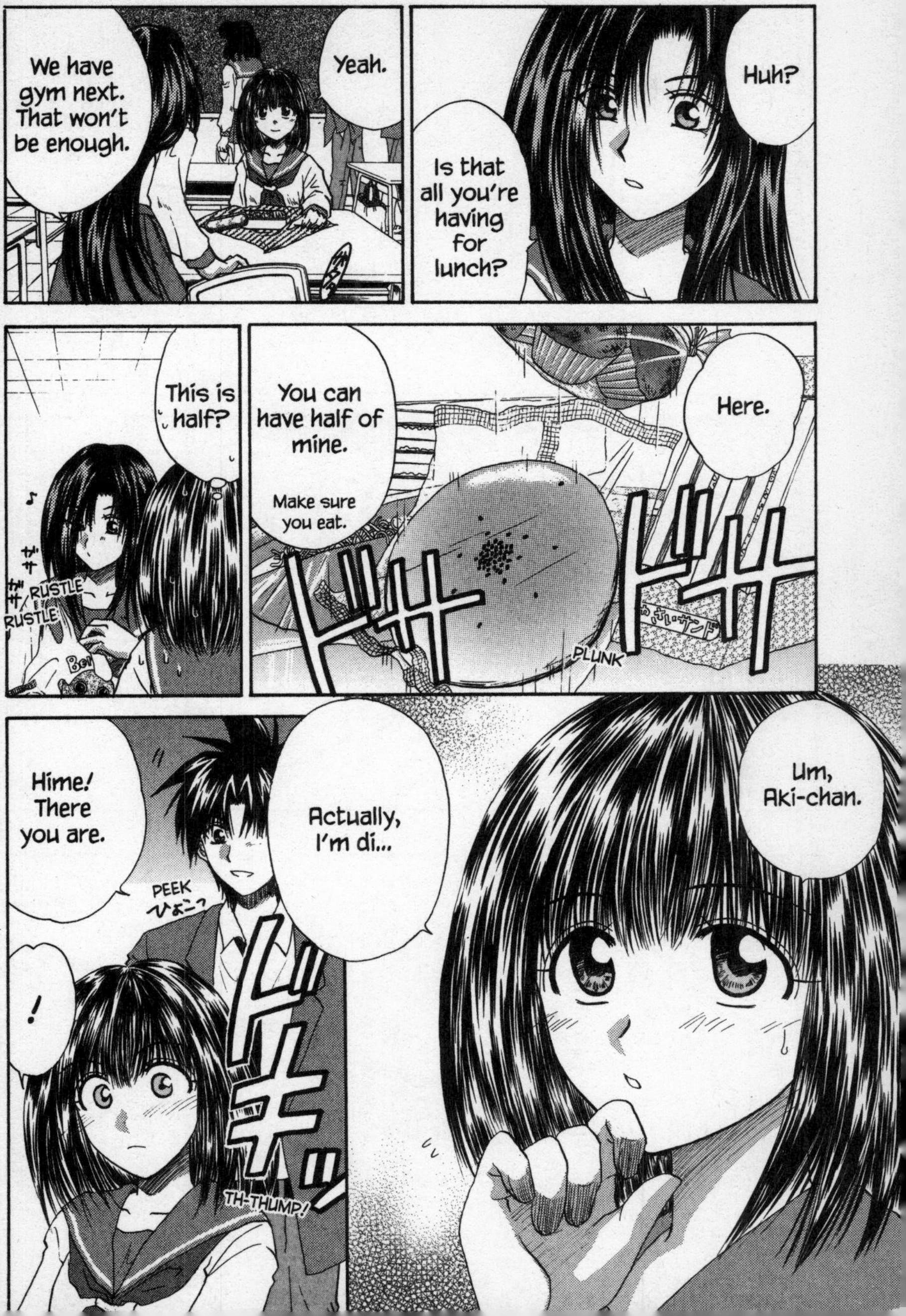
Huh?
Is that all you're having for lunch?
Yeah.
We have gym next. That won't be enough.
Here.
ドサ
ドサ
PLUNK
You can have half of mine.
Make sure you eat.
This is half?
RUSTLE RUSTLE
Um, Aki-chan.
Actually, I'm di...
Hime! There you are.
PEEK
ひょこっ
!
ドキッ
TH-THUMP!

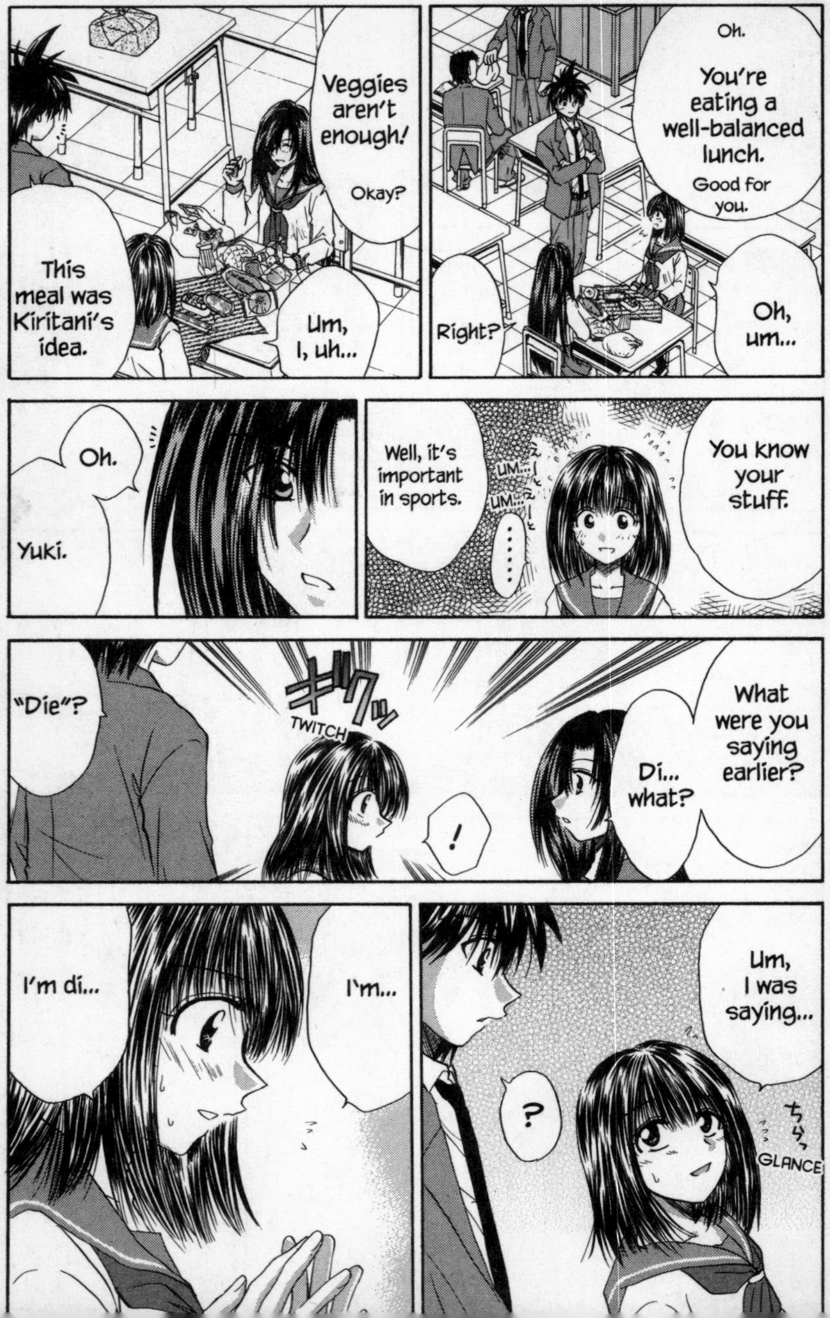
Oh.
You're eating a well-balanced lunch.
Good for you.
Oh, um...
Right?
Veggies aren't enough!
Okay?
Um, I, uh...
This meal was Kiritani's idea.
You know your stuff.
UM...
UM...
......
Well, it's important in sports.
Oh.
Yuki.
What were you saying earlier?
Di... what?
!
TWITCH
"Die"?
Um, I was saying...
GLANCE
?
I'm...
I'm di...

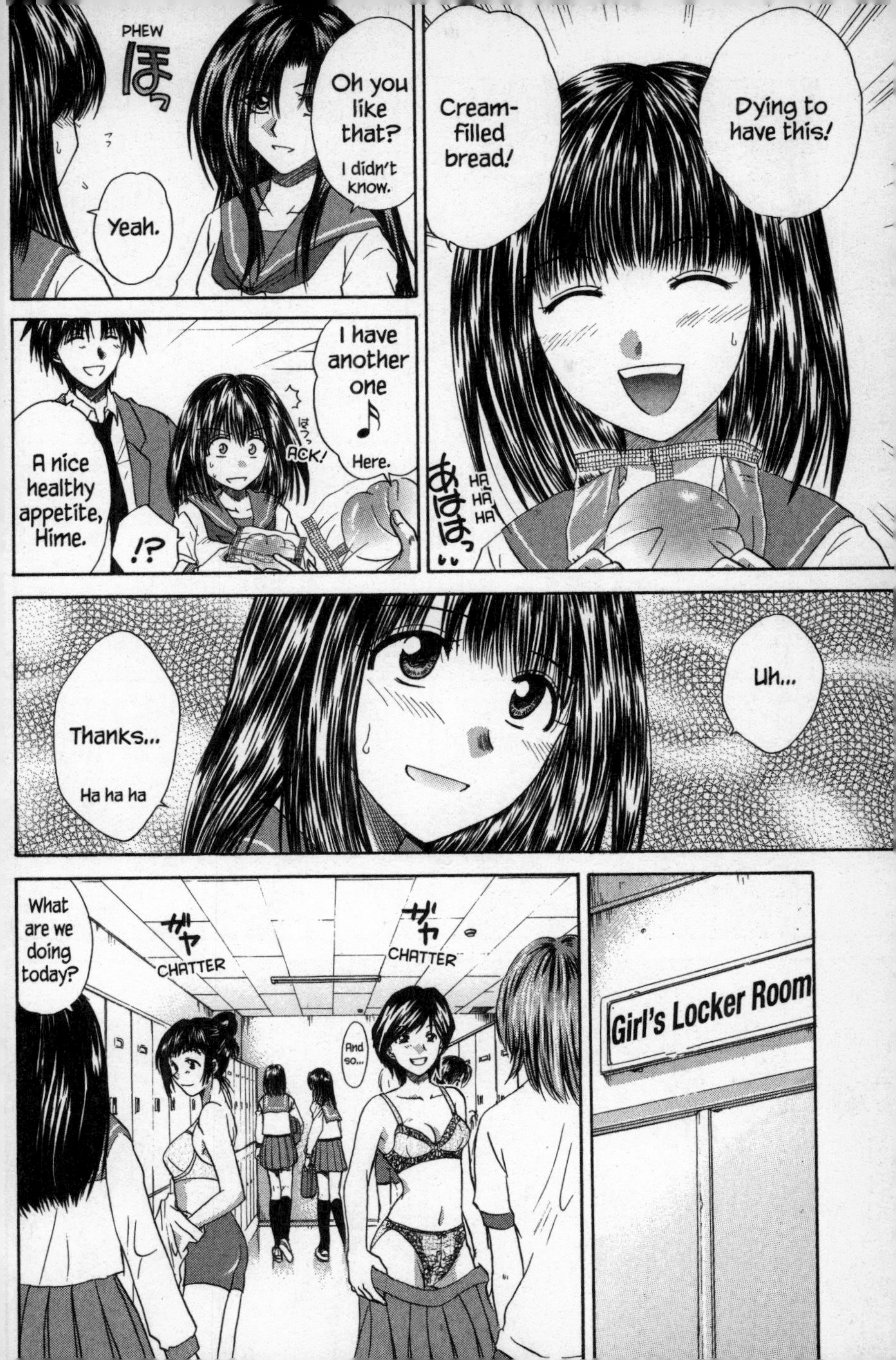
Dying to have this!
Cream-filled bread!
あははっ
HA HA HA
Oh you like that? I didn't know.
ほっ
PHEW
Yeah.
I have another one ♪
Here.
はっ
ACK!
A nice healthy appetite, Hime.
!?
Uh...
Thanks...
Ha ha ha
Girl's Locker Room
ザワ
CHATTER
And so...
ザワ
CHATTER
What are we doing today?

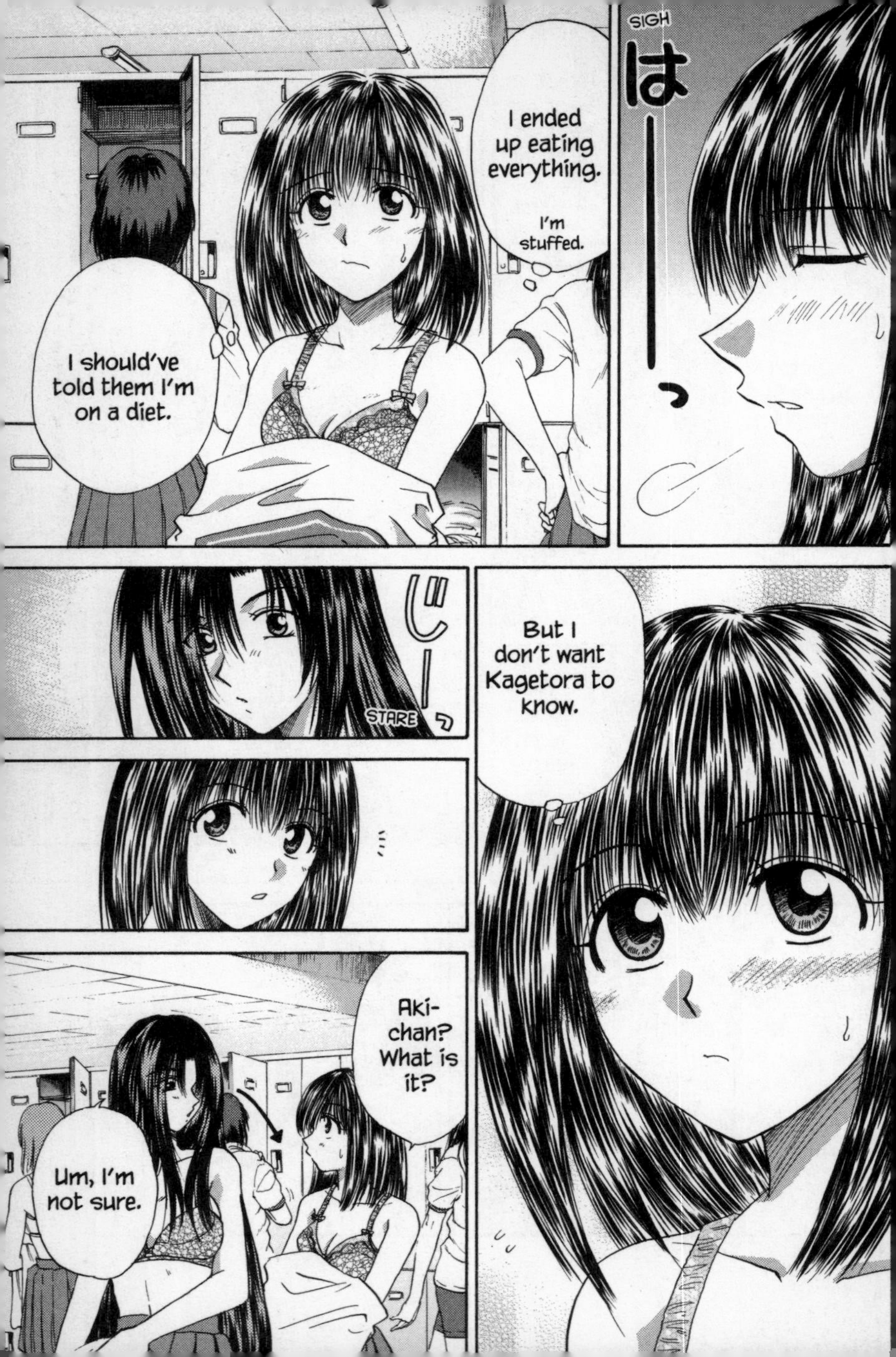
SIGH
はーっ
I ended up eating everything.
I'm stuffed.
I should've told them I'm on a diet.
But I don't want Kagetora to know.
じーっ
STARE
Aki-chan? What is it?
Um, I'm not sure.

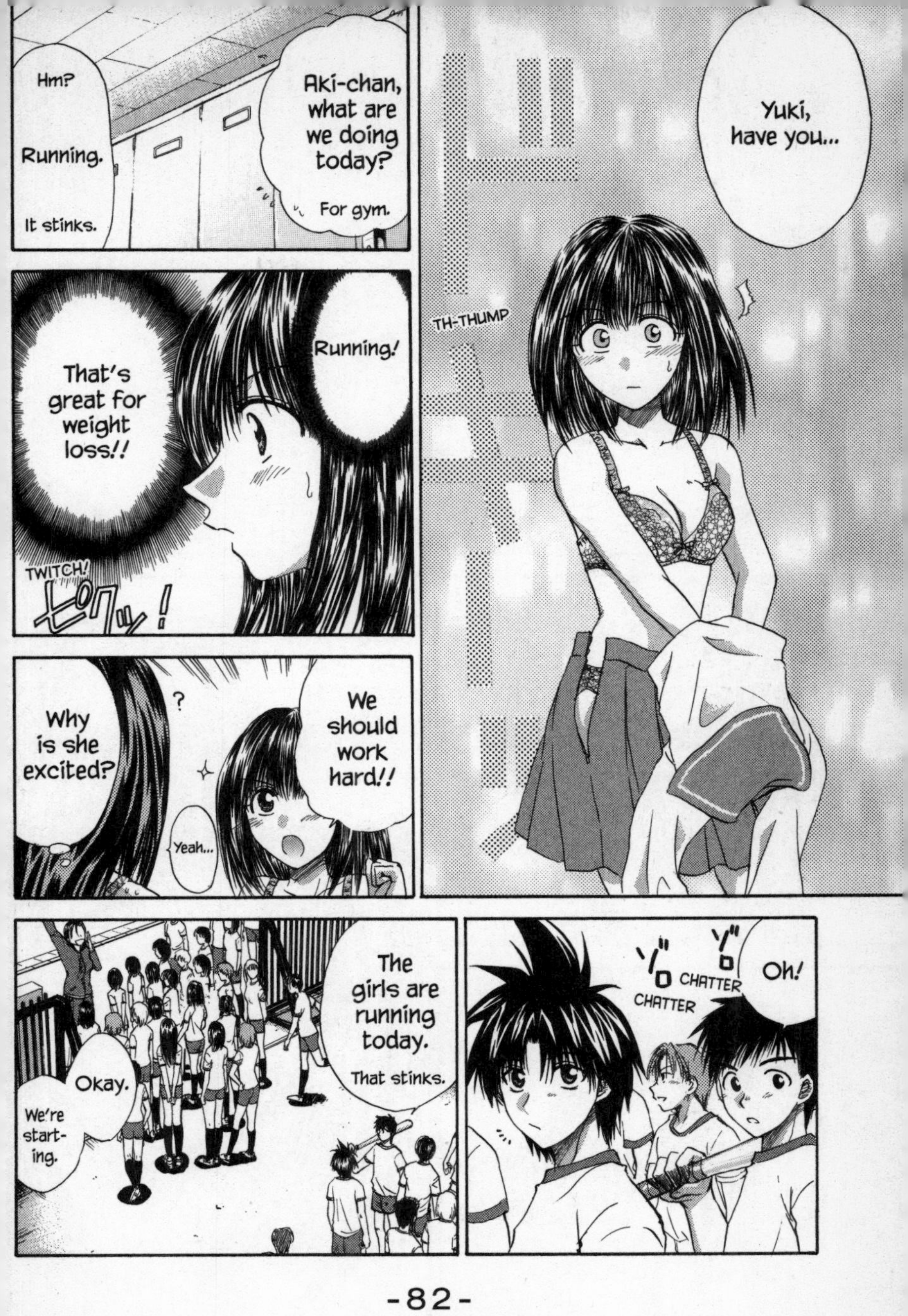

Yuki, have you...
TH-THUMP
Aki-chan, what are we doing today?
For gym.
Hm?
Running.
It stinks.
Running!
That's great for weight loss!!
TWITCH!
ピクッ!
We should work hard!!
Yeah...
?
Why is she excited?
Oh!
ゾロ
CHATTER
ゾロ
CHATTER
The girls are running today.
That stinks.
Okay.
We're start-ing.

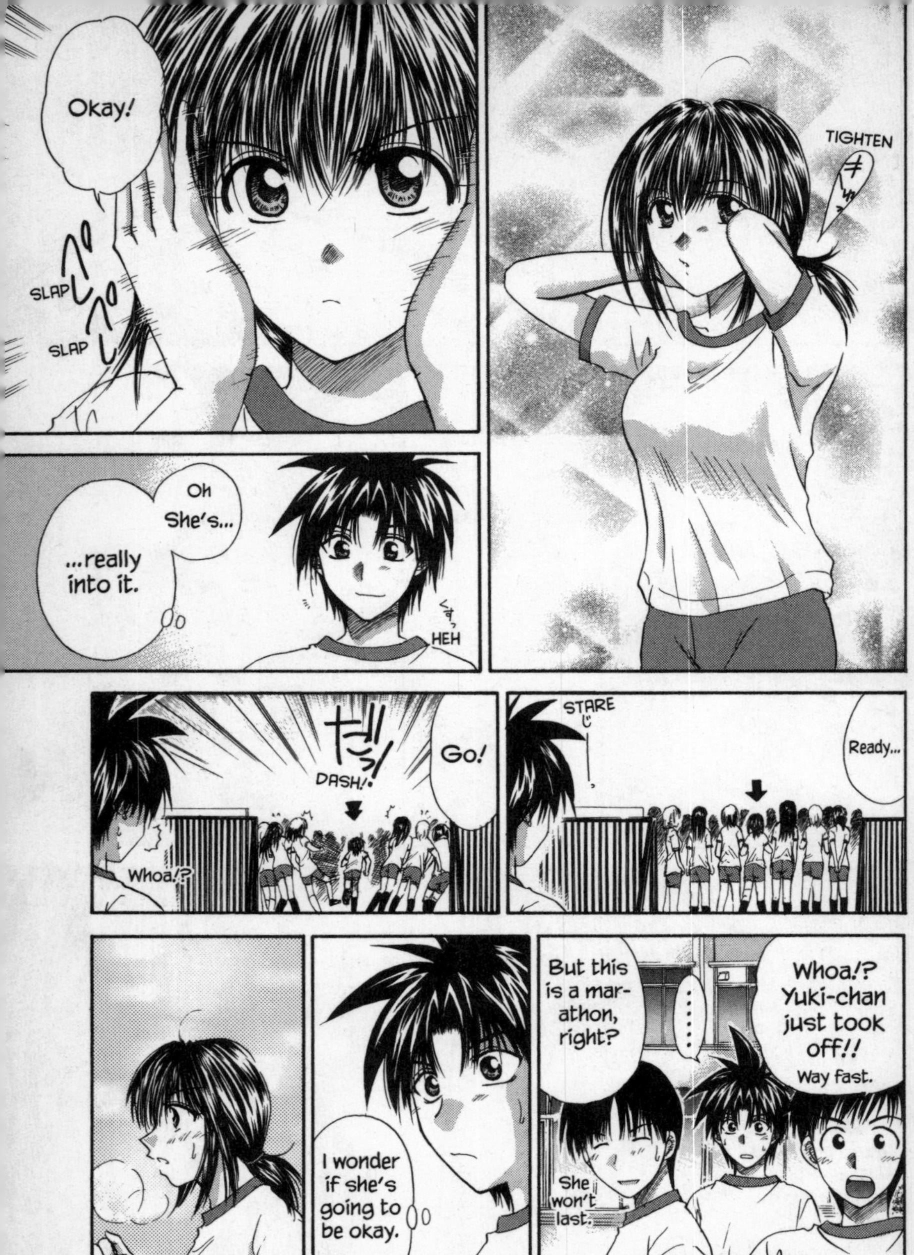
TIGHTEN
Okay!
SLAP
SLAP
Oh She's...
...really into it.
HEH
STARE
Ready...
Go!
DASH!
Whoa!?
Whoa!? Yuki-chan just took off!! Way fast.
...
But this is a marathon, right?
She won't last.
I wonder if she's going to be okay.

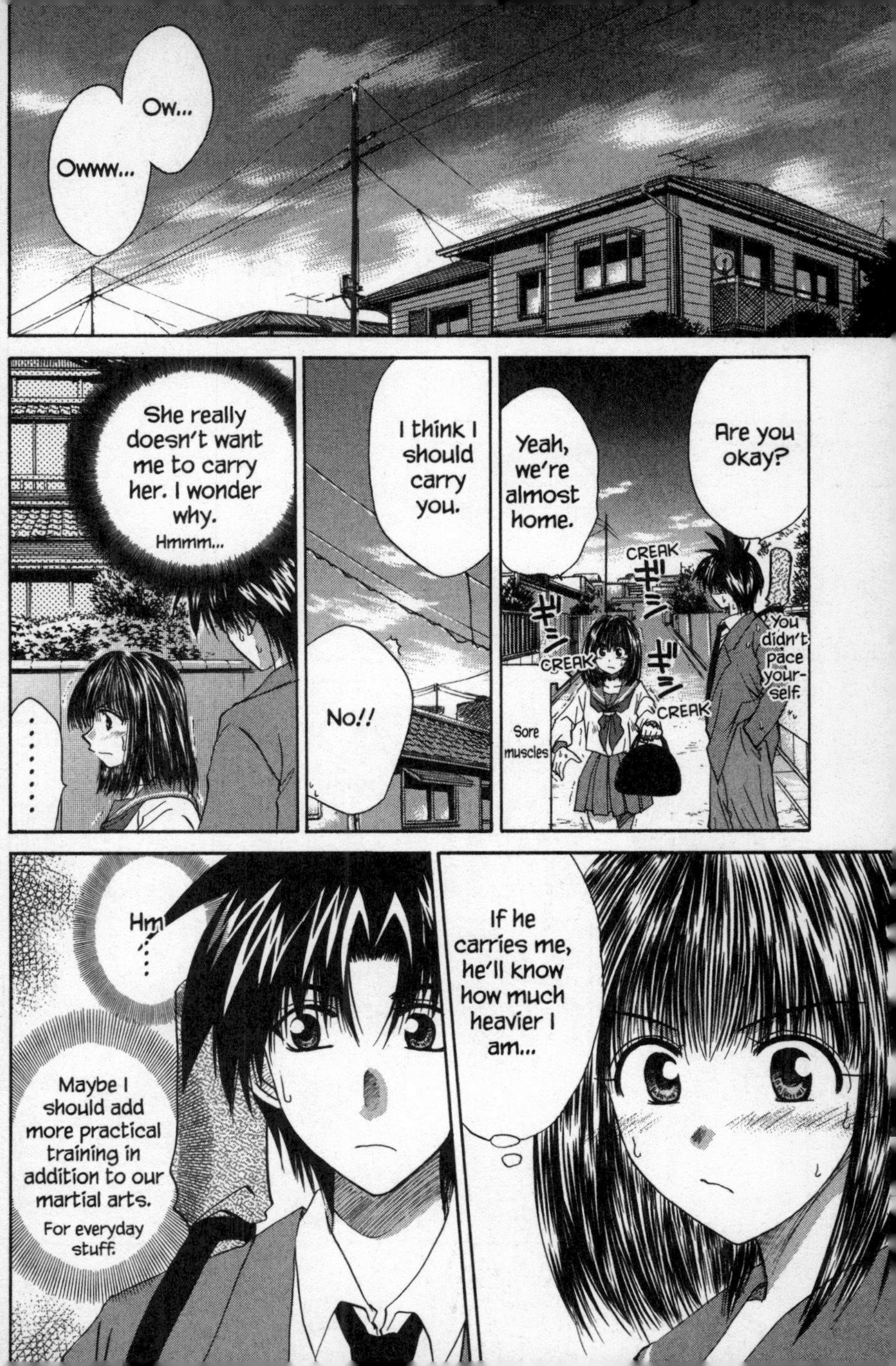
Ow...
Owww...
Are you okay?
Yeah, we're almost home.
CREAK
ギシ
ギシ
CREAK
ギシ
CREAK
You didn't pace yourself.
Sore muscles
I think I should carry you.
No!!
She really doesn't want me to carry her. I wonder why.
Hmmm...
......
If he carries me, he'll know how much heavier I am...
Hm...
Maybe I should add more practical training in addition to our martial arts.
For everyday stuff.

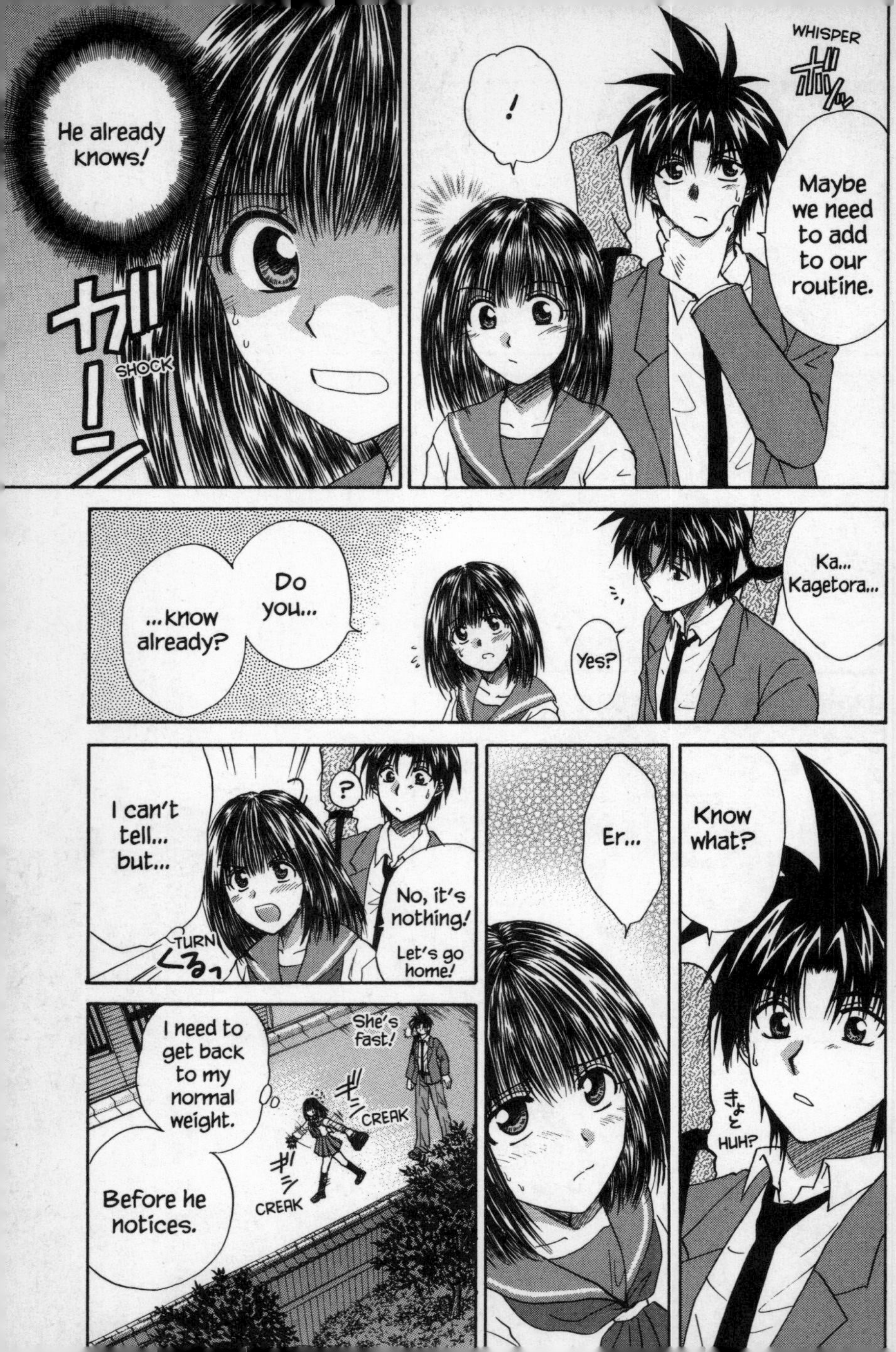

WHISPER
!
Maybe we need to add to our routine.
He already knows!
SHOCK
Ka... Kagetora...
Yes?
Do you...
...know already?
Know what?
HUH?
Er...
I can't tell... but...
?
No, it's nothing!
Let's go home!
TURN
She's fast!
I need to get back to my normal weight.
CREAK
Before he notices.
CREAK

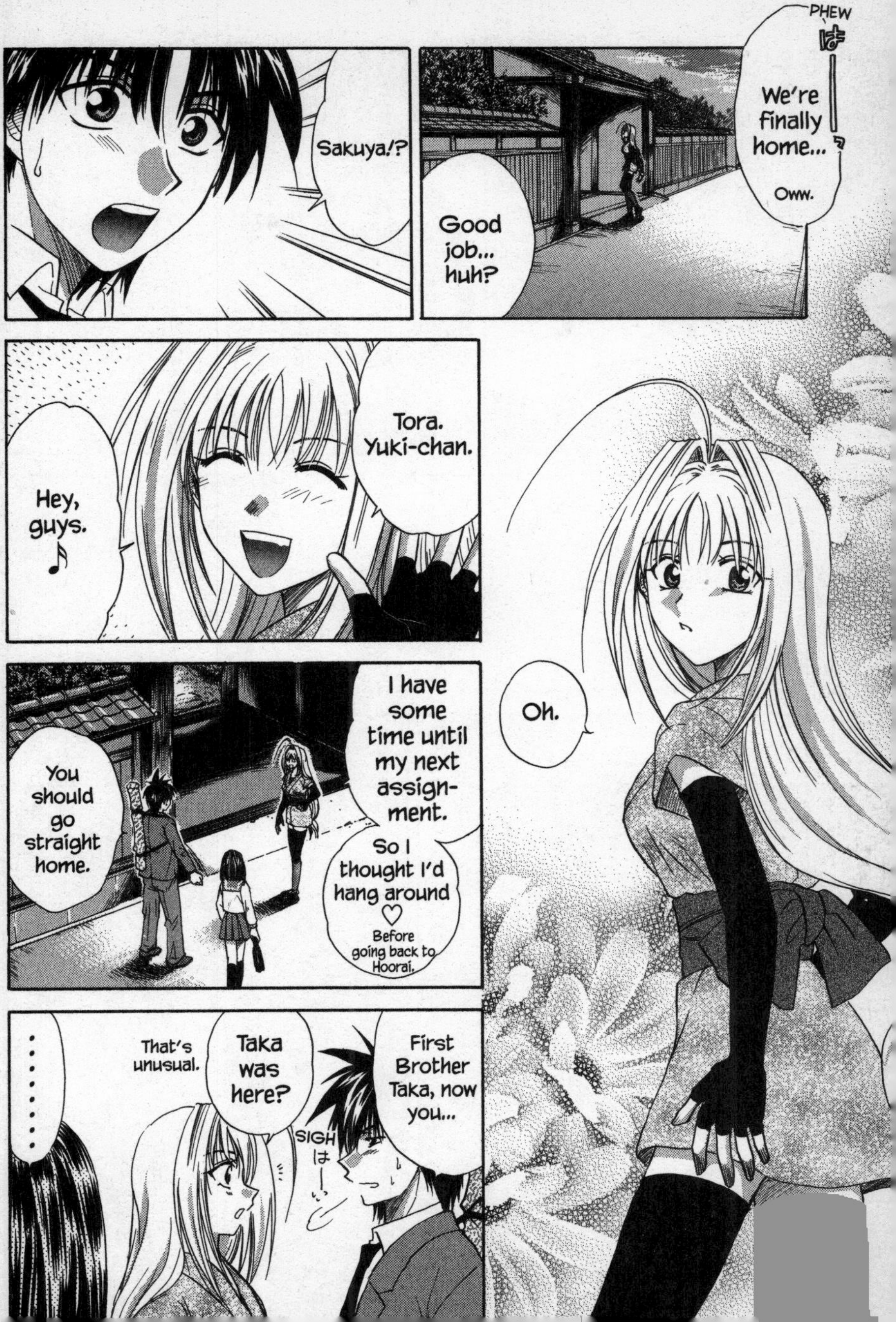

PHEW
は
We're finally home...
Oww.
Good job... huh?
Sakuya!?
Oh.
Tora. Yuki-chan.
Hey, guys. ♪
I have some time until my next assignment.
So I thought I'd hang around ♡
Before going back to Hoorai.
You should go straight home.
First Brother Taka, now you...
SIGH
は
Taka was here?
That's unusual.
....

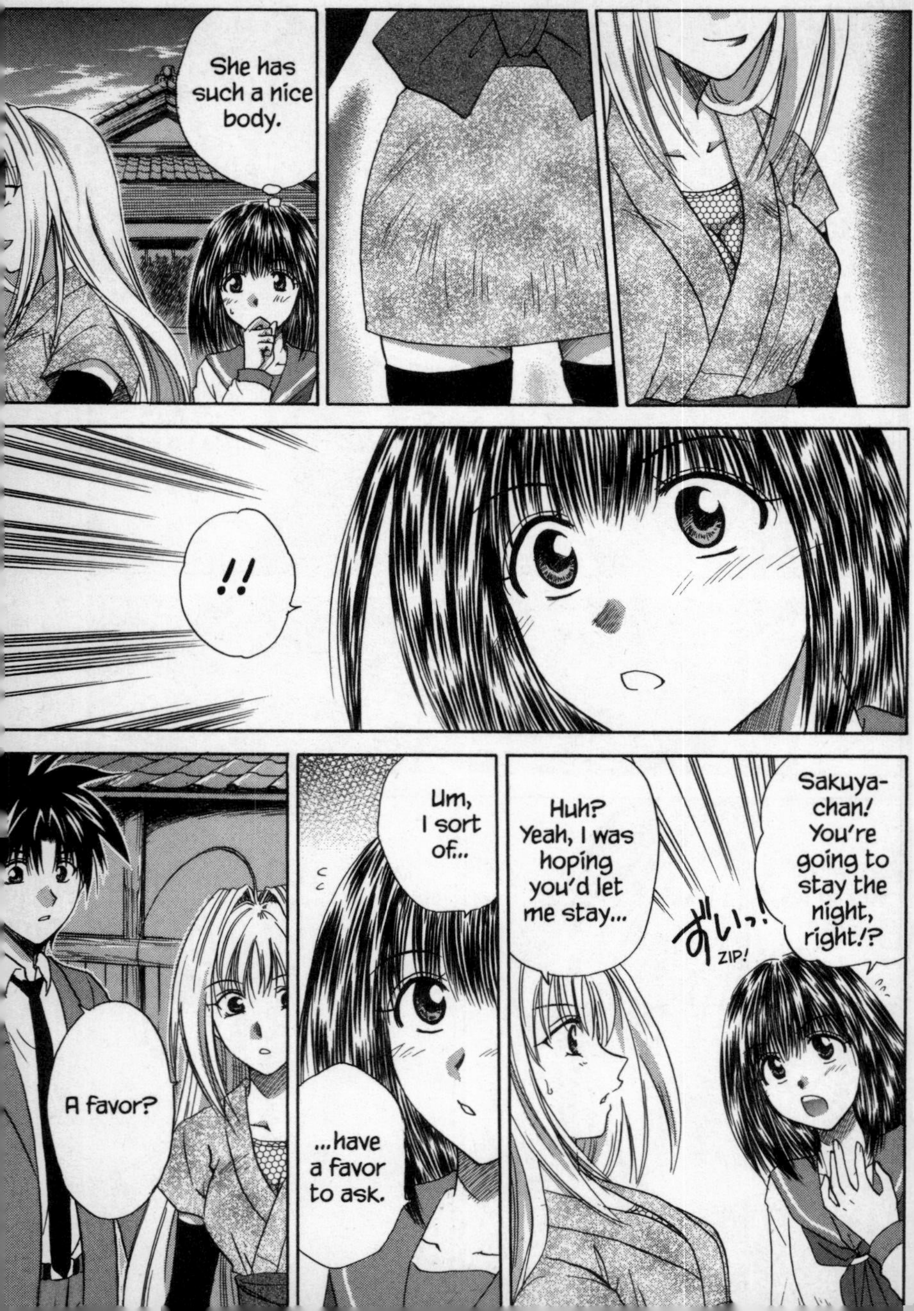
She has such a nice body.
!!
Sakuya-chan! You're going to stay the night, right!?
ずいっ!
ZIP!
Huh? Yeah, I was hoping you'd let me stay...
Um, I sort of...
...have a favor to ask.
A favor?

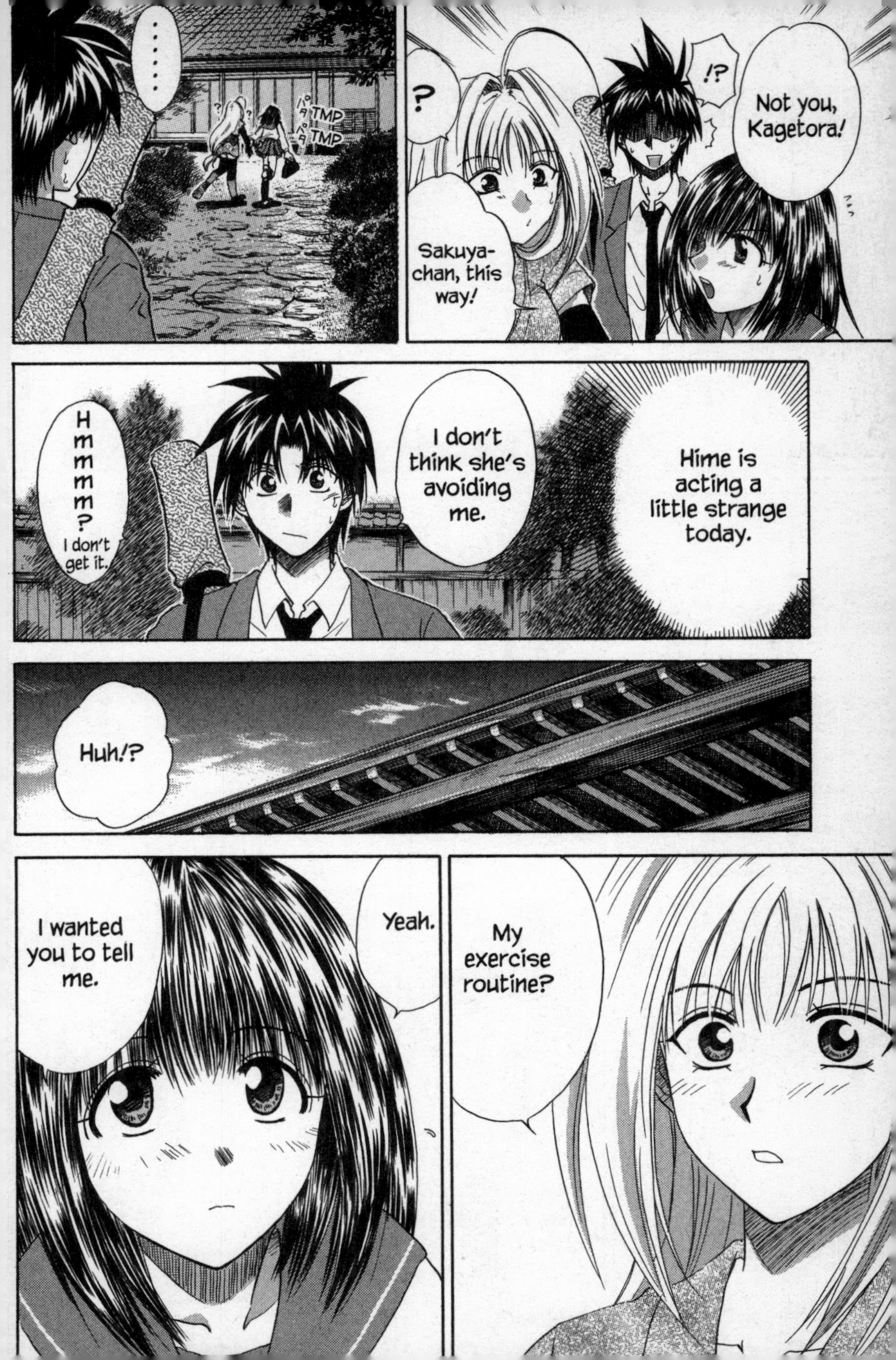
Not you, Kagetora!
!?
?
Sakuya-chan, this way!
......
TMP
TMP
Hime is acting a little strange today.
I don't think she's avoiding me.
Hmmmm?
I don't get it.
Huh!?
My exercise routine?
Yeah.
I wanted you to tell me.

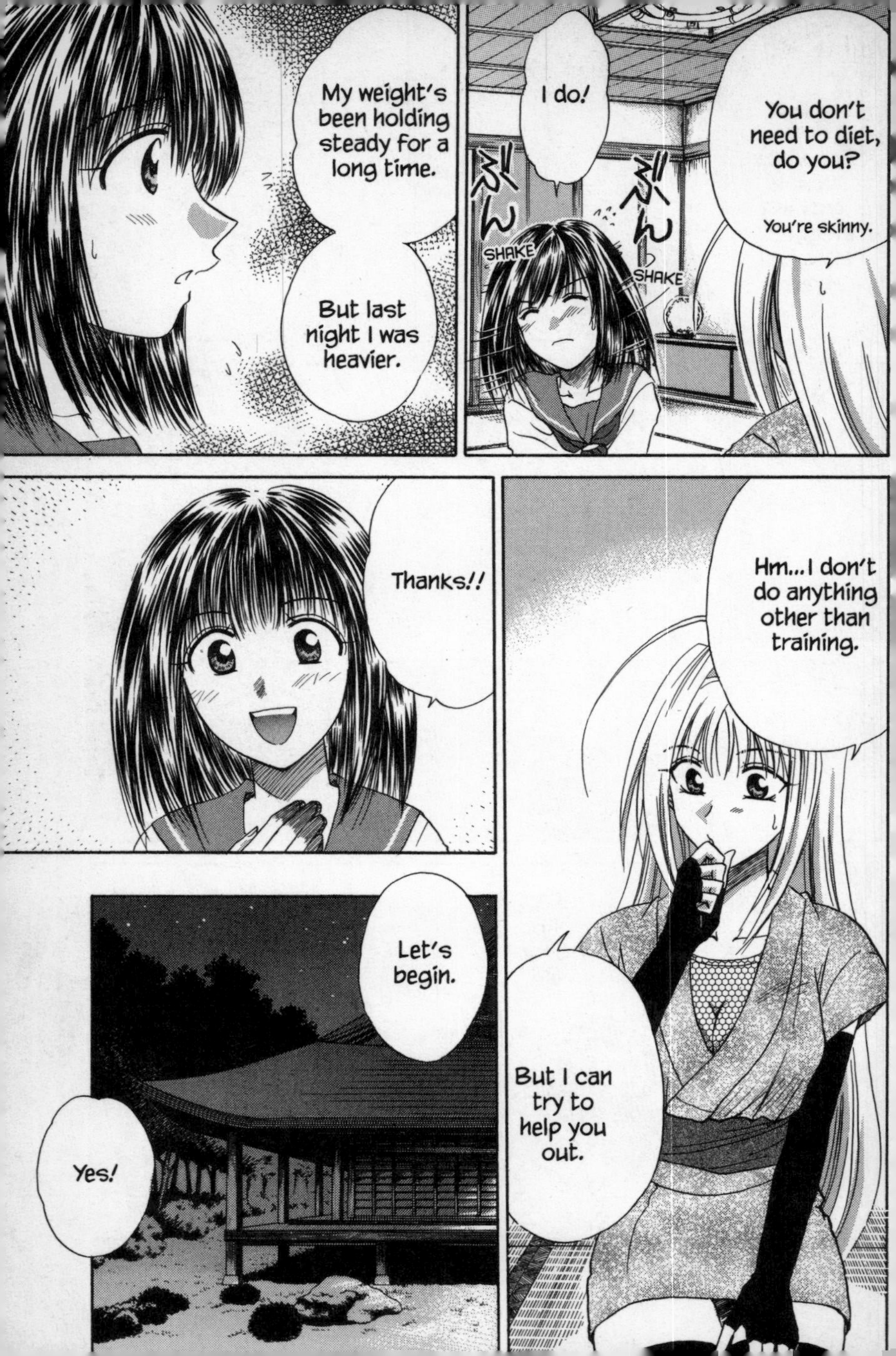
You don't need to diet, do you?
You're skinny.
I do!
ぶん
SHAKE
ぶん
SHAKE
My weight's been holding steady for a long time.
But last night I was heavier.
Hm...I don't do anything other than training.
But I can try to help you out.
Thanks!!
Let's begin.
Yes!

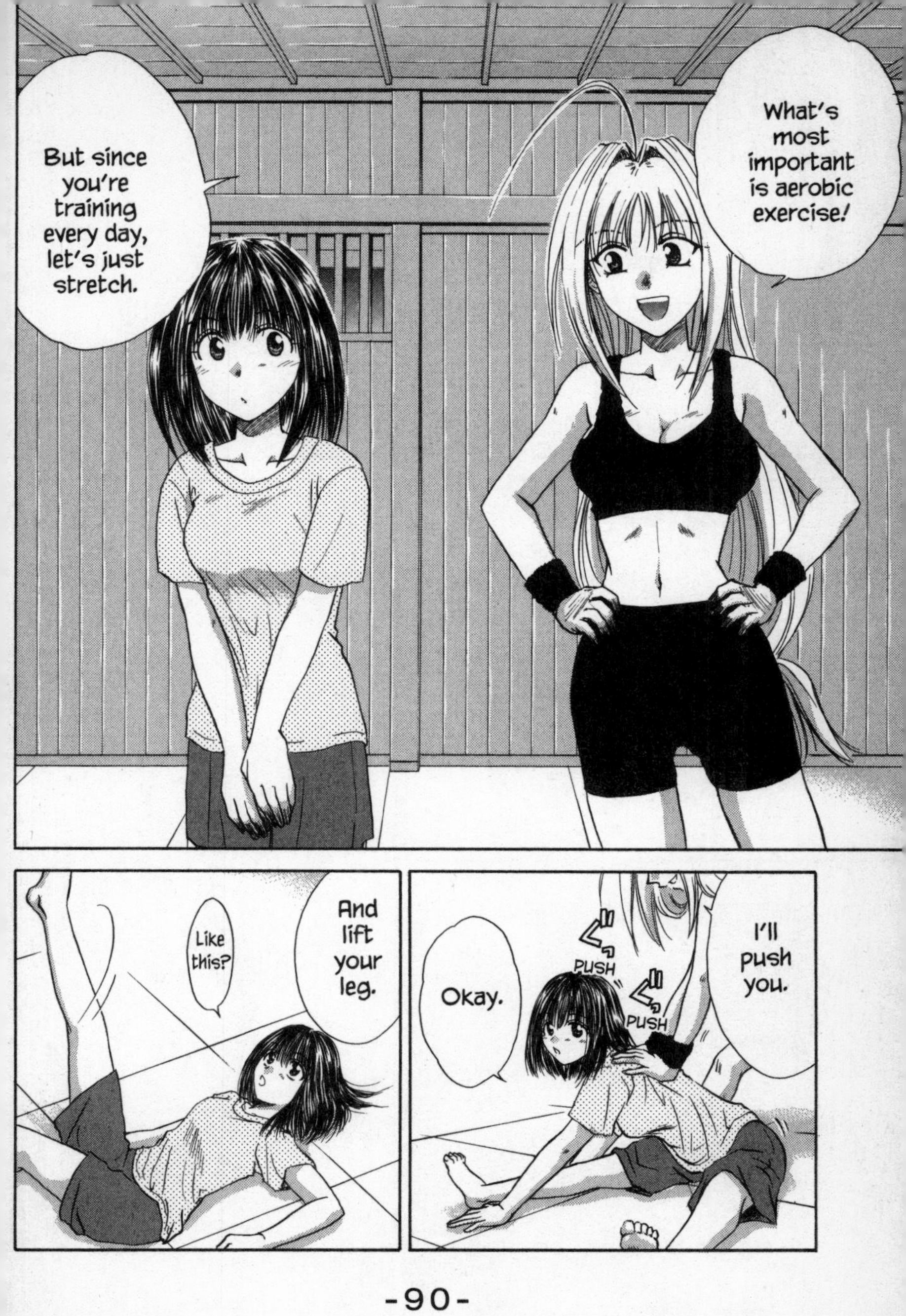
What's most important is aerobic exercise!
But since you're training every day, let's just stretch.
I'll push you.
PUSH
PUSH
Okay.
And lift your leg.
Like this?

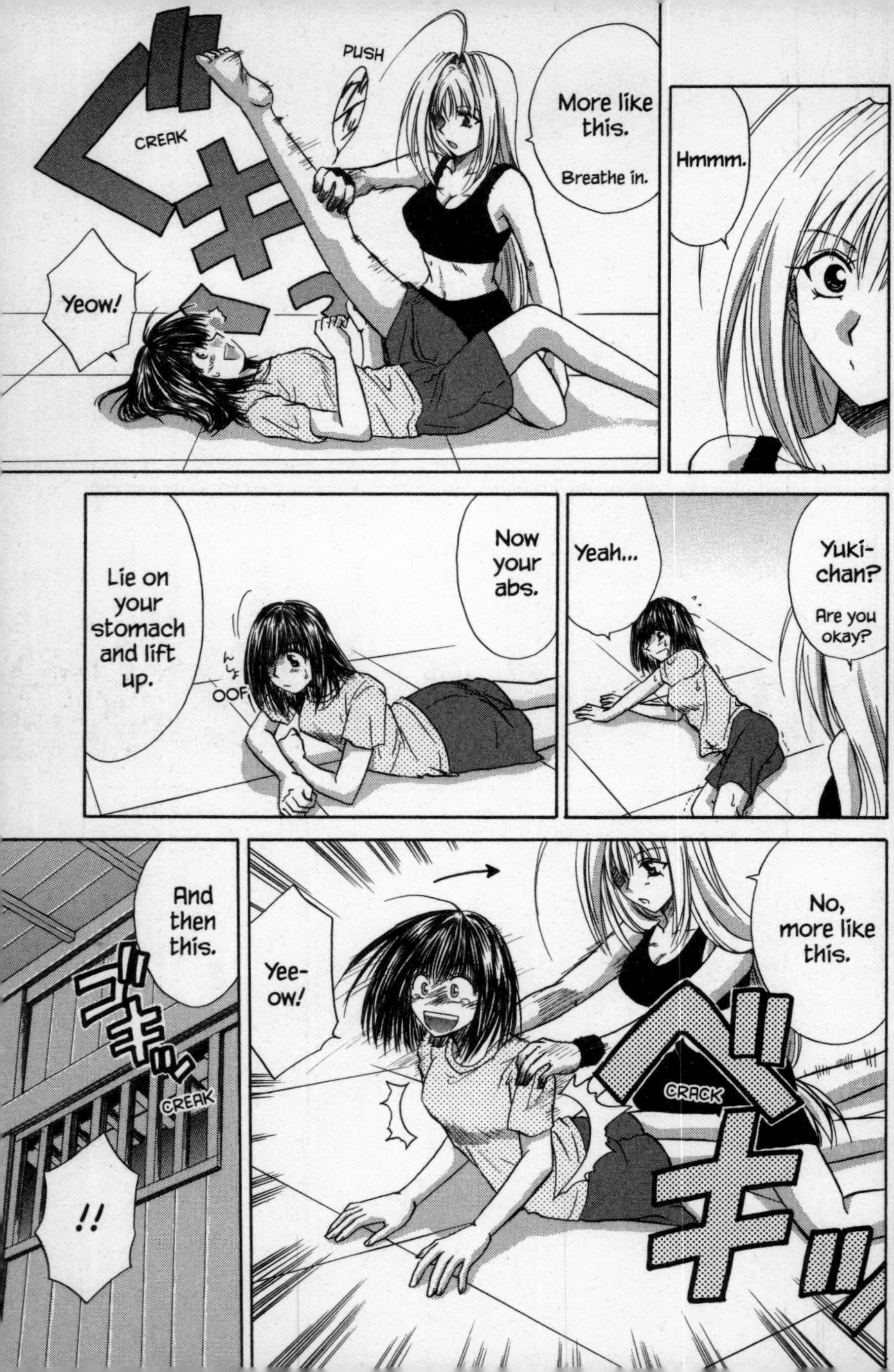

Hmmm.
More like this.
Breathe in.
PUSH
CREAK
Yeow!
Yuki-chan?
Are you okay?
Yeah...
Now your abs.
Lie on your stomach and lift up.
OOF
No, more like this.
Yee-ow!
CRACK
And then this.
CREAK
!!

Okay...

I guess that should do it.

WEAK

Sakuya-chan is pretty harsh.

Next?

And now on to the next thing.

Let's see...

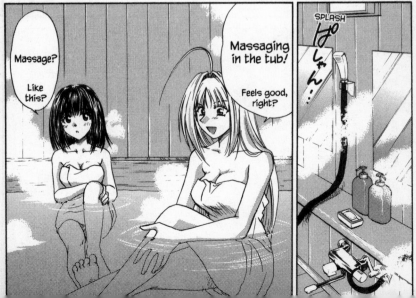

Massage?

Like this?

Massaging in the tub!

Feels good, right?

SPLASH

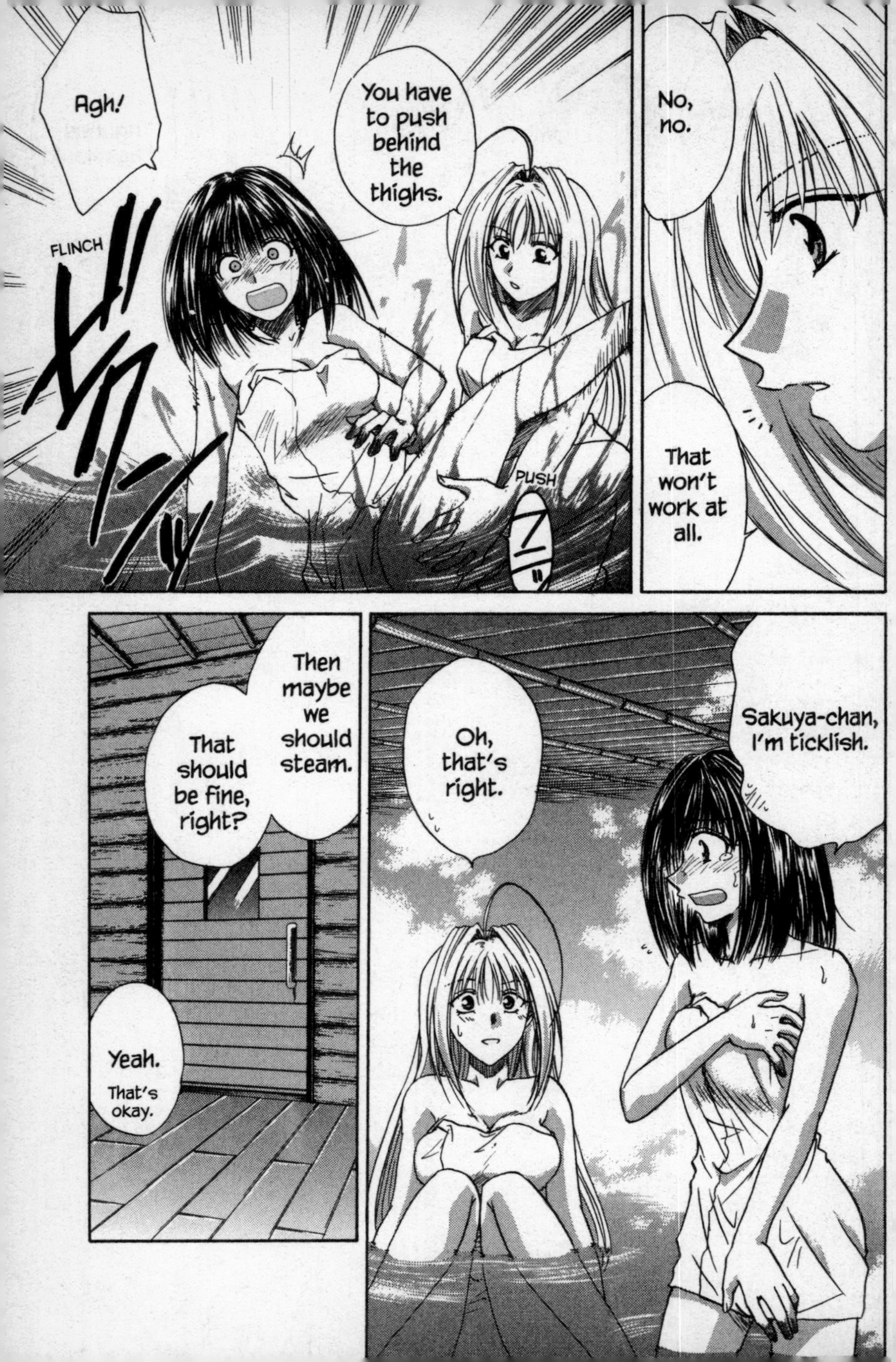
No, no.
That won't work at all.
You have to push behind the thighs.
Agh!
FLINCH
PUSH
Sakuya-chan, I'm ticklish.
Oh, that's right.
Then maybe we should steam.
That should be fine, right?
Yeah.
That's okay.

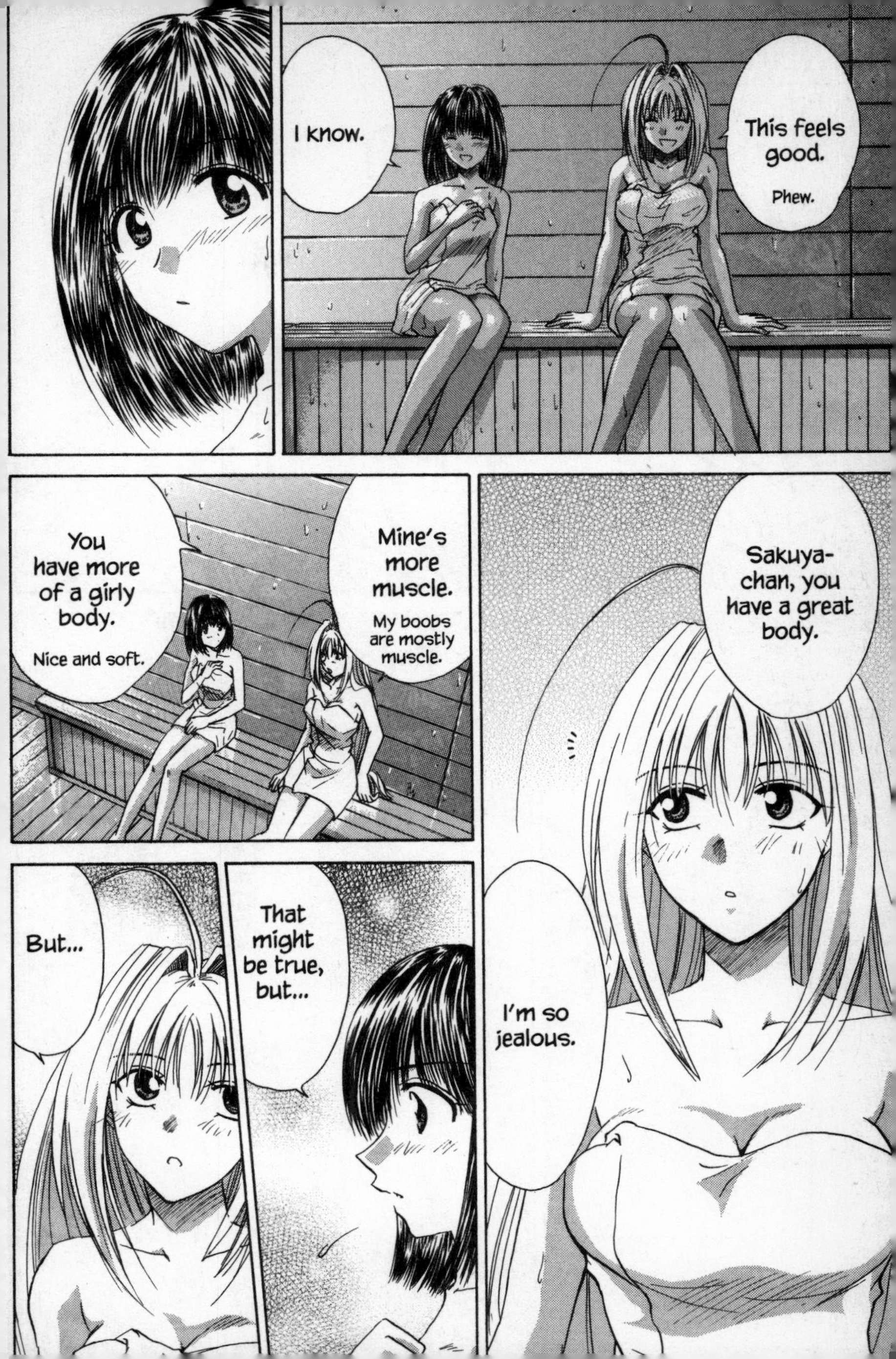
This feels good.
Phew.
I know.
Sakuya-chan, you have a great body.
I'm so jealous.
Mine's more muscle.
My boobs are mostly muscle.
You have more of a girly body.
Nice and soft.
That might be true, but...
But...

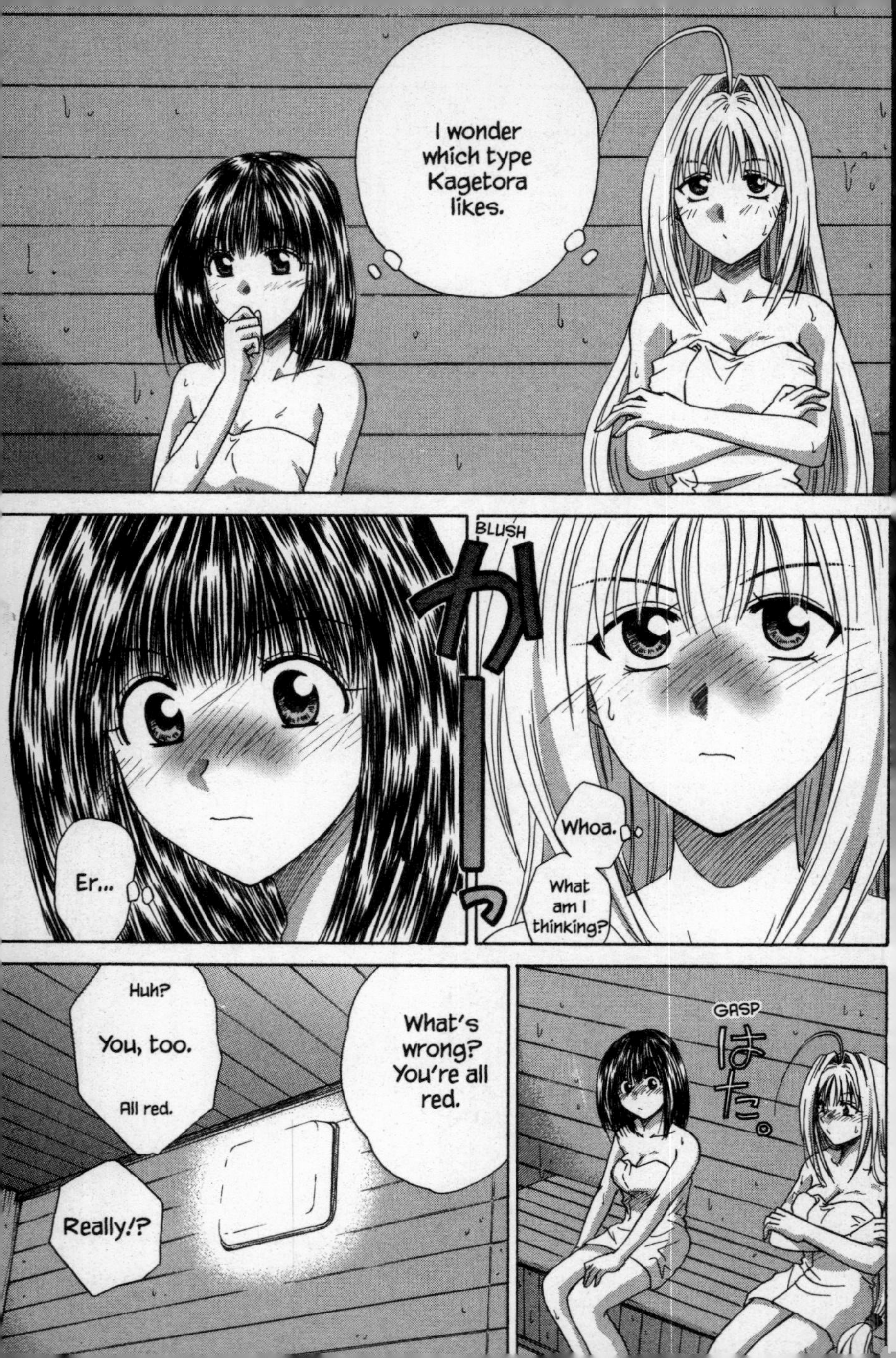
I wonder which type Kagetora likes.
BLUSH
かーっ
Whoa.
What am I thinking?
Er...
GASP
はっ。
What's wrong? You're all red.
Huh?
You, too.
All red.
Really!?

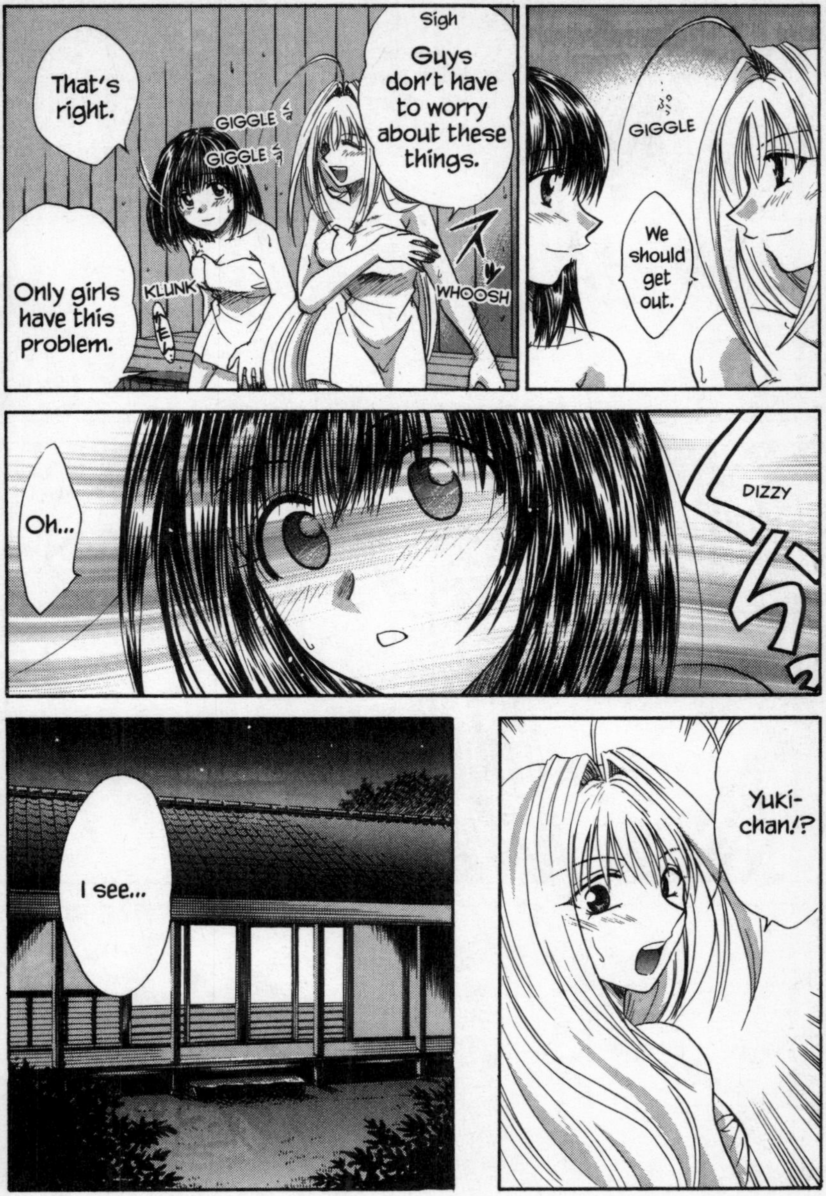
GIGGLE
We should get out.
Sigh
Guys don't have to worry about these things.
That's right.
GIGGLE
GIGGLE
WHOOSH
KLUNK
Only girls have this problem.
DIZZY
Oh...
Yuki-chan!?
I see...

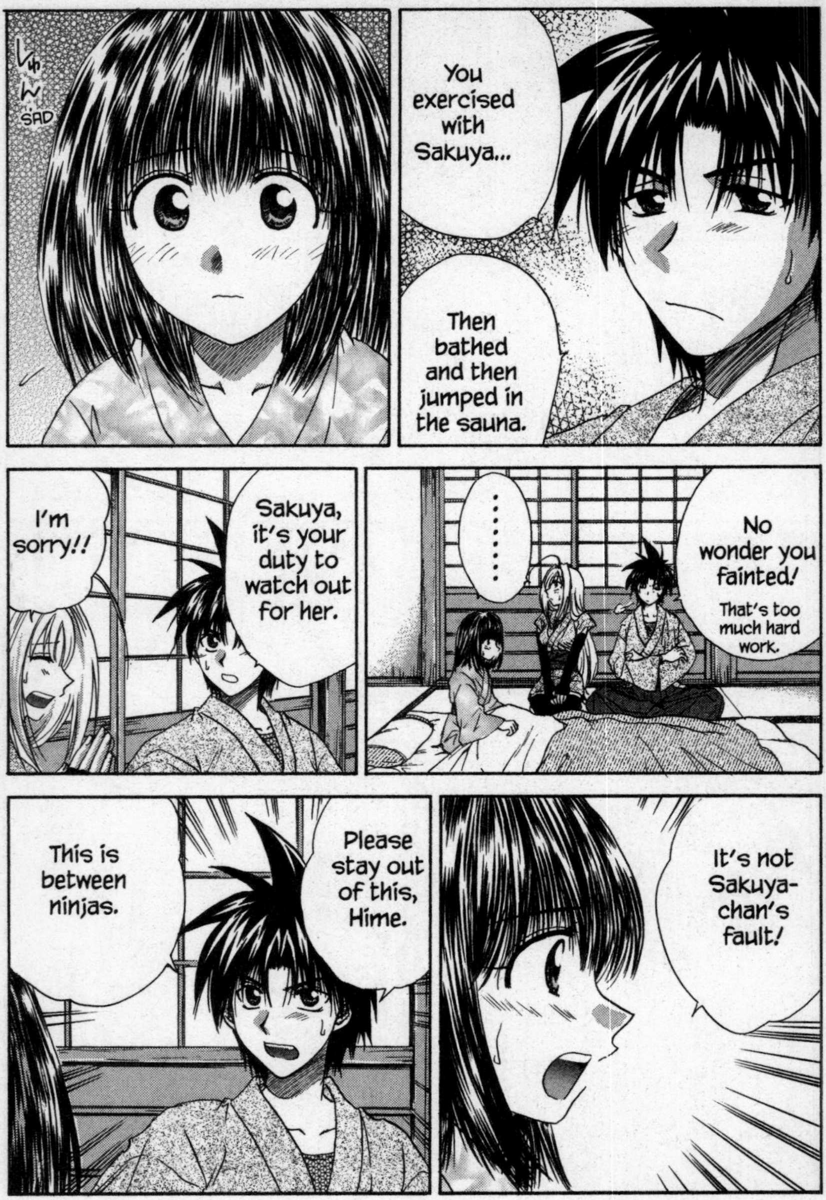
You exercised with Sakuya...
Then bathed and then jumped in the sauna.
しゅん
SAD
No wonder you fainted!
That's too much hard work.
......
Sakuya, it's your duty to watch out for her.
I'm sorry!!
It's not Sakuya-chan's fault!
Please stay out of this, Hime.
This is between ninjas.

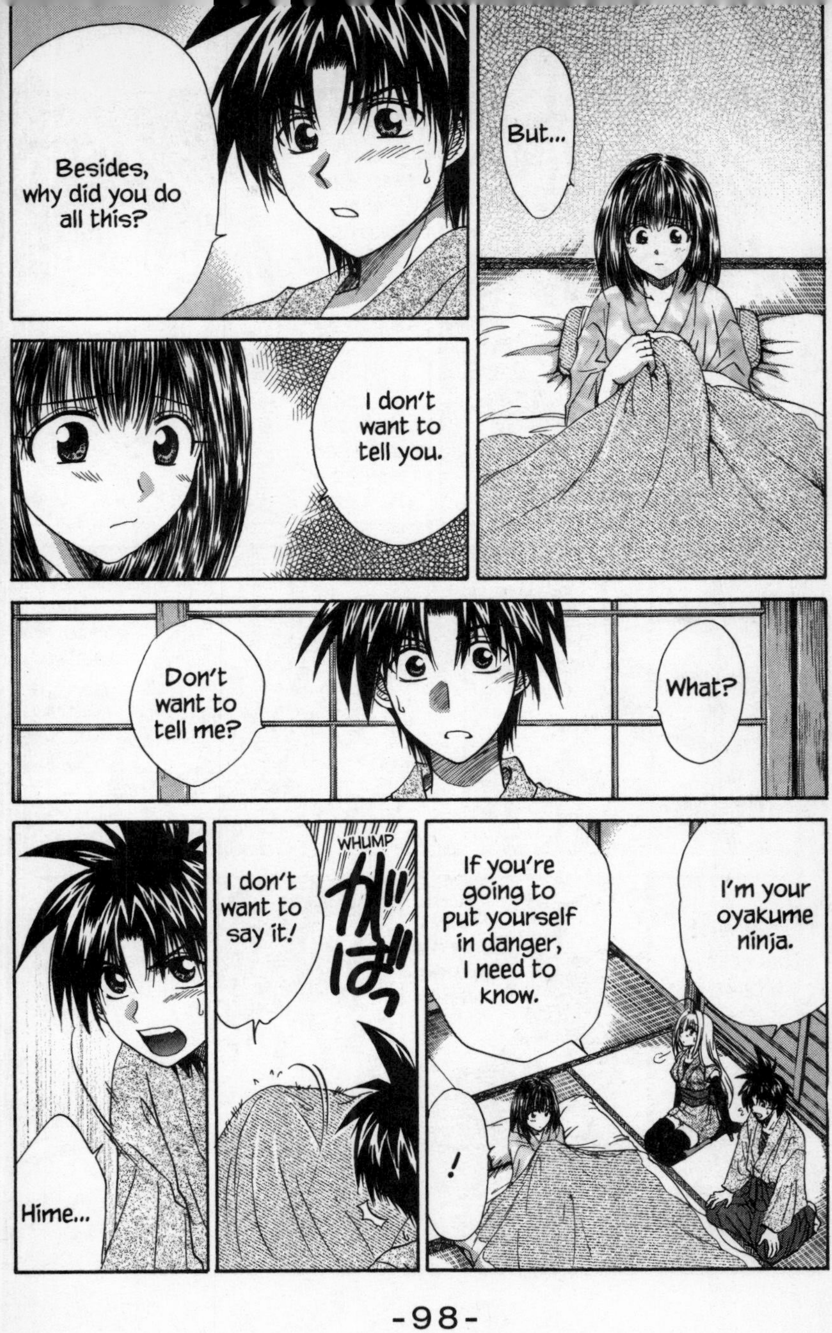
But...
Besides, why did you do all this?
I don't want to tell you.
What?
Don't want to tell me?
I'm your oyakume ninja.
If you're going to put yourself in danger, I need to know.
!
WHUMP
がばっ
I don't want to say it!
Hime...

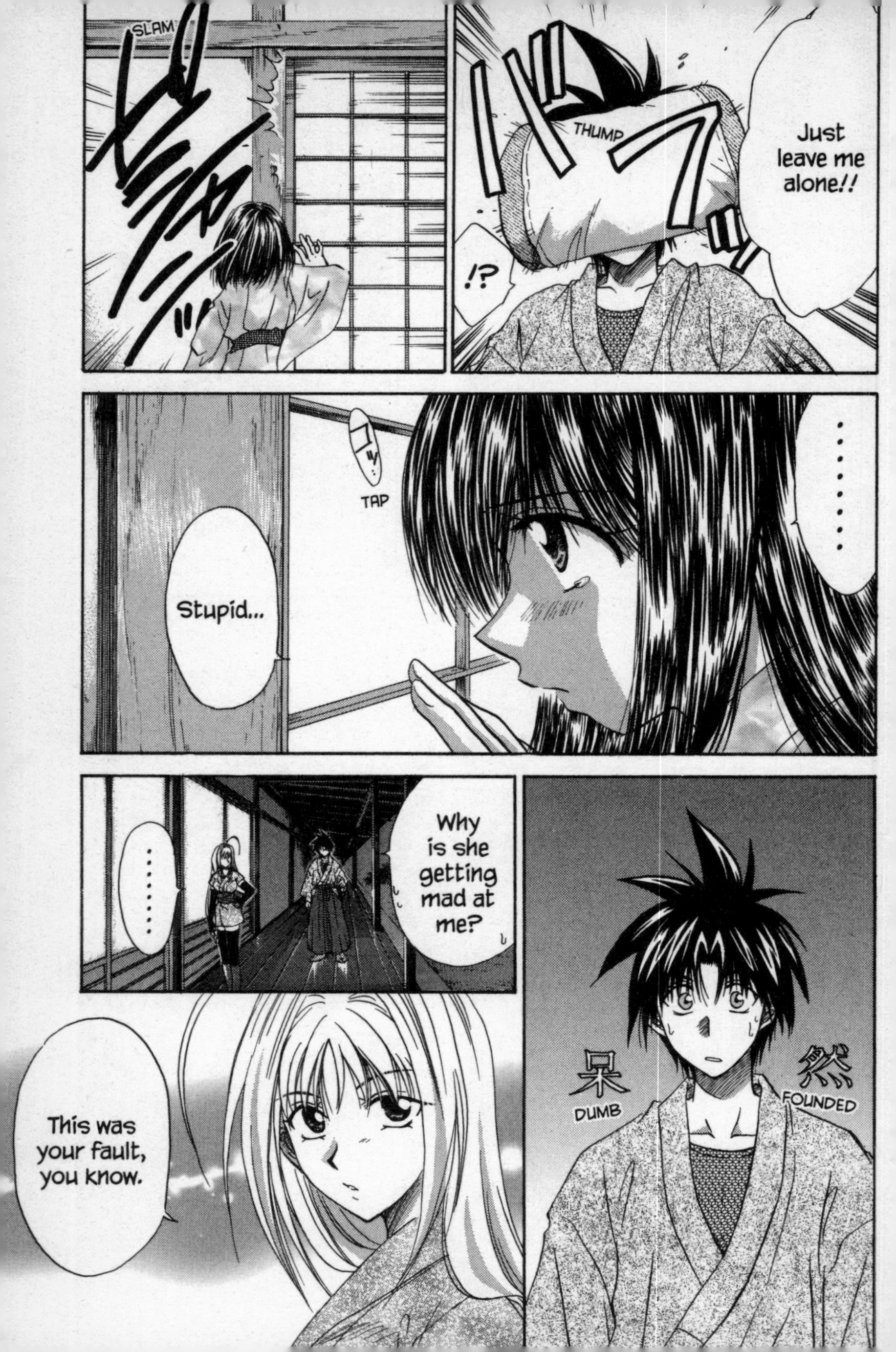

Just leave me alone!!
THUMP
!?
SLAM
......
TAP
Stupid...
呆然
DUMB FOUNDED
Why is she getting mad at me?
......
This was your fault, you know.

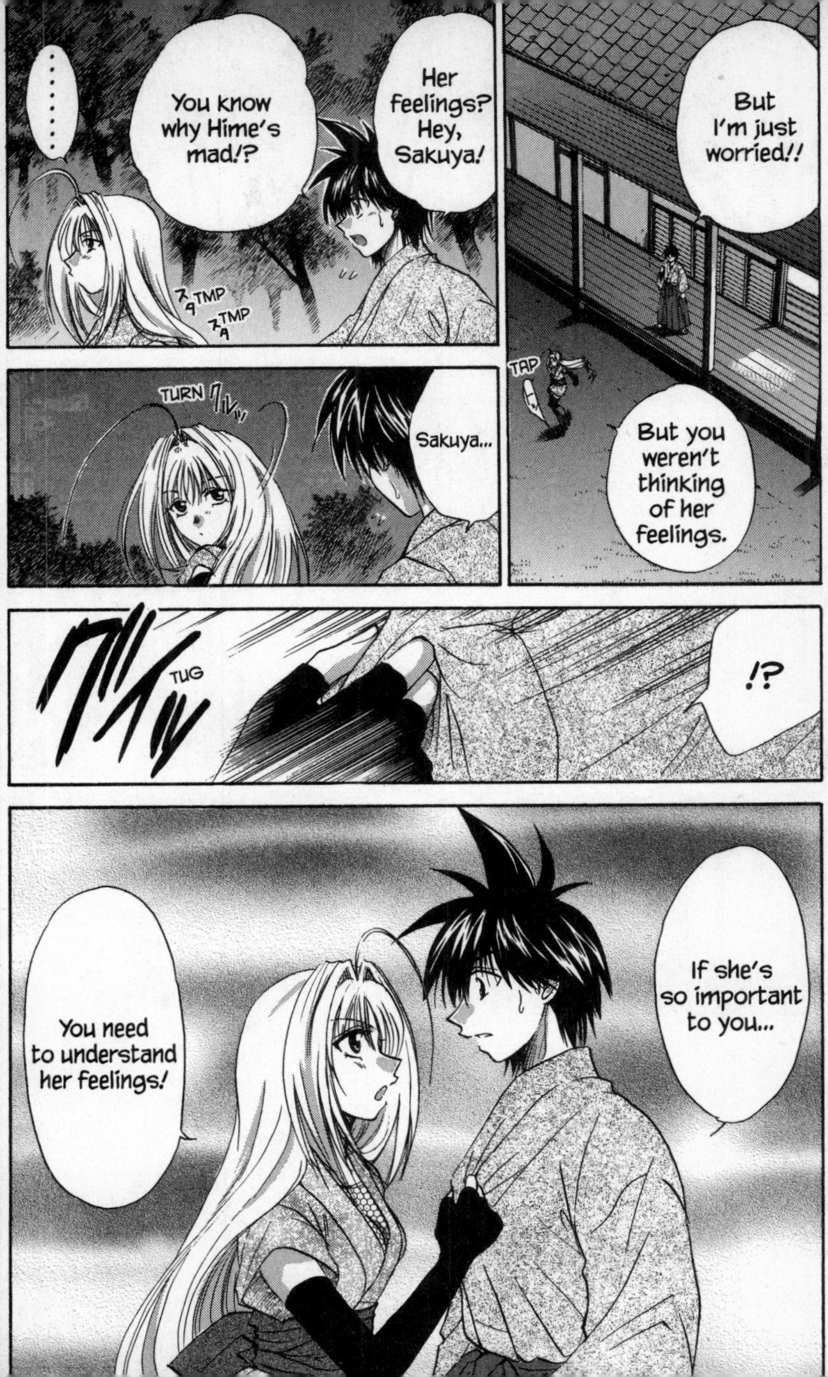

But I'm just worried!!
TAP
But you weren't thinking of her feelings.
Her feelings? Hey, Sakuya!
You know why Hime's mad!?
. . . . . .
TMP
TMP
Sakuya...
TURN
!?
TUG
If she's so important to you...
You need to understand her feelings!

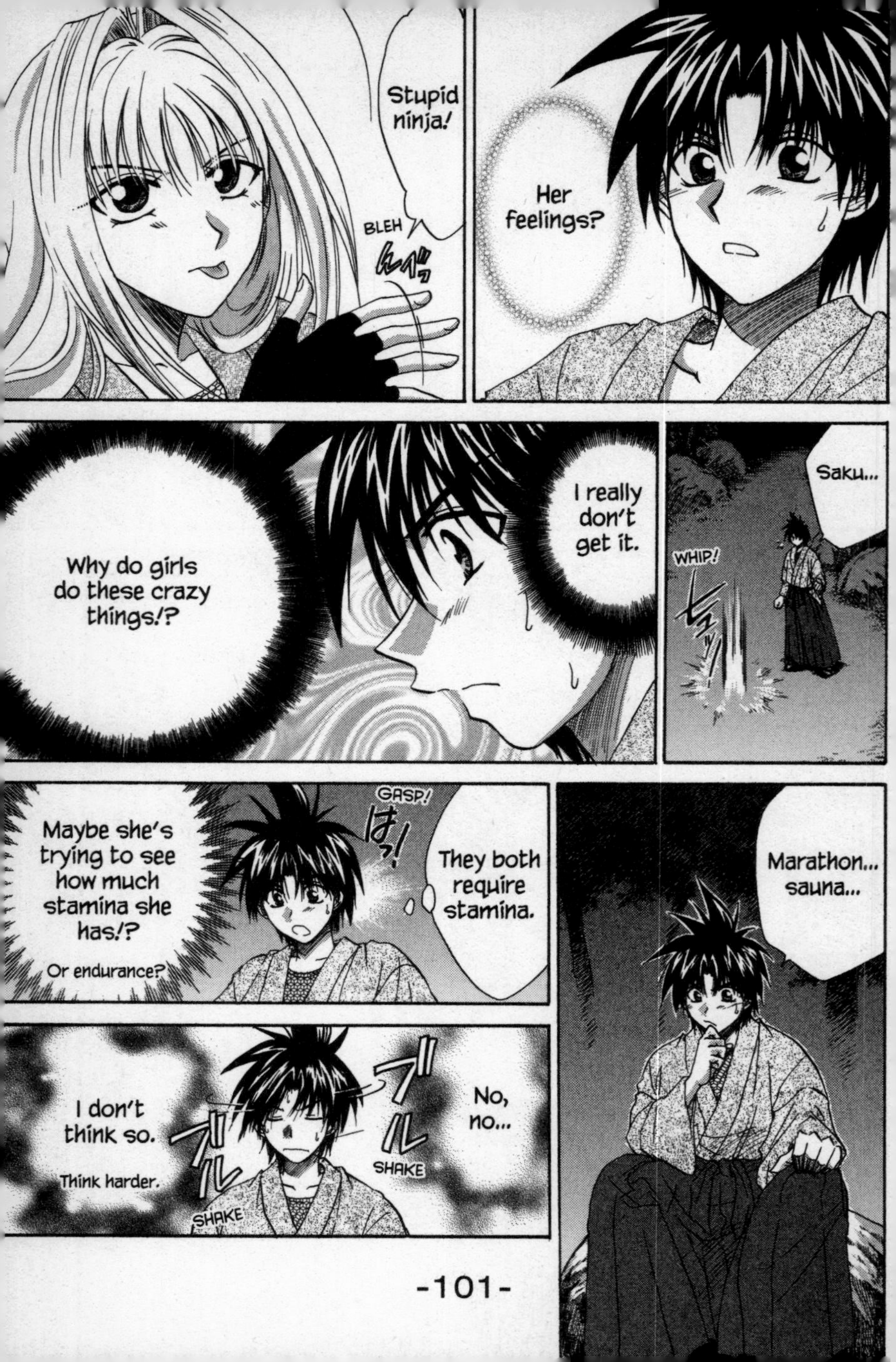
Her feelings?
BLEH
Stupid ninja!
Saku...
WHIP!
I really don't get it.
Why do girls do these crazy things!?
Marathon... sauna...
GASP!
はっ!
They both require stamina.
Maybe she's trying to see how much stamina she has!?
Or endurance?
No, no...
ブル
SHAKE
I don't think so.
Think harder.
ブル
SHAKE

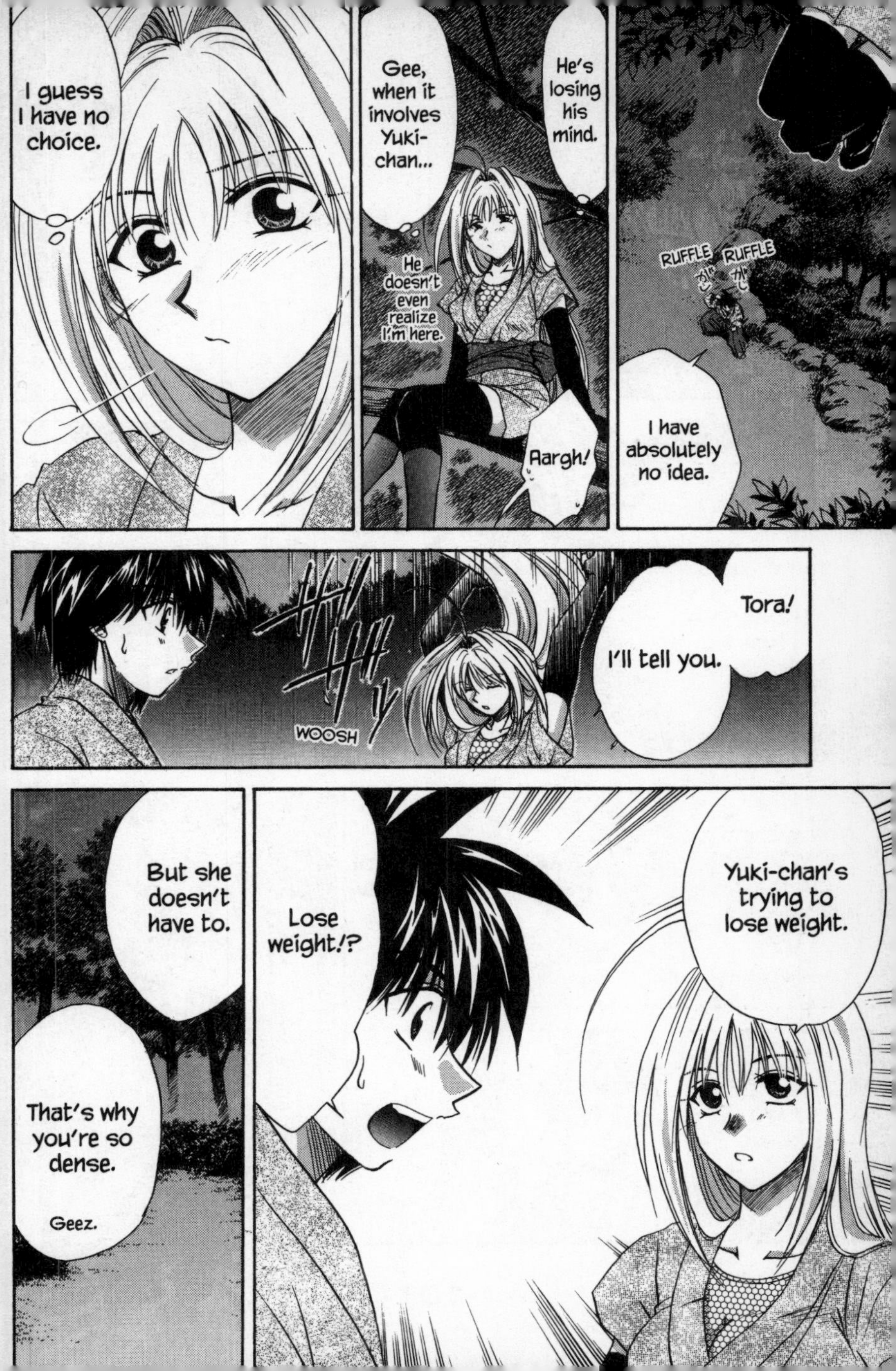
RUFFLE RUFFLE
I have absolutely no idea.
He's losing his mind.
Gee, when it involves Yuki-chan...
He doesn't even realize I'm here.
Aargh!
I guess I have no choice.
Tora!
I'll tell you.
WOOSH
Yuki-chan's trying to lose weight.
Lose weight!?
But she doesn't have to.
That's why you're so dense.
Geez.

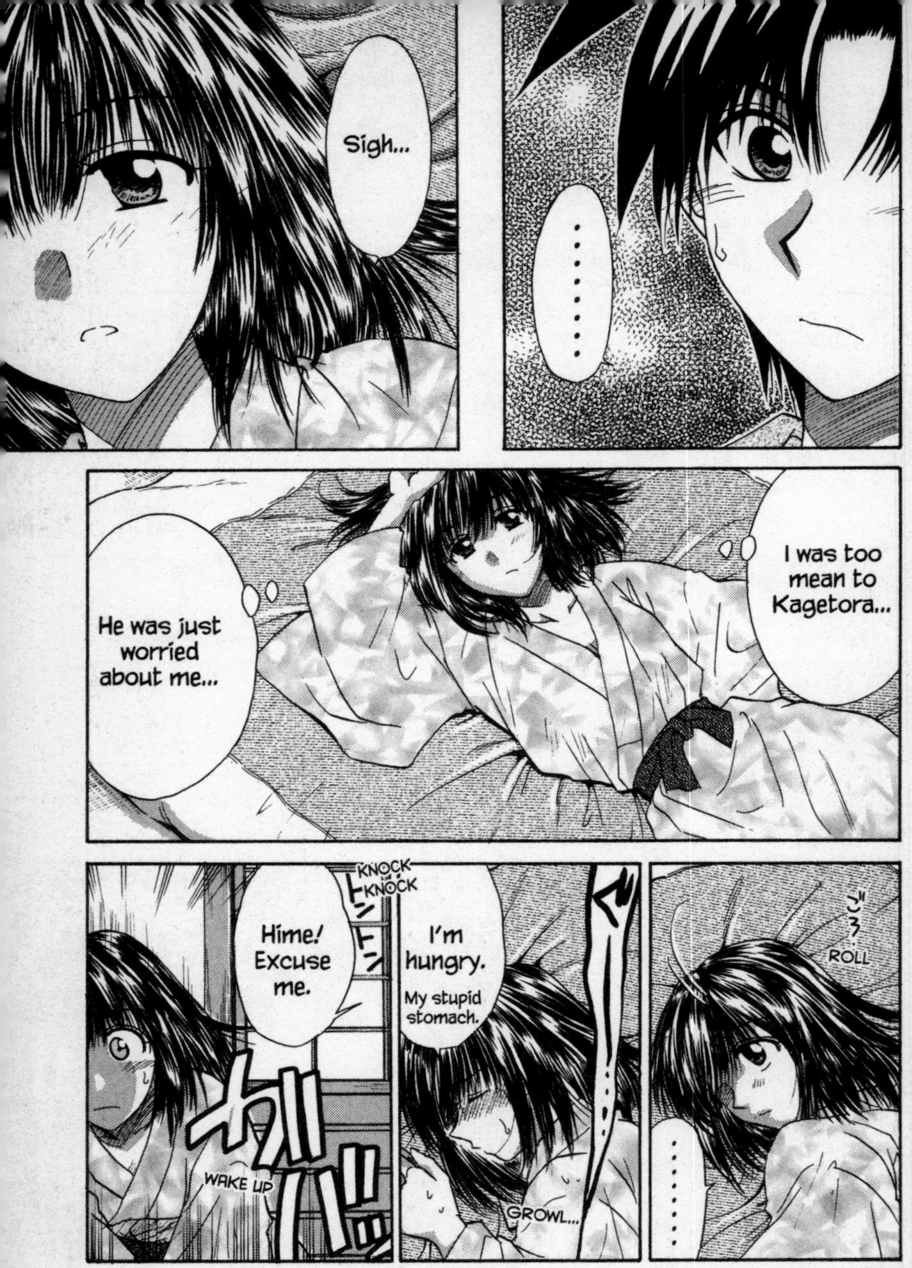

......
Sigh...
I was too mean to Kagetora...
He was just worried about me...
ごろ
ROLL
......
I'm hungry.
My stupid stomach.
GROWL...
KNOCK KNOCK
Hime! Excuse me.
WAKE UP

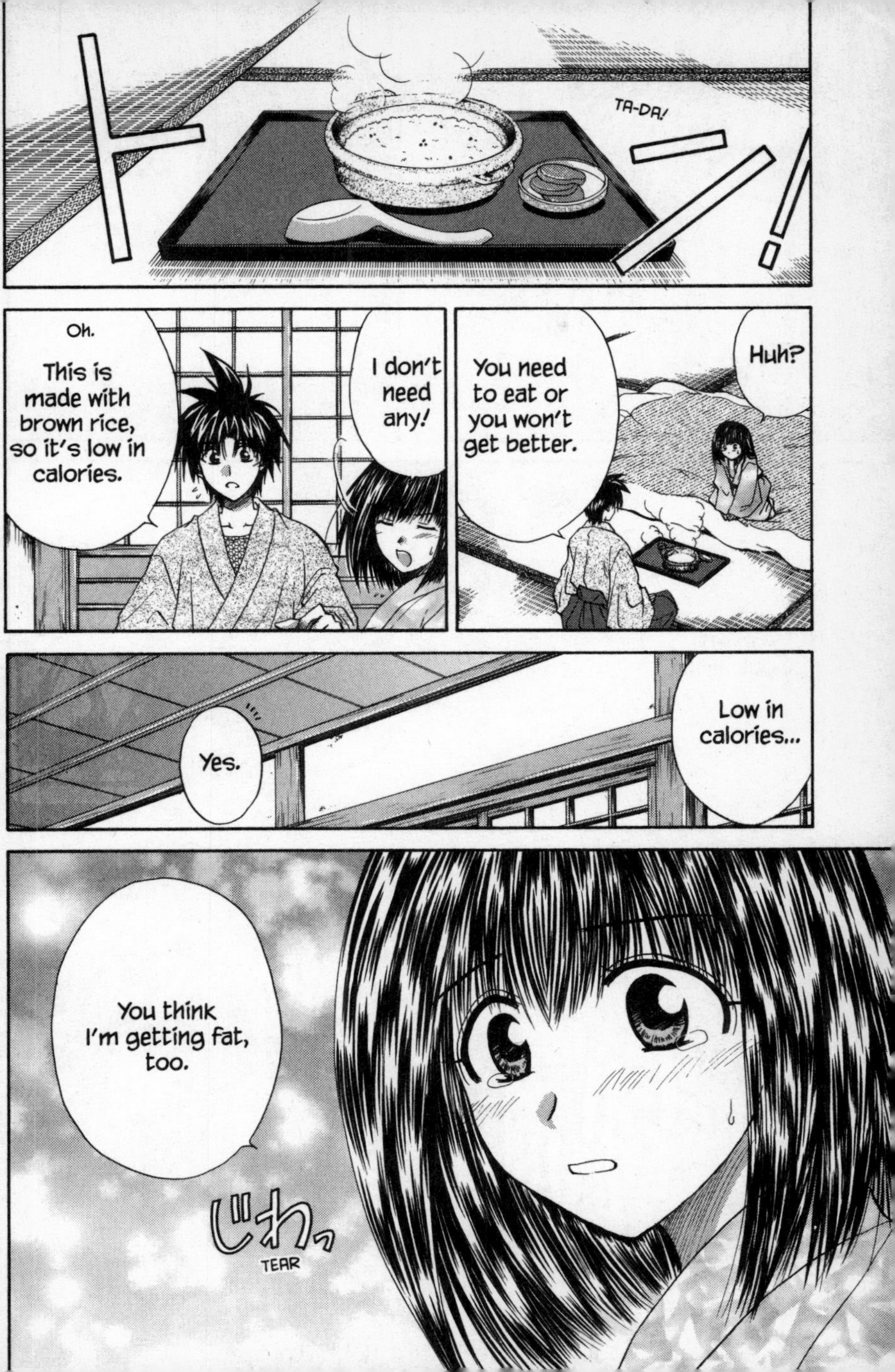

TA-DA!
Huh?
You need to eat or you won't get better.
I don't need any!
Oh.
This is made with brown rice, so it's low in calories.
Low in calories...
Yes.
You think I'm getting fat, too.
じわっ
TEAR

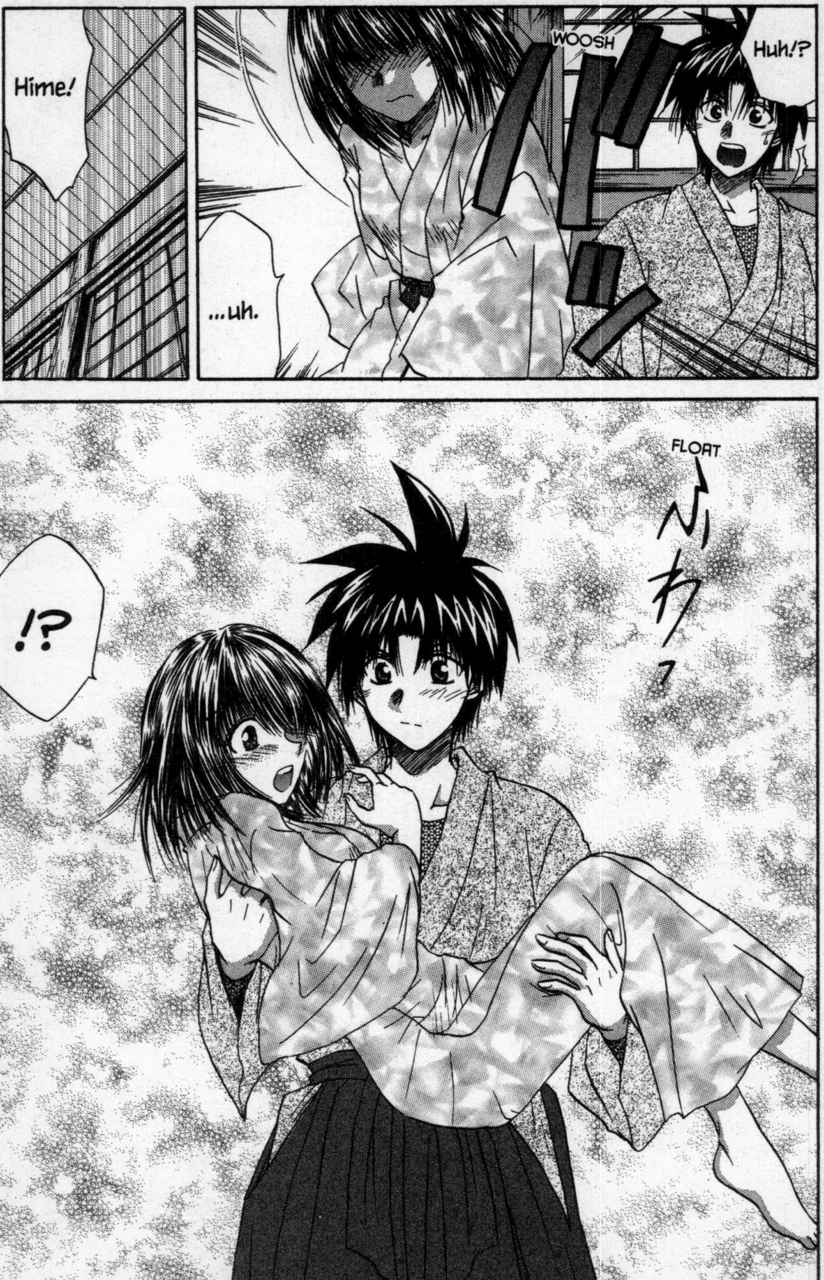
Huh!?
WOOSH
...uh.
Hime!
FLOAT
ふわっ
!?

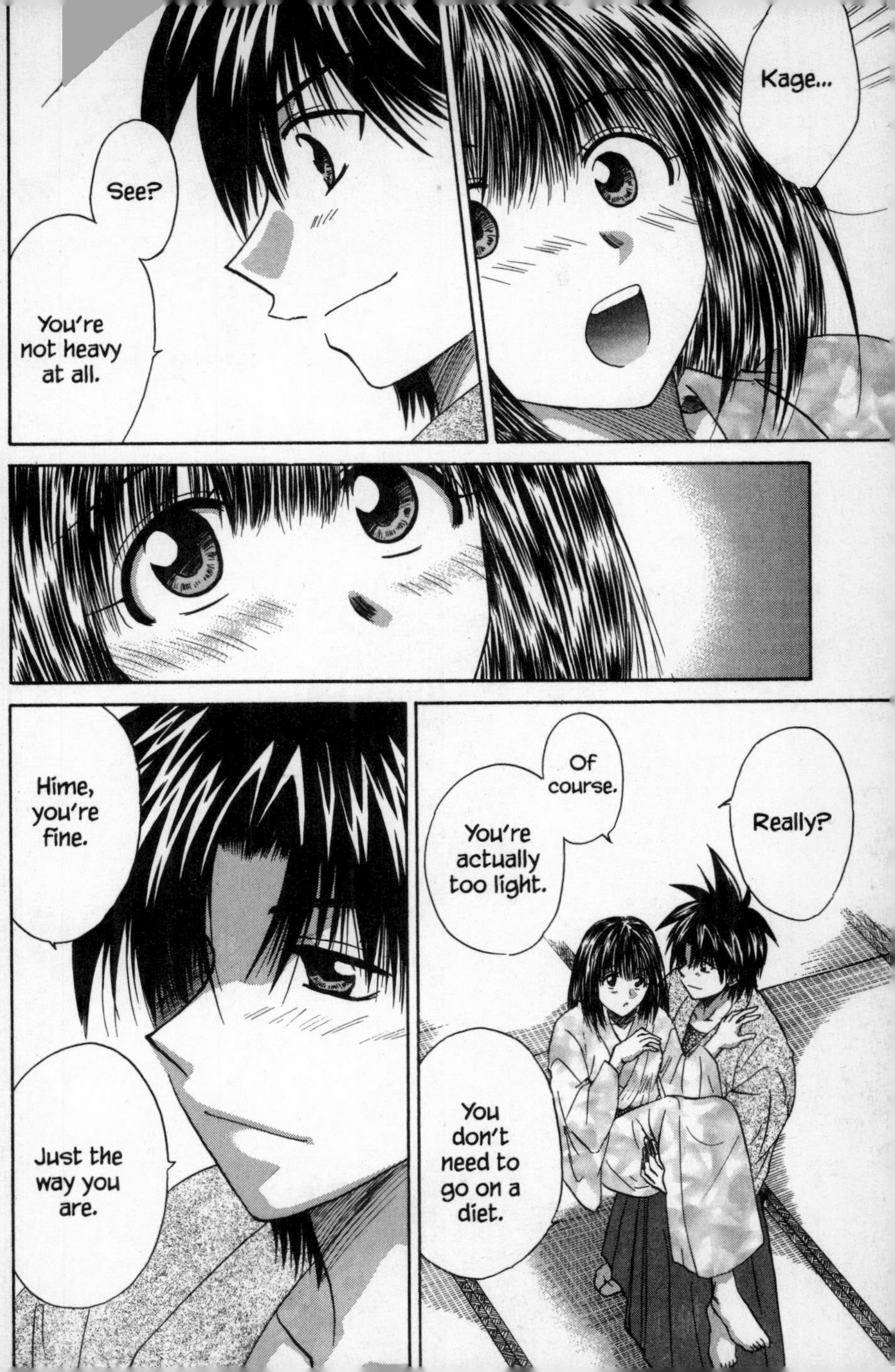
Kage...
See?
You're not heavy at all.
Really?
Of course.
You're actually too light.
You don't need to go on a diet.
Hime, you're fine.
Just the way you are.

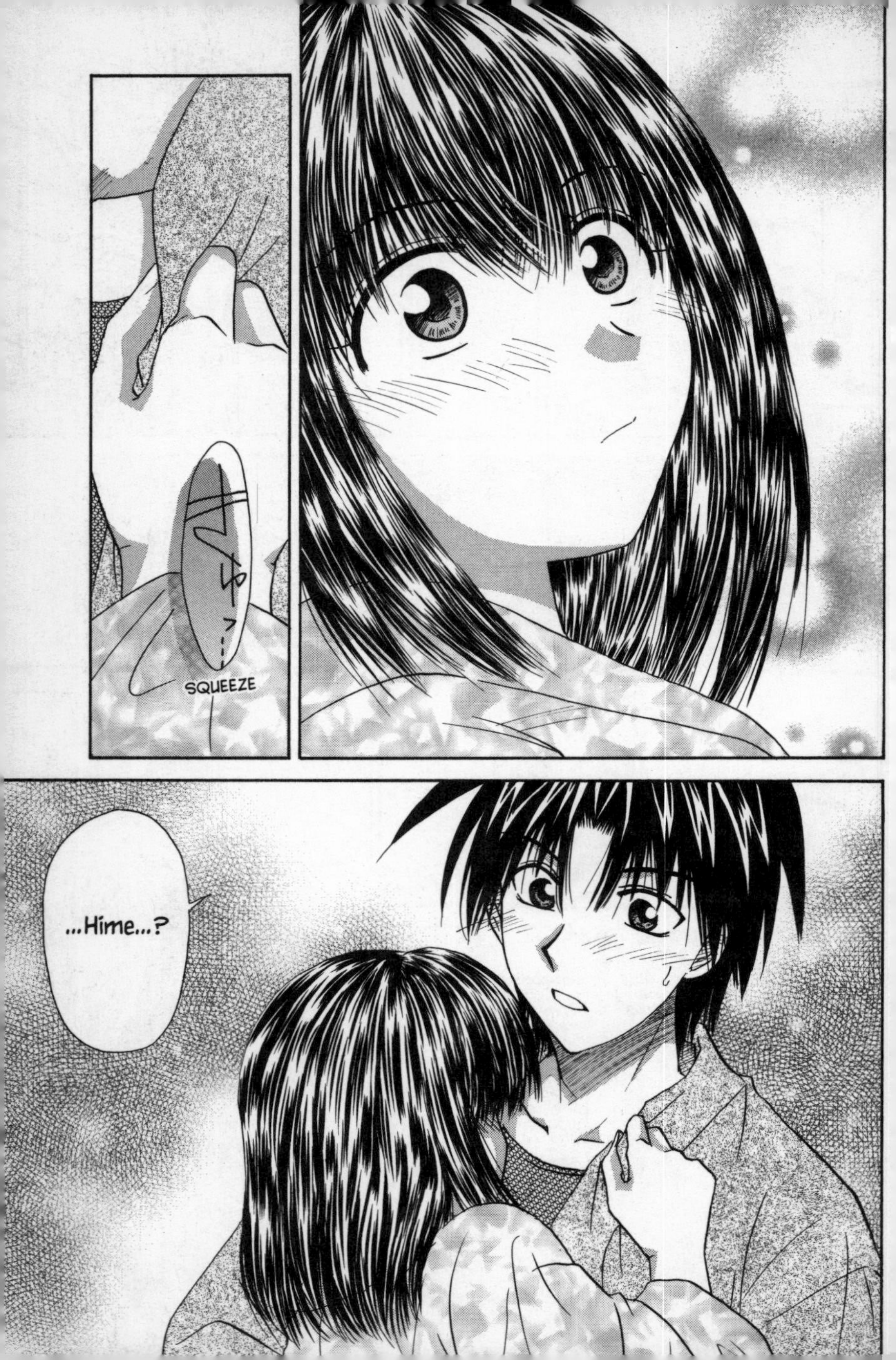
SQUEEZE
...Hime...?

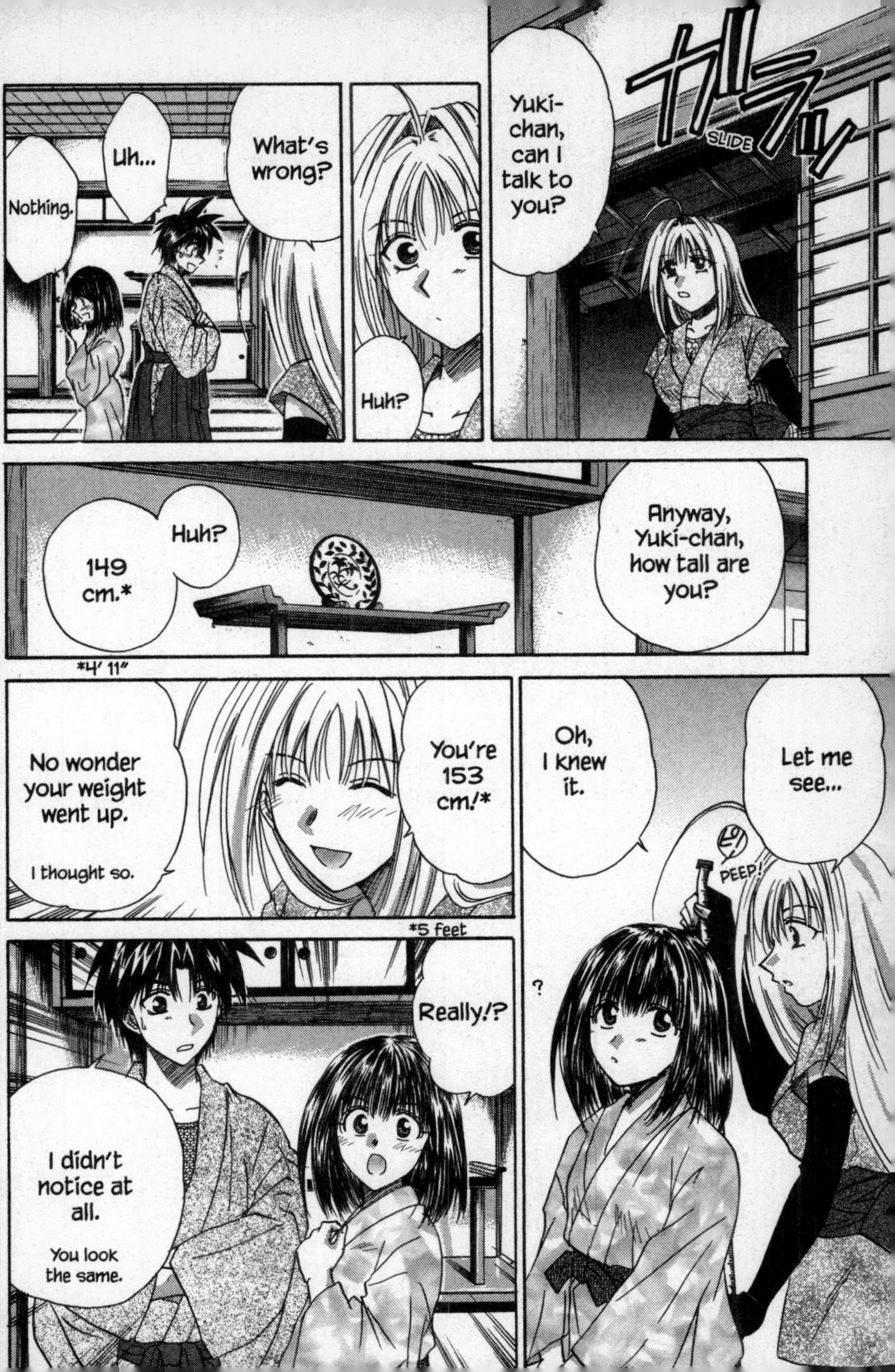

ガラッ
SLIDE
Yuki-chan, can I talk to you?
Huh?
What's wrong?
Uh...
Nothing.
Anyway, Yuki-chan, how tall are you?
Huh?
149 cm.*
*4' 11"
Let me see...
PEEP!
Oh, I knew it.
?
You're 153 cm!*
No wonder your weight went up.
I thought so.
*5 feet
Really!?
I didn't notice at all.
You look the same.

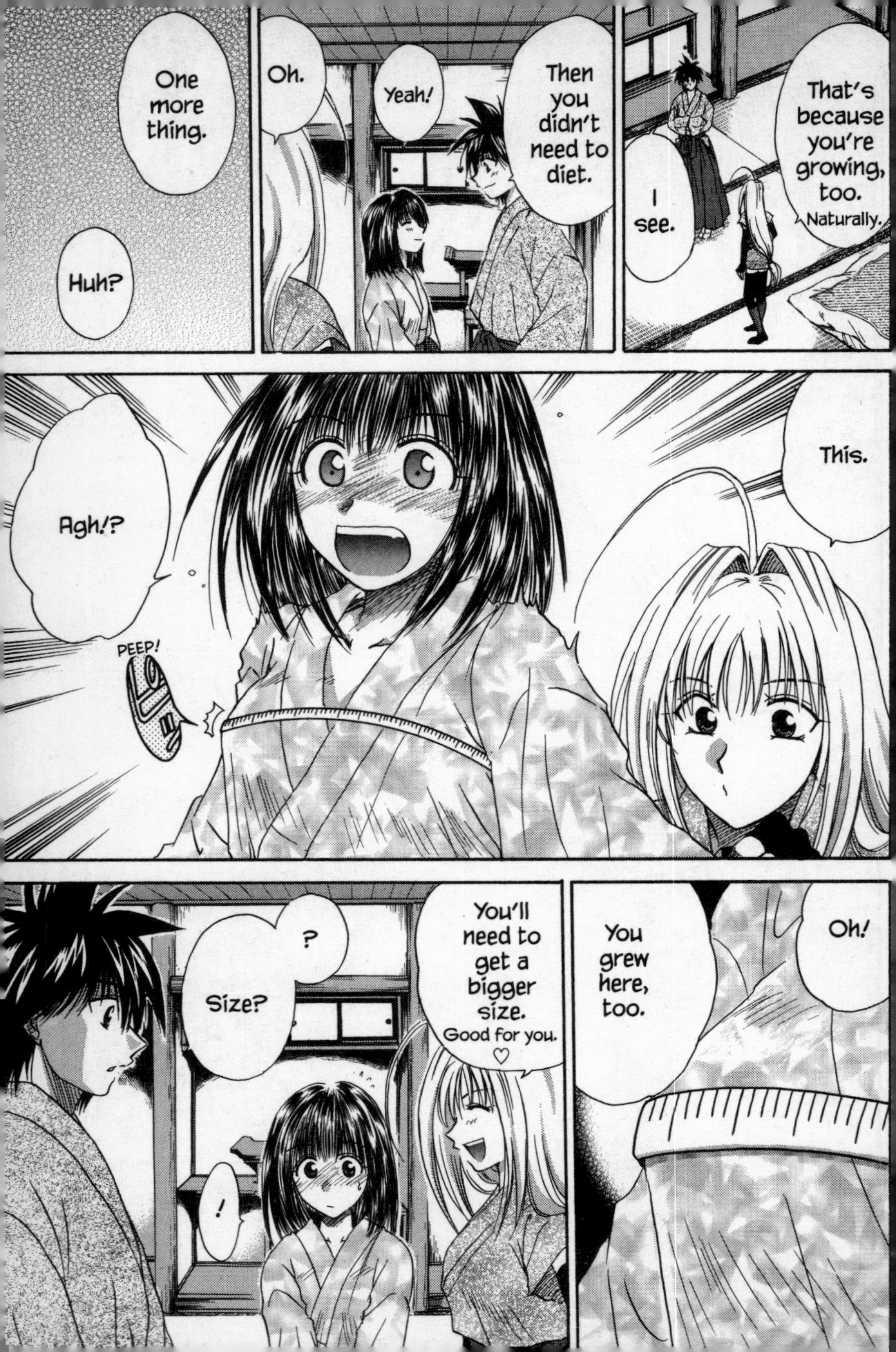
That's because you're growing, too.
Naturally.
I see.
Then you didn't need to diet.
Yeah!
Oh.
One more thing.
Huh?
This.
Agh!?
PEEP!
Oh!
You grew here, too.
You'll need to get a bigger size.
Good for you. ♡
?
Size?
!

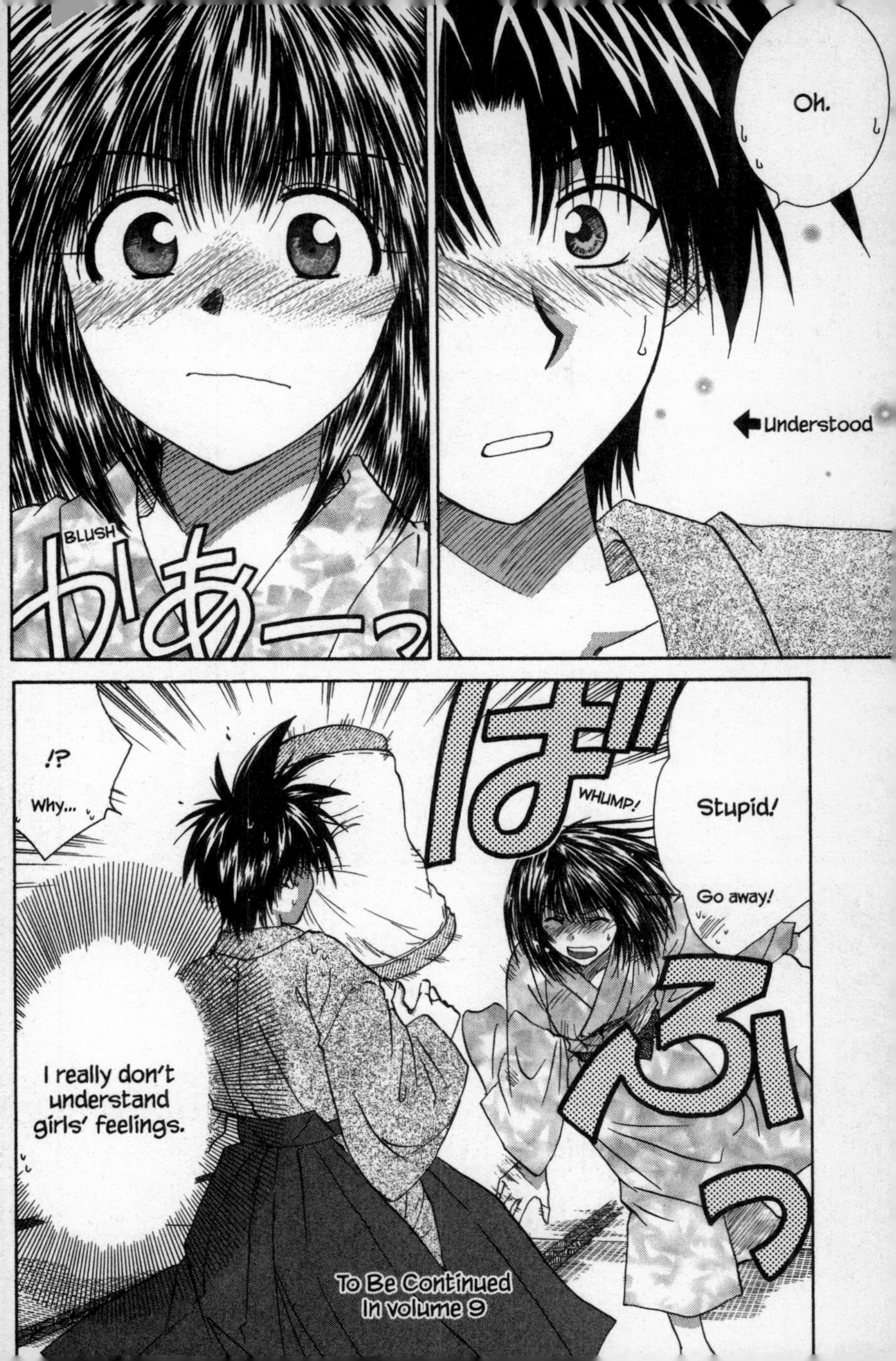

Oh.
Understood
BLUSH
かあーっ
ぼふっ
WHUMP!
Stupid!
Go away!
!?
Why...
I really don't understand girls' feelings.
To Be Continued
In volume 9

Explanation

Um...the chapters that follow are the ones that were featured in *Weekly Shonen Magazine* for a short period of time. It's like... maybe a side story? (laugh)

Kagetora and Yuki are in their senior year, but in the side story they are still juniors. It's set during the winter, so it takes place around #21 and #22. Maybe you can enjoy it while reading volume 5.

By the way, I did this feature in the *Weekly Shonen Magazine* on very short notice. I had to scramble with my staff to finish it. To have a weekly deadline... it was very thrilling and I feel like I gained a lot of experience (laugh).

I thought that with this, I had mastered the concept of deadlines. But when I went back to monthly deadlines, I realized I had completely forgotten the feeling of a deadline that slowly creeps up on you. Well, I guess that can't be helped...

So please enjoy the *Weekly Shonen Magazine* version of KAGETORA. ♪

I feel like I had better experiences in the *Weekly Magazine* version...

◄ He had difficulties and hardships in volume 8 (laugh)

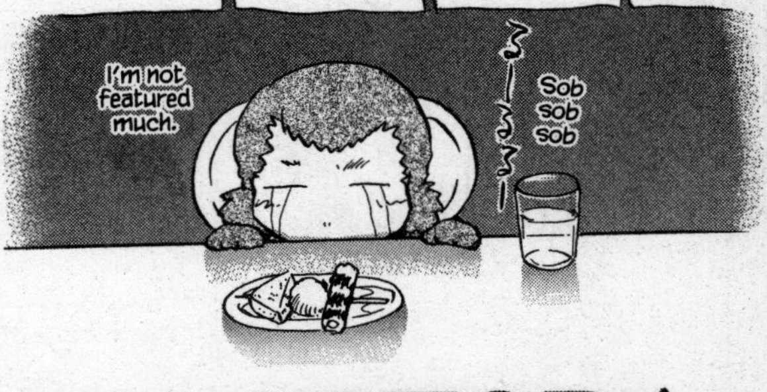
Sob sob sob
I'm not featured much.

KAGETORA

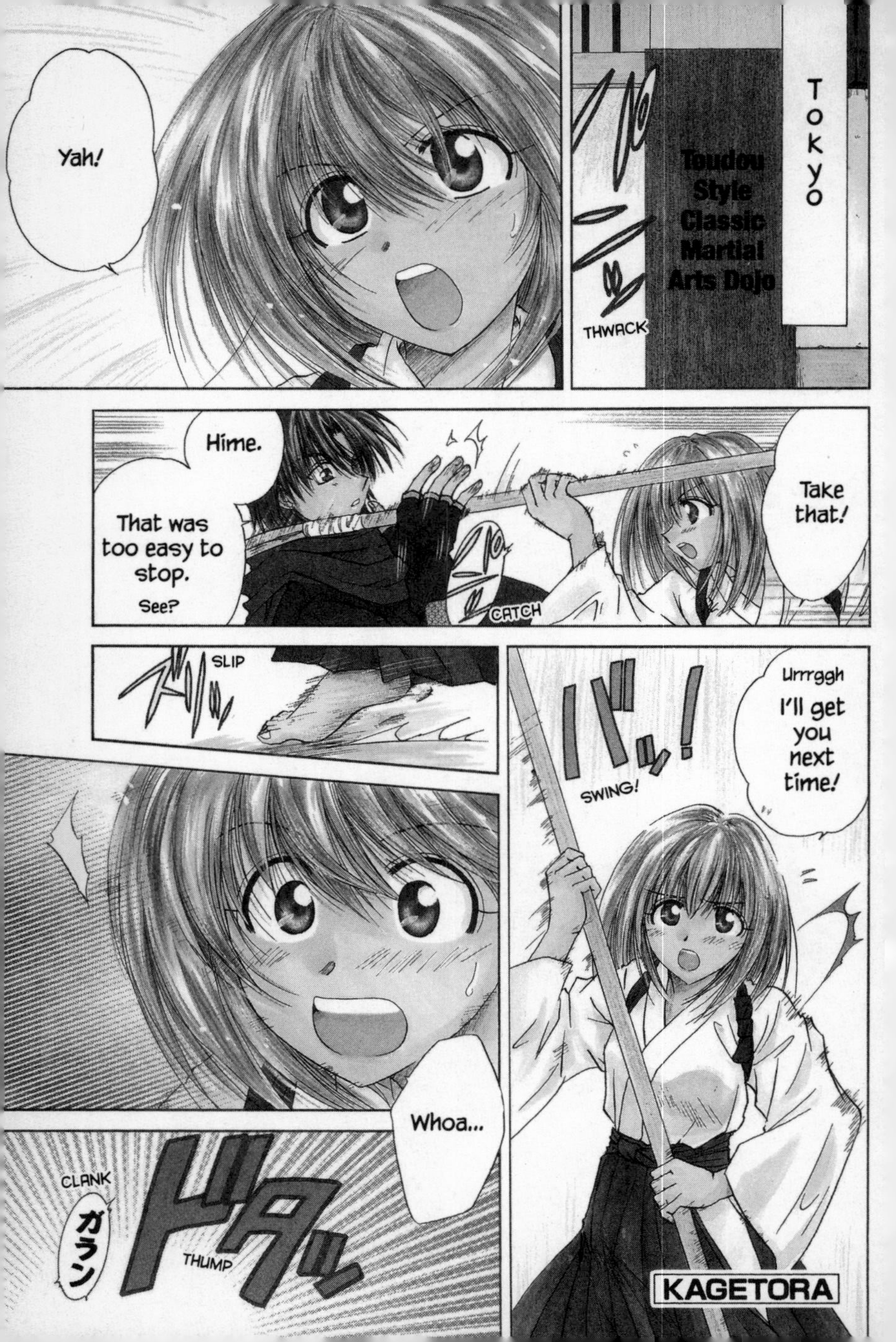
Tokyo
Toudou Style Classic Martial Arts Dojo
THWACK
Yah!
Take that!
Hime.
That was too easy to stop.
See?
CATCH
Urrrggh
I'll get you next time!
バッ!
SWING!
KAGETORA
SLIP
Whoa...
CLANK
ガラン
ドタッ
THUMP

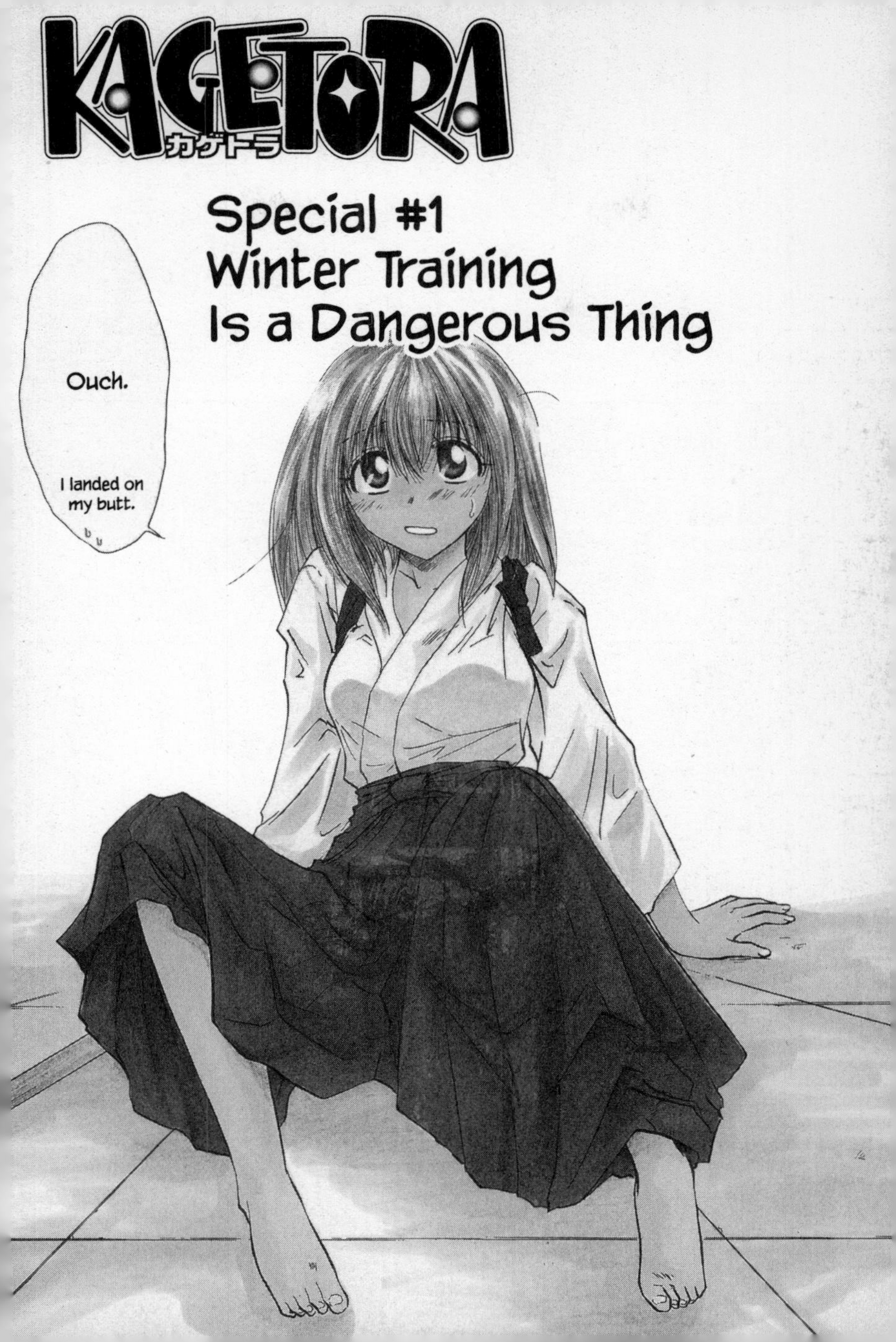
KAGETORA
カゲトラ
Special #1
Winter Training
Is a Dangerous Thing
Ouch.
I landed on my butt.

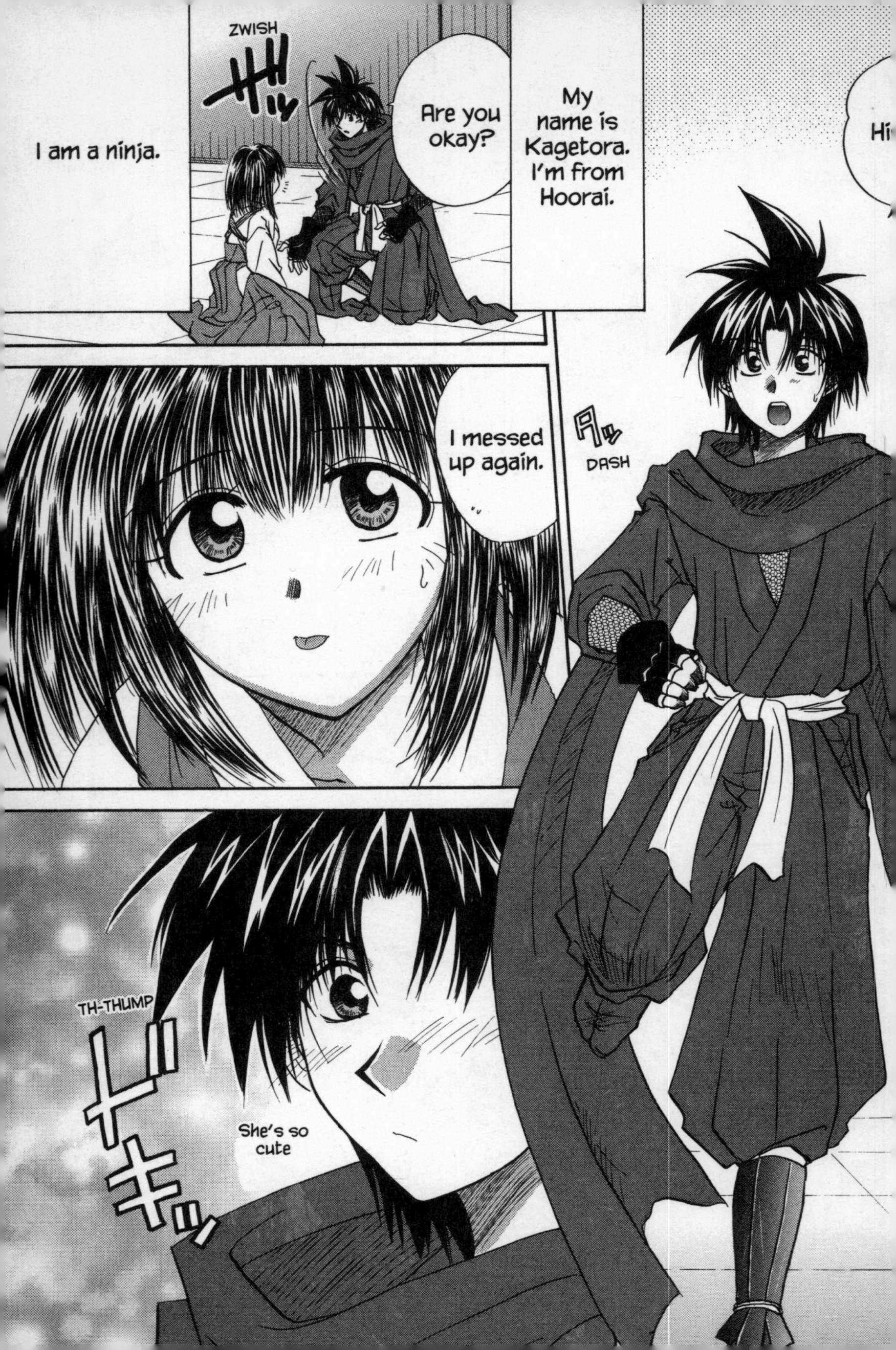
DASH
My name is Kagetora. I'm from Hoorai.
Are you okay?
ZWISH
I am a ninja.
I messed up again.
She's so cute
TH-THUMP

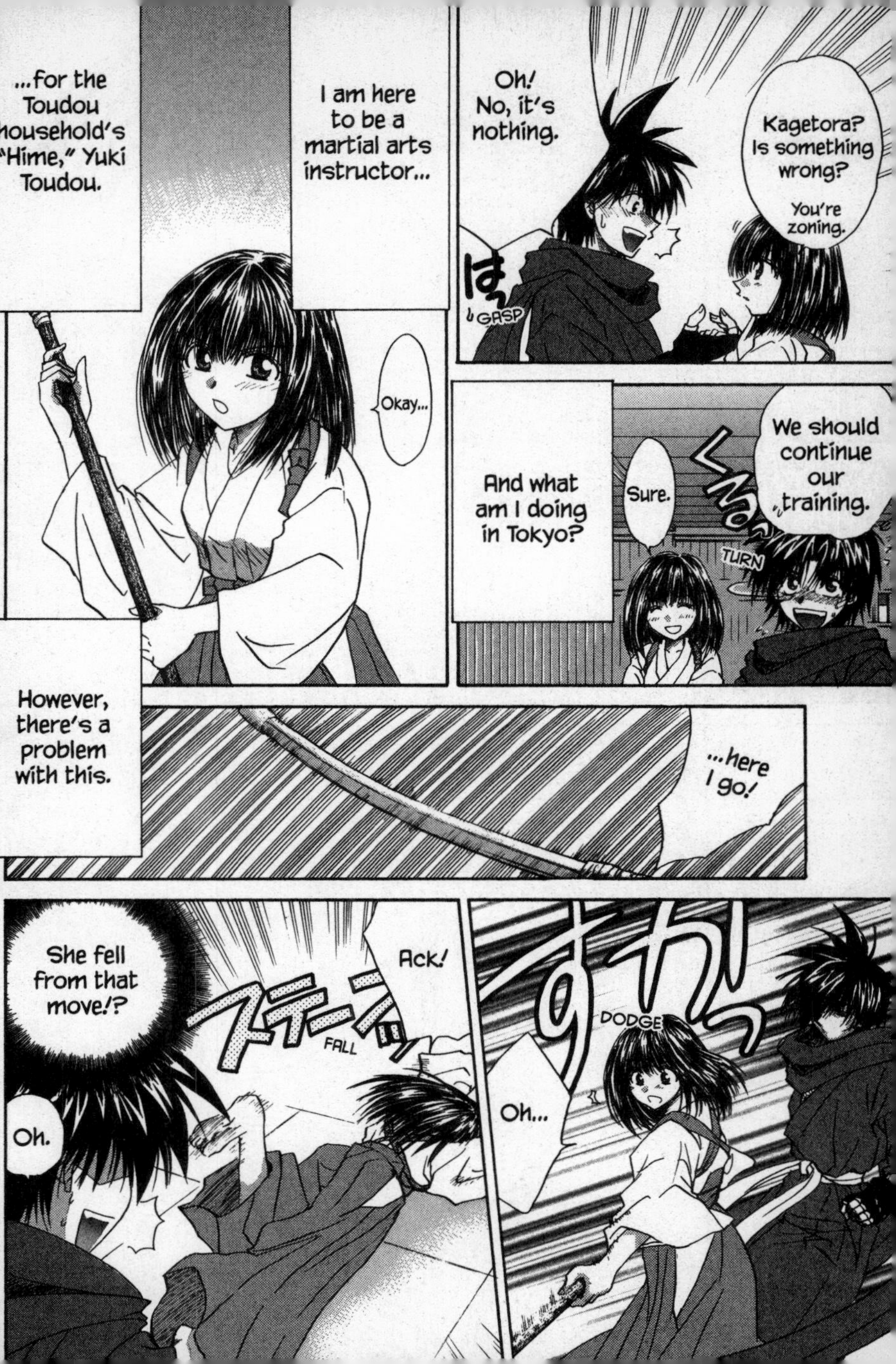
Kagetora? Is something wrong?
You're zoning.
GASP
Oh! No, it's nothing.
We should continue our training.
TURN
Sure.
And what am I doing in Tokyo?
I am here to be a martial arts instructor...
...for the Toudou household's "Hime," Yuki Toudou.
Okay...
...here I go!
However, there's a problem with this.
DODGE
Oh...
Ack!
FALL
She fell from that move!?
Oh.

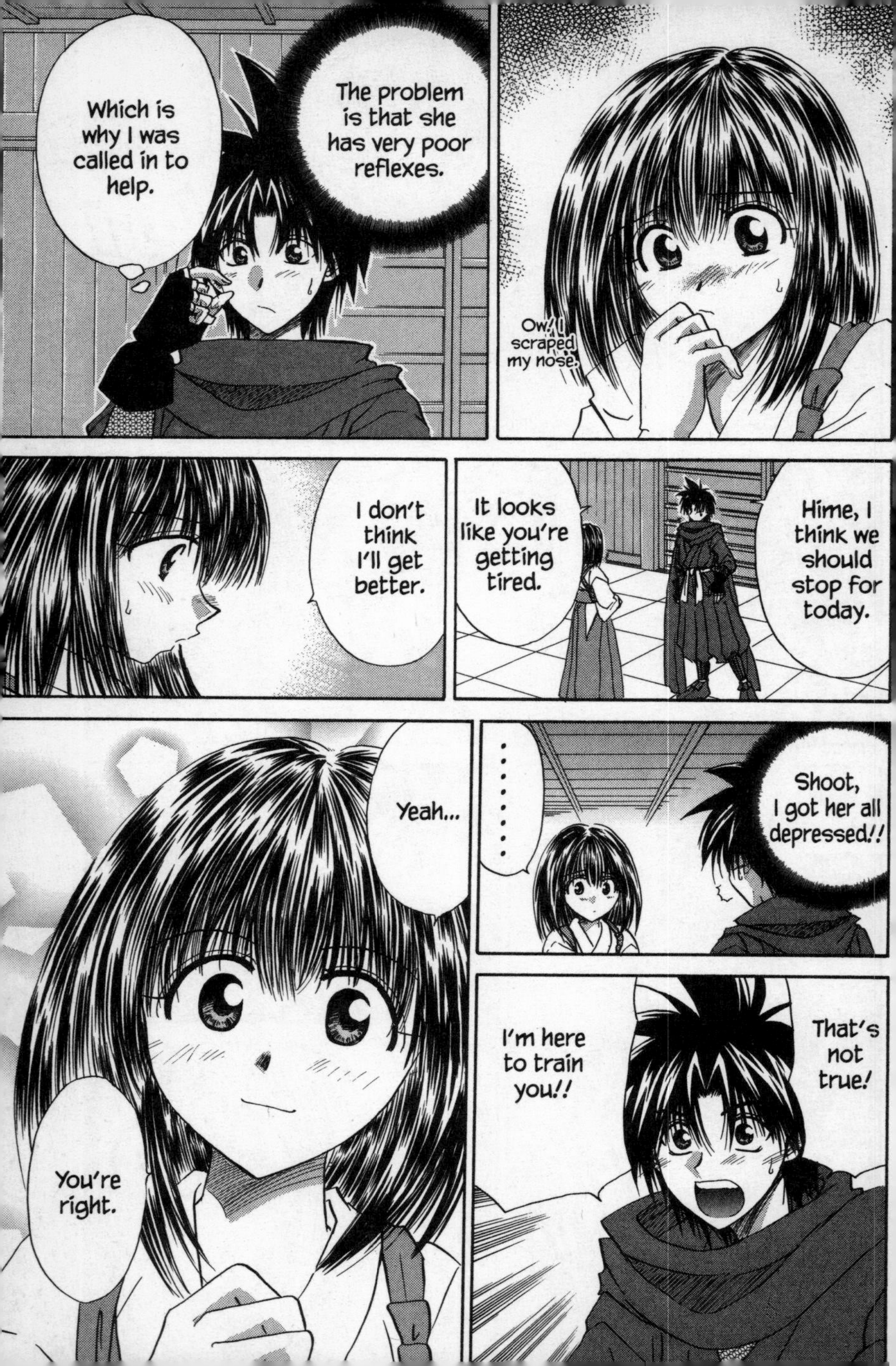
Ow! I scraped my nose.
The problem is that she has very poor reflexes.
Which is why I was called in to help.
Hime, I think we should stop for today.
It looks like you're getting tired.
I don't think I'll get better.
Shoot, I got her all depressed!!
......
That's not true!
I'm here to train you!!
Yeah...
You're right.

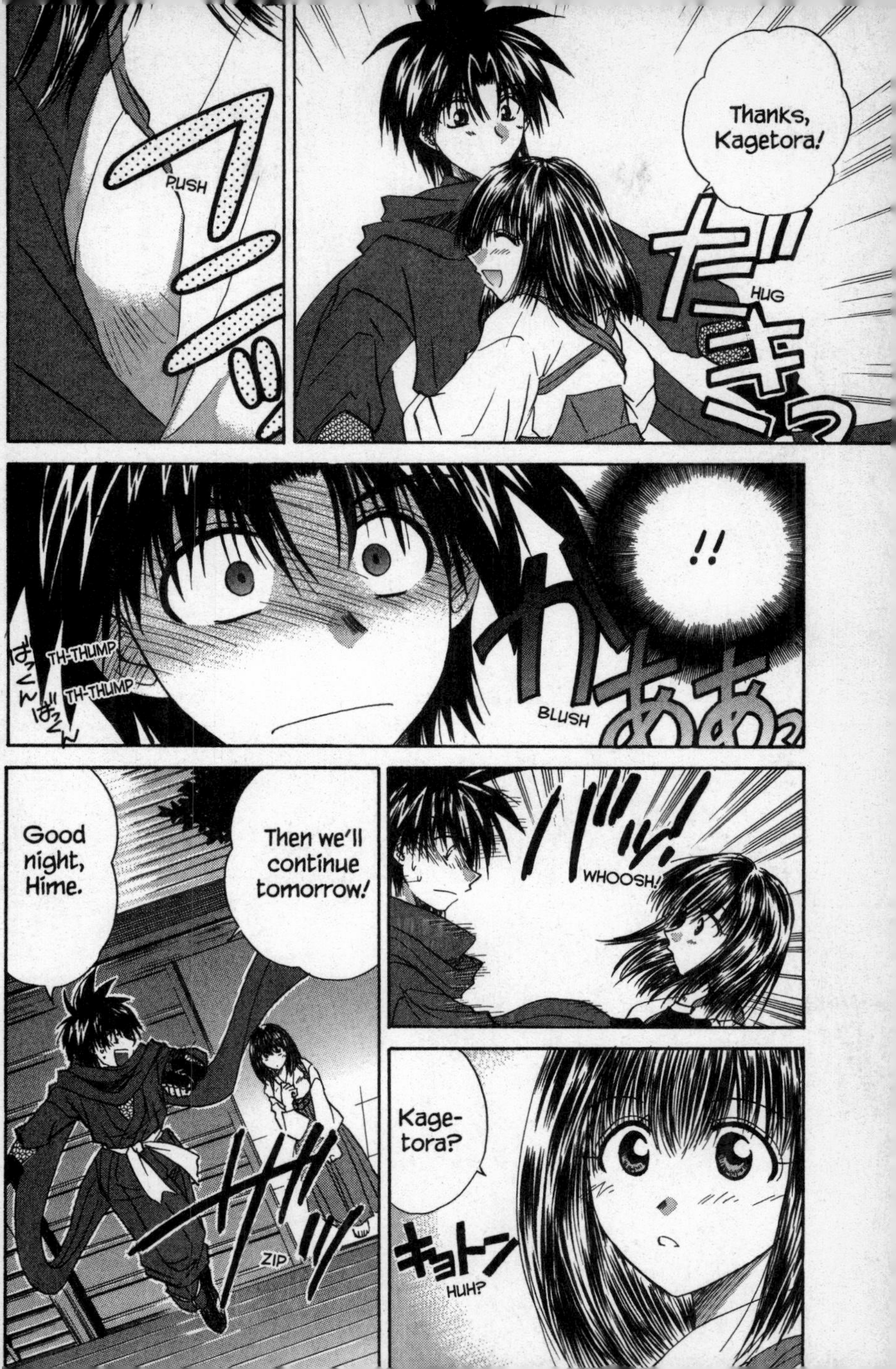
Thanks, Kagetora!
だきっ
HUG
PUSH
!!
かぁぁっ
BLUSH
ばっくん ばっくん
TH-THUMP
TH-THUMP
バッ!
WHOOSH!
Kage-tora?
キョトン
HUH?
Then we'll continue tomorrow!
Good night, Hime.
ZIP

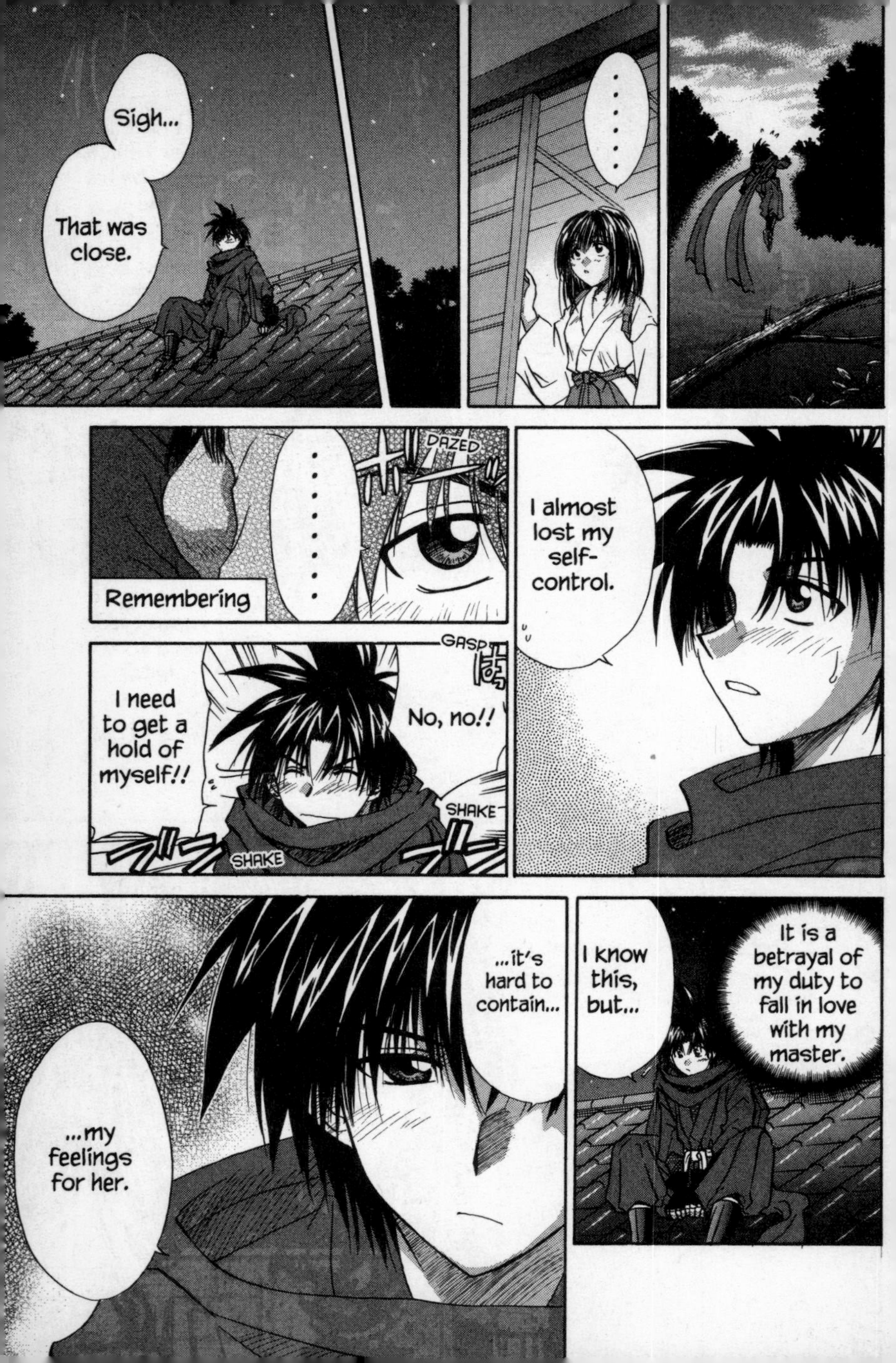
. . . . . .
Sigh...
That was close.
I almost lost my self-control.
DAZED
. . . .
Remembering
GASP
No, no!!
SHAKE
I need to get a hold of myself!!
SHAKE
It is a betrayal of my duty to fall in love with my master.
I know this, but...
...it's hard to contain...
...my feelings for her.

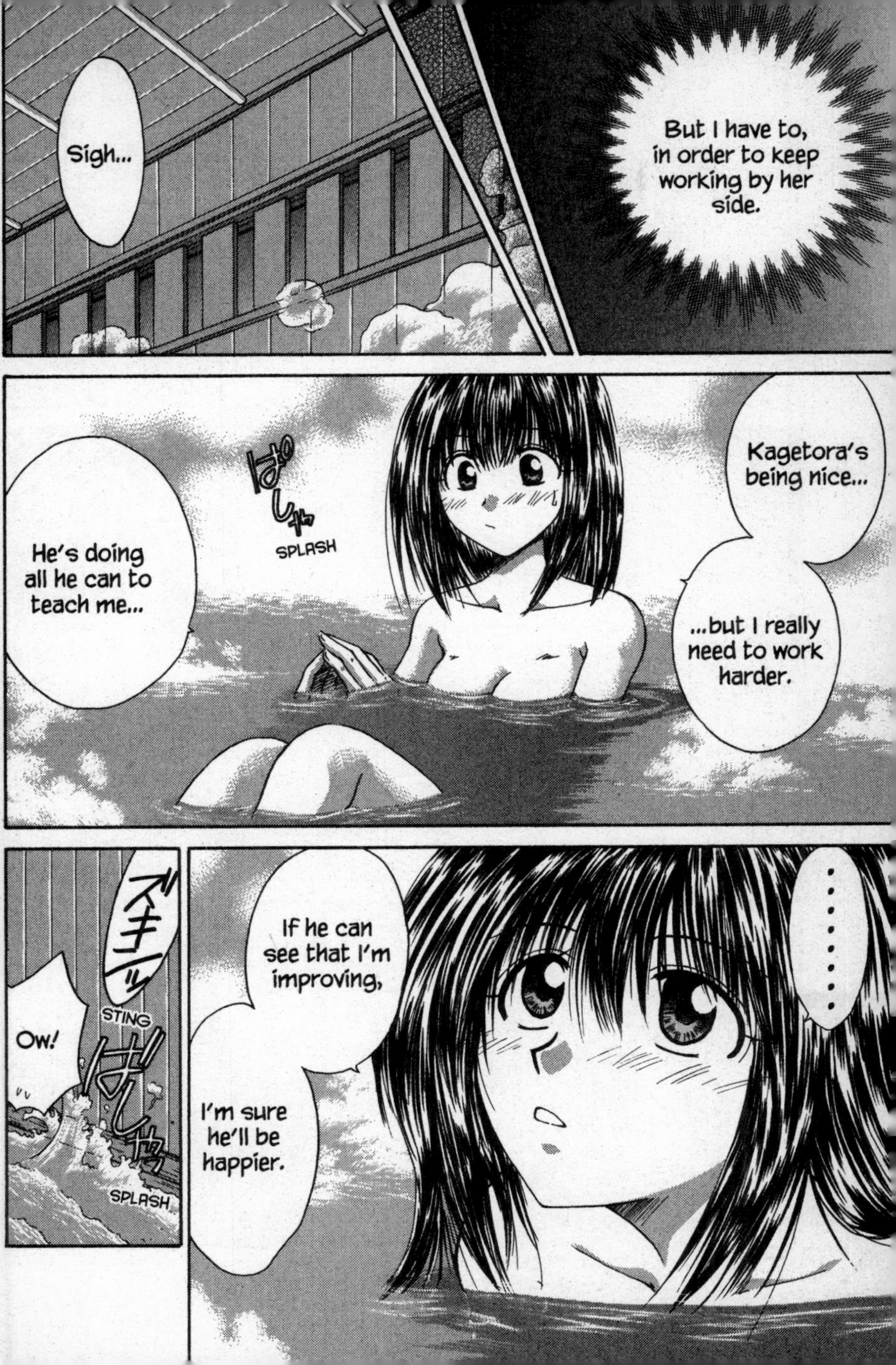
But I have to, in order to keep working by her side.
Sigh...
Kagetora's being nice...
...but I really need to work harder.
ぱしゃ
SPLASH
He's doing all he can to teach me...
......
If he can see that I'm improving,
I'm sure he'll be happier.
ズキッ
STING
Ow!
ぱしゃ
SPLASH

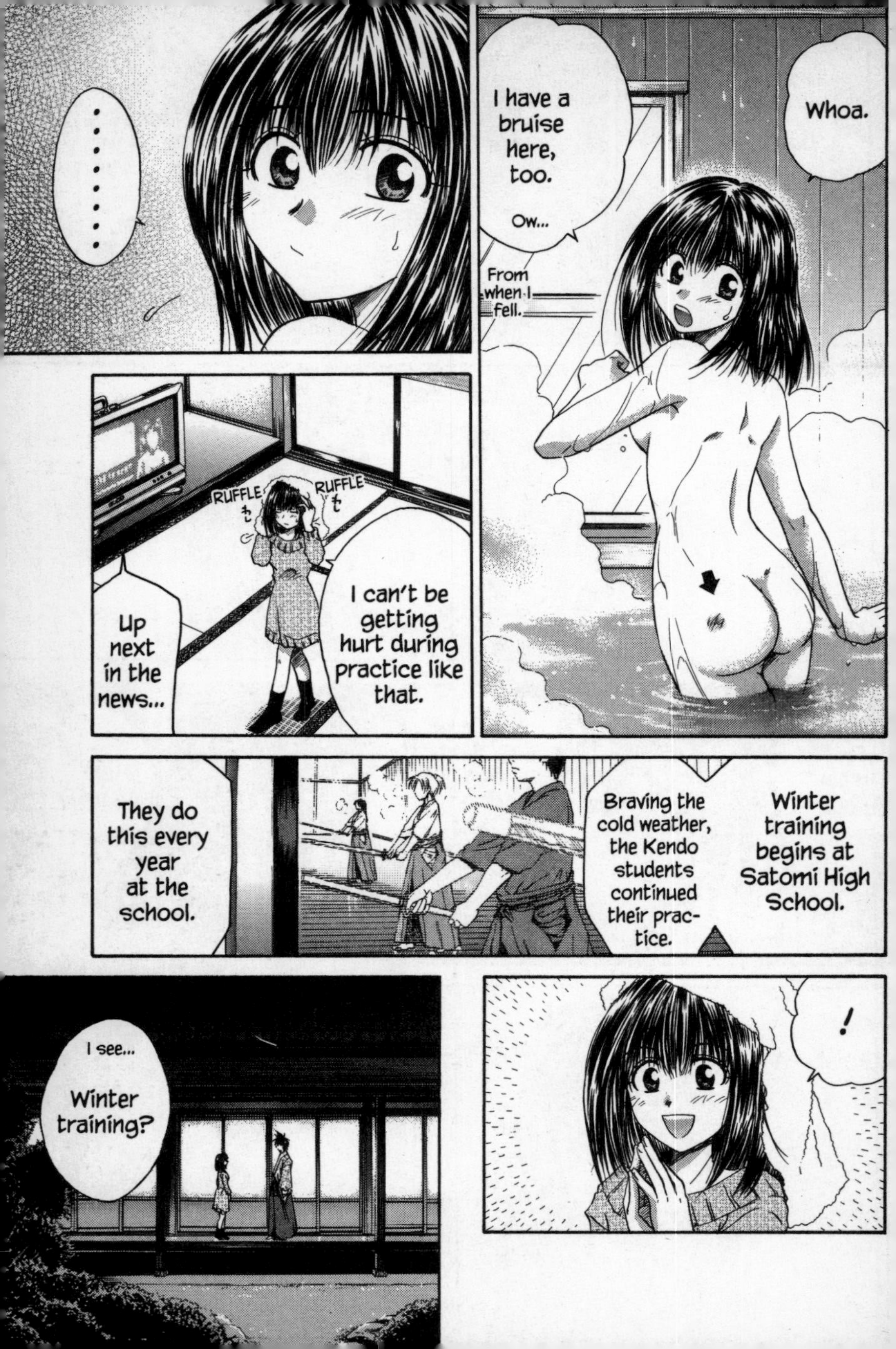
Whoa.
I have a bruise here, too.
Ow...
From when I fell.
......
RUFFLE
RUFFLE
I can't be getting hurt during practice like that.
Up next in the news...
Winter training begins at Satomi High School.
Braving the cold weather, the Kendo students continued their practice.
They do this every year at the school.
!
I see...
Winter training?

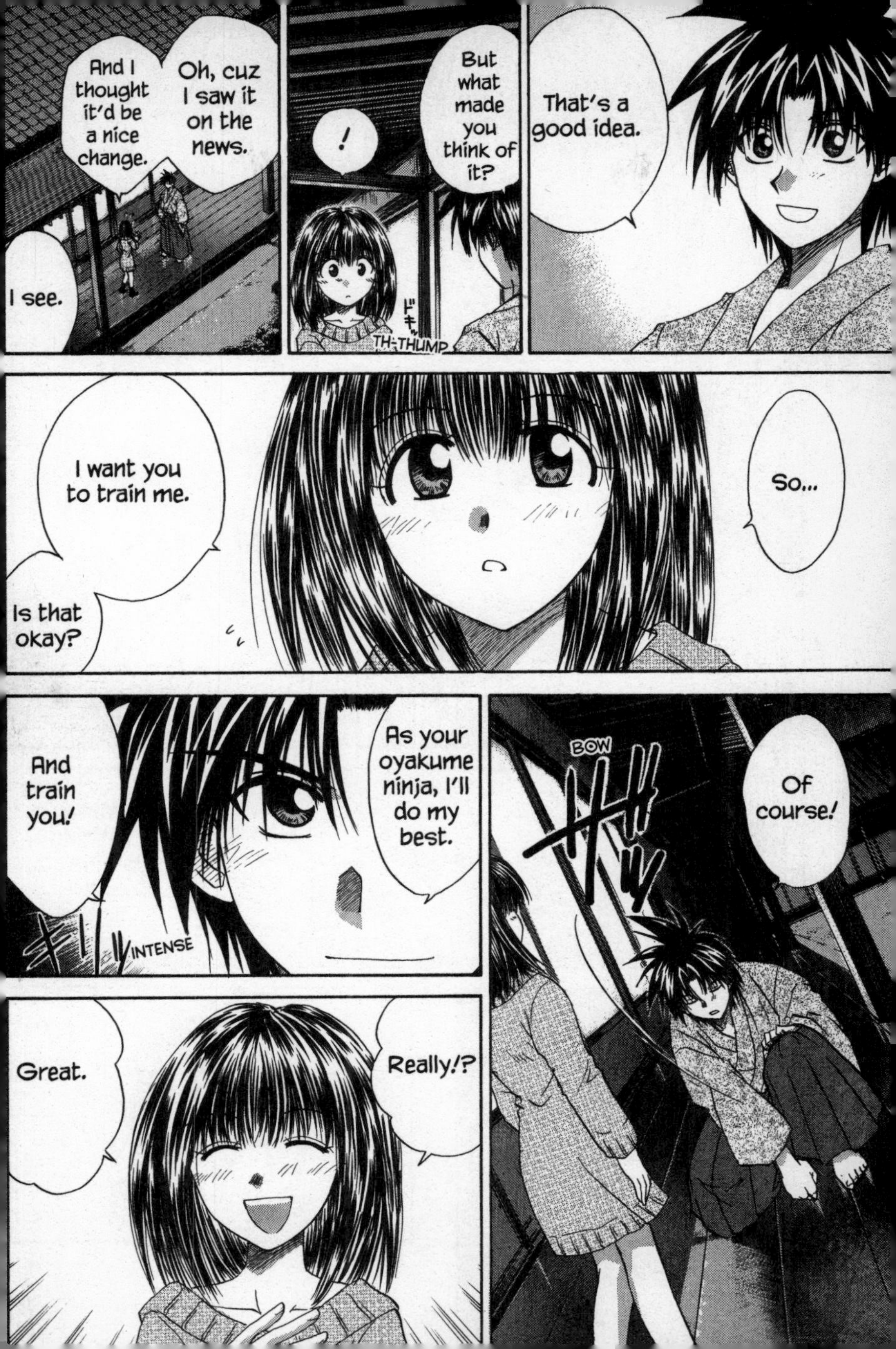
That's a good idea.
But what made you think of it?
!
ドキッ
TH-THUMP
Oh, cuz I saw it on the news.
And I thought it'd be a nice change.
I see.
So...
I want you to train me.
Is that okay?
Of course!
BOW
As your oyakume ninja, I'll do my best.
And train you!
INTENSE
Really!?
Great.

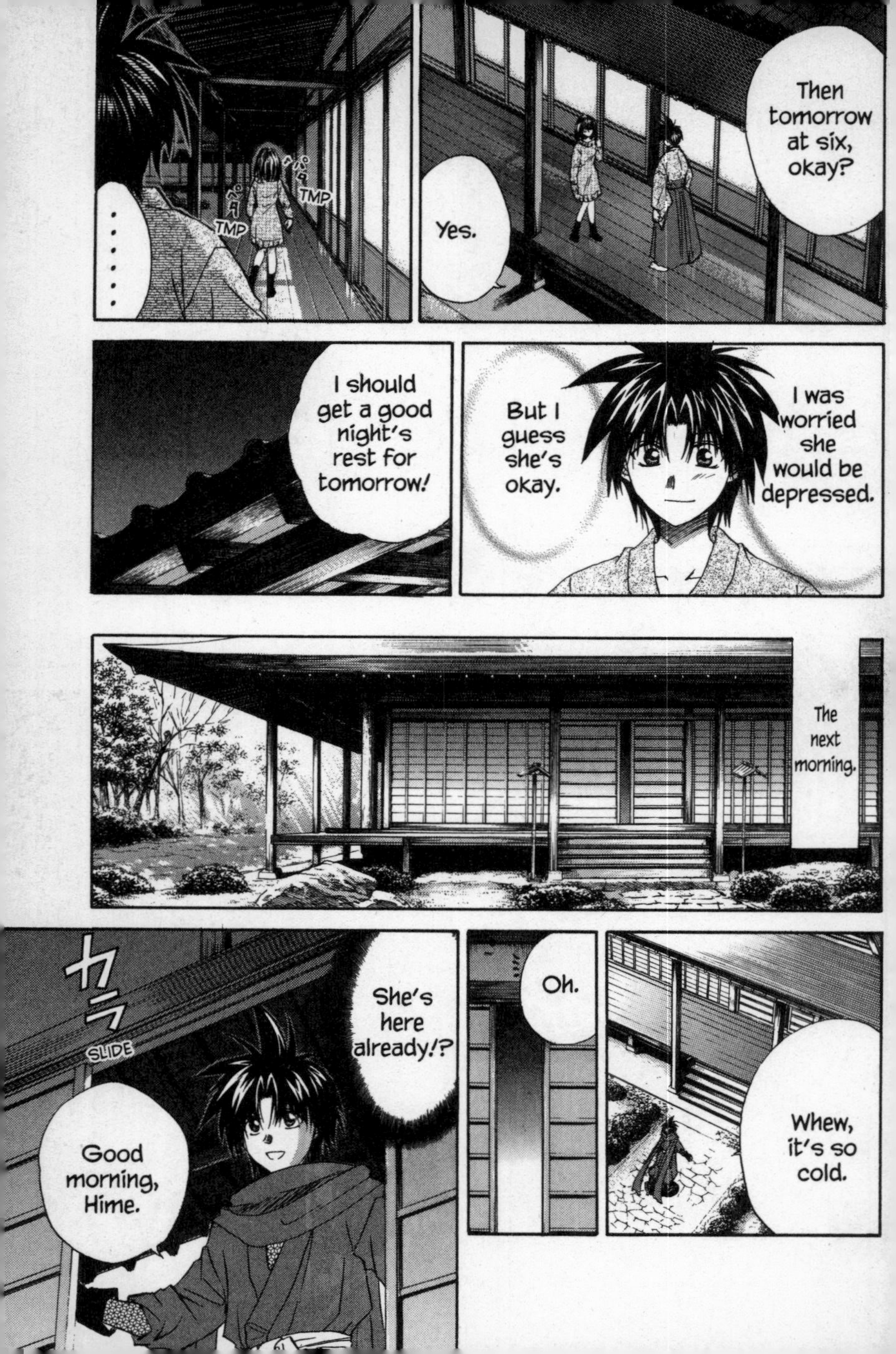
Then tomorrow at six, okay?
Yes.
TMP
TMP
......
I was worried she would be depressed.
But I guess she's okay.
I should get a good night's rest for tomorrow!
The next morning.
Whew, it's so cold.
Oh.
She's here already!?
カラ
SLIDE
Good morning, Hime.

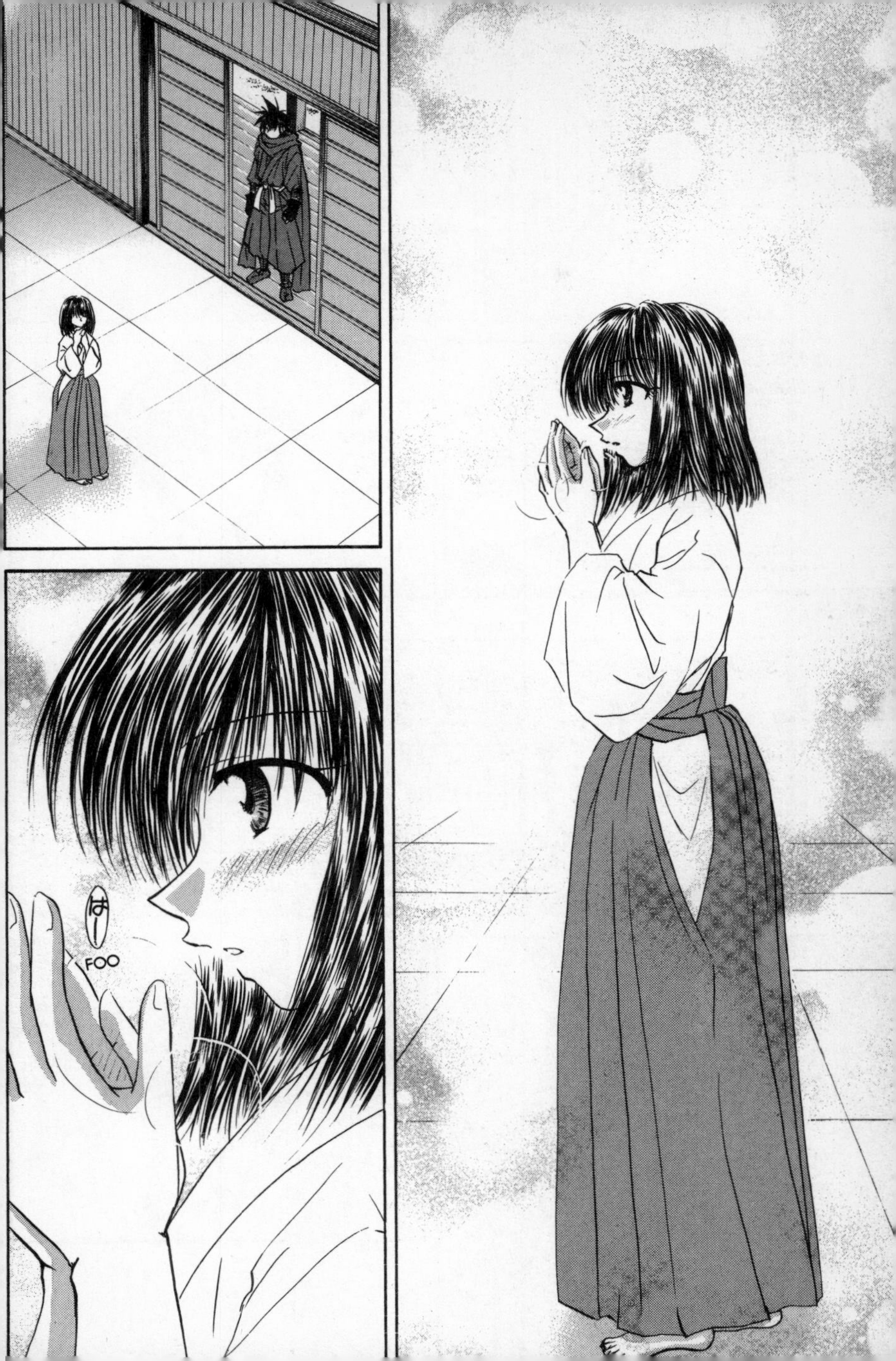
はー
FOO

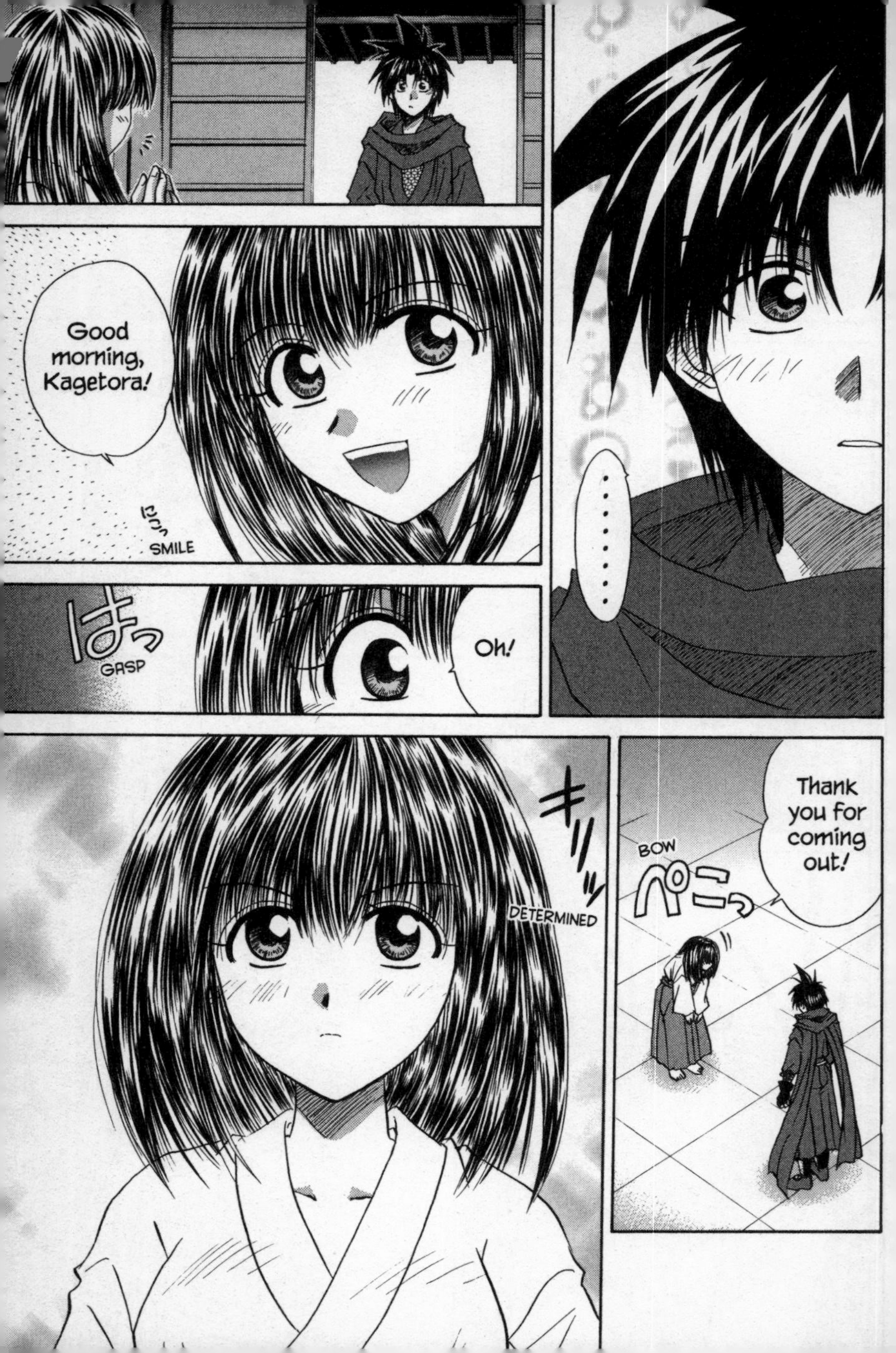
......
Good morning, Kagetora!
にこっ
SMILE
はっ
GASP
Oh!
ぺこっ
BOW
Thank you for coming out!
キリッ
DETERMINED

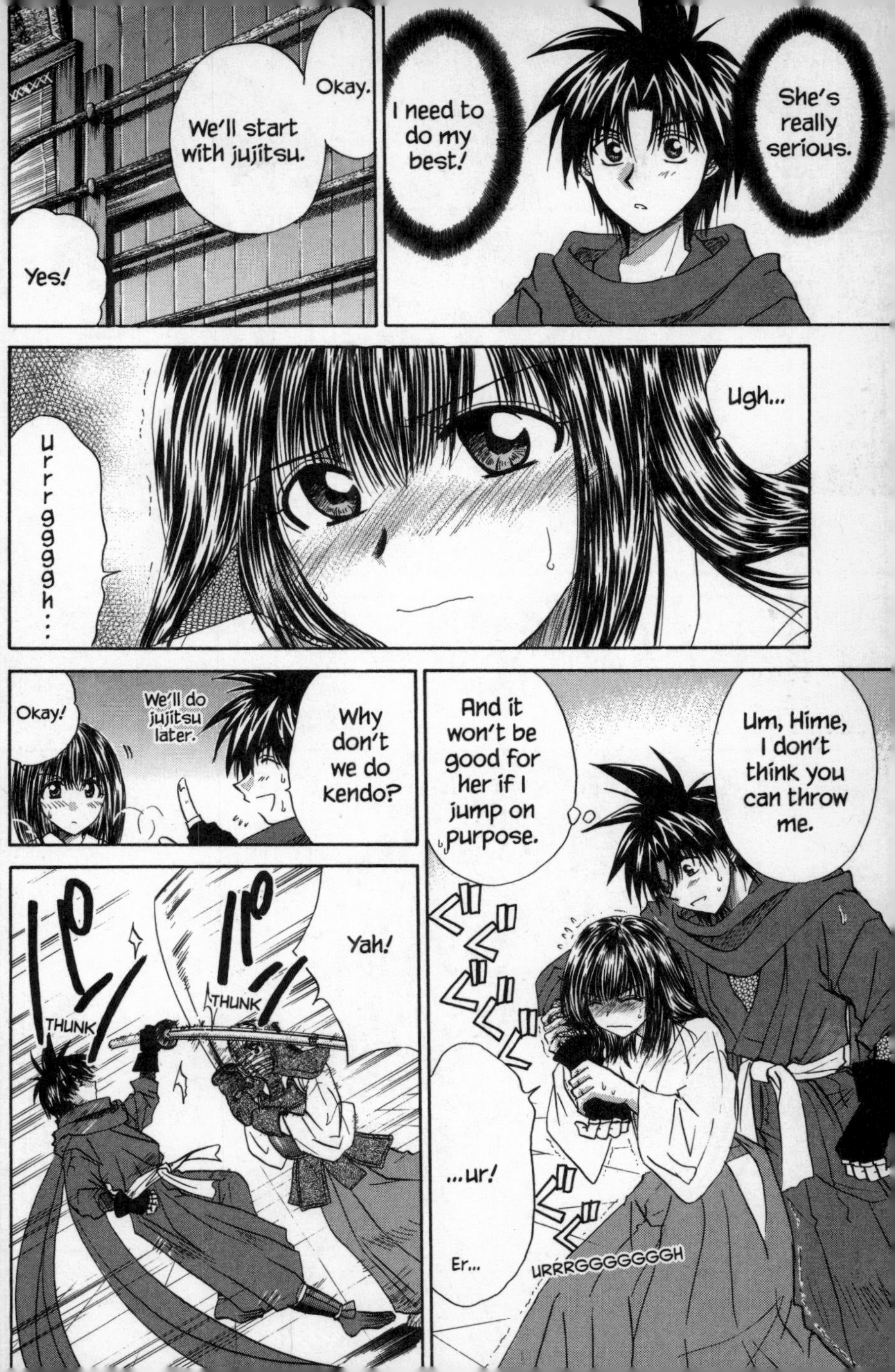
She's really serious.
I need to do my best!
Okay.
We'll start with jujitsu.
Yes!
Ugh...
Urrrggggh...
Um, Hime, I don't think you can throw me.
And it won't be good for her if I jump on purpose.
...ur!
Er...
URRRGGGGGGGH
Why don't we do kendo?
We'll do jujitsu later.
Okay!
Yah!
THUNK
THUNK

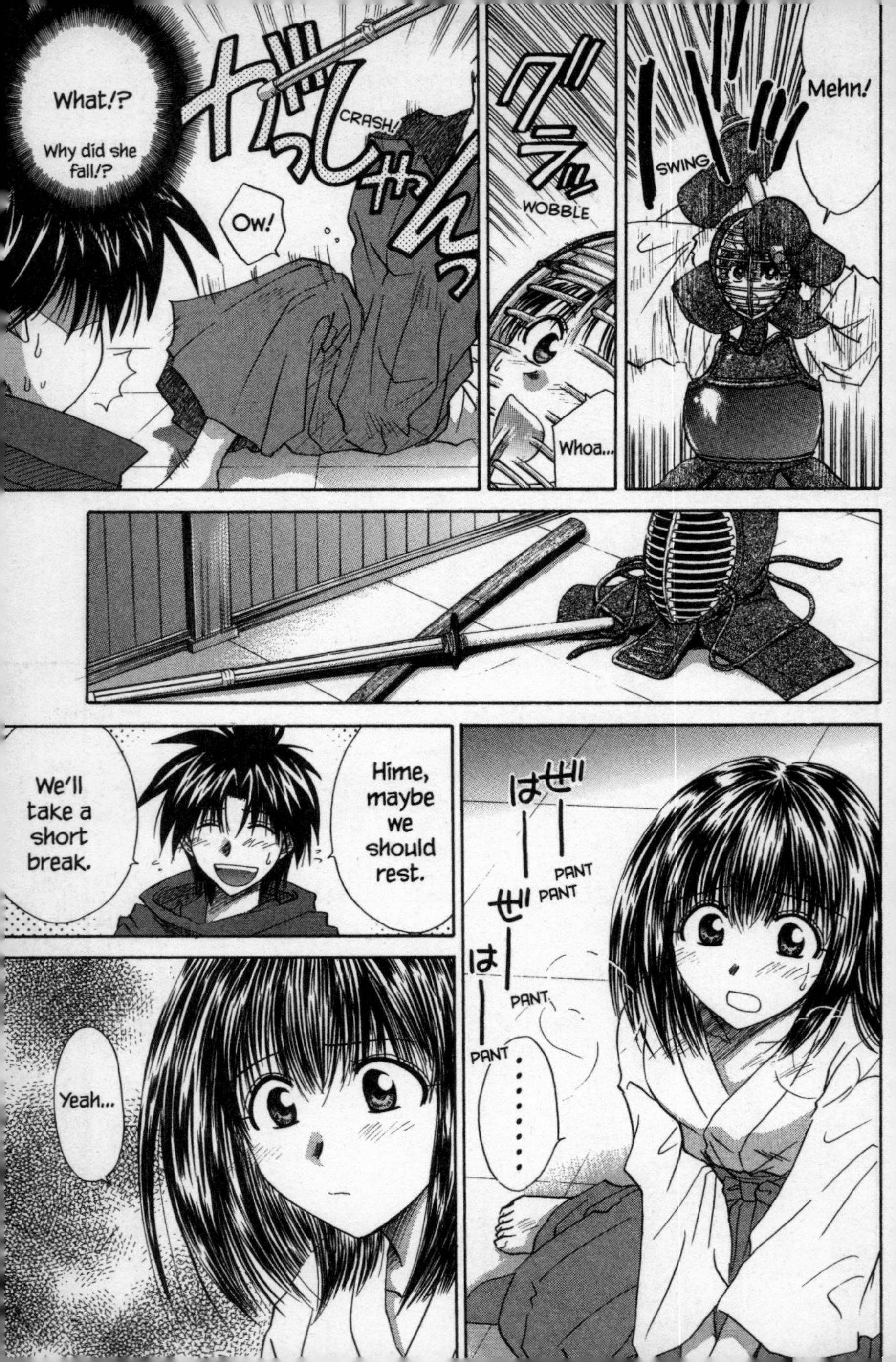
Mehn!
SWING
WOBBLE
Whoa...
CRASH!
Ow!
What!?
Why did she fall!?
PANT
PANT
PANT
PANT
......
Hime, maybe we should rest.
We'll take a short break.
Yeah...

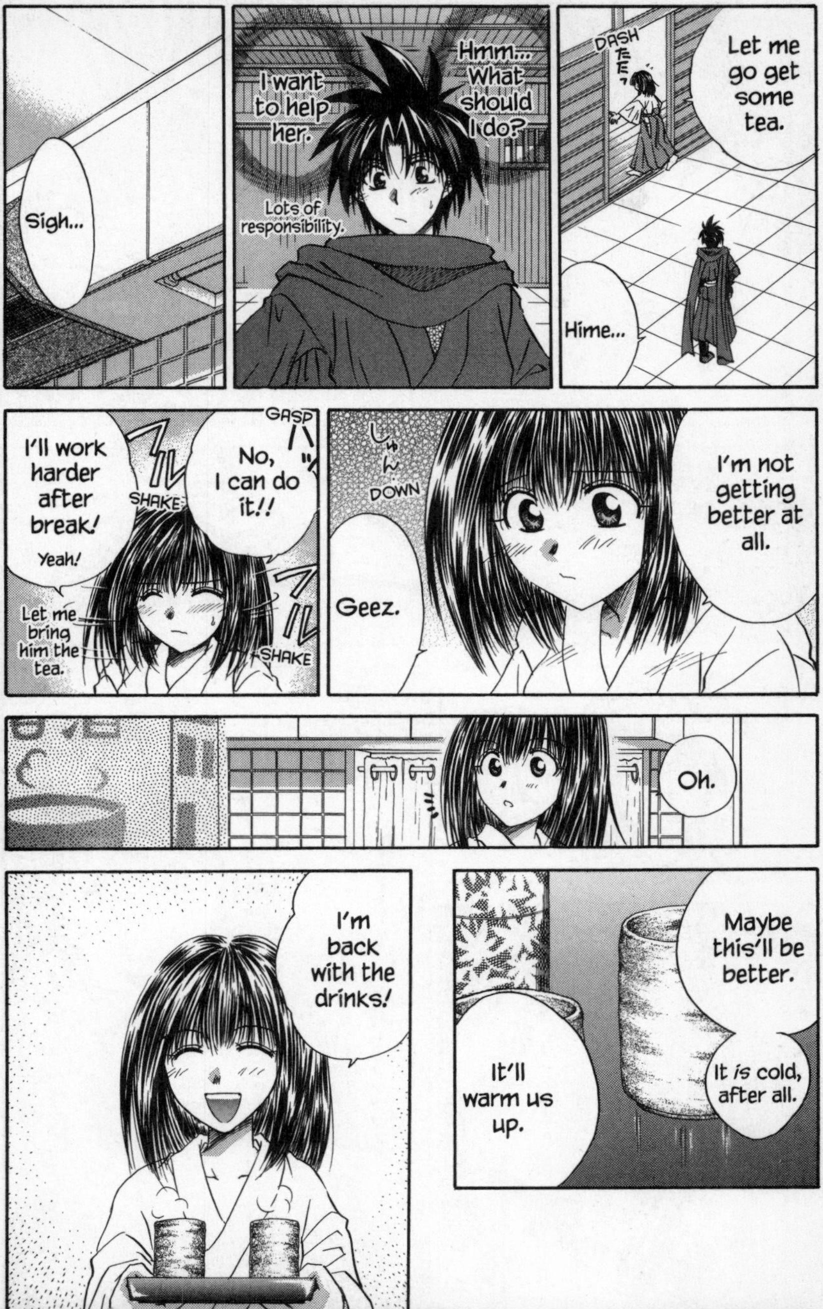
DASH
Let me go get some tea.
Hime...
Hmm... What should I do?
I want to help her.
Lots of responsibility.
Sigh...
I'm not getting better at all.
しゅん
DOWN
Geez.
GASP
ハッ
No, I can do it!!
SHAKE
I'll work harder after break!
Yeah!
Let me bring him the tea.
SHAKE
Oh.
Maybe this'll be better.
It *is* cold, after all.
It'll warm us up.
I'm back with the drinks!

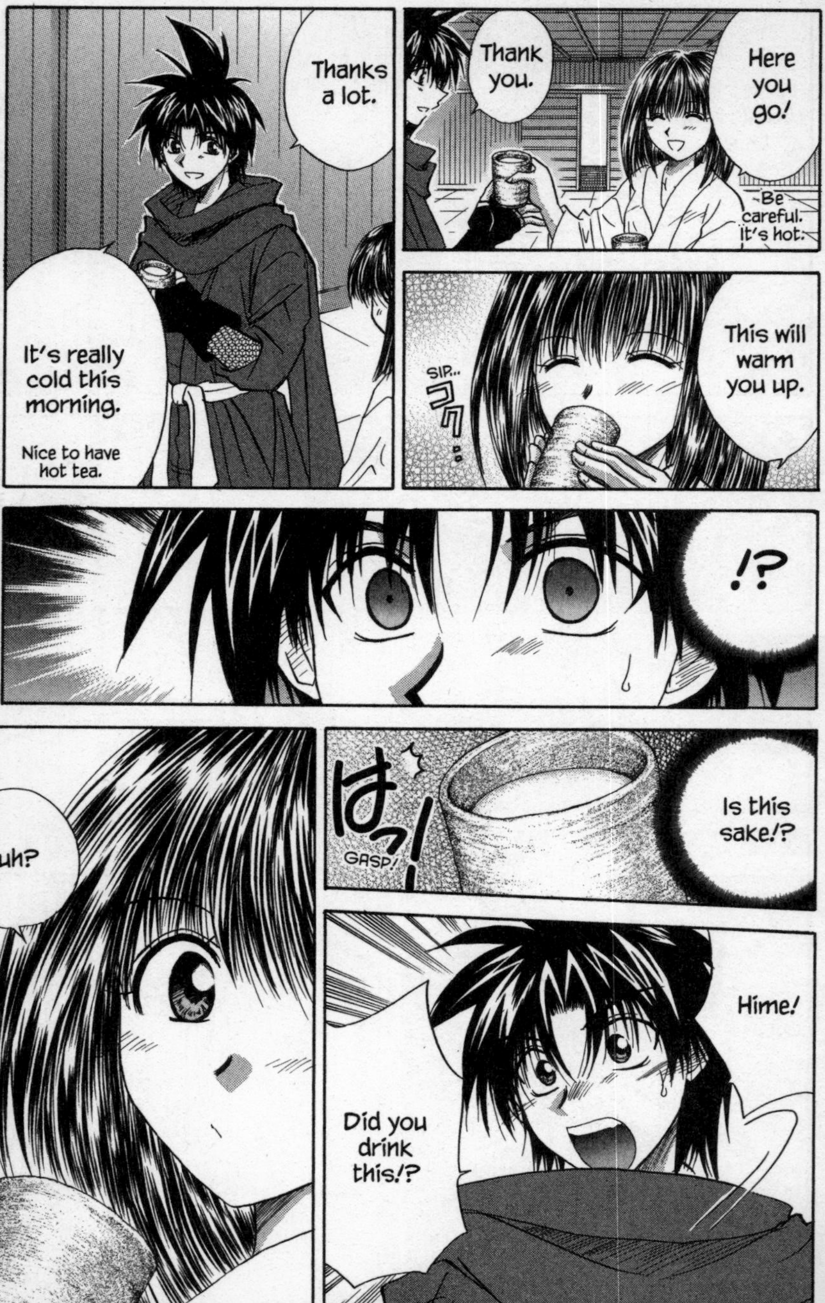
Here you go!
Be careful. It's hot.
Thank you.
This will warm you up.
SIP... コク
Thanks a lot.
It's really cold this morning.
Nice to have hot tea.
!?
Is this sake!?
はっ GASP!
Hime!
Did you drink this!?
Huh?

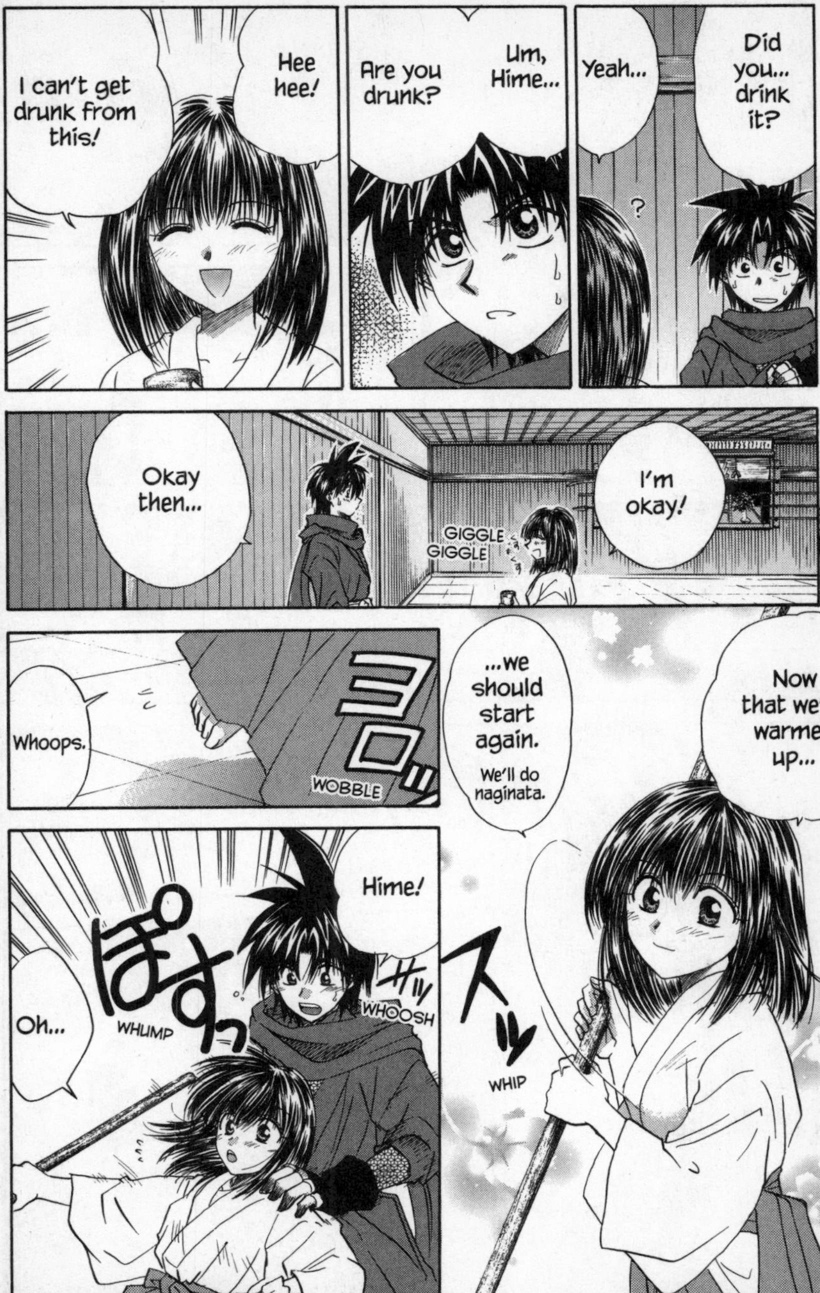
Did you... drink it?
?
Yeah...
Um, Hime...
Are you drunk?
Hee hee!
I can't get drunk from this!
I'm okay!
GIGGLE GIGGLE
Okay then...
Now that we're warmed up...
...we should start again.
We'll do naginata.
WOBBLE
Whoops.
Hime!
WHOOSH
WHIP
WHUMP
Oh...

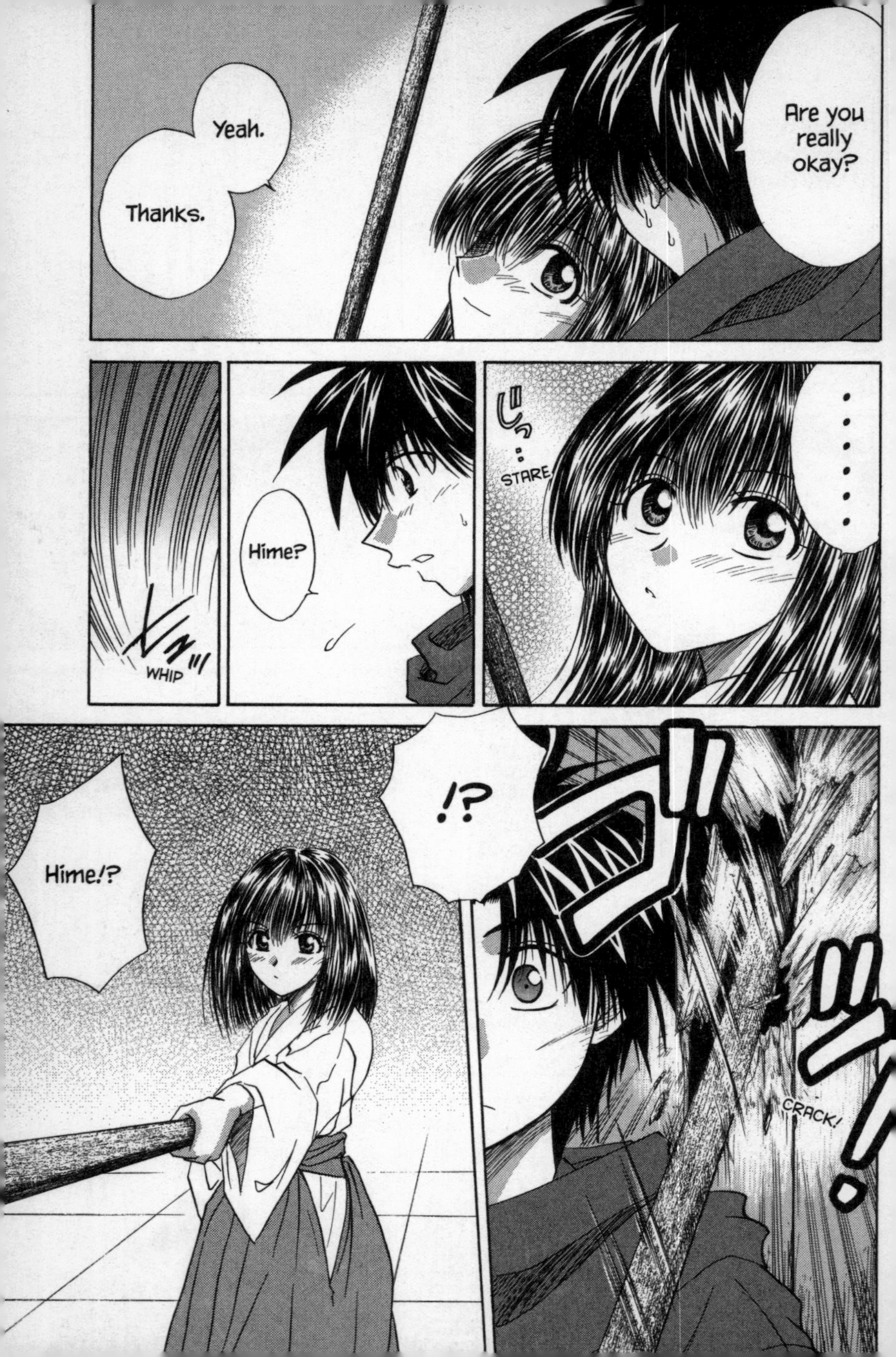
Are you really okay?
Yeah.
Thanks.
じっ
STARE
......
Hime?
WHIP
!?
CRACK!
Hime!?

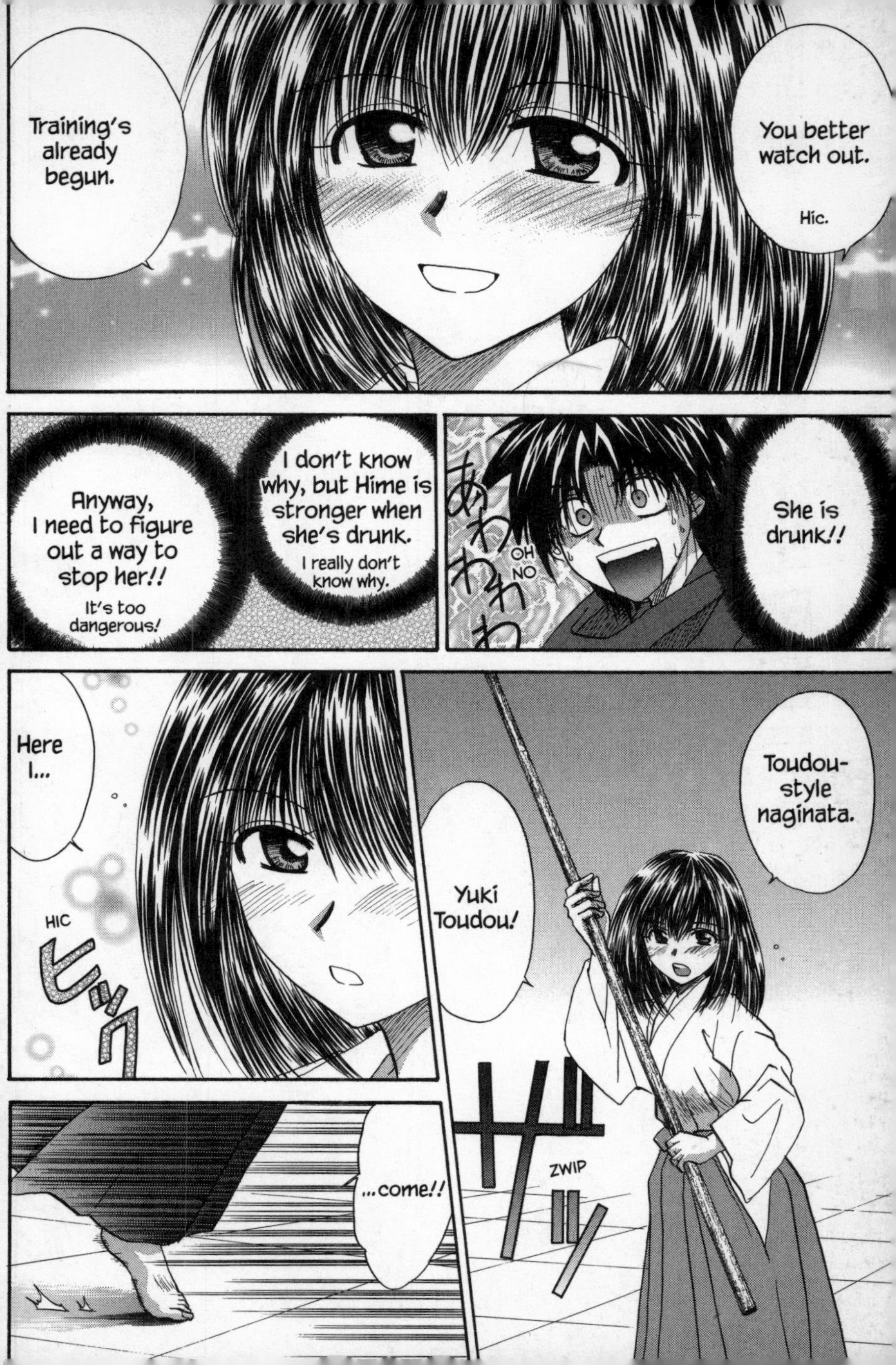
You better watch out.
Hic.
Training's already begun.
She is drunk!!
あわわわ
OH NO
I don't know why, but Hime is stronger when she's drunk.
I really don't know why.
Anyway, I need to figure out a way to stop her!!
It's too dangerous!
Toudou-style naginata.
Yuki Toudou!
ZWIP
Here I...
HIC
ヒック
...come!!

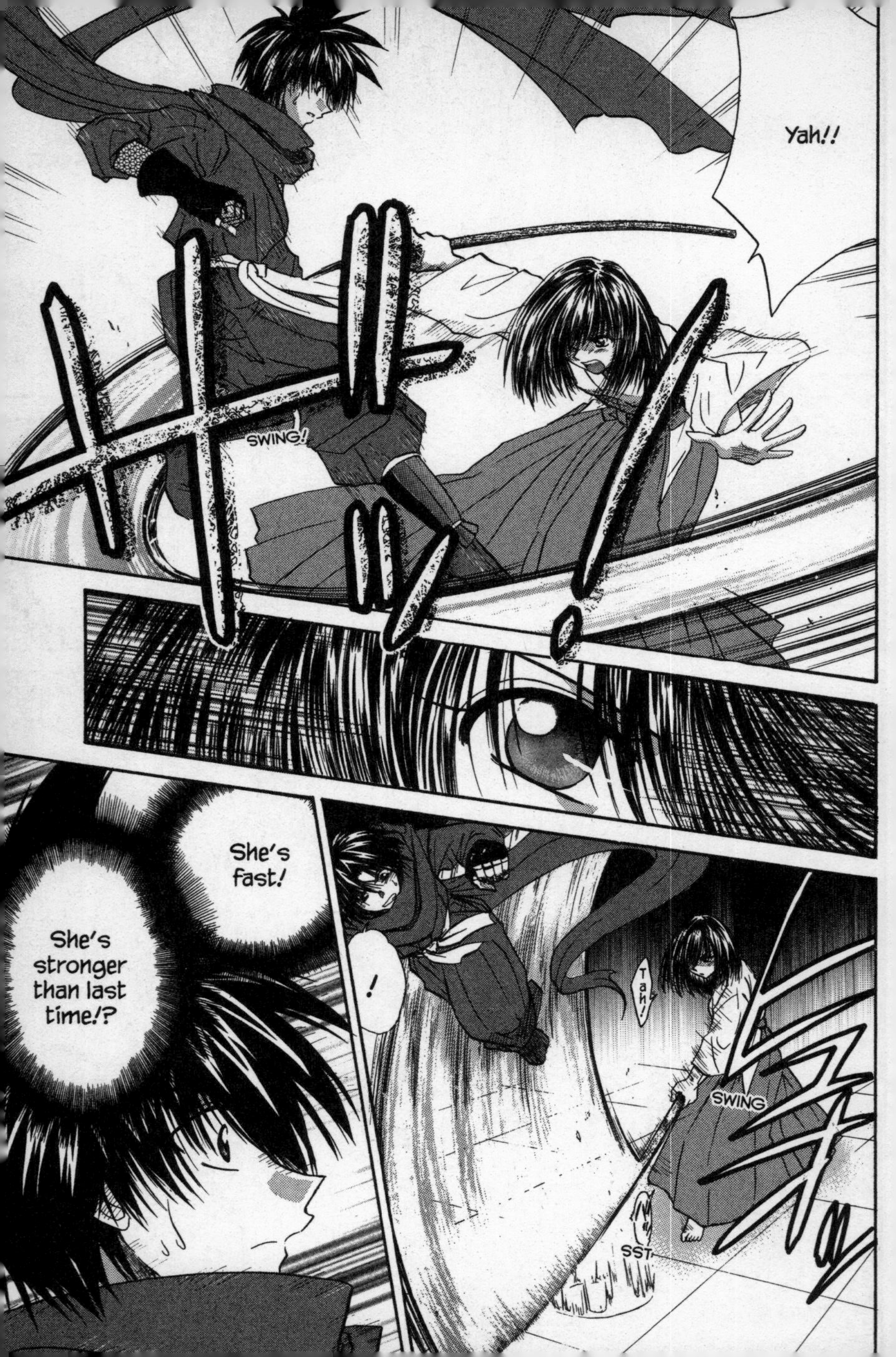
Yah!!
SWING!
Tah!
SWING
SST
!
She's fast!
She's stronger than last time!?

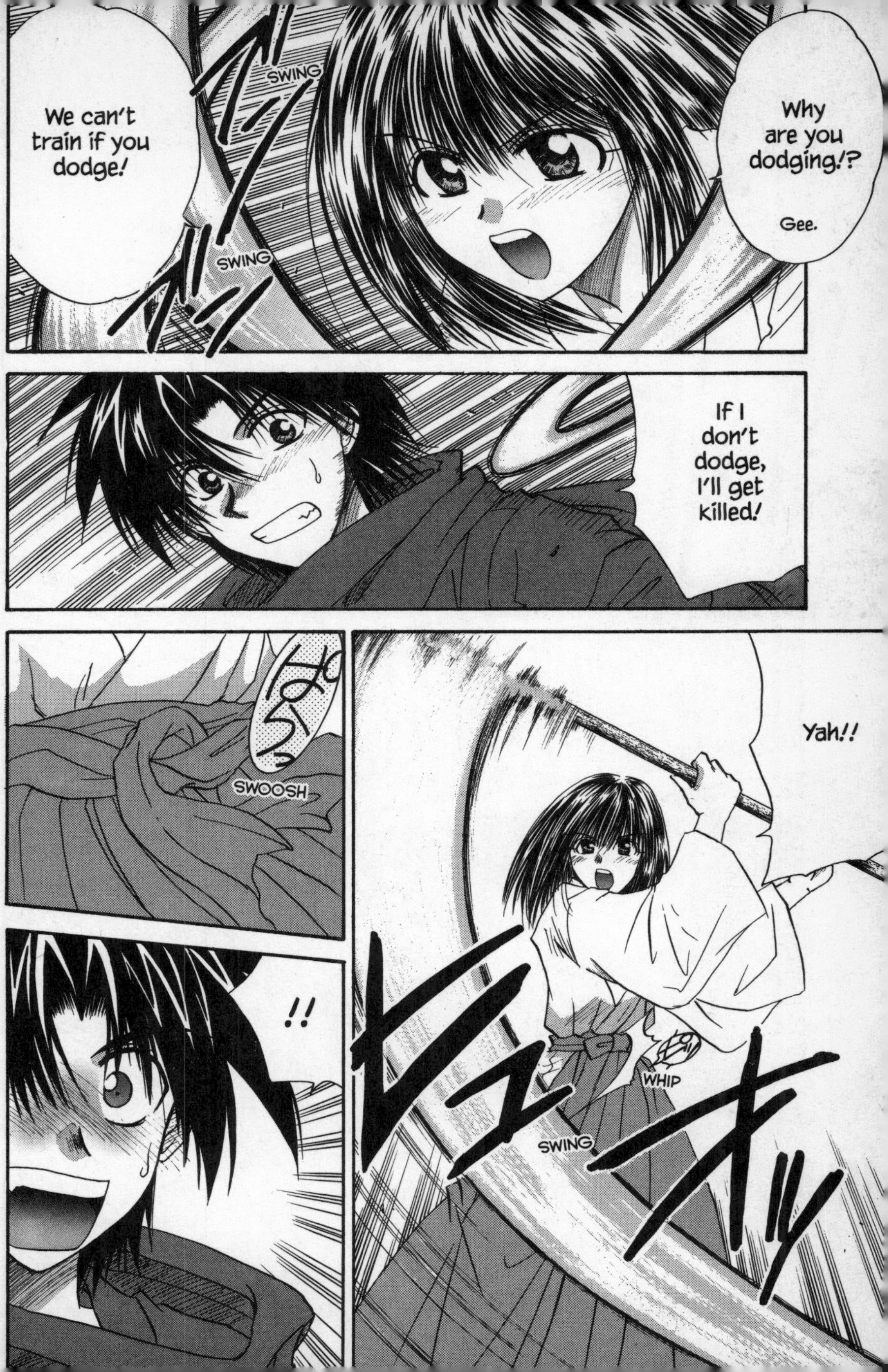
Why are you dodging!?
Gee.
SWING
We can't train if you dodge!
SWING
If I don't dodge, I'll get killed!
Yah!!
WHIP
SWING
SWOOSH
!!

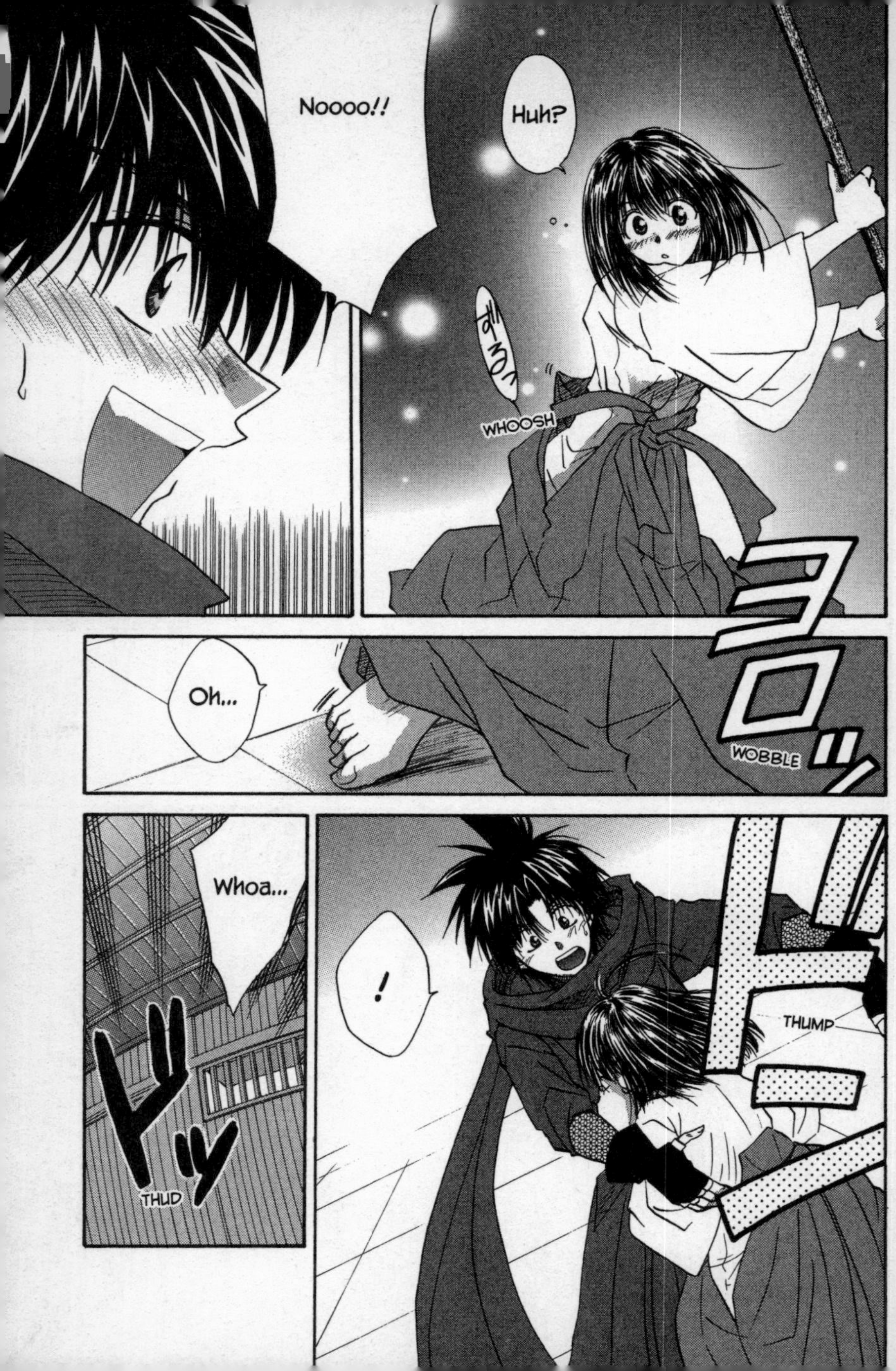
Huh?
ずるっ
WHOOSH
Noooo!!
ヨロッ
WOBBLE
Oh...
!
THUMP
Whoa...
ドッ
THUD

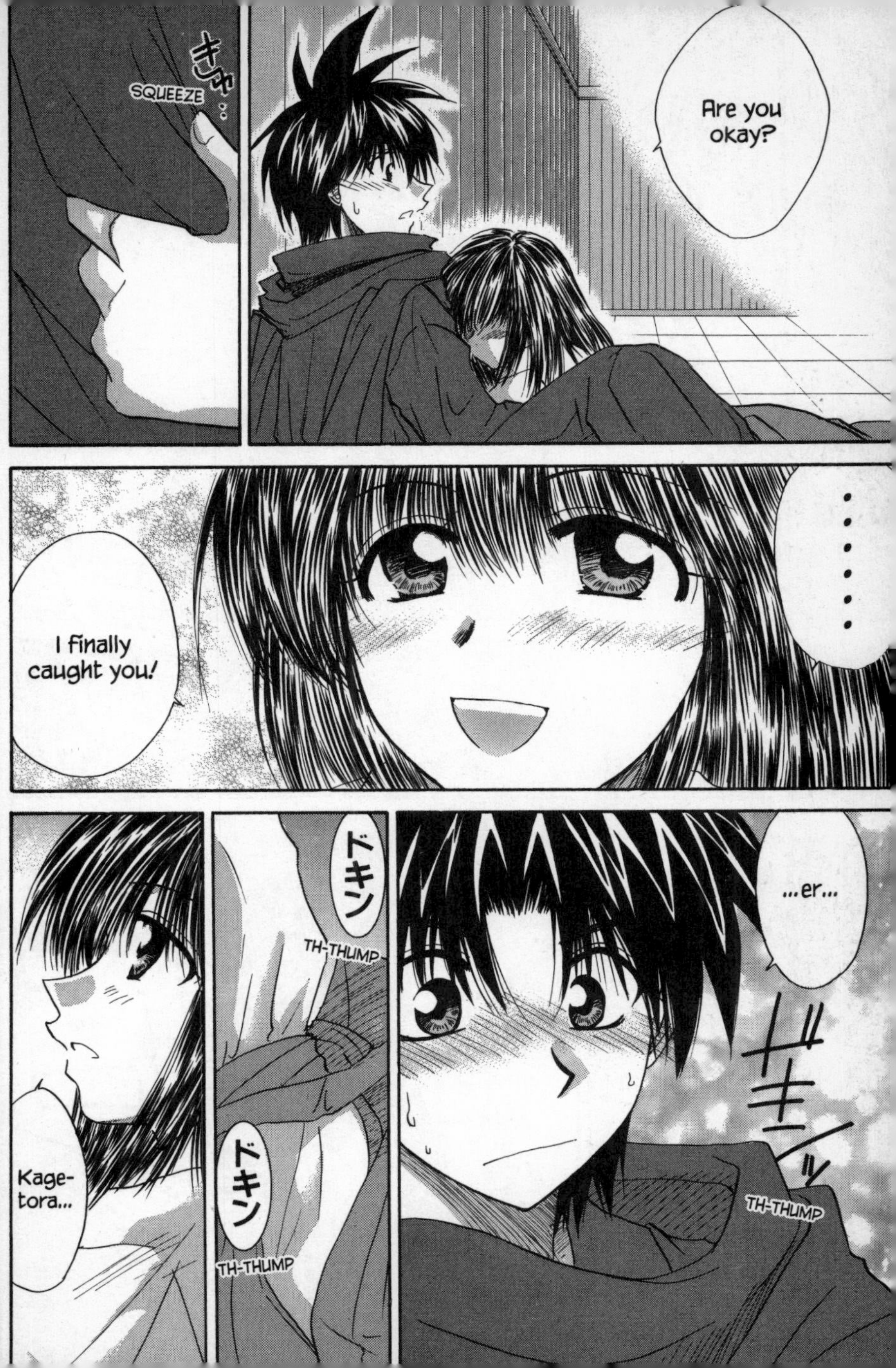
Are you okay?
きゅ…
SQUEEZE
......
I finally caught you!
...er...
TH-THUMP
ドキン
TH-THUMP
ドキン
TH-THUMP
Kage-tora...

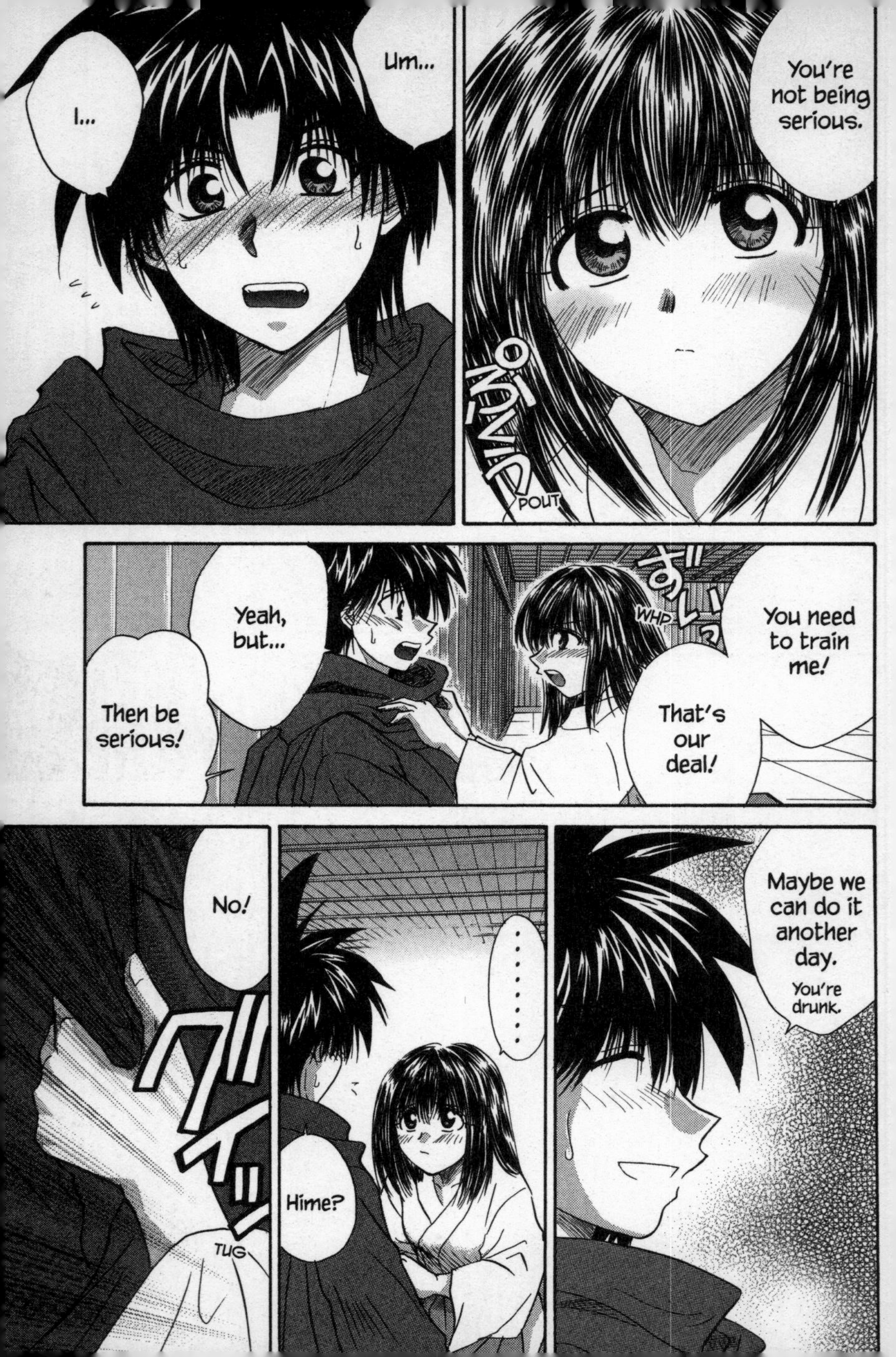
You're not being serious.
POUT
Um...
I...
You need to train me!
WHP
That's our deal!
Yeah, but...
Then be serious!
Maybe we can do it another day.
You're drunk.
......
Hime?
No!
TUG

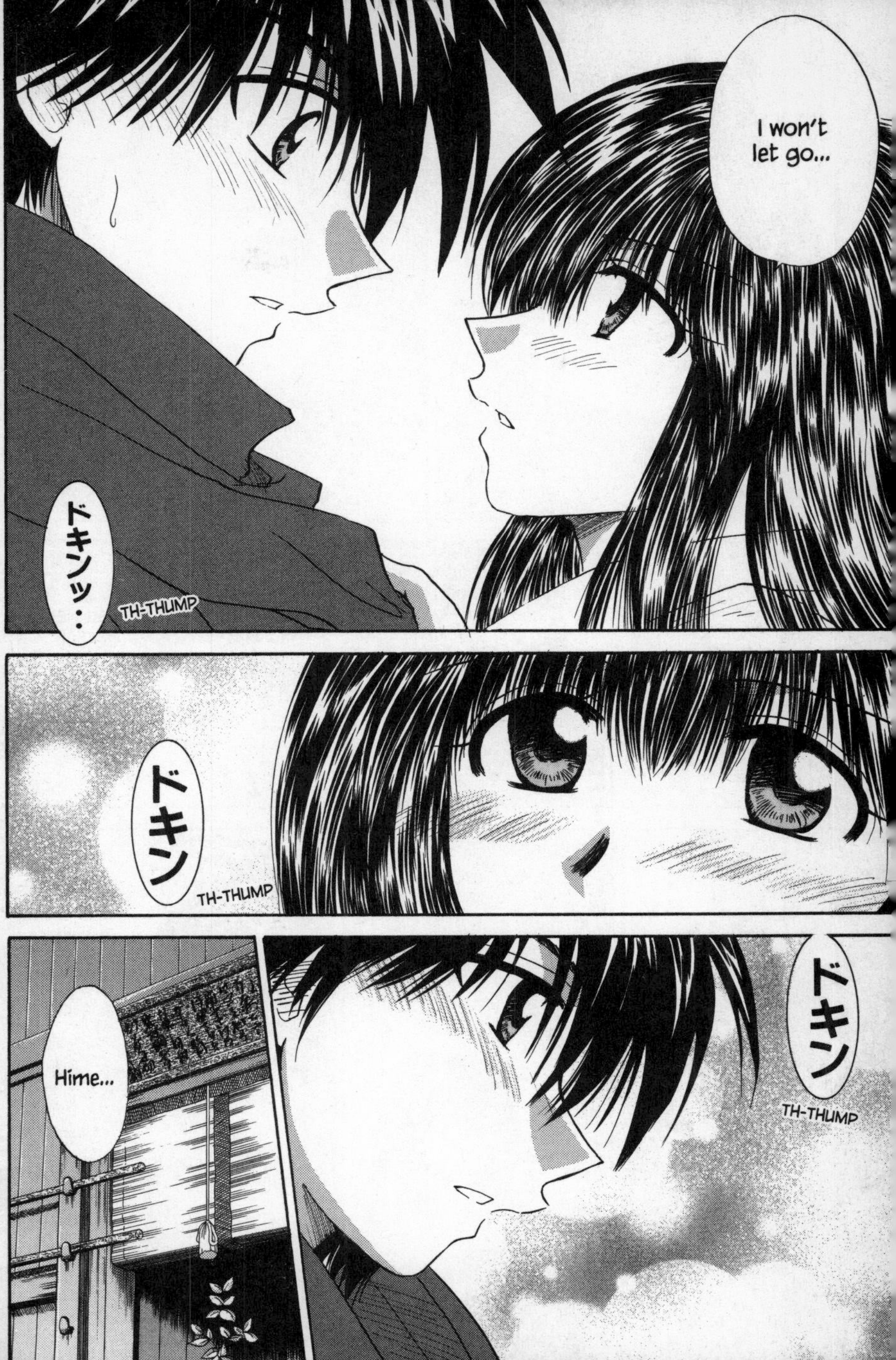
I won't let go...
ドキンッ・・
TH-THUMP
ドキン
TH-THUMP
ドキン
TH-THUMP
Hime...

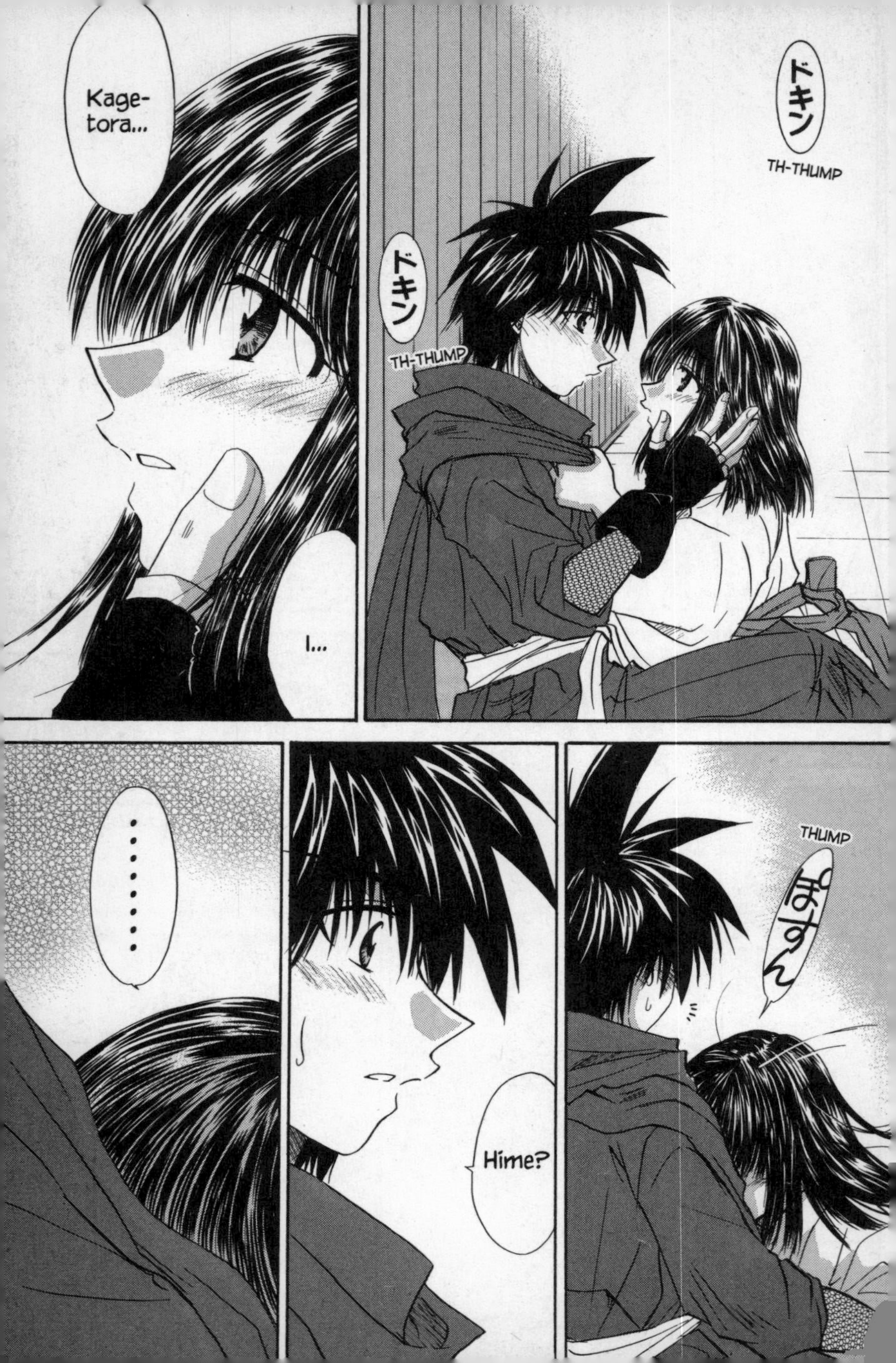
ドキン
TH-THUMP
ドキン
TH-THUMP
Kage-tora...
I...
THUMP
ぽすん
Hime?
......

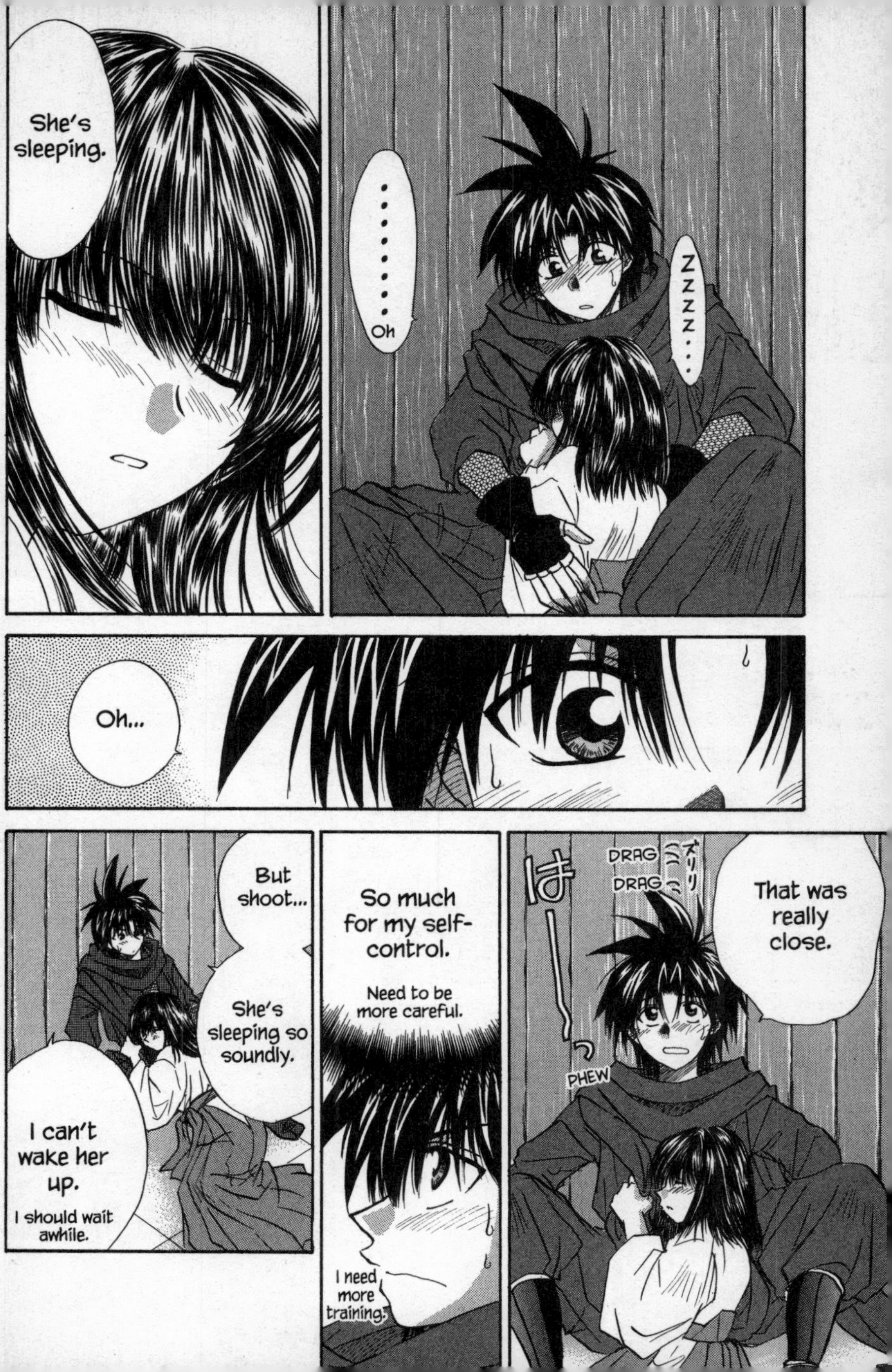
ZZZZ...
......Oh
She's sleeping.
Oh...
That was really close.
DRAG
DRAG
PHEW
So much for my self-control.
Need to be more careful.
I need more training.
But shoot...
She's sleeping so soundly.
I can't wake her up.
I should wait awhile.

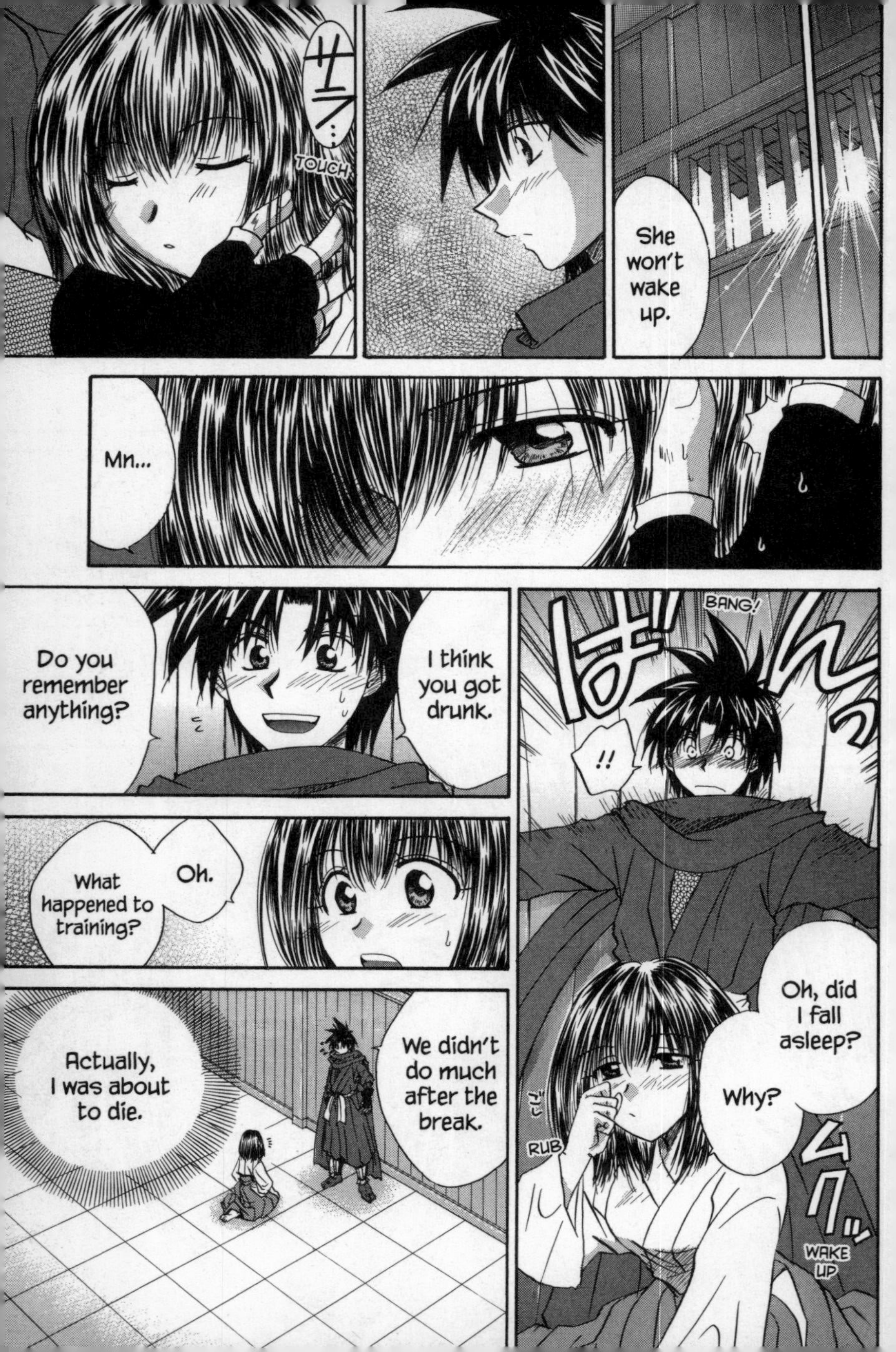
She won't wake up.
サラ…
TOUCH
Mn...
ばんっ
BANG!
!!
Oh, did I fall asleep?
Why?
ムクッ
WAKE UP
ごし
RUB
I think you got drunk.
Do you remember anything?
Oh.
What happened to training?
We didn't do much after the break.
Actually, I was about to die.

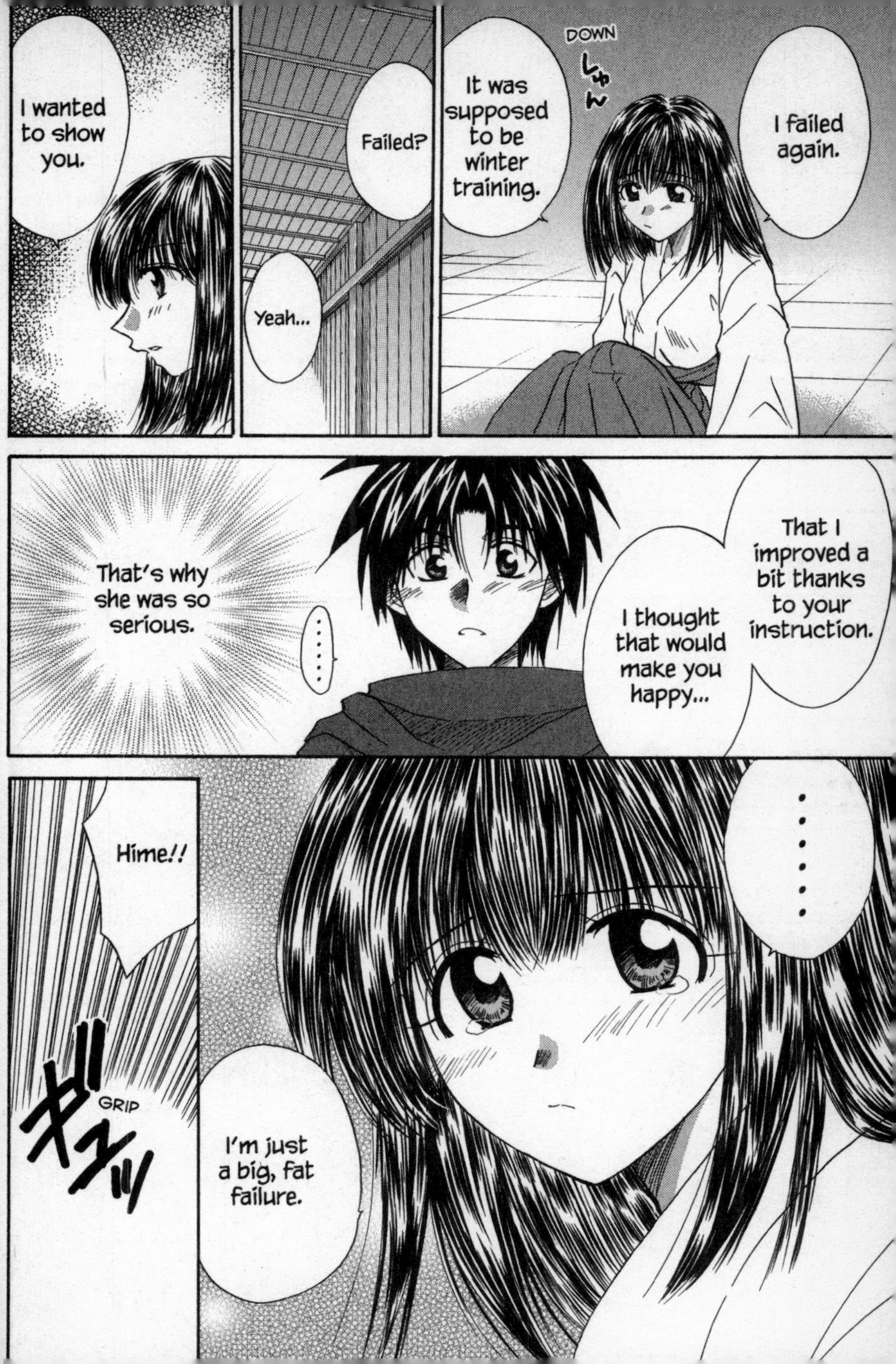
I failed again.
DOWN
しゅん
It was supposed to be winter training.
Failed?
Yeah...
I wanted to show you.
That I improved a bit thanks to your instruction.
I thought that would make you happy...
......
That's why she was so serious.
......
I'm just a big, fat failure.
Hime!!
GRIP
ギュッ

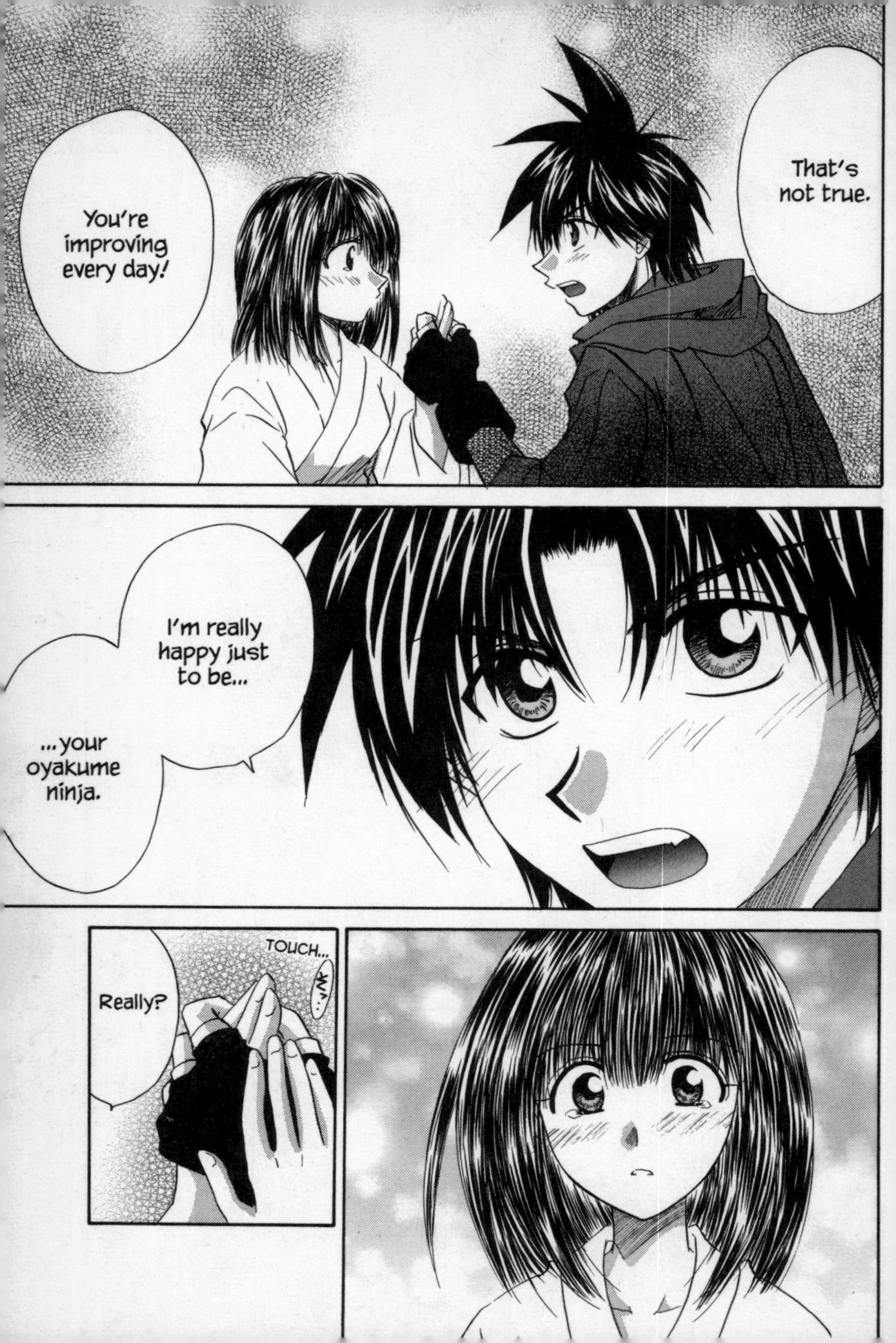
That's not true.
You're improving every day!
I'm really happy just to be...
...your oyakume ninja.
TOUCH...
Really?

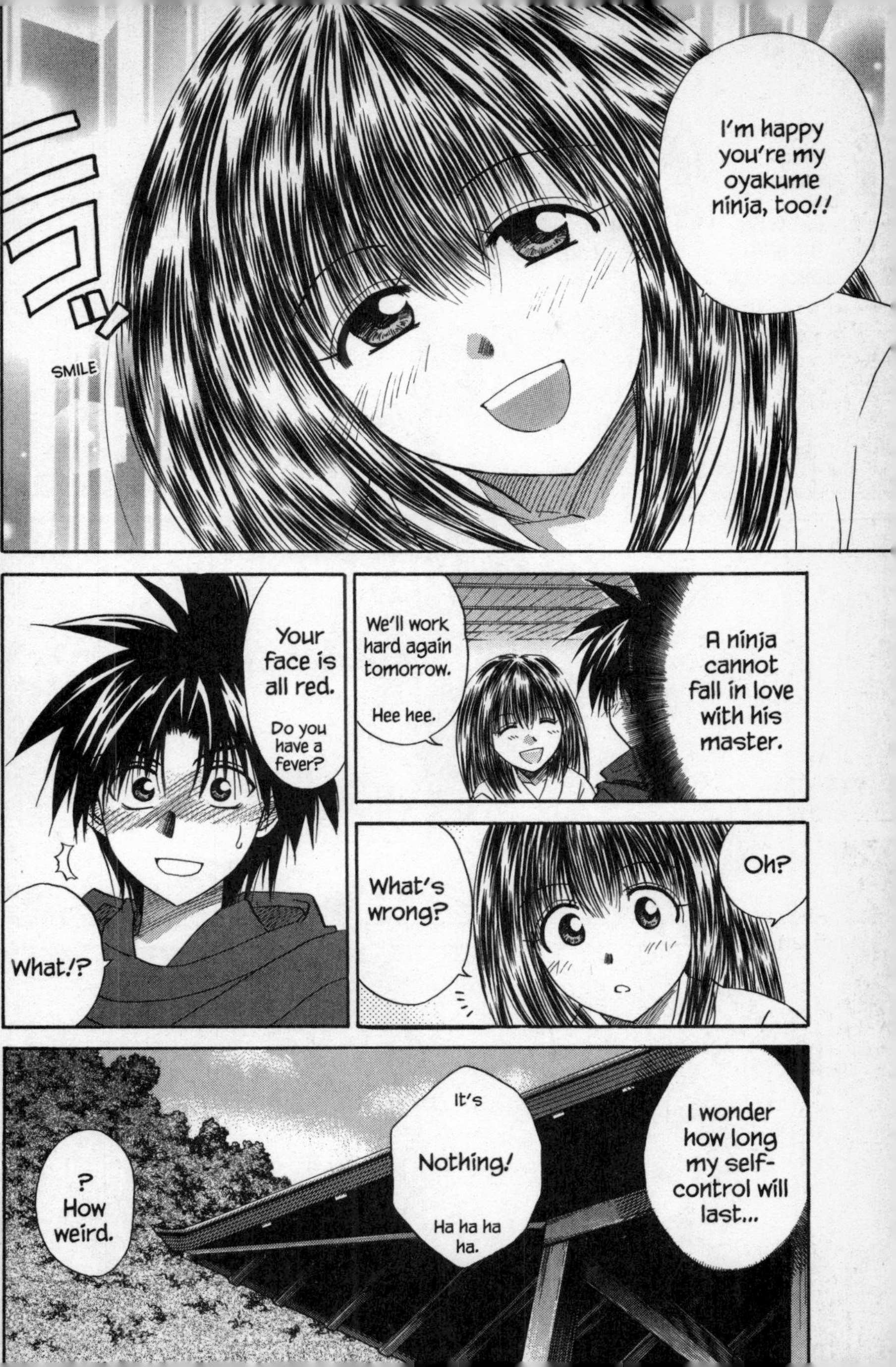
I'm happy you're my oyakume ninja, too!!
SMILE
A ninja cannot fall in love with his master.
We'll work hard again tomorrow.
Hee hee.
Oh?
What's wrong?
Your face is all red.
Do you have a fever?
What!?
I wonder how long my self-control will last...
It's
Nothing!
Ha ha ha ha.
? How weird.

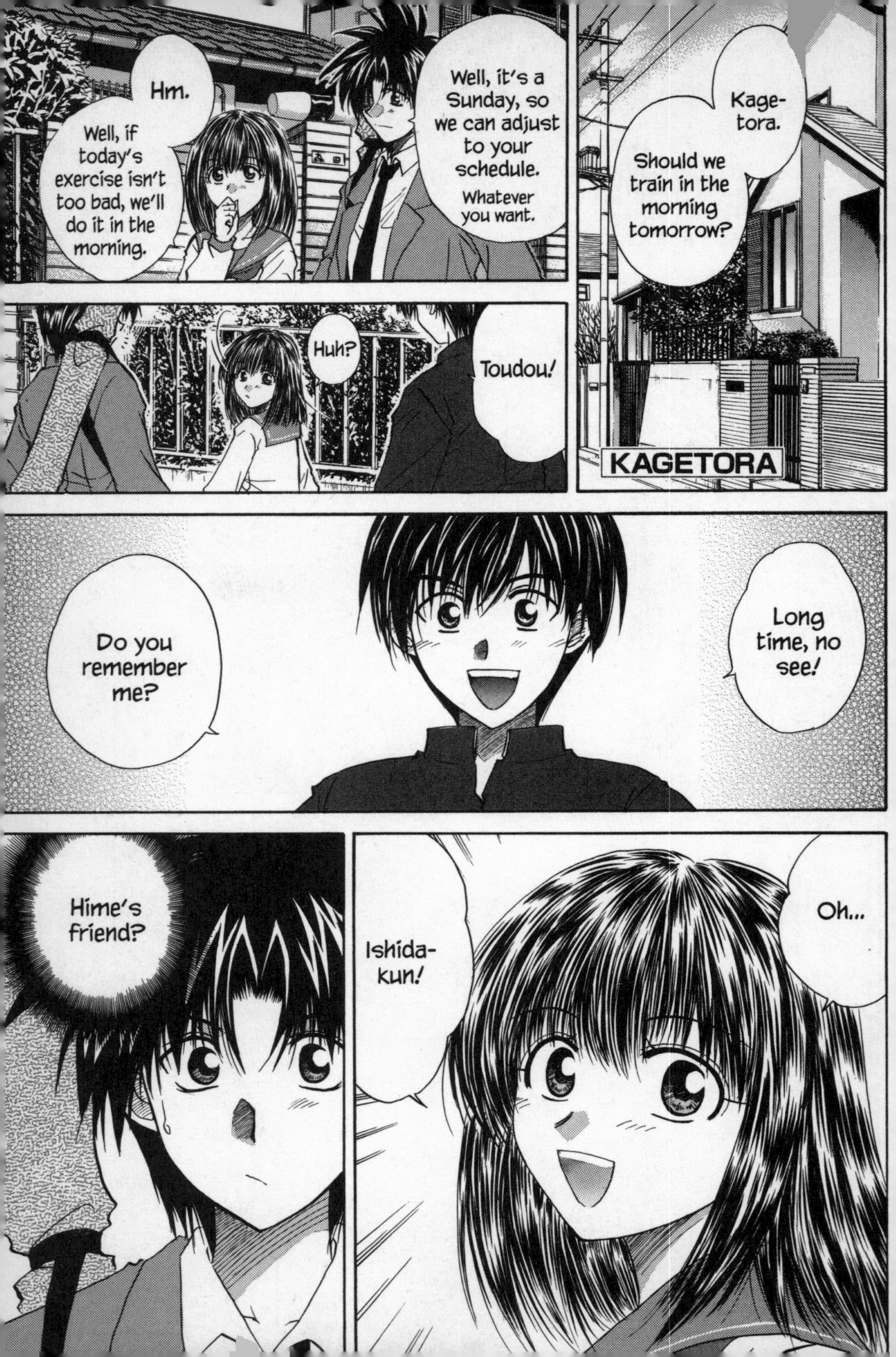
Kage-tora.
Should we train in the morning tomorrow?
KAGETORA
Well, it's a Sunday, so we can adjust to your schedule.
Whatever you want.
Hm.
Well, if today's exercise isn't too bad, we'll do it in the morning.
Toudou!
Huh?
Long time, no see!
Do you remember me?
Oh...
Ishida-kun!
Hime's friend?

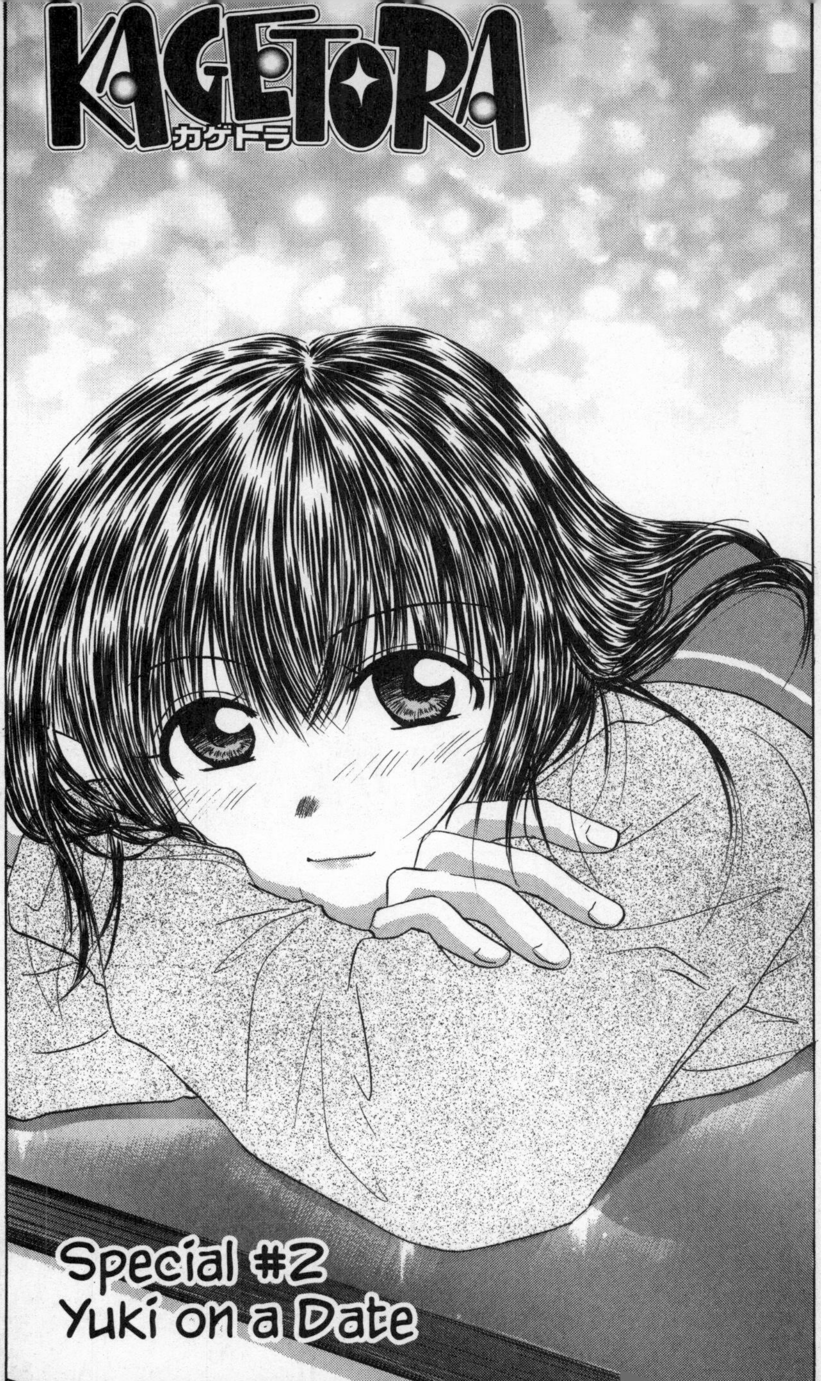
KAGETORA
カゲトラ
Special #2
Yuki on a Date

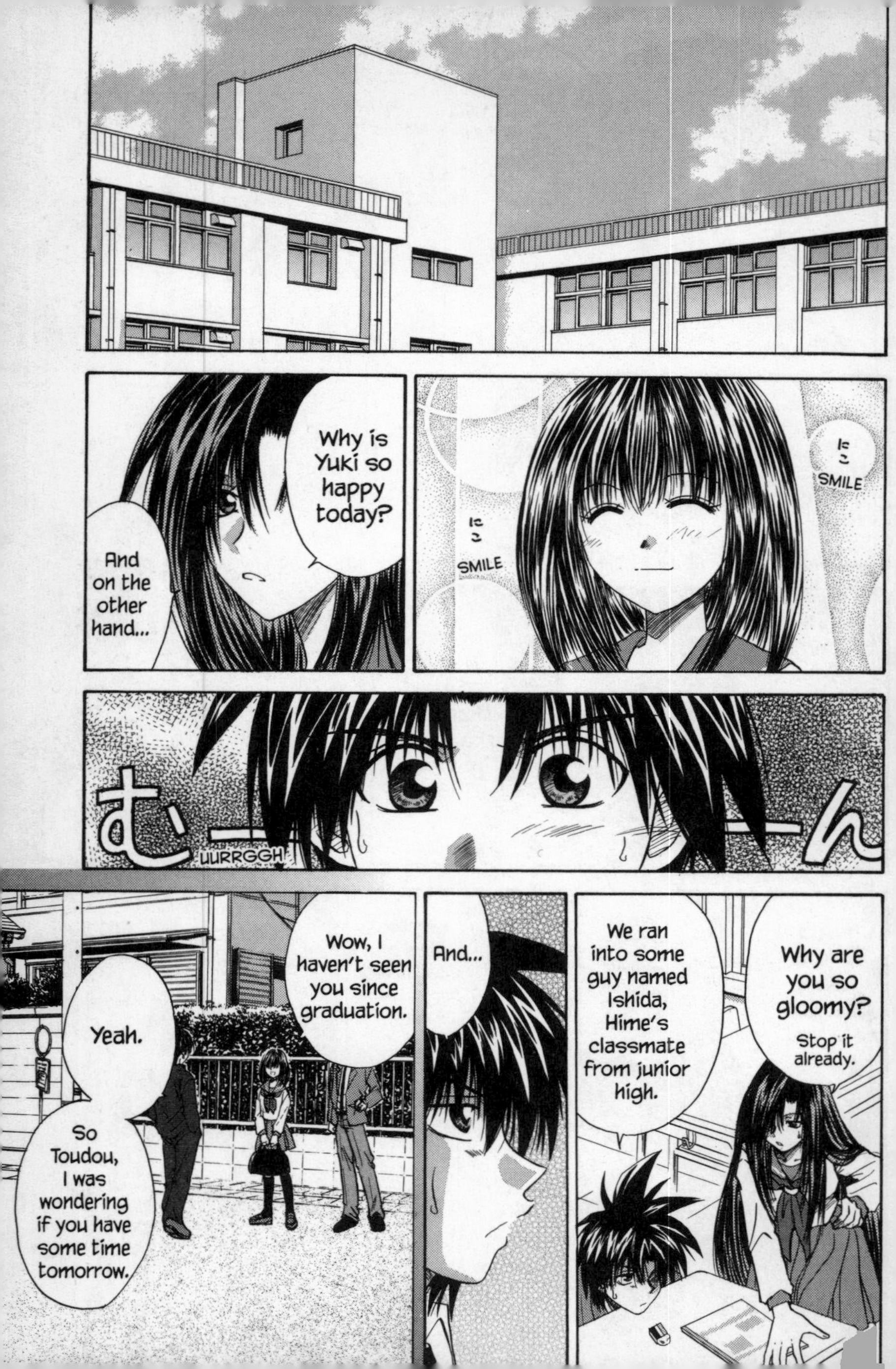
にこ
SMILE
にこ
SMILE
Why is Yuki so happy today?
And on the other hand...
むーーん
UURRGGH
Why are you so gloomy?
Stop it already.
We ran into some guy named Ishida, Hime's classmate from junior high.
And...
Wow, I haven't seen you since graduation.
Yeah.
So Toudou, I was wondering if you have some time tomorrow.

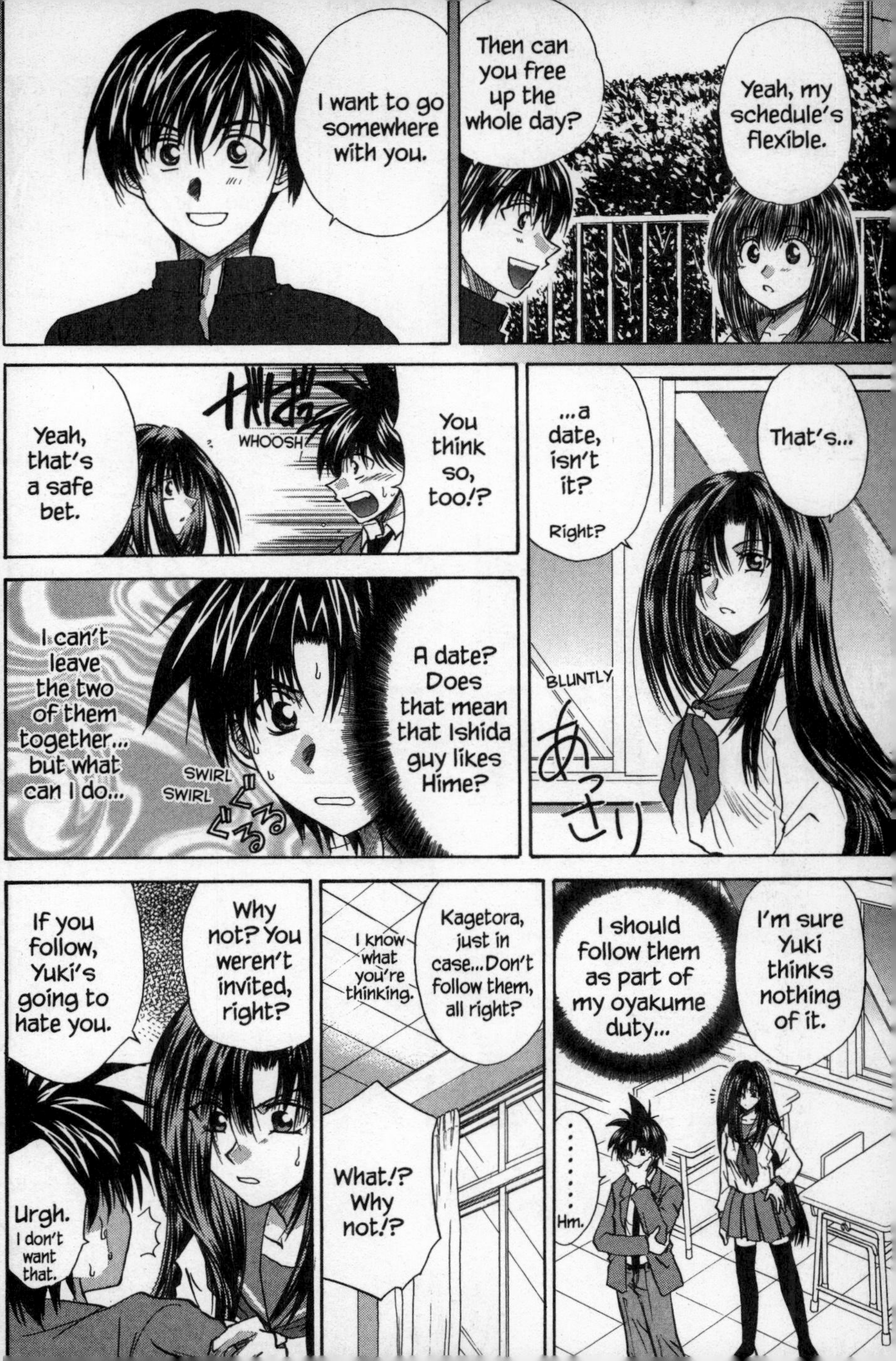

Yeah, my schedule's flexible.
Then can you free up the whole day?
I want to go somewhere with you.
That's...
...a date, isn't it?
Right?
BLUNTLY
あっさり
You think so, too!?
WHOOSH
Yeah, that's a safe bet.
A date? Does that mean that Ishida guy likes Hime?
SWIRL SWIRL
ぐるぐる
I can't leave the two of them together... but what can I do...
I'm sure Yuki thinks nothing of it.
I should follow them as part of my oyakume duty...
......
Hm.
Kagetora, just in case...Don't follow them, all right?
I know what you're thinking.
What!? Why not!?
Why not? You weren't invited, right?
If you follow, Yuki's going to hate you.
Urgh.
I don't want that.

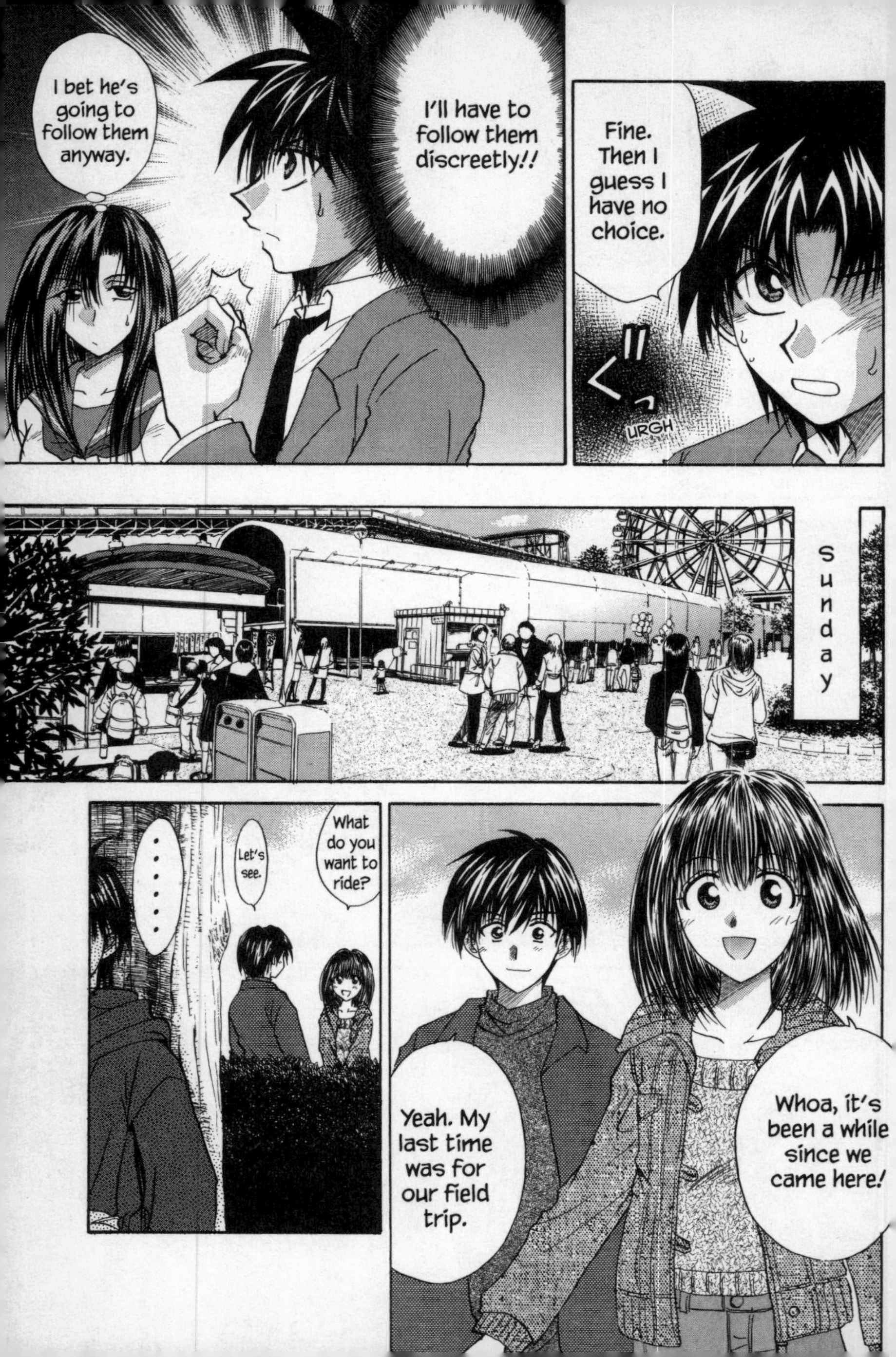
Fine. Then I guess I have no choice.
URGH
I'll have to follow them discreetly!!
I bet he's going to follow them anyway.
Sunday
Whoa, it's been a while since we came here!
Yeah. My last time was for our field trip.
What do you want to ride?
Let's see.
......

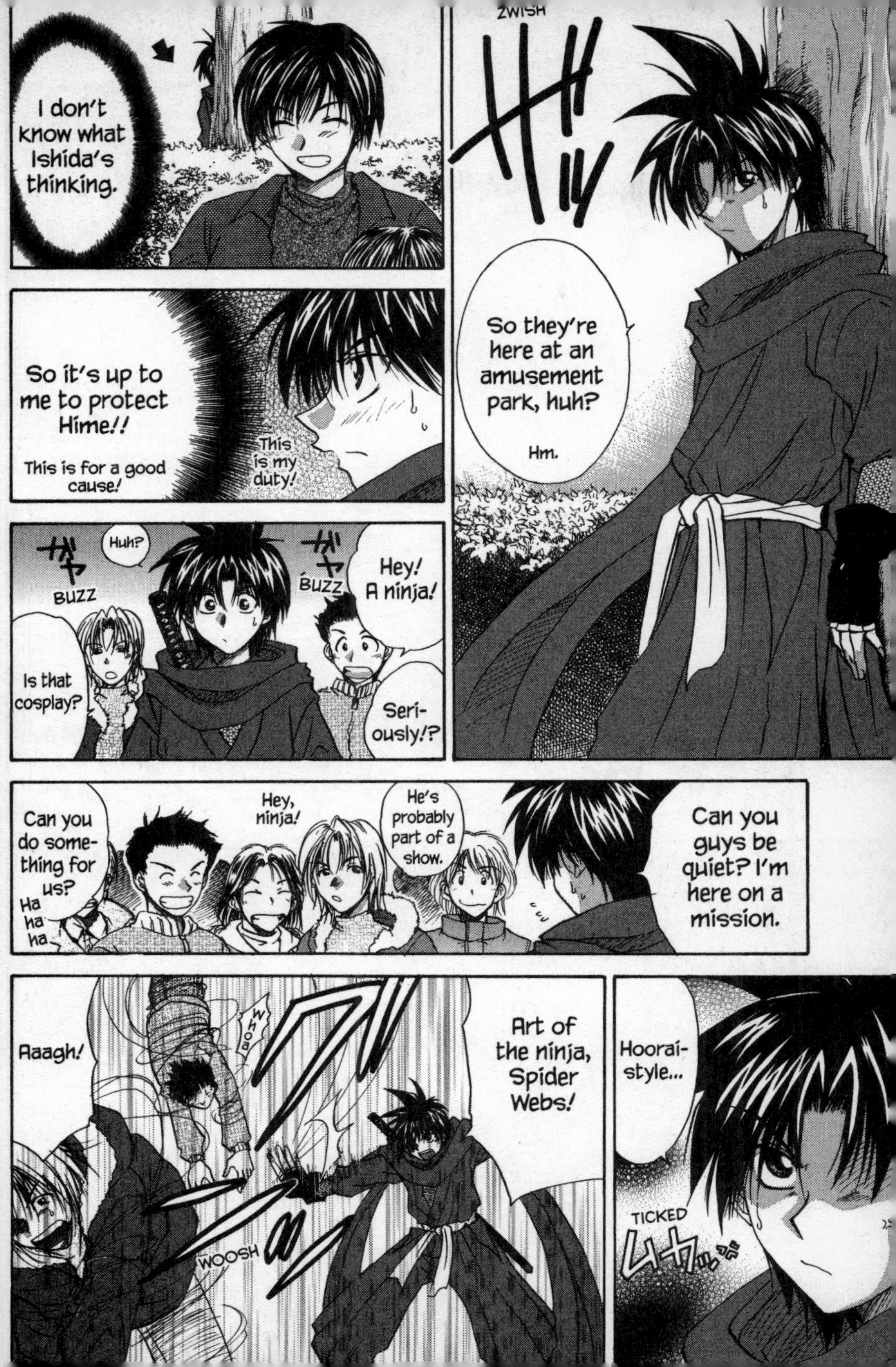
ZWISH
So they're here at an amusement park, huh?
Hm.
I don't know what Ishida's thinking.
So it's up to me to protect Hime!!
This is my duty!
This is for a good cause!
BUZZ
Hey! A ninja!
Seri- ously!?
Huh?
BUZZ
Is that cosplay?
Can you guys be quiet? I'm here on a mission.
He's probably part of a show.
Hey, ninja!
Can you do some- thing for us?
Ha ha ha
Hoorai- style...
TICKED
Art of the ninja, Spider Webs!
Whoa
Aaagh!
WOOSH

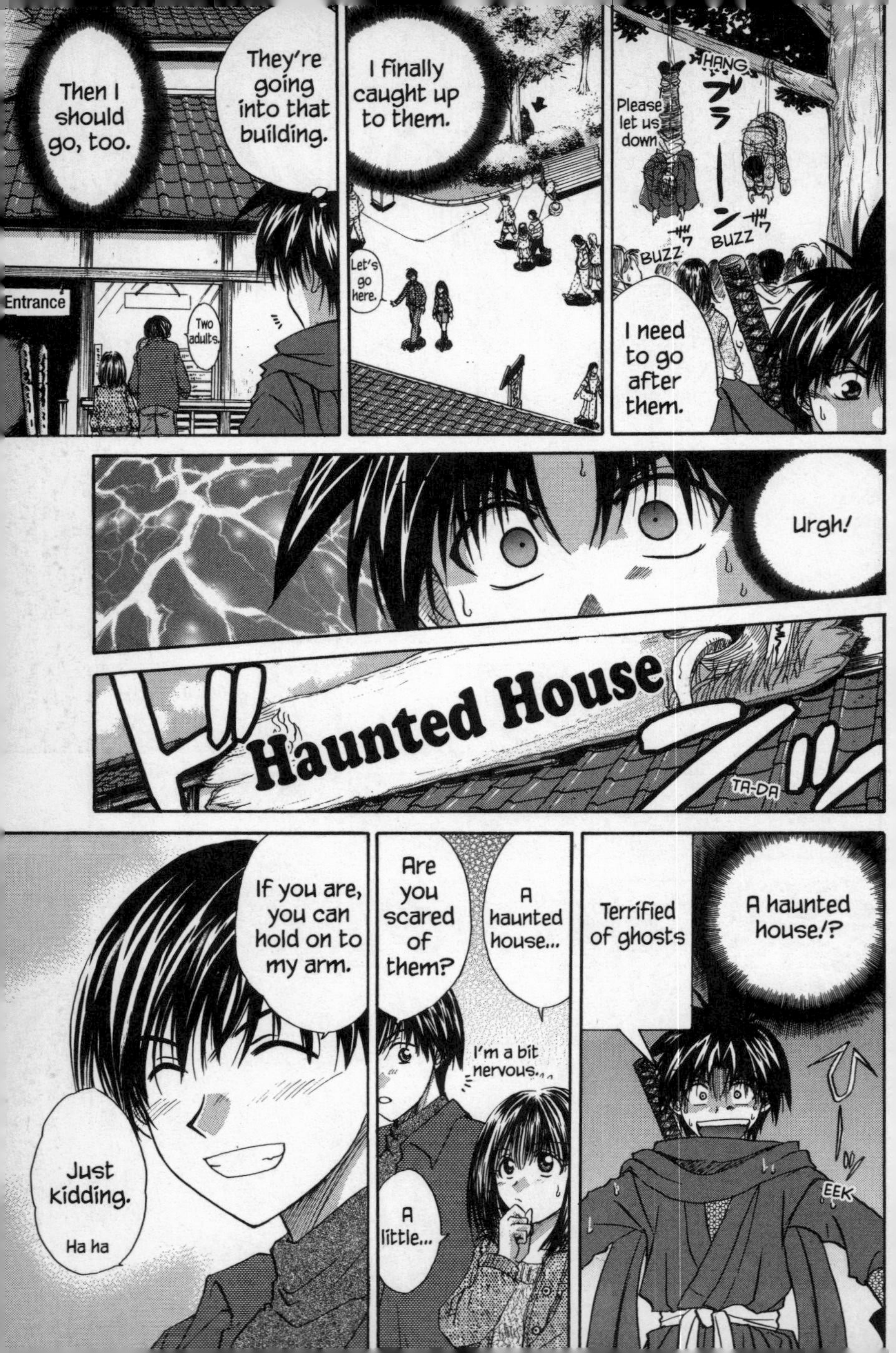

HANG
ブラーン
Please let us down
BUZZ
BUZZ
I need to go after them.
I finally caught up to them.
Let's go here.
They're going into that building.
Then I should go, too.
Entrance
Two adults.
Urgh!
Haunted House
TA-DA
A haunted house!?
EEK
Terrified of ghosts
A haunted house...
Are you scared of them?
I'm a bit nervous...
A little...
If you are, you can hold on to my arm.
Just kidding.
Ha ha

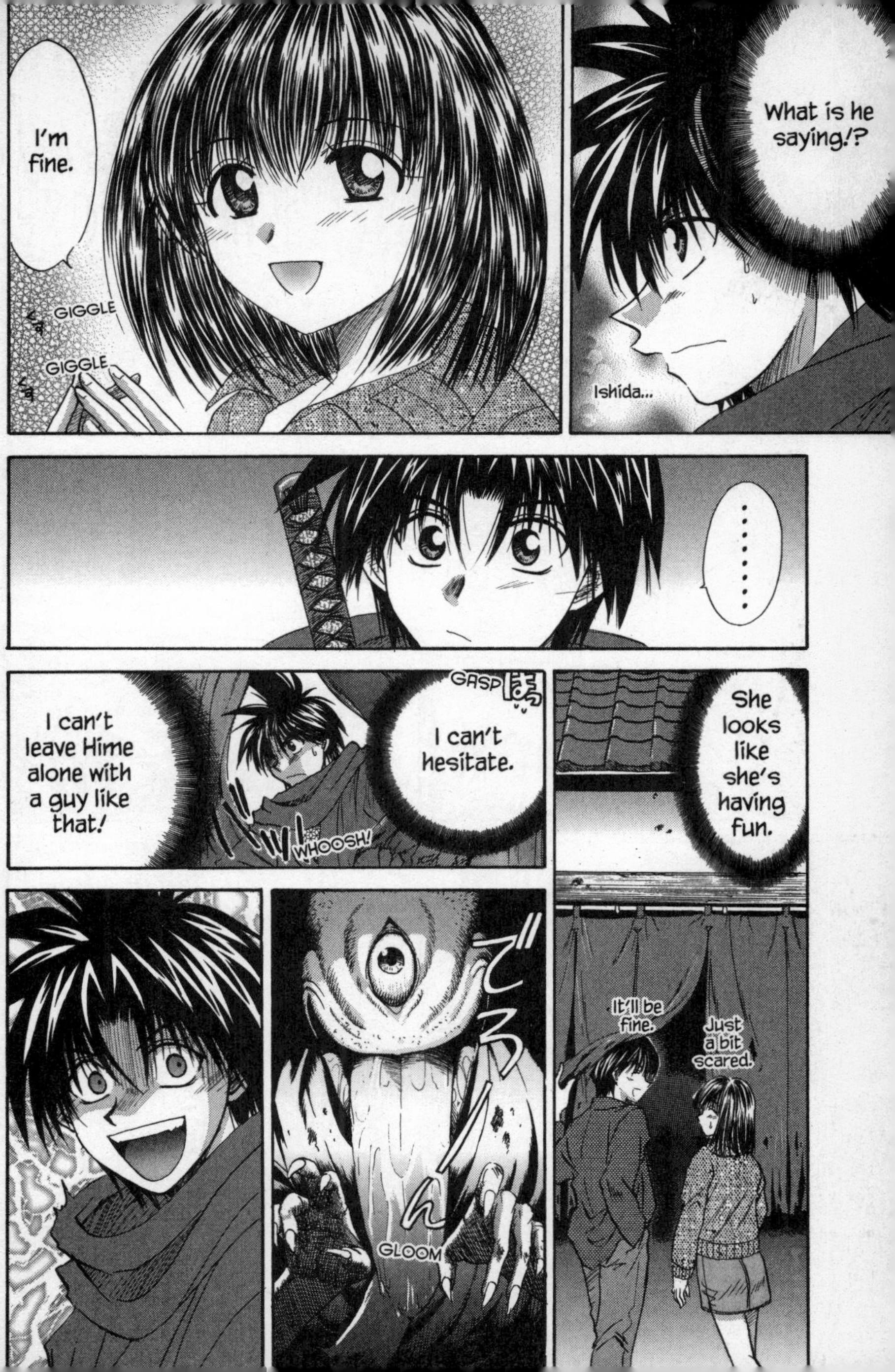

What is he saying!?
Ishida...
I'm fine.
GIGGLE
GIGGLE
......
She looks like she's having fun.
It'll be fine.
Just a bit scared.
GASP
I can't hesitate.
I can't leave Hime alone with a guy like that!
WHOOSH!
GLOOM

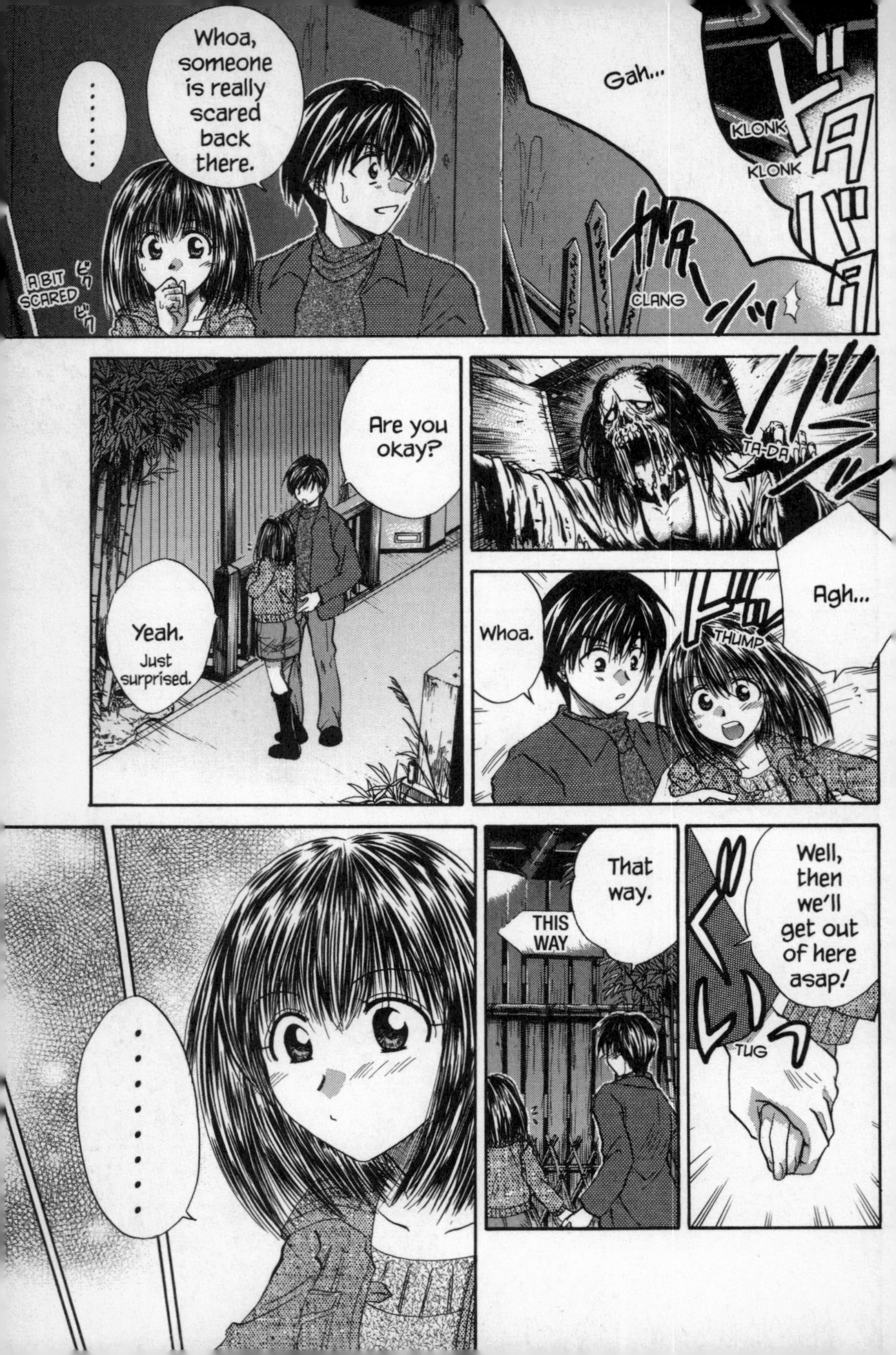

Gah...
KLONK
KLONK
CLANG
Whoa, someone is really scared back there.
......
A BIT SCARED
TA-DA
Agh...
THUMP
Whoa.
Are you okay?
Yeah. Just surprised.
Well, then we'll get out of here asap!
TUG
That way.
THIS WAY
......

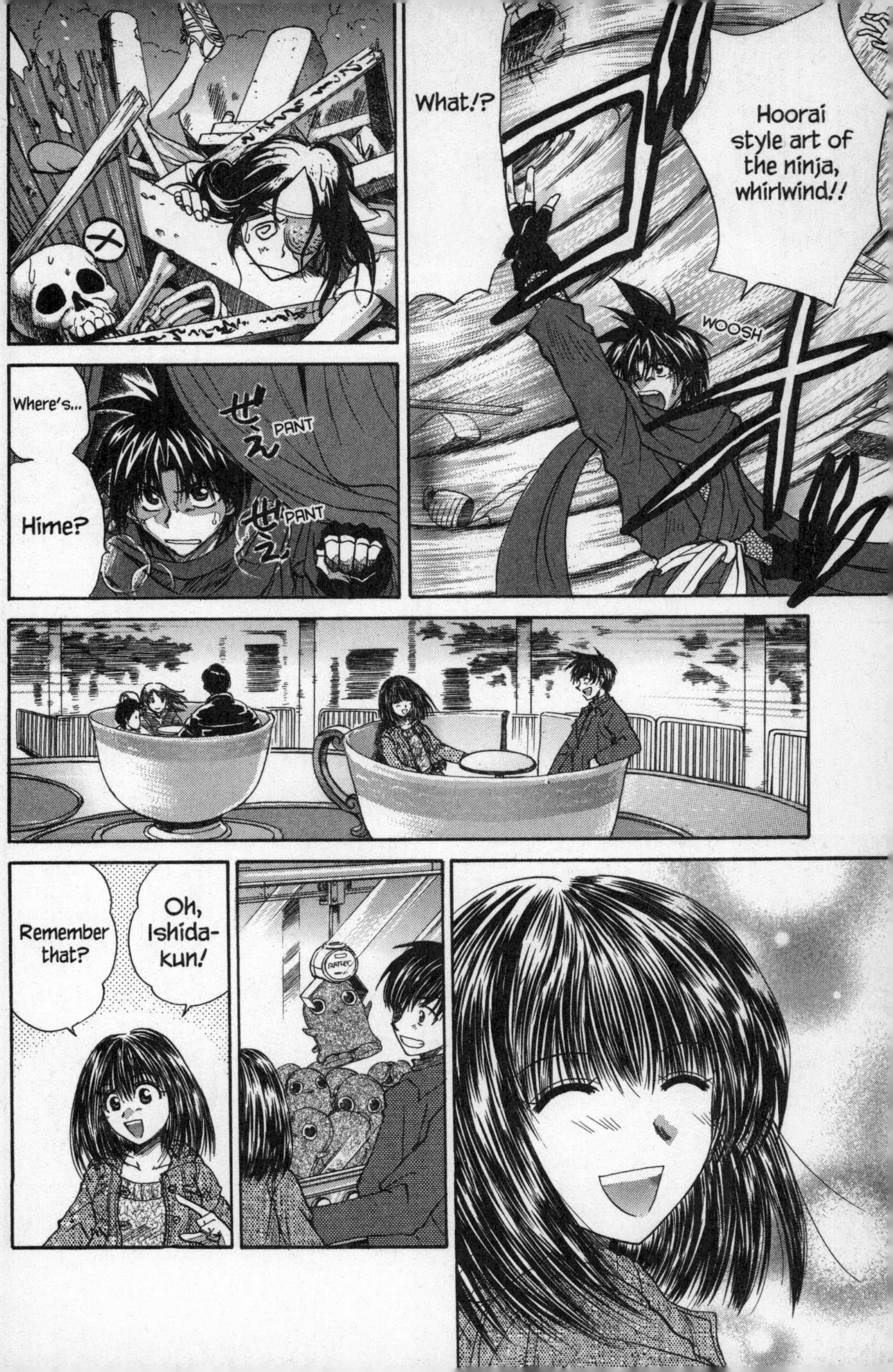
Hoorai style art of the ninja, whirlwind!!
What!?
WOOSH
Where's...
Hime?
ぜえ
PANT
ぜえ
PANT
Oh, Ishida-kun!
Remember that?

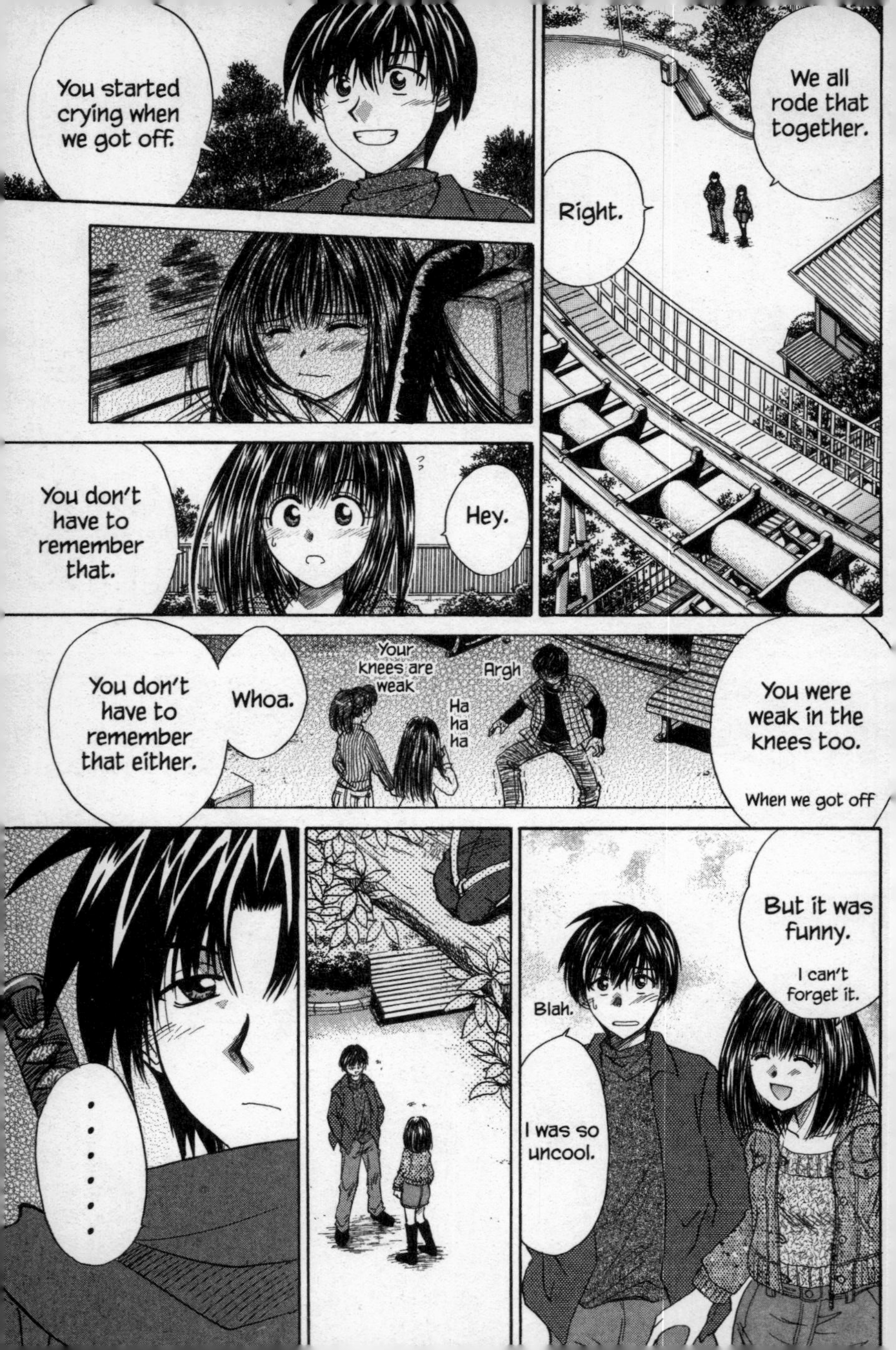
We all rode that together.
Right.
You started crying when we got off.
Hey.
You don't have to remember that.
You were weak in the knees too.
When we got off
Argh
Your knees are weak
Ha ha ha
Whoa.
You don't have to remember that either.
But it was funny.
I can't forget it.
Blah.
I was so uncool.
......

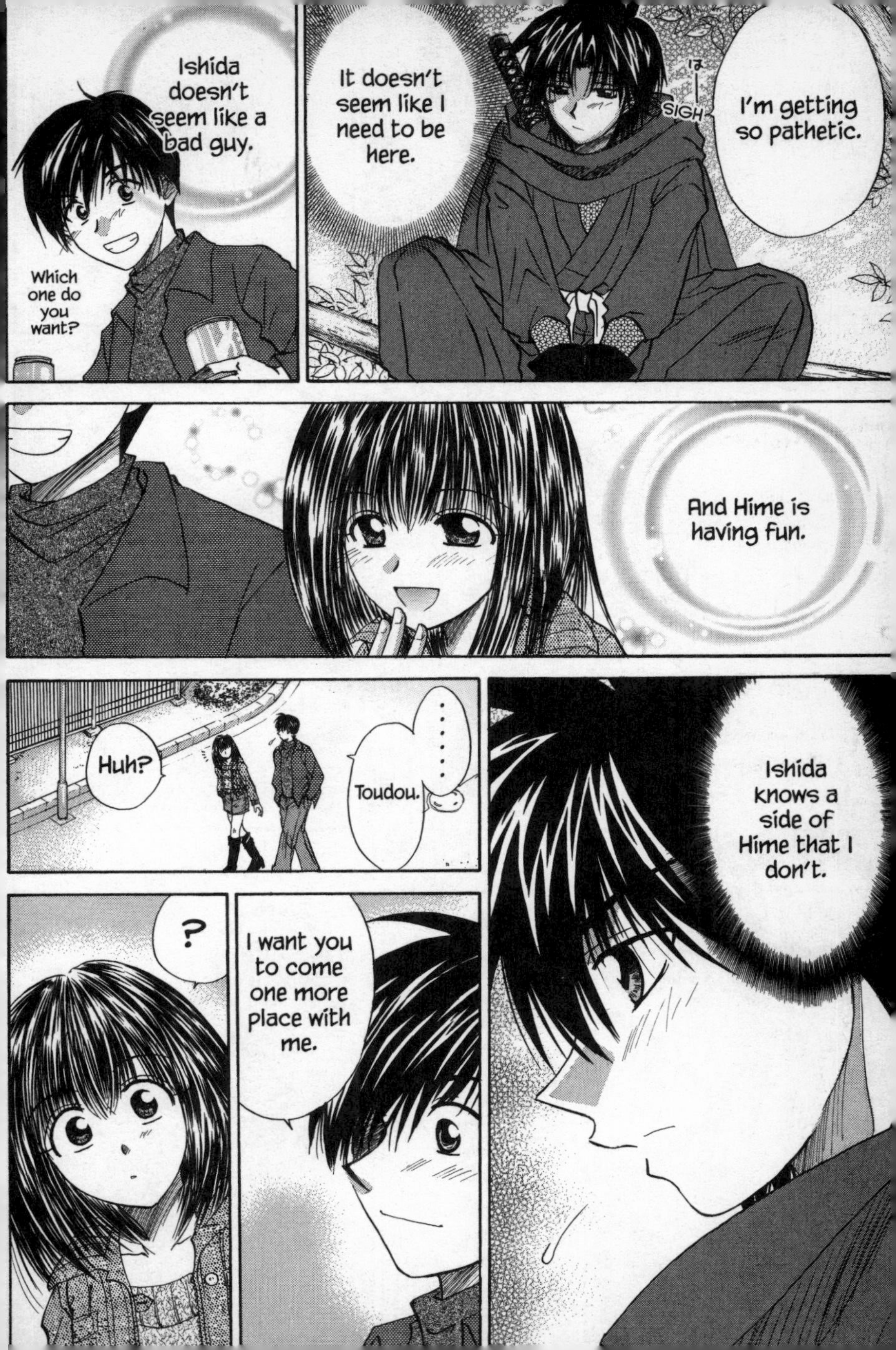
I'm getting so pathetic.
SIGH
It doesn't seem like I need to be here.
Ishida doesn't seem like a bad guy.
Which one do you want?
And Hime is having fun.
Ishida knows a side of Hime that I don't.
......
Toudou.
Huh?
I want you to come one more place with me.
?

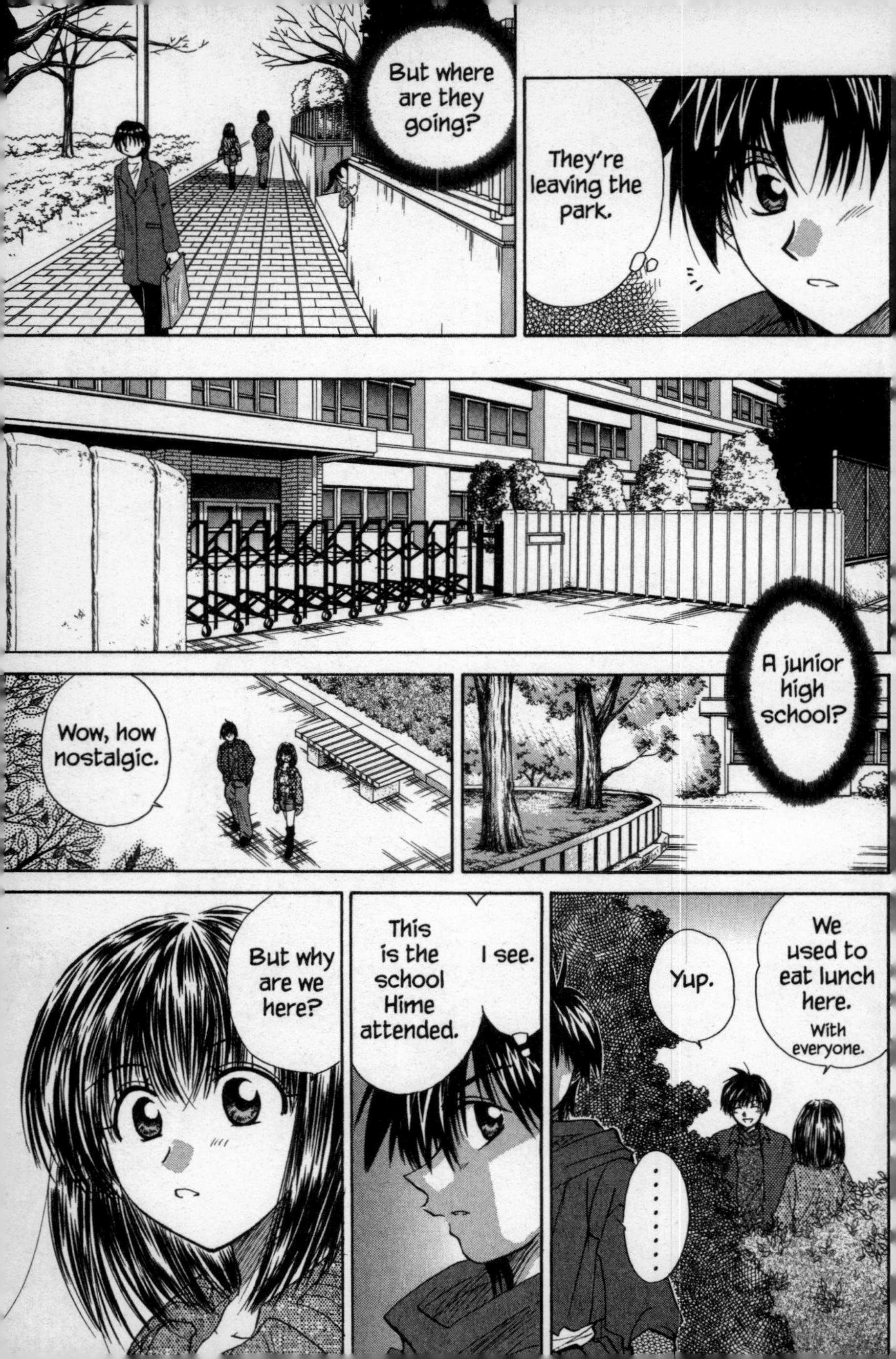
They're leaving the park.
But where are they going?
A junior high school?
Wow, how nostalgic.
We used to eat lunch here.
With everyone.
Yup.
......
I see.
This is the school Hime attended.
But why are we here?

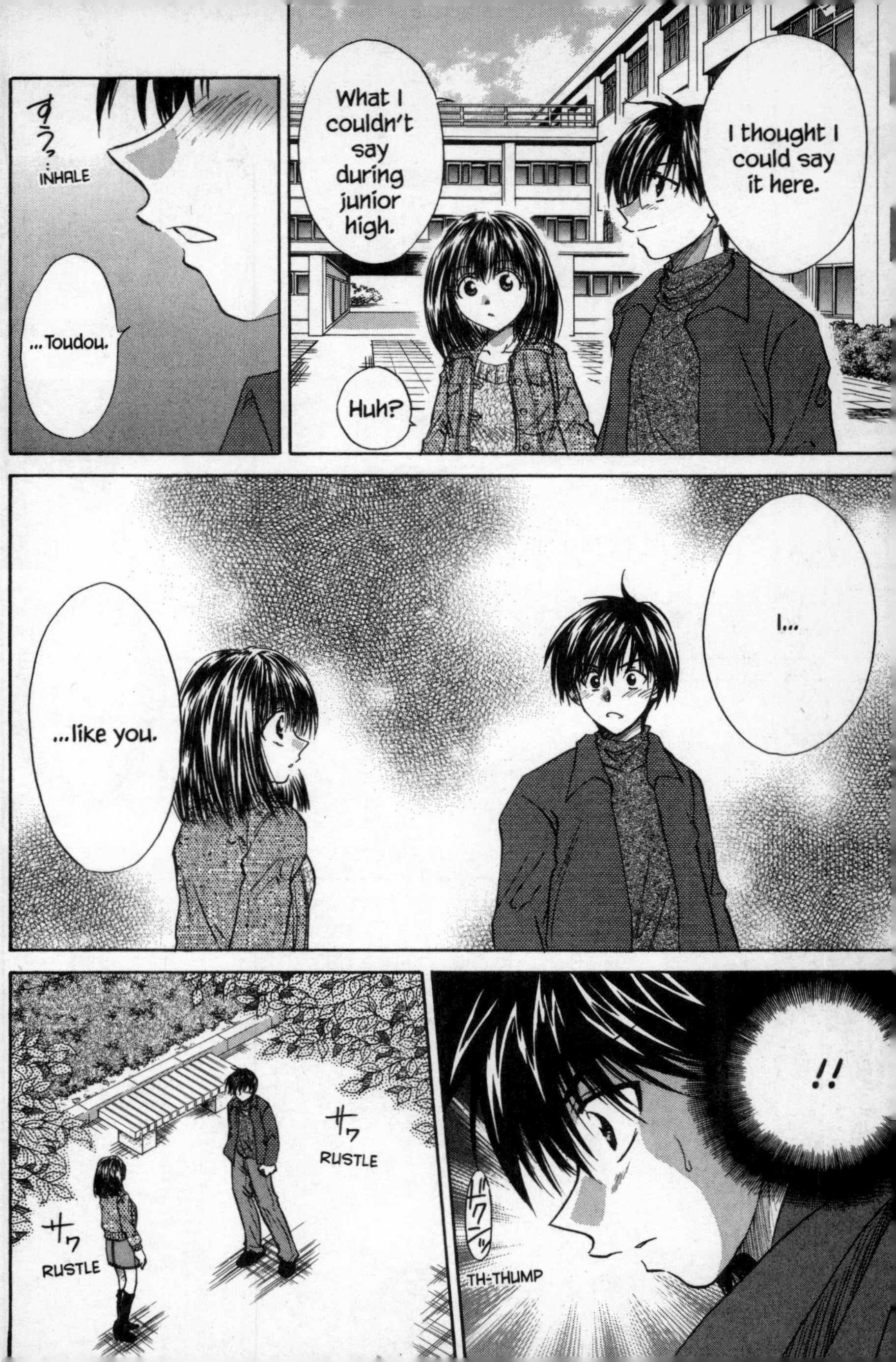

I thought I could say it here.
What I couldn't say during junior high.
Huh?
INHALE
...Toudou.
I...
...like you.
!!
TH-THUMP
RUSTLE
RUSTLE

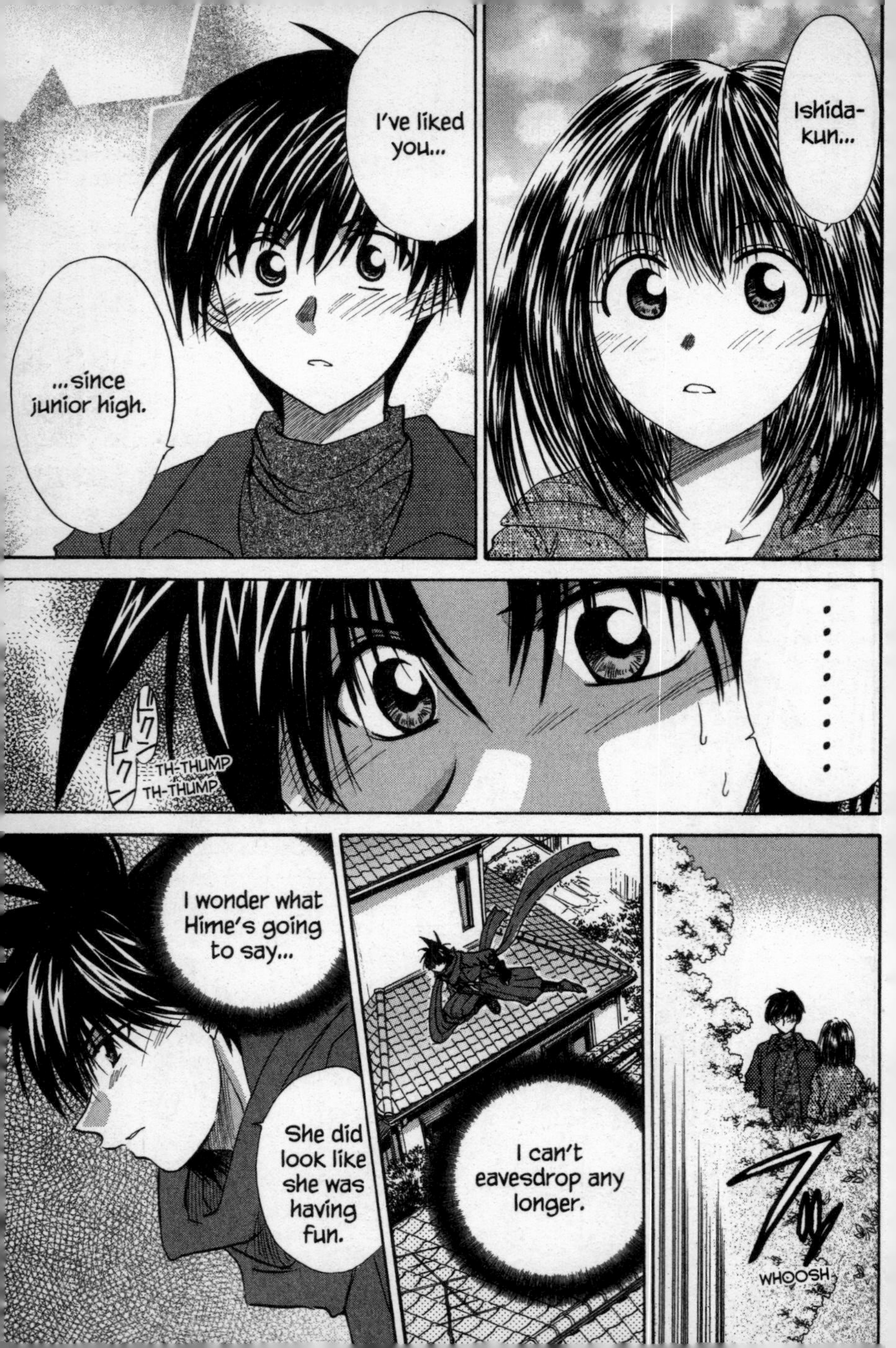

Ishida-kun...
I've liked you...
...since junior high.
....
TH-THUMP
TH-THUMP
WHOOSH
I can't eavesdrop any longer.
I wonder what Hime's going to say...
She did look like she was having fun.

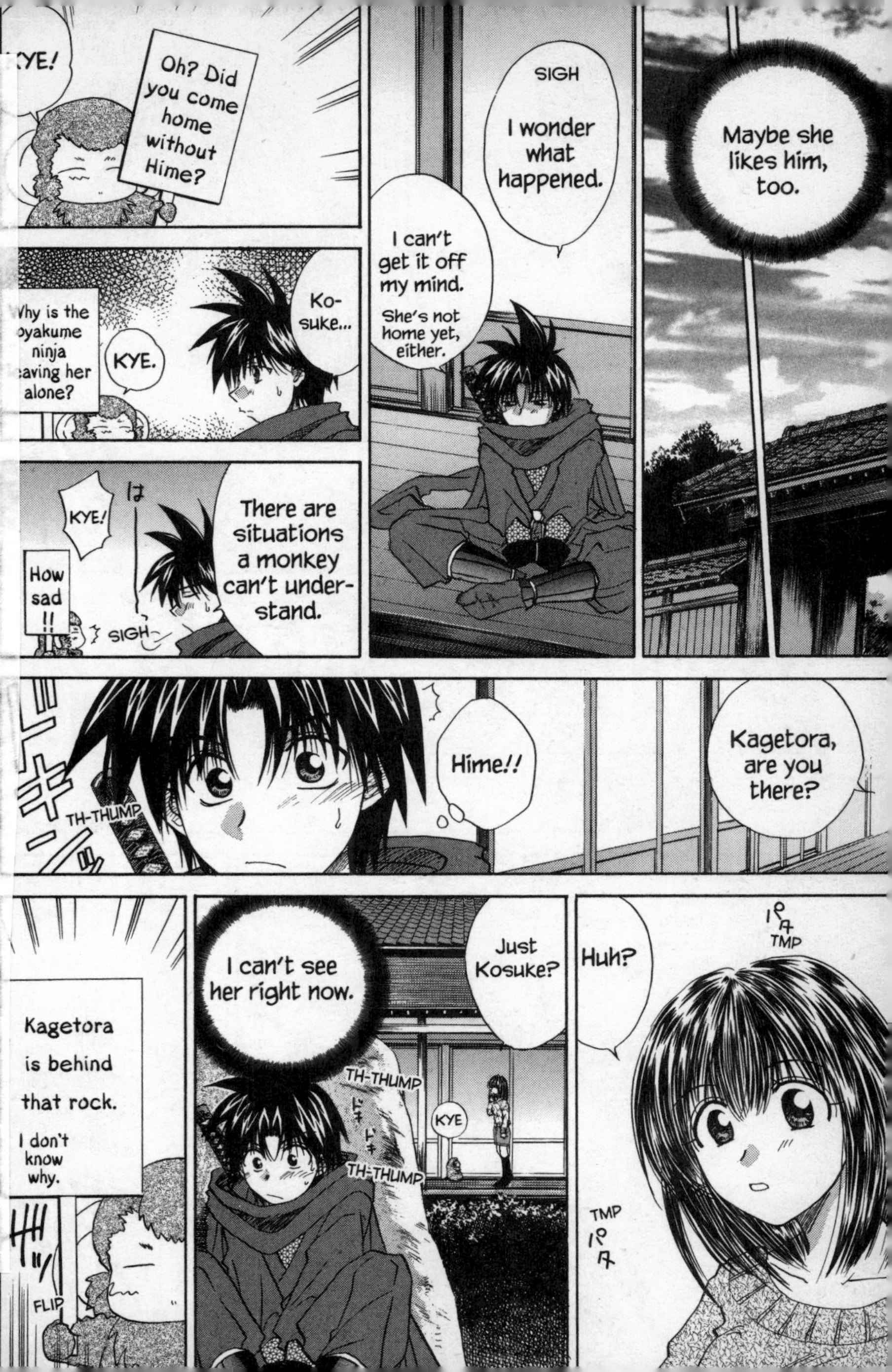
Maybe she likes him, too.
SIGH
I wonder what happened.
I can't get it off my mind.
She's not home yet, either.
KYE!
Oh? Did you come home without Hime?
Ko-suke...
KYE.
Why is the oyakume ninja leaving her alone?
There are situations a monkey can't under-stand.
は
KYE!
How sad !!
SIGH
Kagetora, are you there?
Hime!!
TH-THUMP
パタ TMP
Huh?
TMP パタ
Just Kosuke?
I can't see her right now.
TH-THUMP
ドキ ドキ
KYE
TH-THUMP
Kagetora is behind that rock.
I don't know why.
FLIP

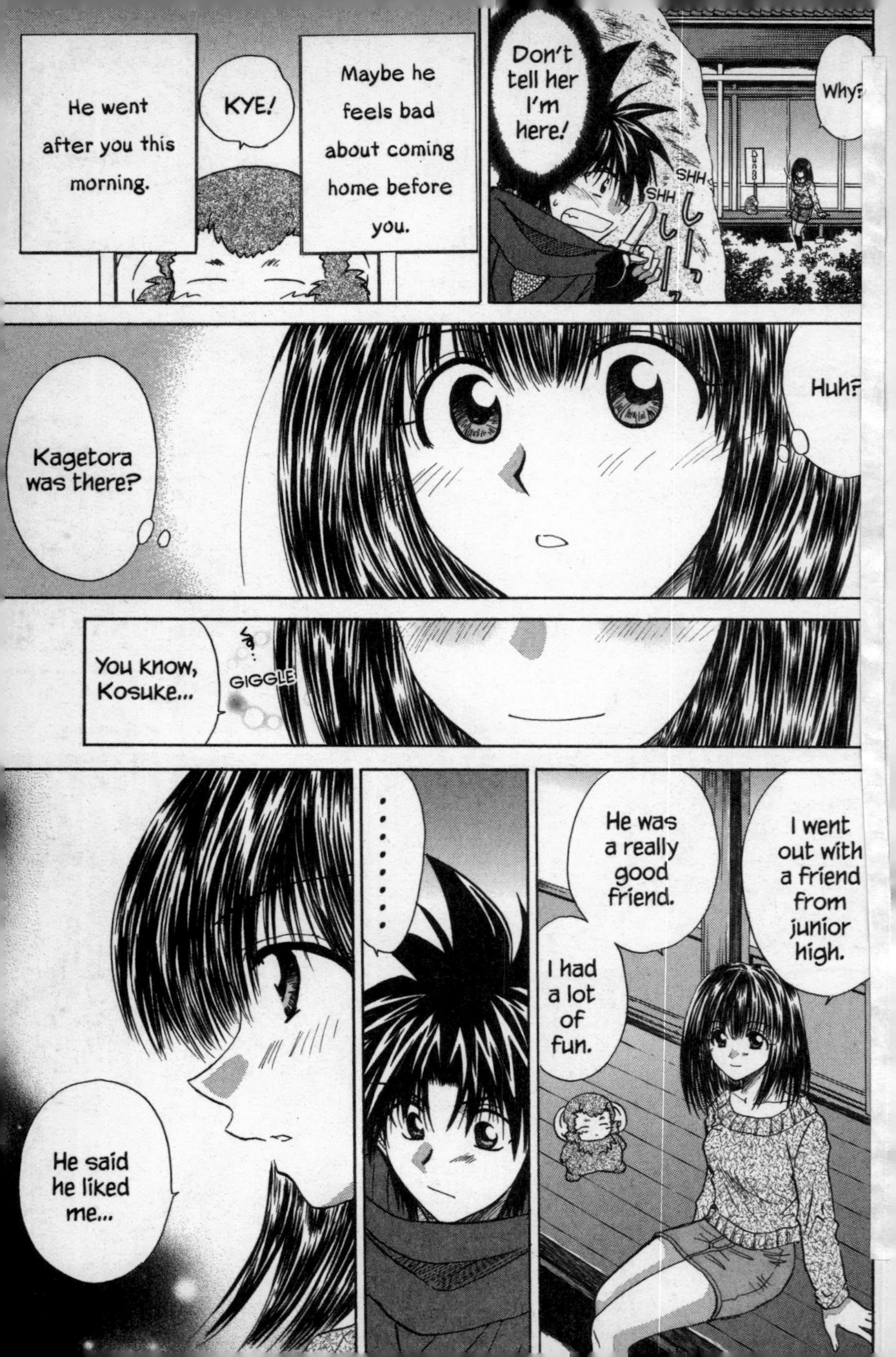
Why?
Don't tell her I'm here!
SHH
SHH
Maybe he feels bad about coming home before you.
KYE!
He went after you this morning.
Huh?
Kagetora was there?
GIGGLE
You know, Kosuke...
I went out with a friend from junior high.
He was a really good friend.
I had a lot of fun.
....
He said he liked me...

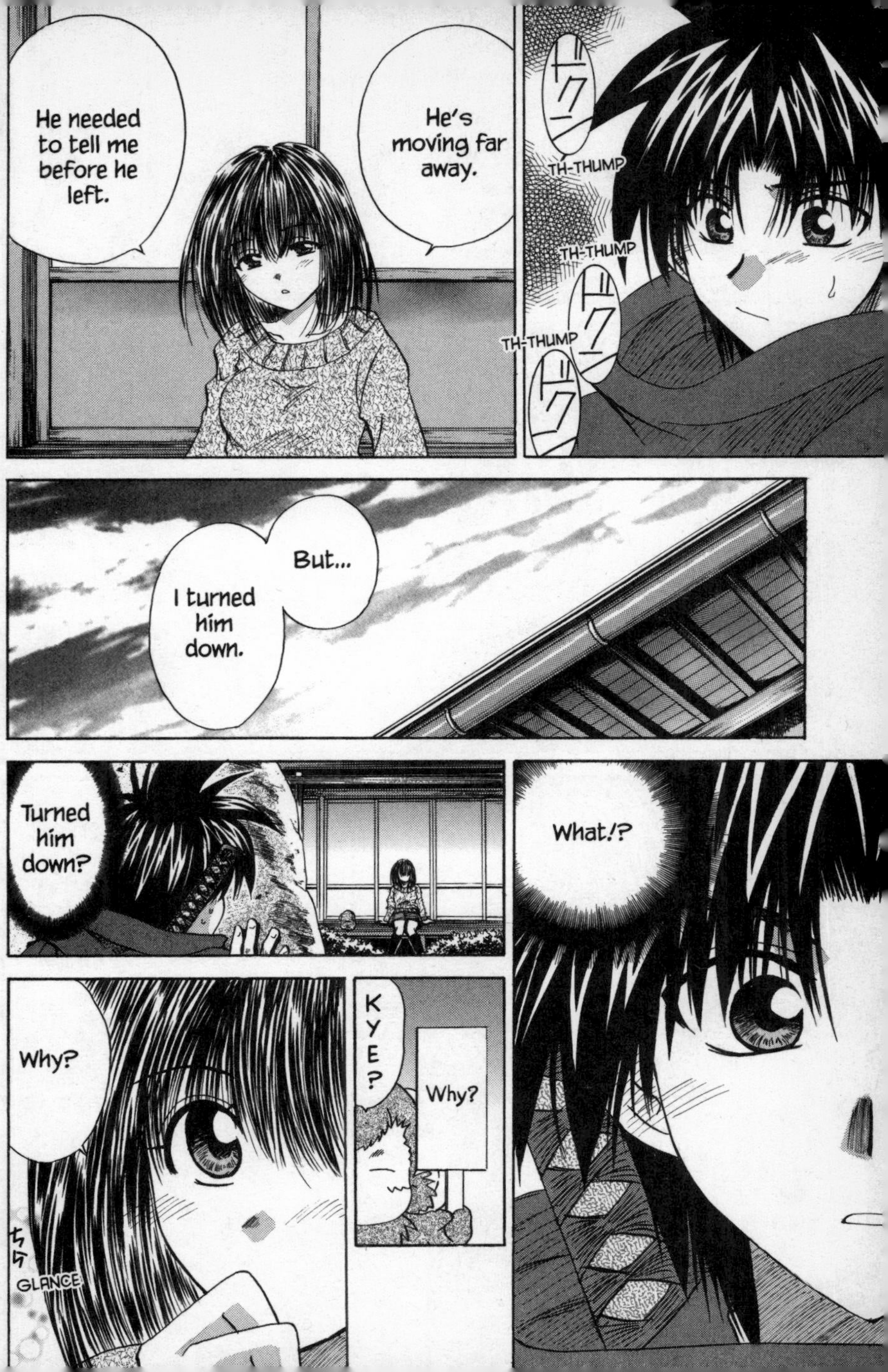
ドクン
TH-THUMP
TH-THUMP
ドクン
TH-THUMP
ドクン
He's moving far away.
He needed to tell me before he left.
But...
I turned him down.
What!?
Turned him down?
KYE?
Why?
Why?
ちら
GLANCE

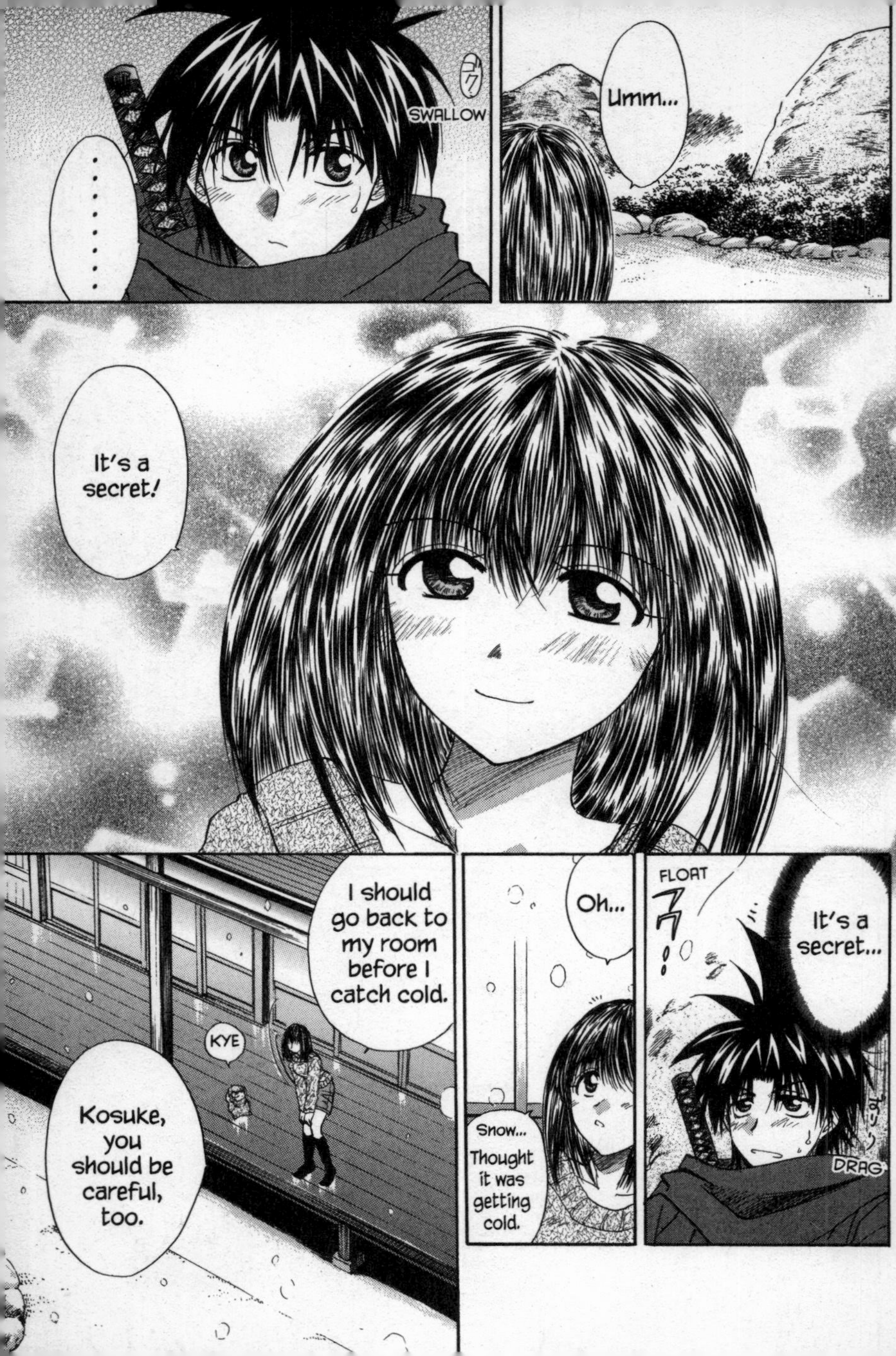
Umm...
SWALLOW
......
It's a secret!
FLOAT
It's a secret...
DRAG
Oh...
Snow... Thought it was getting cold.
I should go back to my room before I catch cold.
KYE
Kosuke, you should be careful, too.

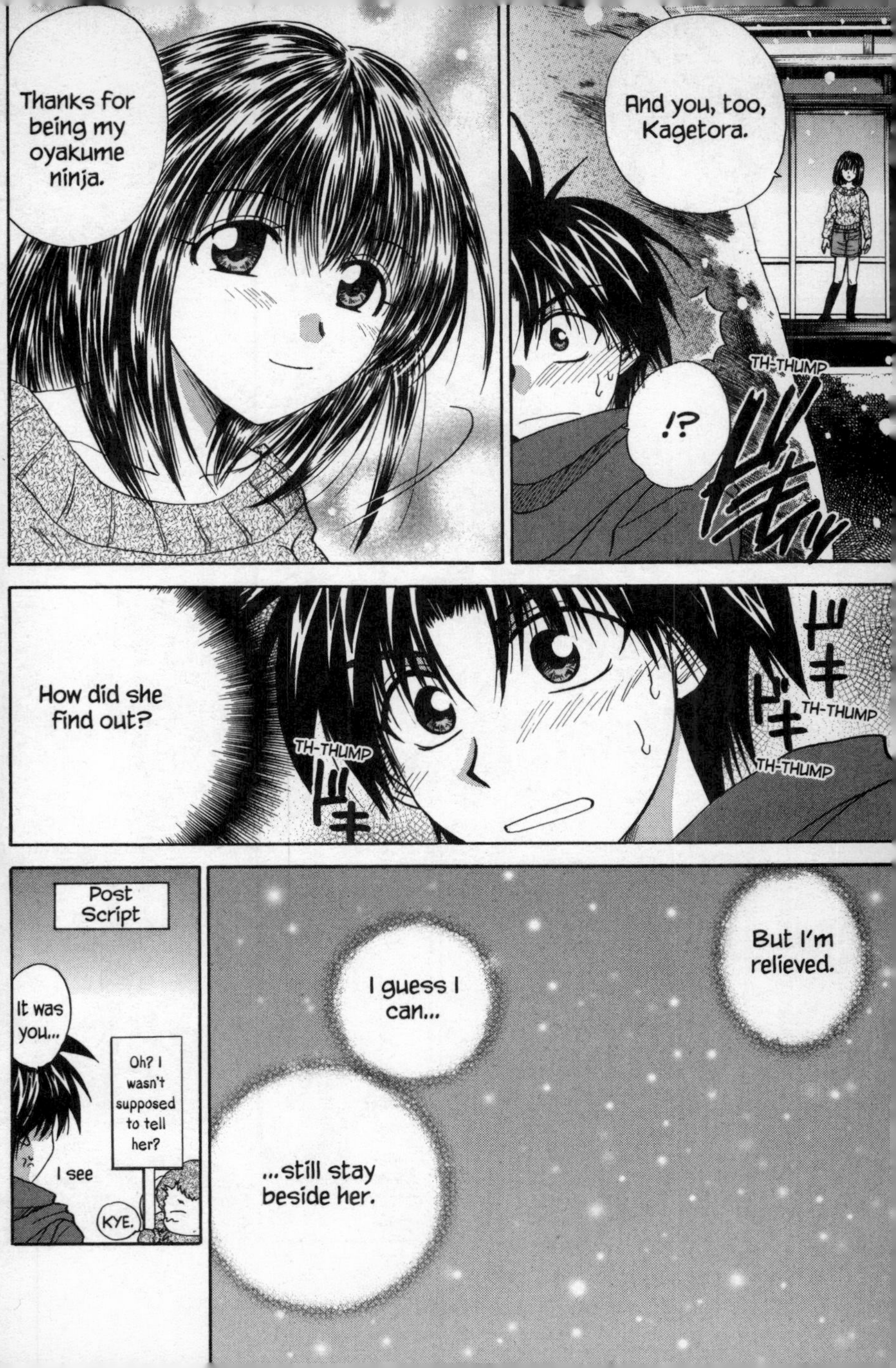

And you, too, Kagetora.
!?
TH-THUMP
Thanks for being my oyakume ninja.
How did she find out?
TH-THUMP
TH-THUMP
TH-THUMP
But I'm relieved.
I guess I can...
...still stay beside her.
Post Script
It was you...
Oh? I wasn't supposed to tell her?
I see
KYE.

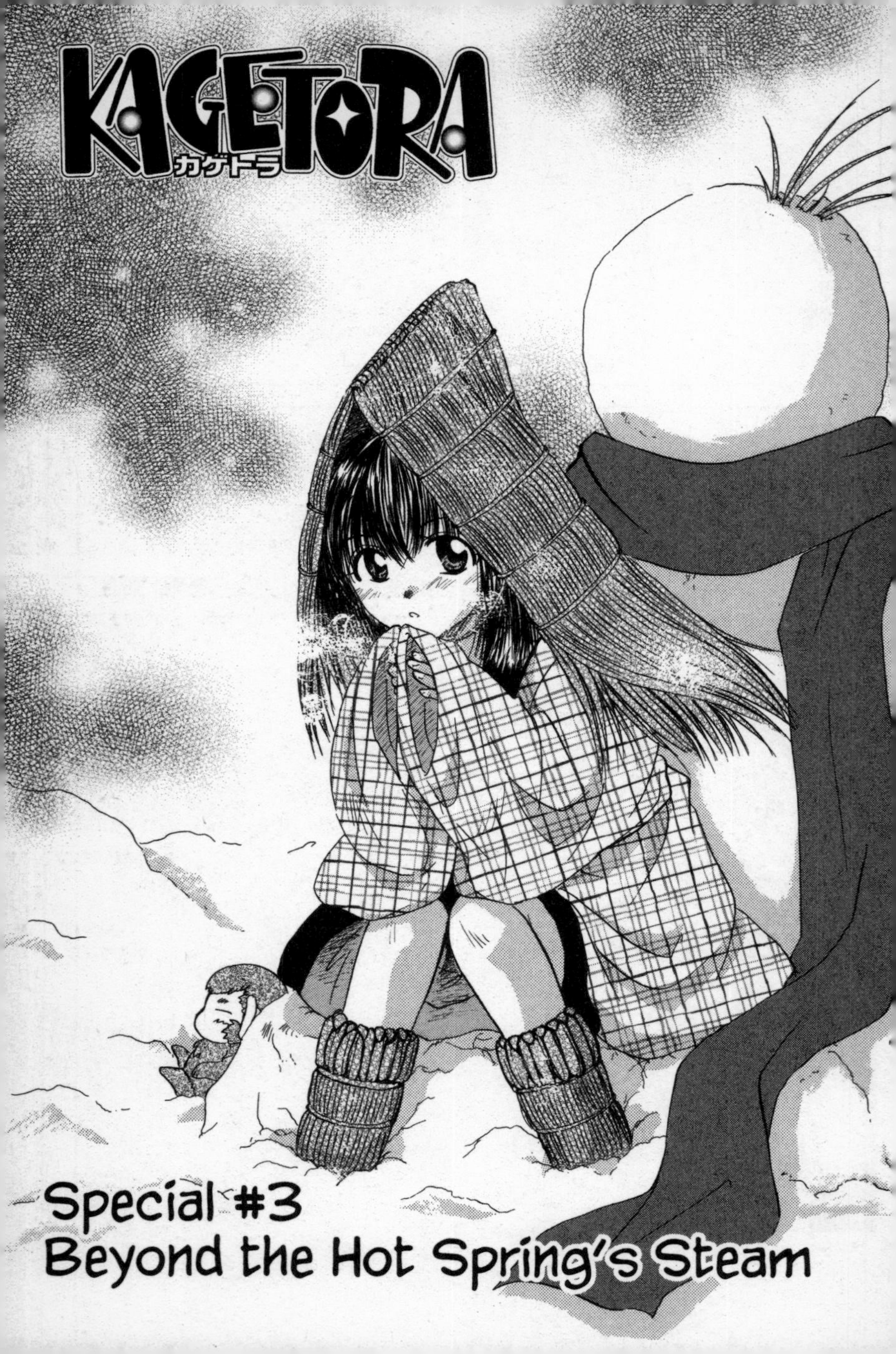
KAGETORA
カゲトラ
Special #3
Beyond the Hot Spring's Steam

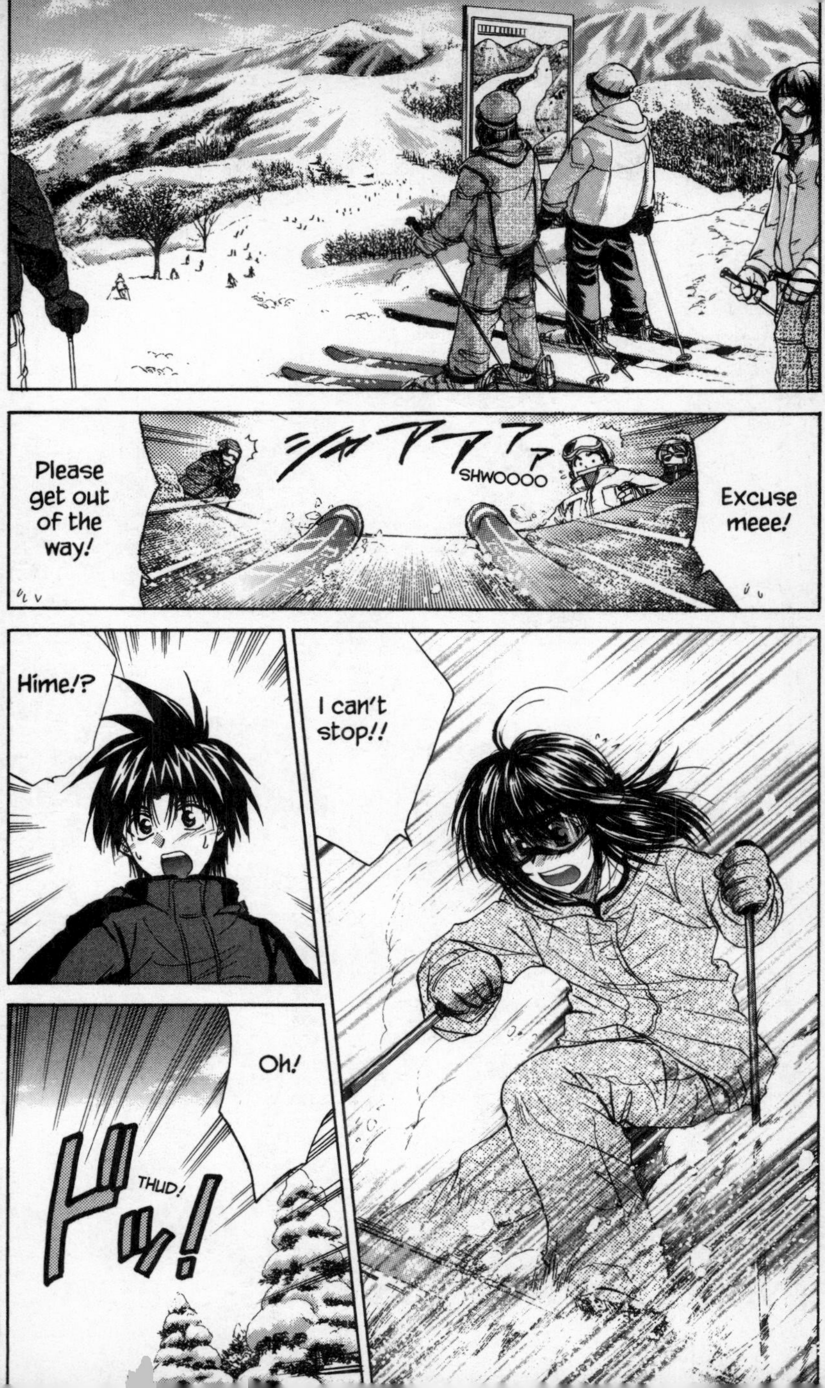
Excuse meee!
シャアアアア
SHWOOOO
Please get out of the way!
I can't stop!!
Hime!?
Oh!
ドッ!
THUD!

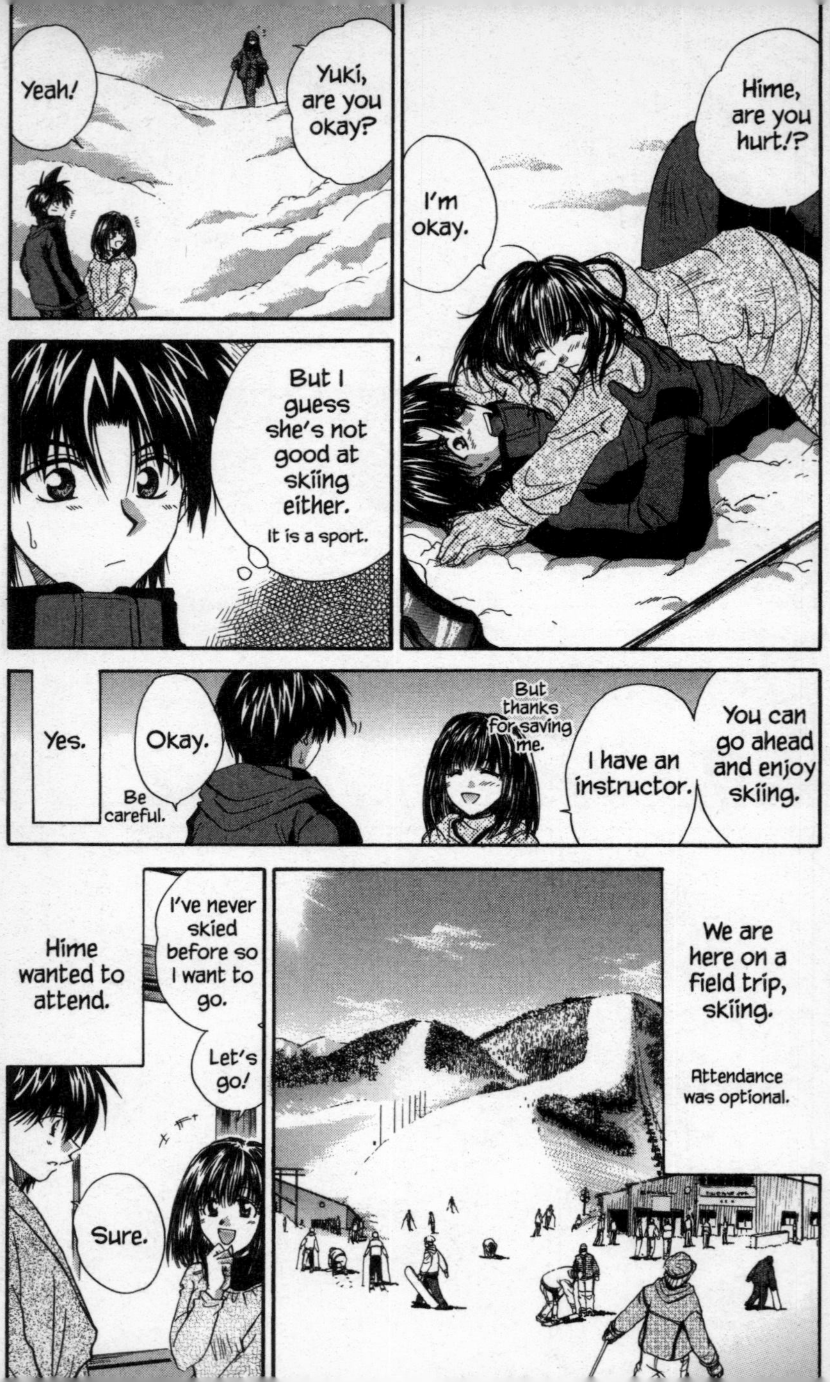
Hime, are you hurt!?
I'm okay.
Yuki, are you okay?
Yeah!
But I guess she's not good at skiing either.
It is a sport.
You can go ahead and enjoy skiing.
I have an instructor.
But thanks for saving me.
Okay.
Be careful.
Yes.
We are here on a field trip, skiing.
Attendance was optional.
I've never skied before so I want to go.
Hime wanted to attend.
Let's go!
Sure.

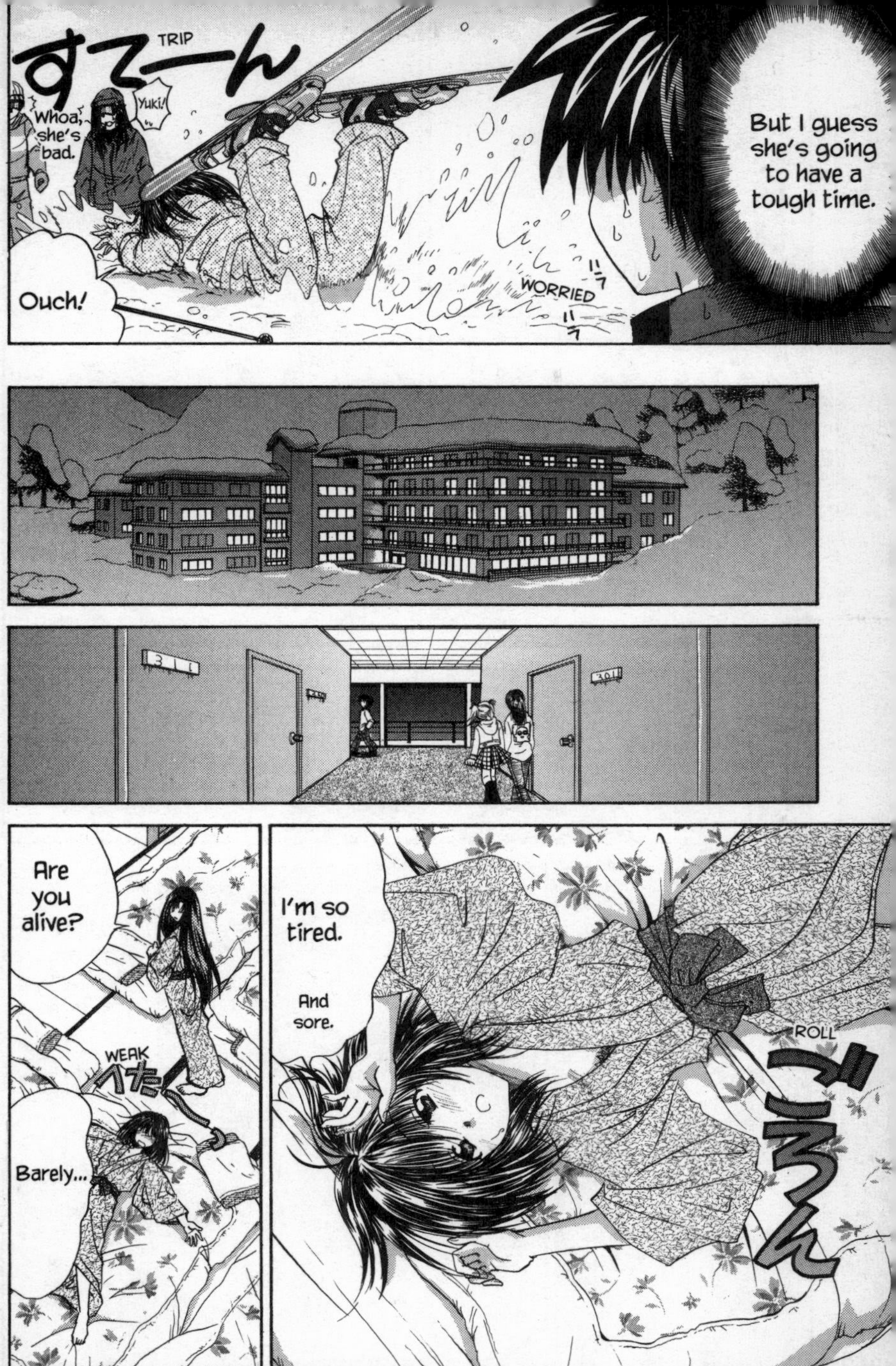
But I guess she's going to have a tough time.
すてーん
TRIP
Yuki!
Whoa, she's bad.
WORRIED
Ouch!
ROLL
ごろん
I'm so tired.
And sore.
Are you alive?
WEAK
へたー
Barely...

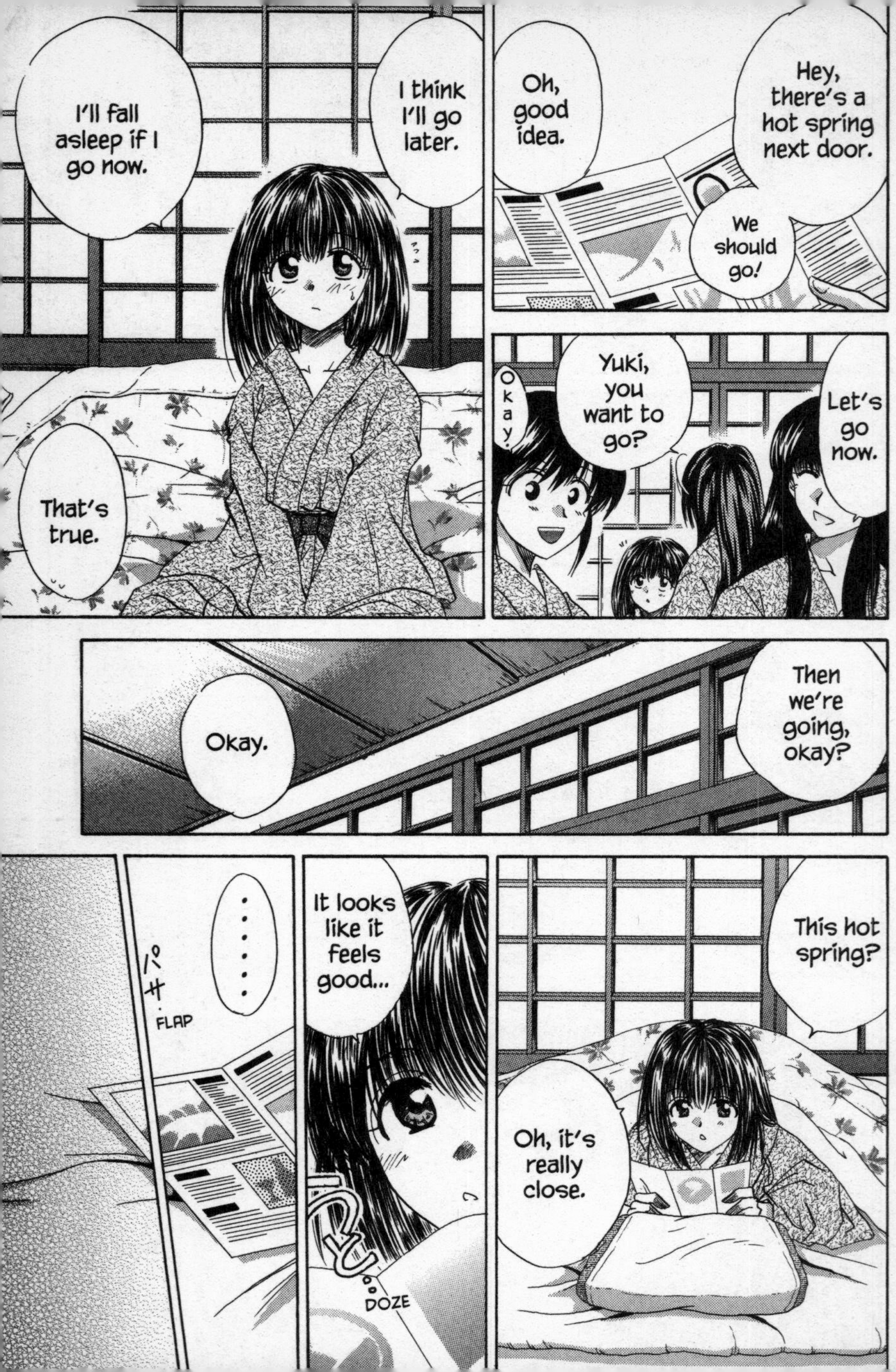
Hey, there's a hot spring next door.
We should go!
Oh, good idea.
Let's go now.
Yuki, you want to go?
Okay.
I think I'll go later.
I'll fall asleep if I go now.
That's true.
Then we're going, okay?
Okay.
This hot spring?
Oh, it's really close.
It looks like it feels good...
DOZE
......
パサ
FLAP

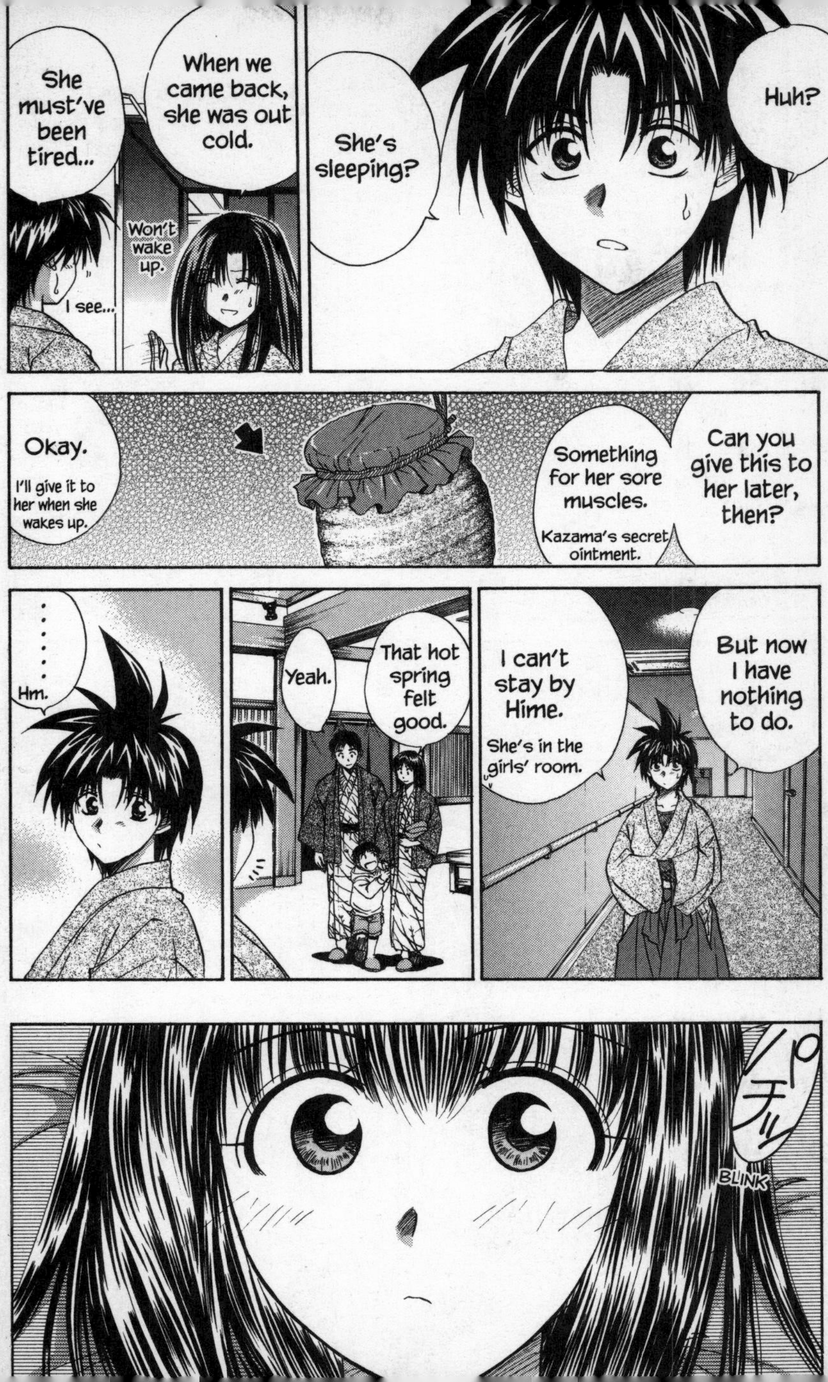
Huh?
She's sleeping?
When we came back, she was out cold.
She must've been tired...
Won't wake up.
I see...
Can you give this to her later, then?
Something for her sore muscles.
Kazama's secret ointment.
Okay.
I'll give it to her when she wakes up.
But now I have nothing to do.
I can't stay by Hime.
She's in the girls' room.
That hot spring felt good.
Yeah.
......
Hm.
BLINK

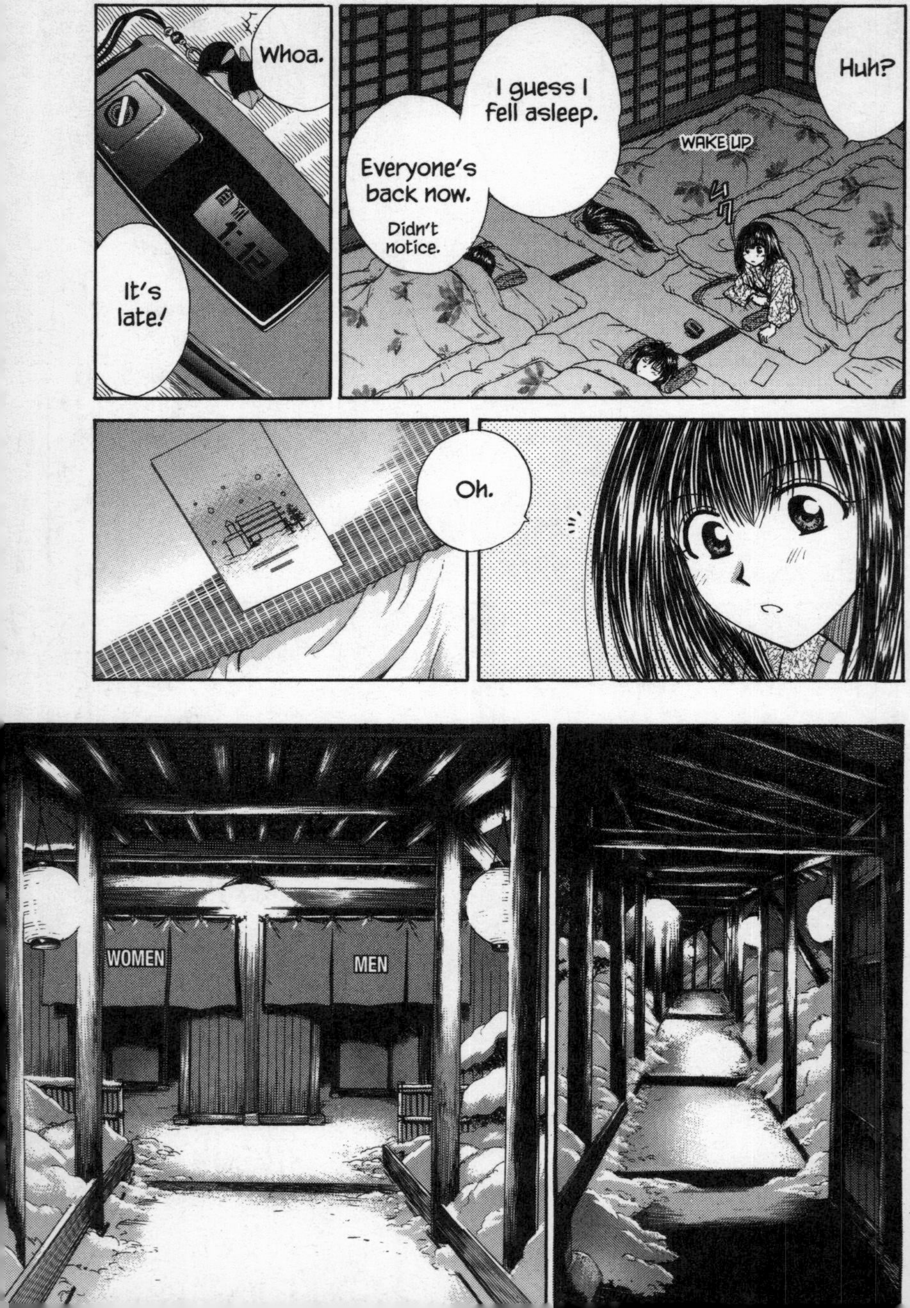
Huh?
WAKE UP
I guess I fell asleep.
Everyone's back now.
Didn't notice.
Whoa.
It's late!
Oh.
MEN
WOMEN

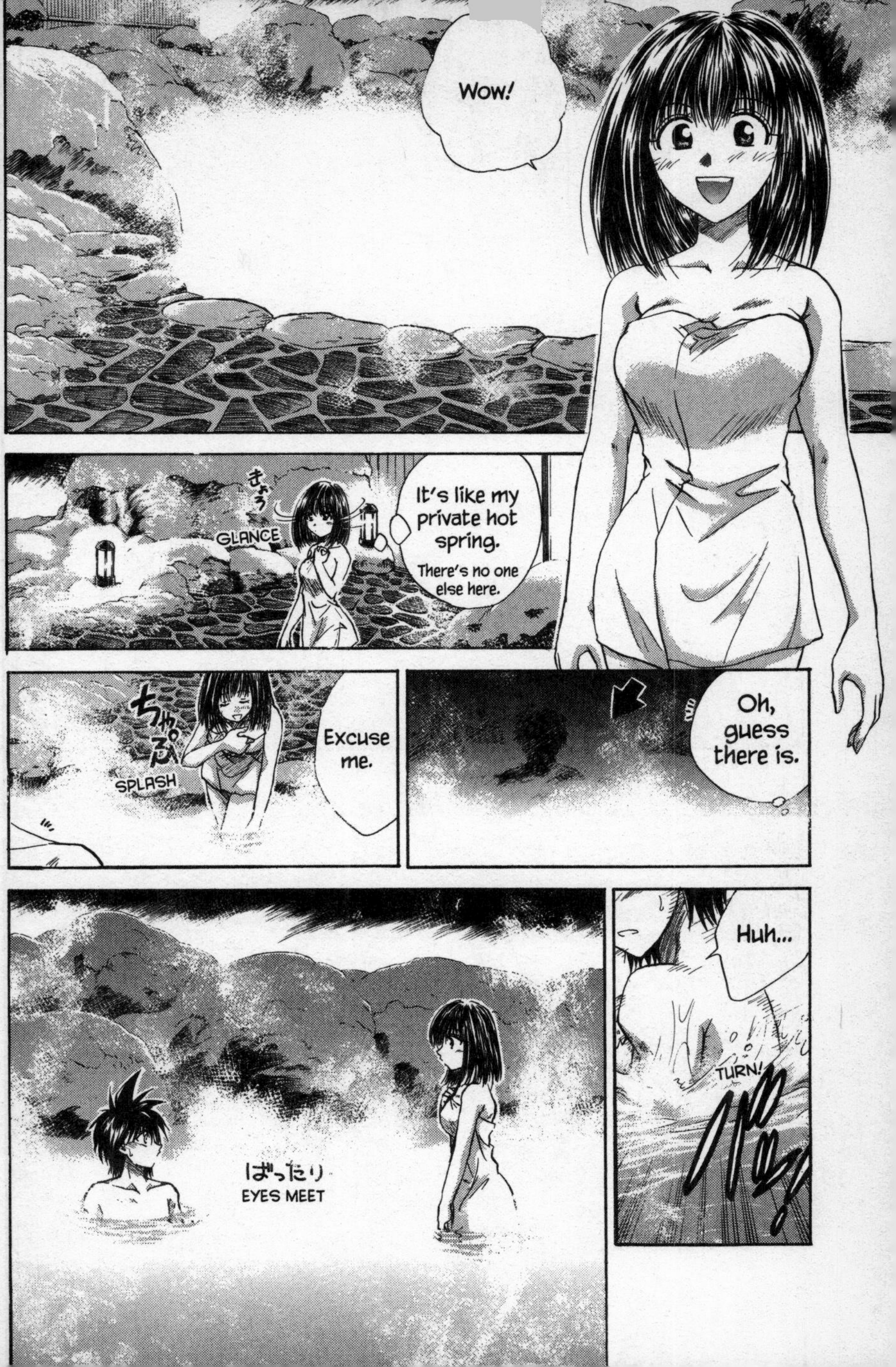
Wow!
It's like my private hot spring.
There's no one else here.
GLANCE
Oh, guess there is.
Excuse me.
SPLASH
Huh...
TURN!
ばったり
EYES MEET

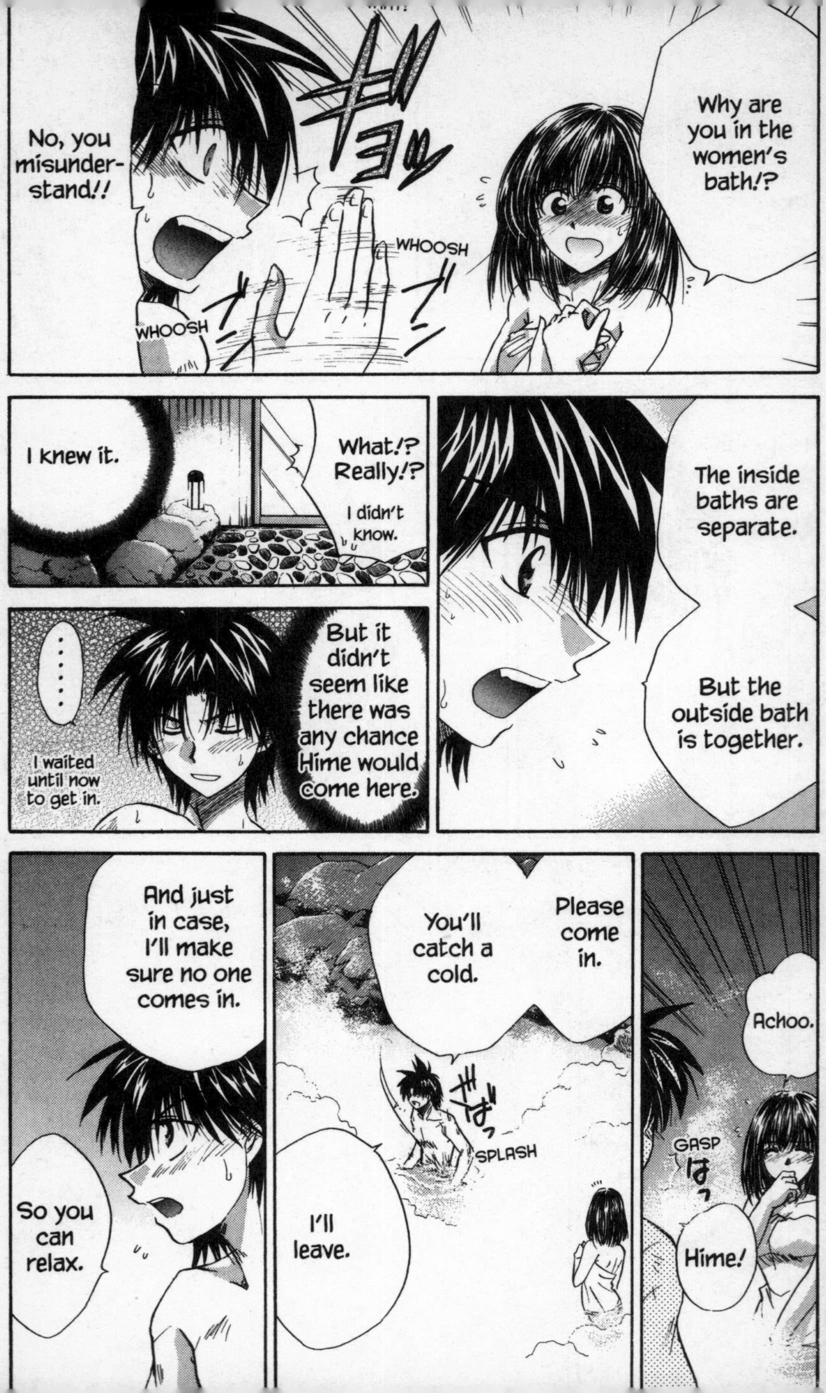

Why are you in the women's bath!?
ギョッ
No, you misunderstand!!
WHOOSH
WHOOSH
The inside baths are separate.
But the outside bath is together.
What!? Really!?
I didn't know.
I knew it.
But it didn't seem like there was any chance Hime would come here.
I waited until now to get in.
......
Achoo.
GASP
Hime!
Please come in.
You'll catch a cold.
SPLASH
I'll leave.
And just in case, I'll make sure no one comes in.
So you can relax.

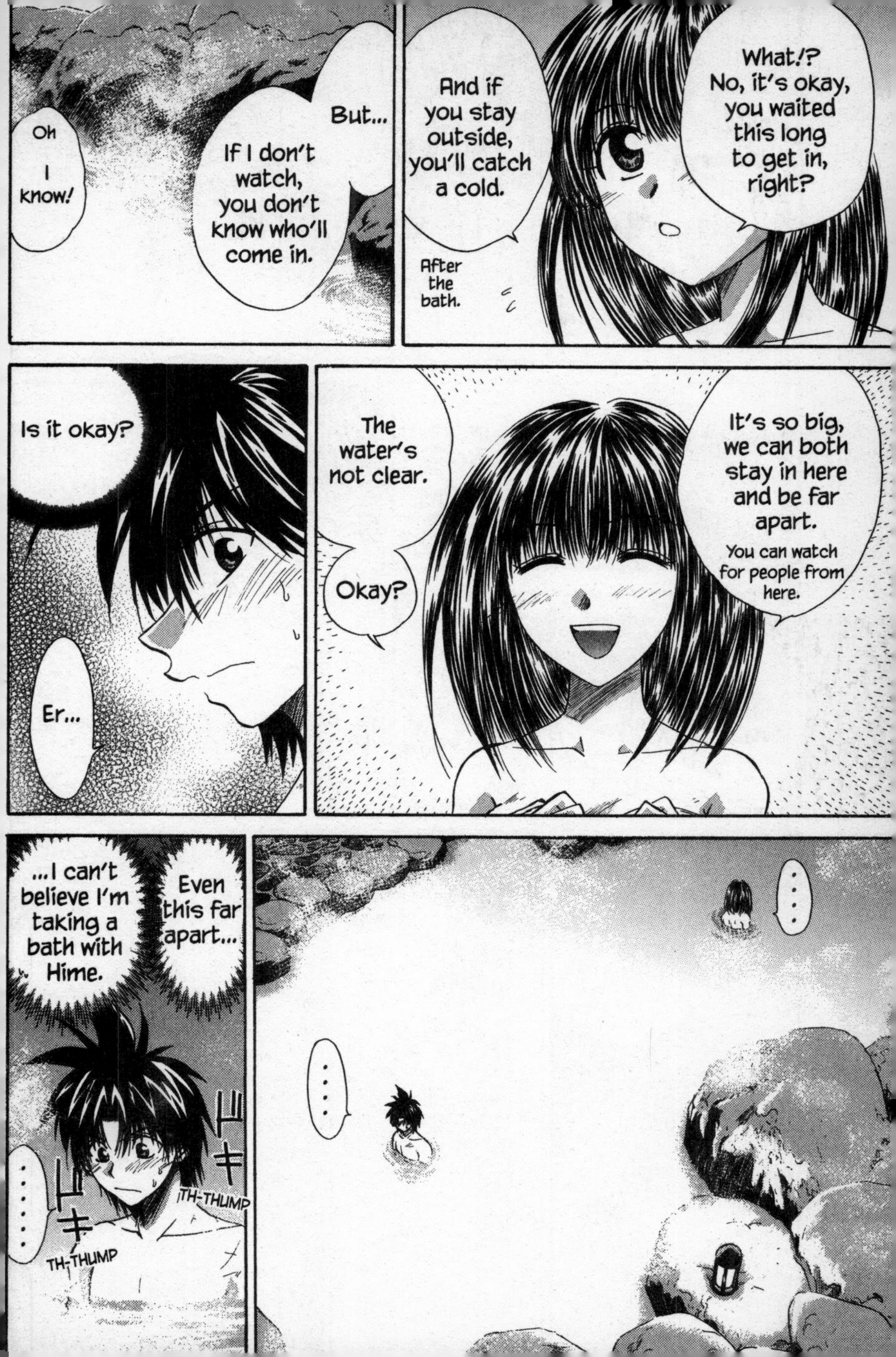
What!? No, it's okay, you waited this long to get in, right?
And if you stay outside, you'll catch a cold.
After the bath.
But...
If I don't watch, you don't know who'll come in.
Oh I know!
It's so big, we can both stay in here and be far apart.
You can watch for people from here.
The water's not clear.
Okay?
Is it okay?
Er...
....
....
Even this far apart...
...I can't believe I'm taking a bath with Hime.
TH-THUMP
TH-THUMP
......

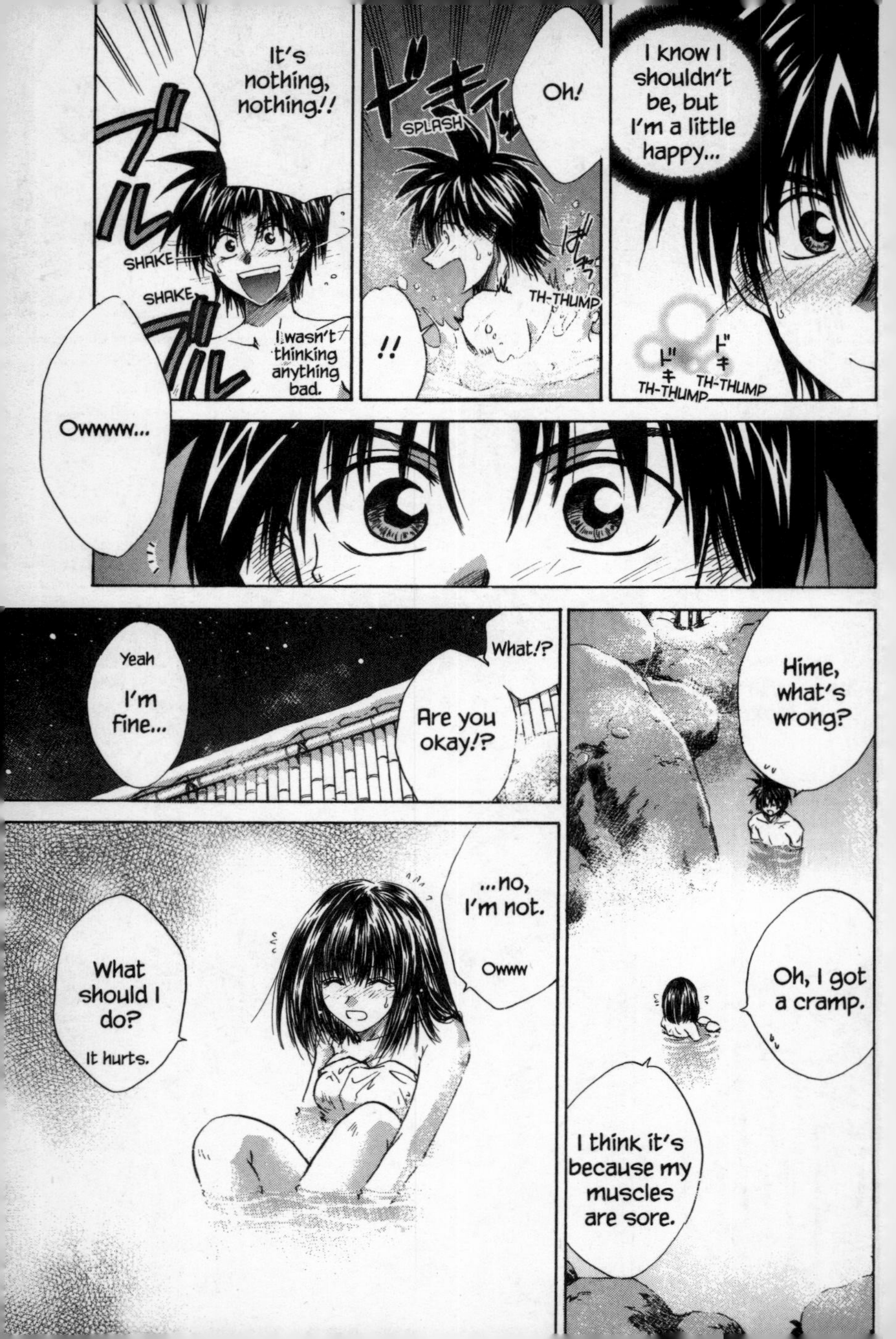
I know I shouldn't be, but I'm a little happy...
ドキ
ドキ
TH-THUMP
TH-THUMP
Oh!
SPLASH
TH-THUMP
!!
It's nothing, nothing!!
SHAKE
SHAKE
I wasn't thinking anything bad.
Owwww...
Hime, what's wrong?
Oh, I got a cramp.
I think it's because my muscles are sore.
What!?
Are you okay!?
Yeah
I'm fine...
...no, I'm not.
Owww
What should I do?
It hurts.

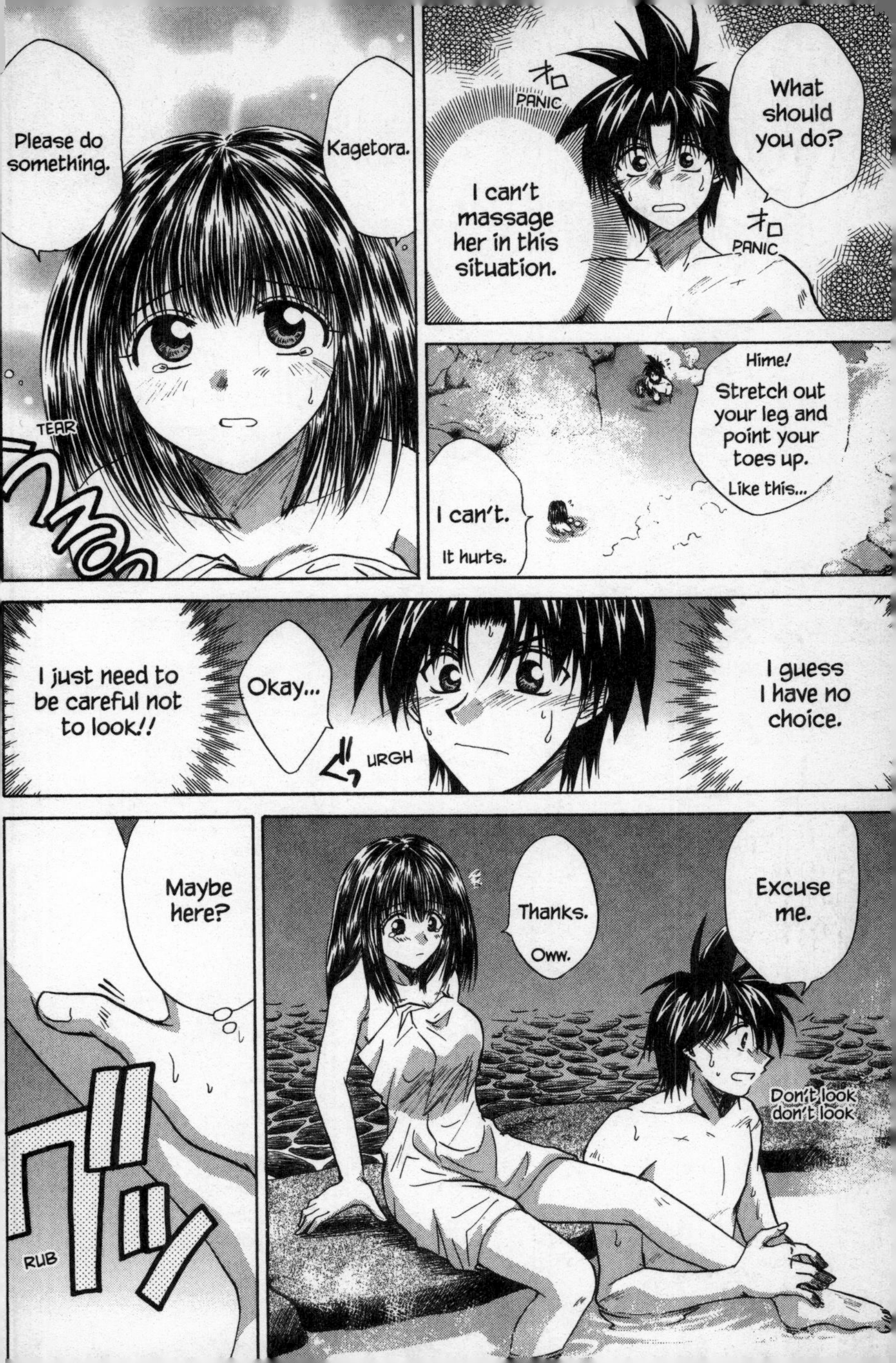

What should you do?
オロ
PANIC
I can't massage her in this situation.
オロ
PANIC
Hime!
Stretch out your leg and point your toes up.
Like this...
I can't.
It hurts.
Kagetora.
Please do something.
TEAR
I guess I have no choice.
Okay...
URGH
I just need to be careful not to look!!
Excuse me.
Thanks.
Oww.
Don't look don't look
Maybe here?
RUB

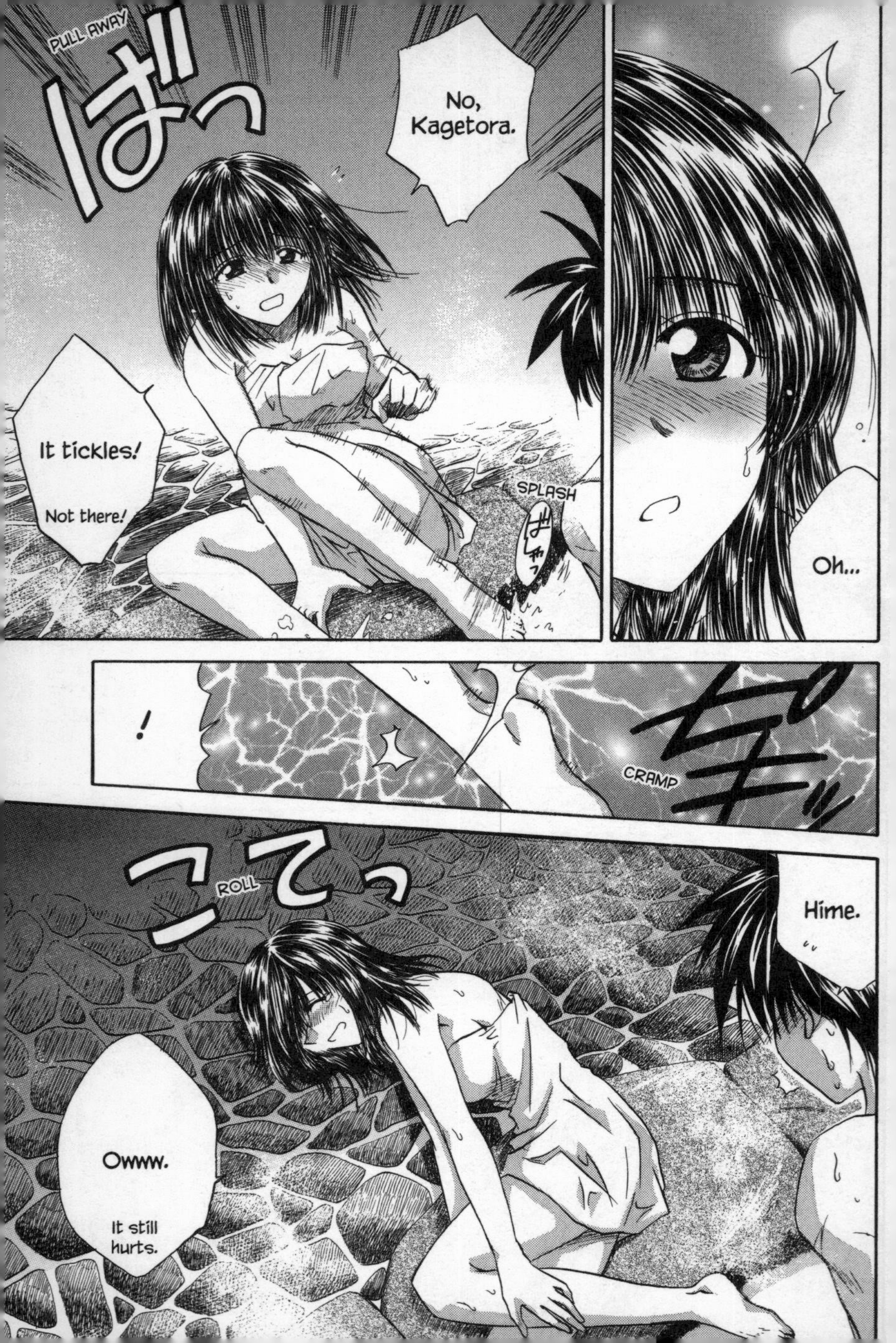

Oh...
PULL AWAY
ばっ
No, Kagetora.
It tickles!
Not there!
SPLASH
ばしゃっ
CRAMP
!
Hime.
こてっ
ROLL
Owww.
It still hurts.

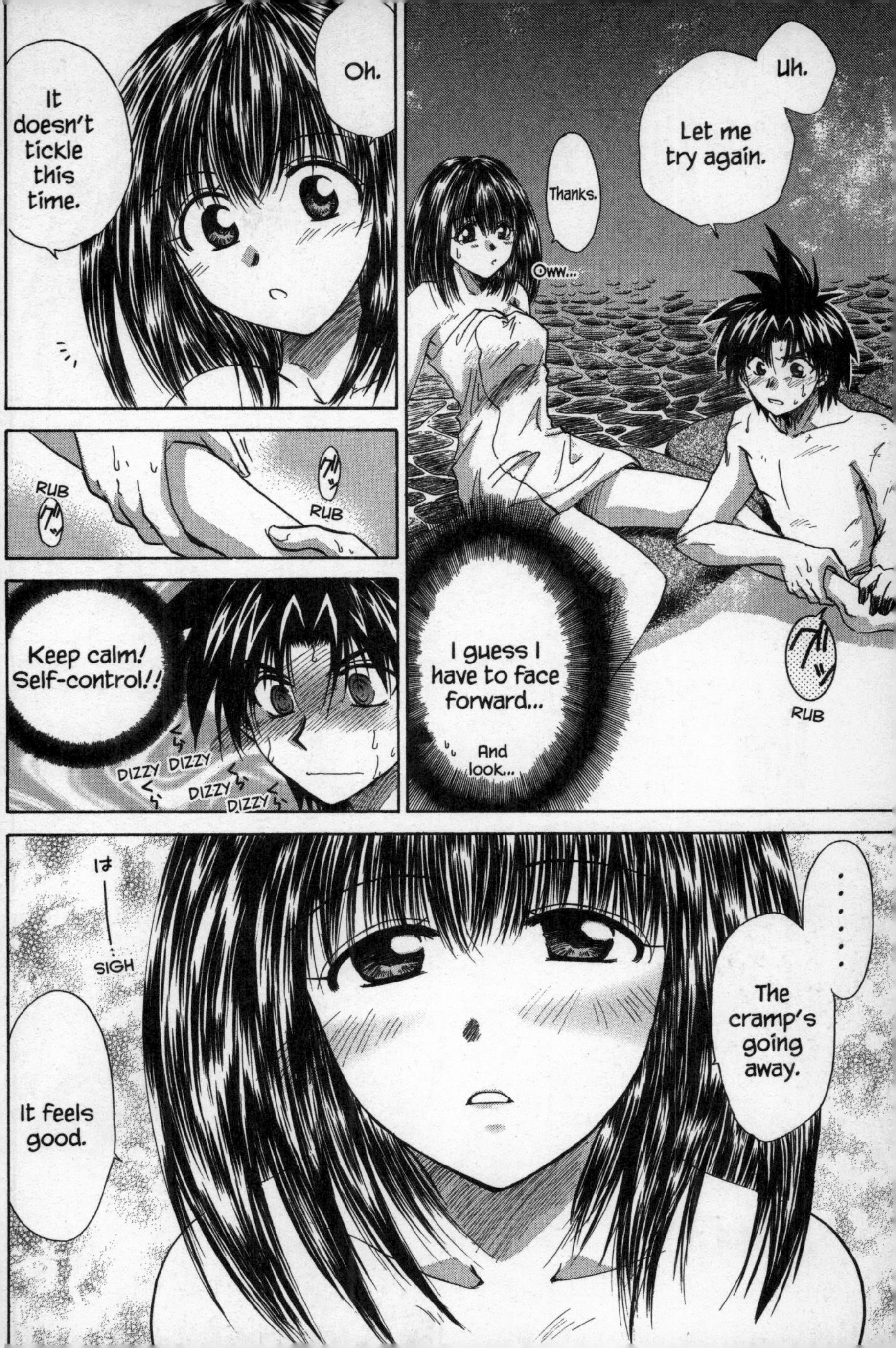
Uh.
Let me try again.
Thanks.
Oww...
RUB
I guess I have to face forward...
And look...
Oh.
It doesn't tickle this time.
RUB
RUB
Keep calm! Self-control!!
DIZZY DIZZY
DIZZY
DIZZY
......
The cramp's going away.
は—
SIGH
It feels good.

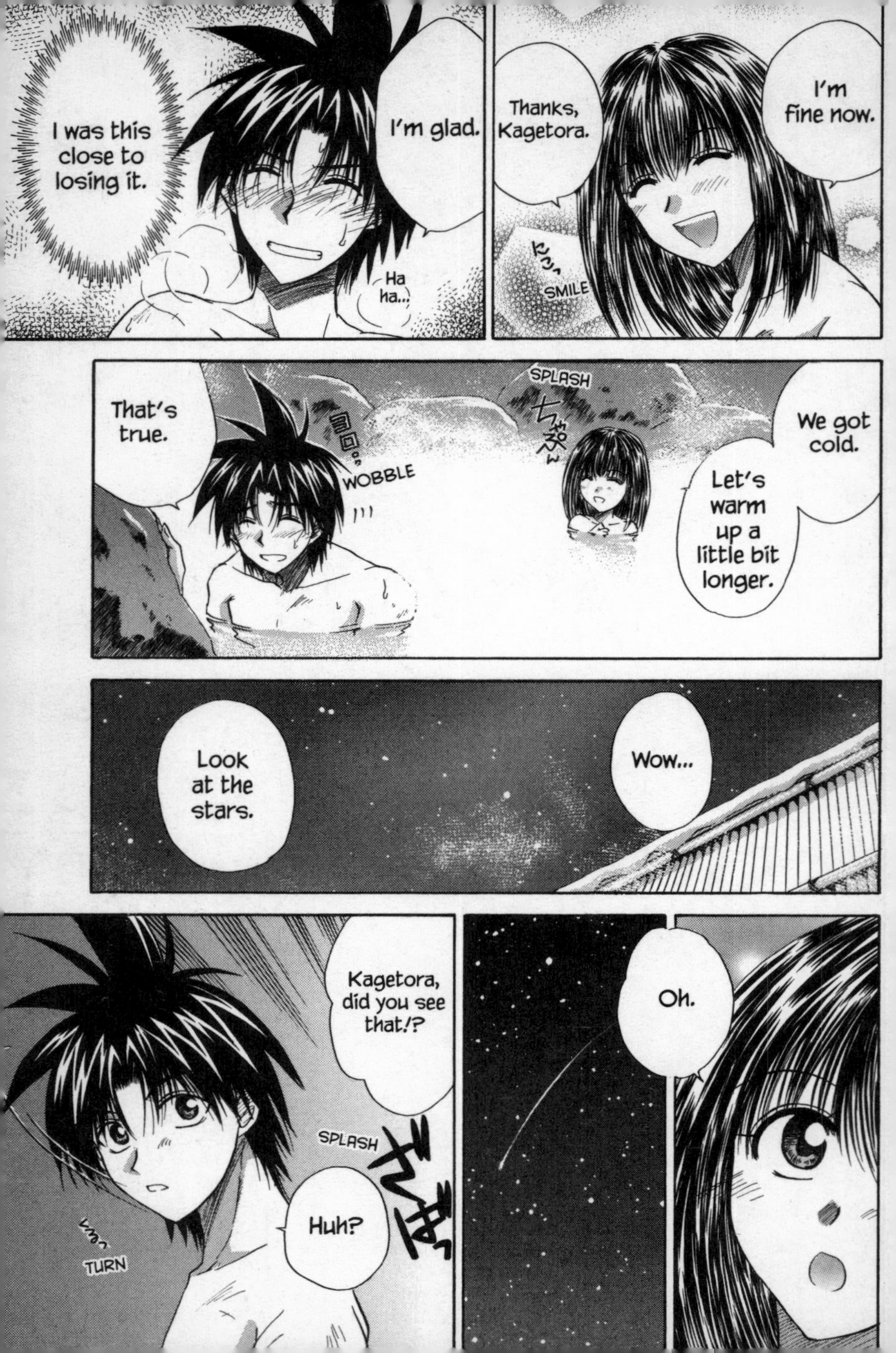
I'm fine now.
Thanks, Kagetora.
SMILE
I'm glad.
I was this close to losing it.
Ha ha...
We got cold.
Let's warm up a little bit longer.
SPLASH
WOBBLE
That's true.
Wow...
Look at the stars.
Oh.
Kagetora, did you see that!?
SPLASH
Huh?
TURN

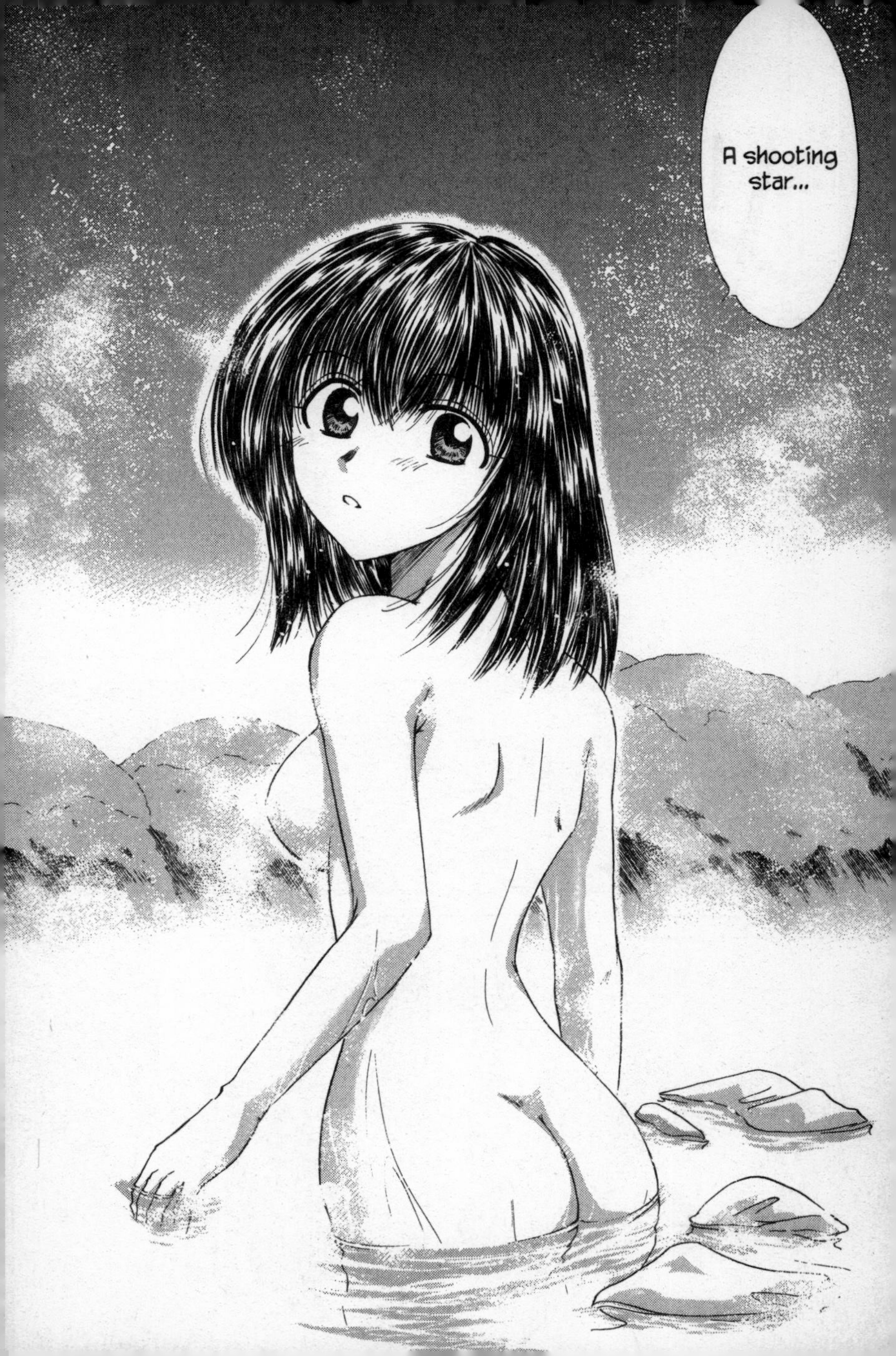
A shooting star...

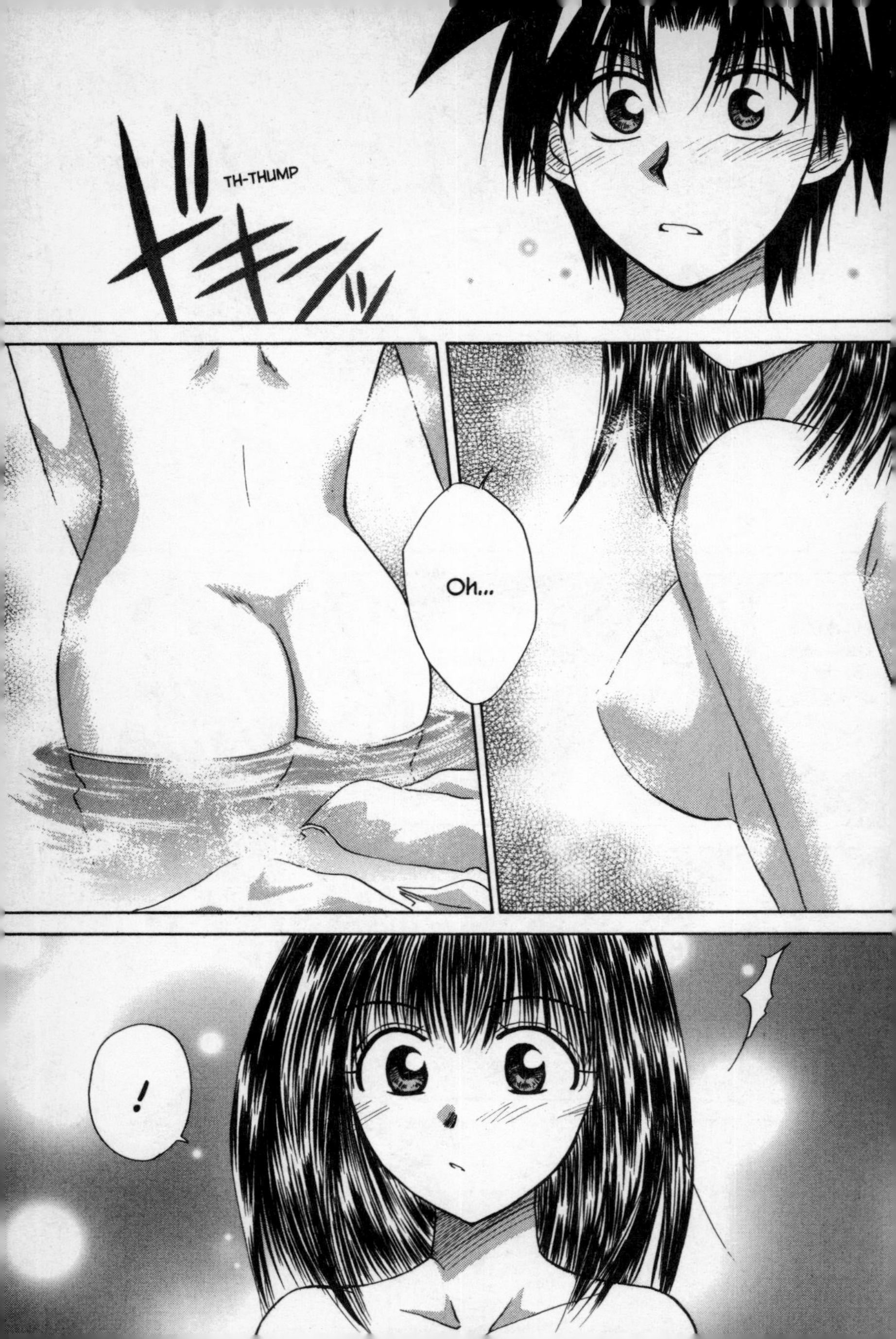
ドキッ
TH-THUMP
Oh...
!

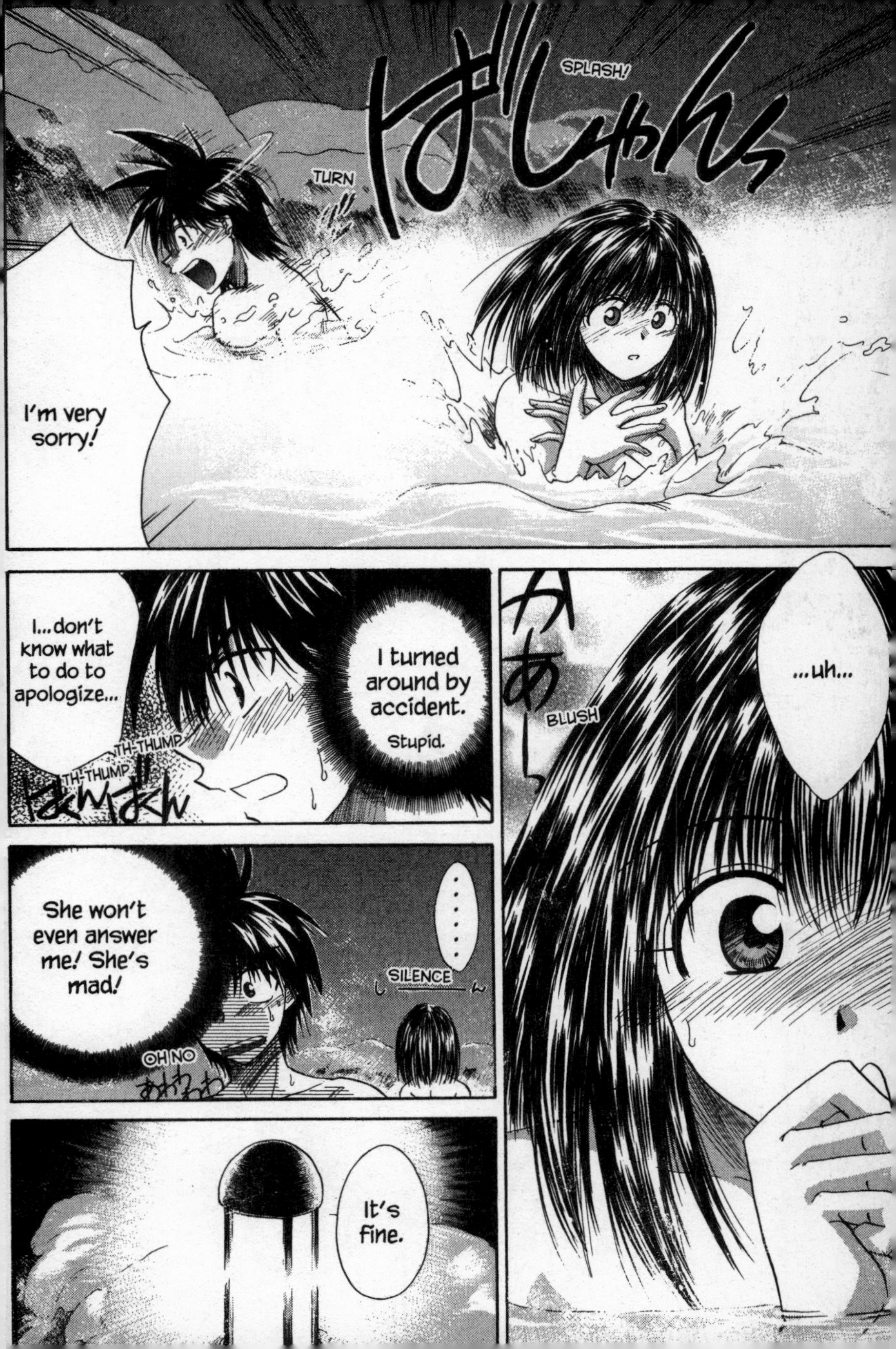

SPLASH!
TURN
I'm very sorry!
...uh...
BLUSH
I turned around by accident.
Stupid.
I...don't know what to do to apologize...
TH-THUMP
TH-THUMP
......
SILENCE
She won't even answer me! She's mad!
OH NO
It's fine.

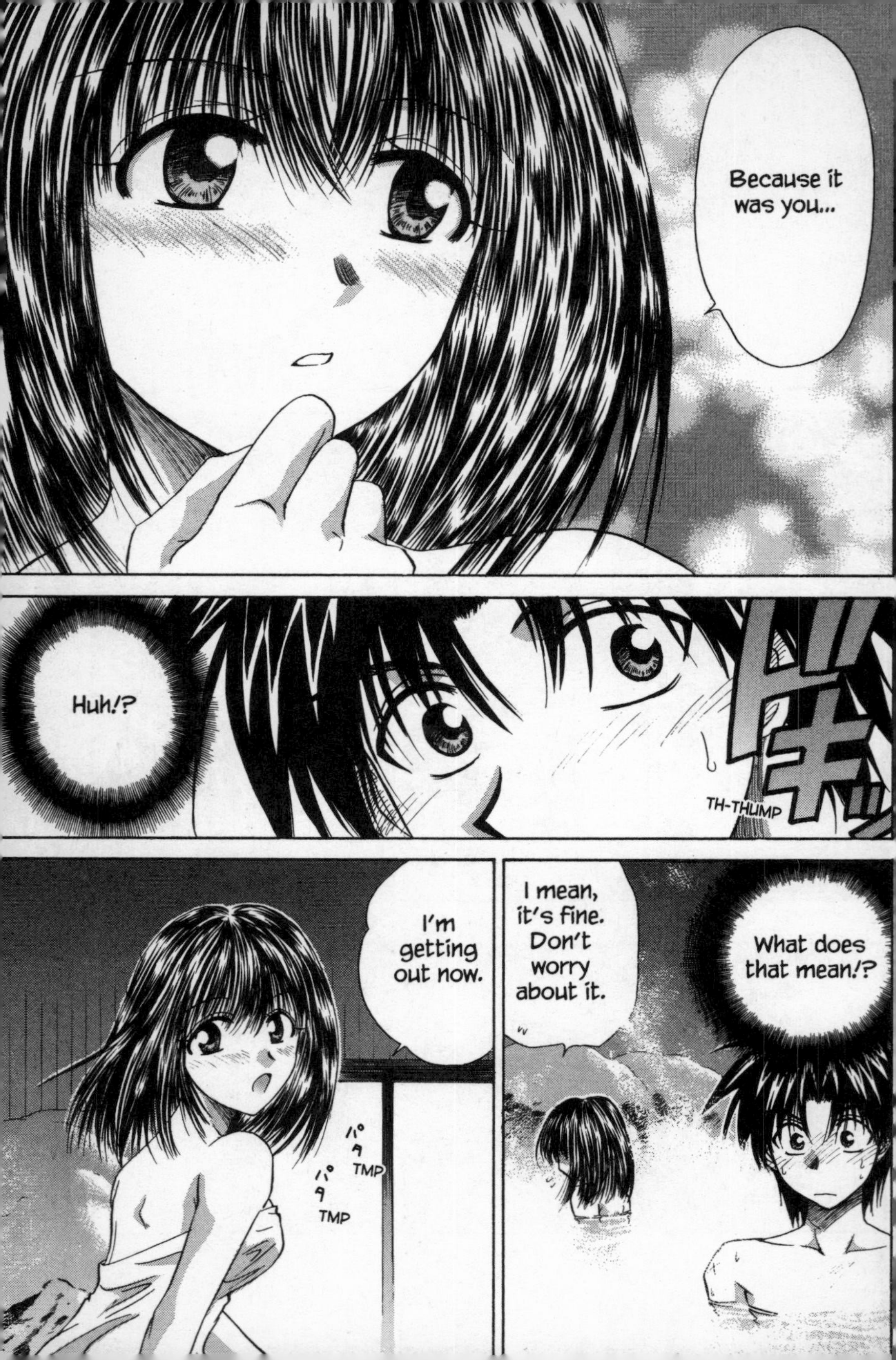
Because it was you...
Huh!?
TH-THUMP
What does that mean!?
I mean, it's fine. Don't worry about it.
I'm getting out now.
パタ
TMP
パタ
TMP

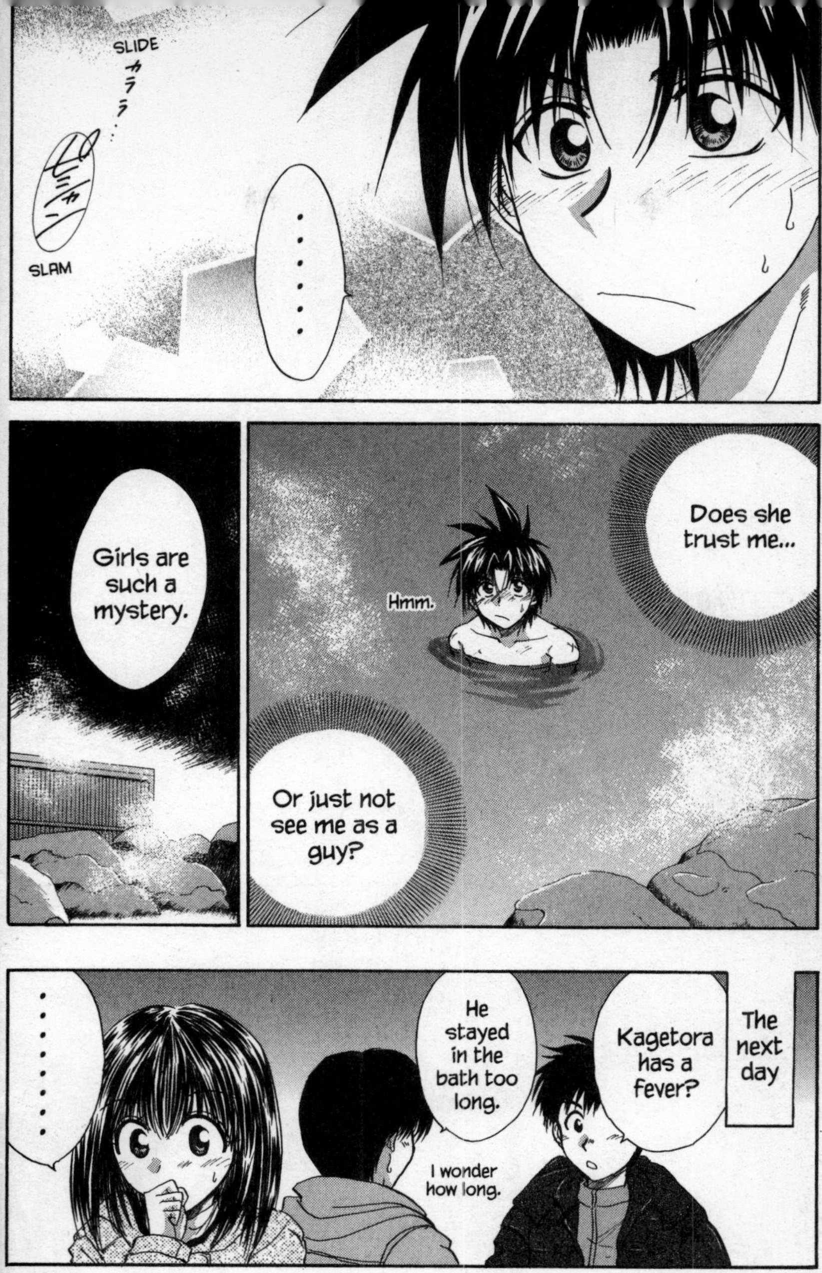
SLIDE
カララ…
SLAM
……
Does she trust me...
Hmm.
Or just not see me as a guy?
Girls are such a mystery.
The next day
Kagetora has a fever?
He stayed in the bath too long.
I wonder how long.
……

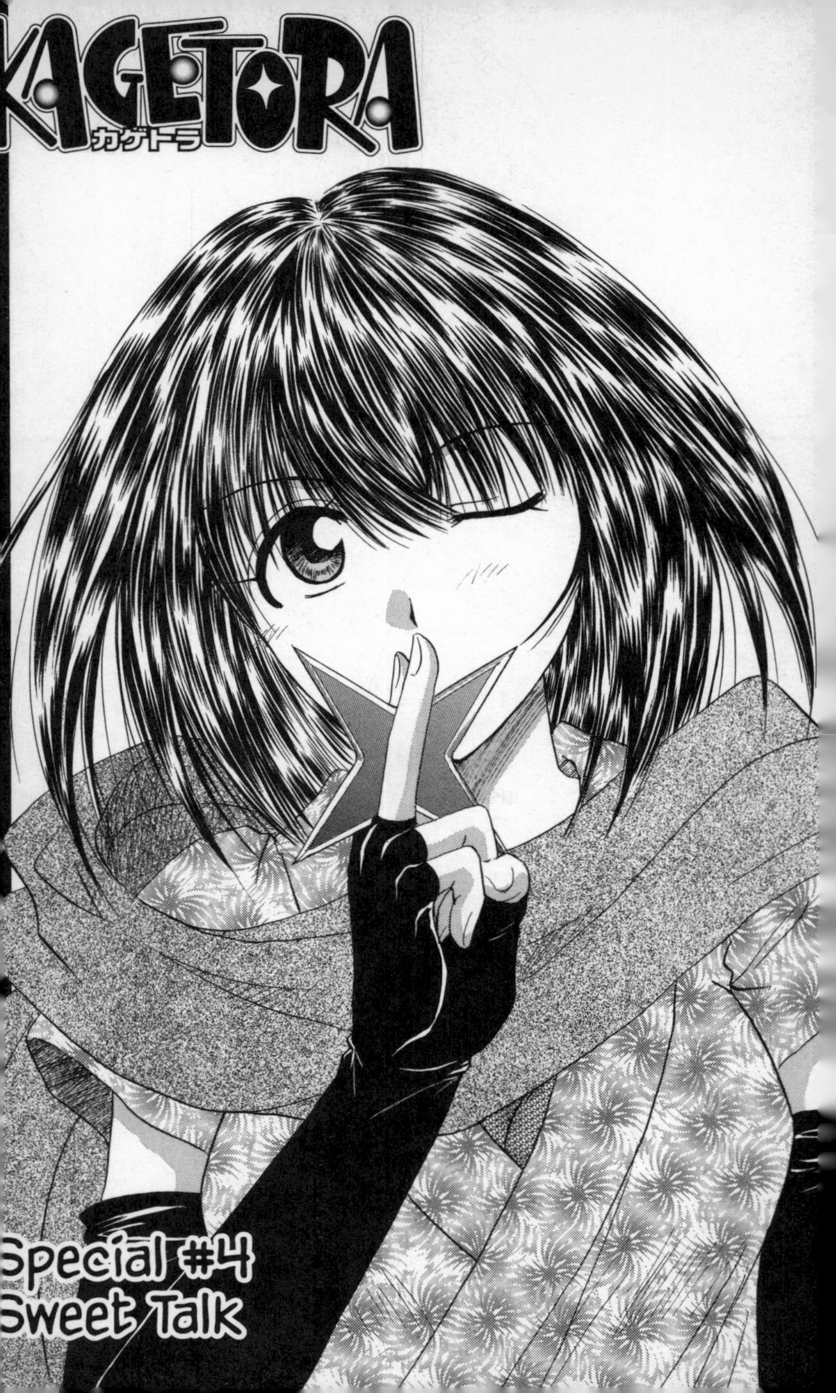
KAGETORA
カゲトラ
Special #4
Sweet Talk

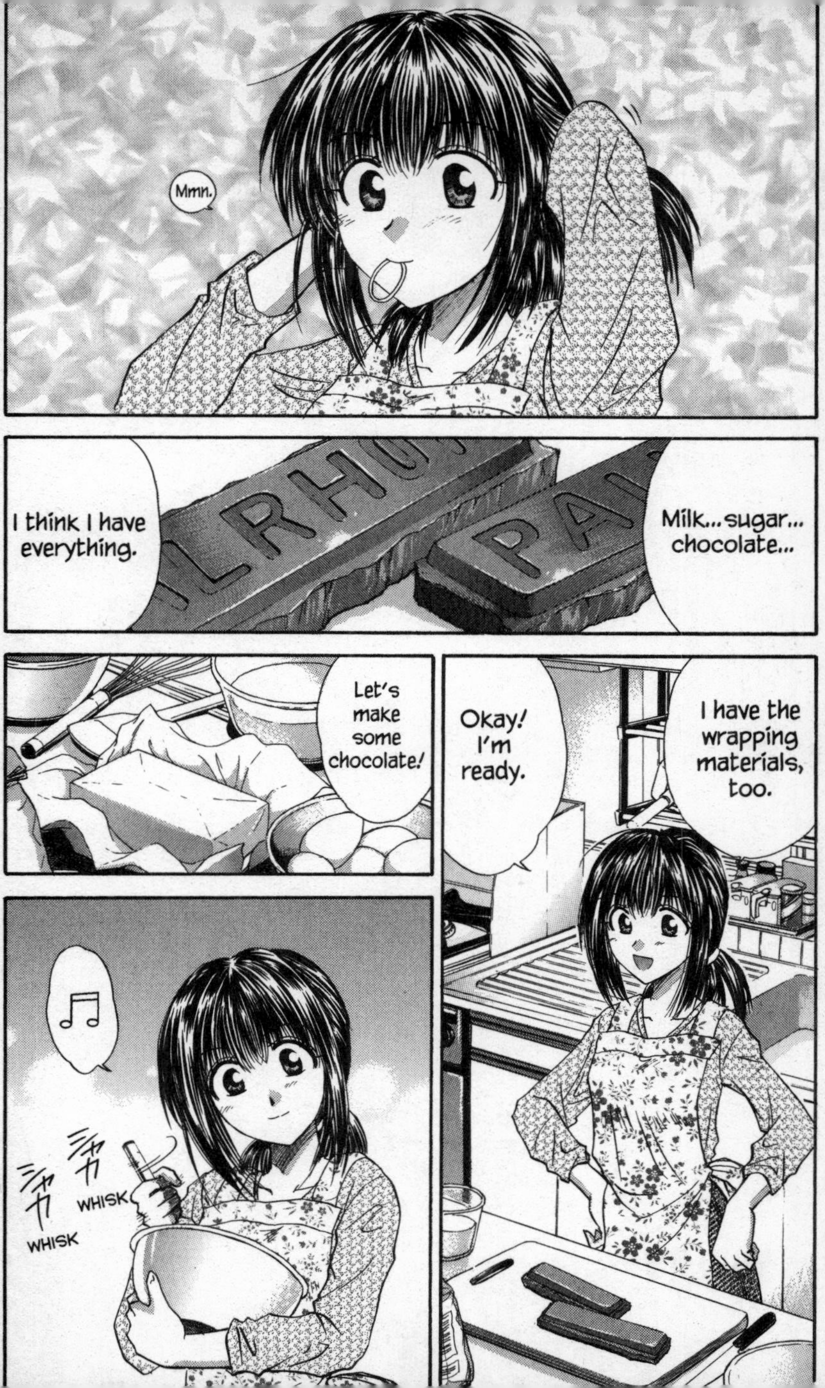
Mmn.
Milk...sugar... chocolate...
I think I have everything.
I have the wrapping materials, too.
Okay! I'm ready.
Let's make some chocolate!
♫
シャカ
WHISK
シャカ
WHISK

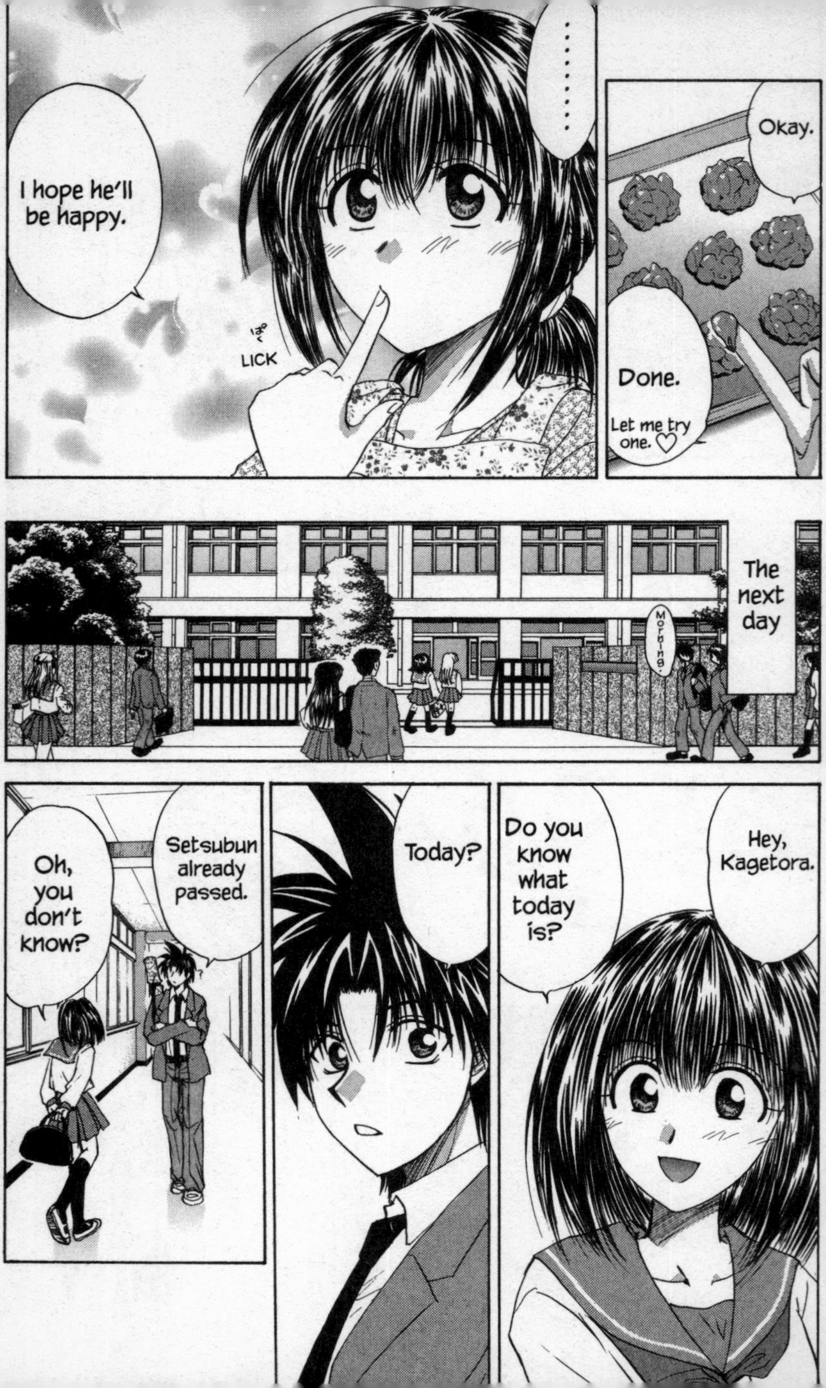
Okay.
Done.
Let me try one. ♡
......
I hope he'll be happy.
LICK
The next day
Morning.
Hey, Kagetora.
Do you know what today is?
Today?
Setsubun already passed.
Oh, you don't know?

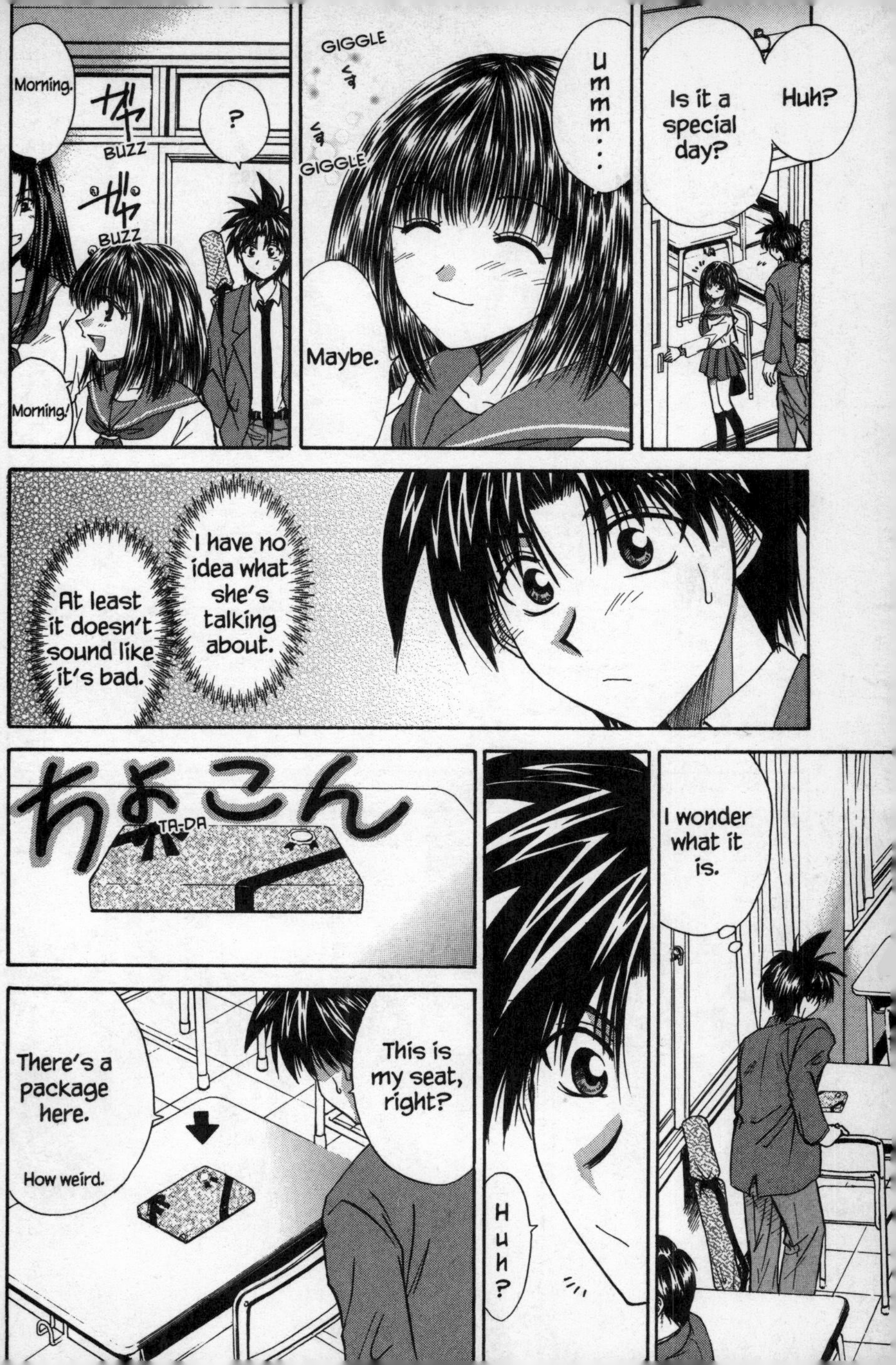

Huh?
Is it a special day?
Ummm...
GIGGLE
くす
くす
GIGGLE
Maybe.
?
BUZZ
BUZZ
Morning.
Morning!
I have no idea what she's talking about.
At least it doesn't sound like it's bad.
I wonder what it is.
Huh?
ちょこん
TA-DA
This is my seat, right?
There's a package here.
How weird.

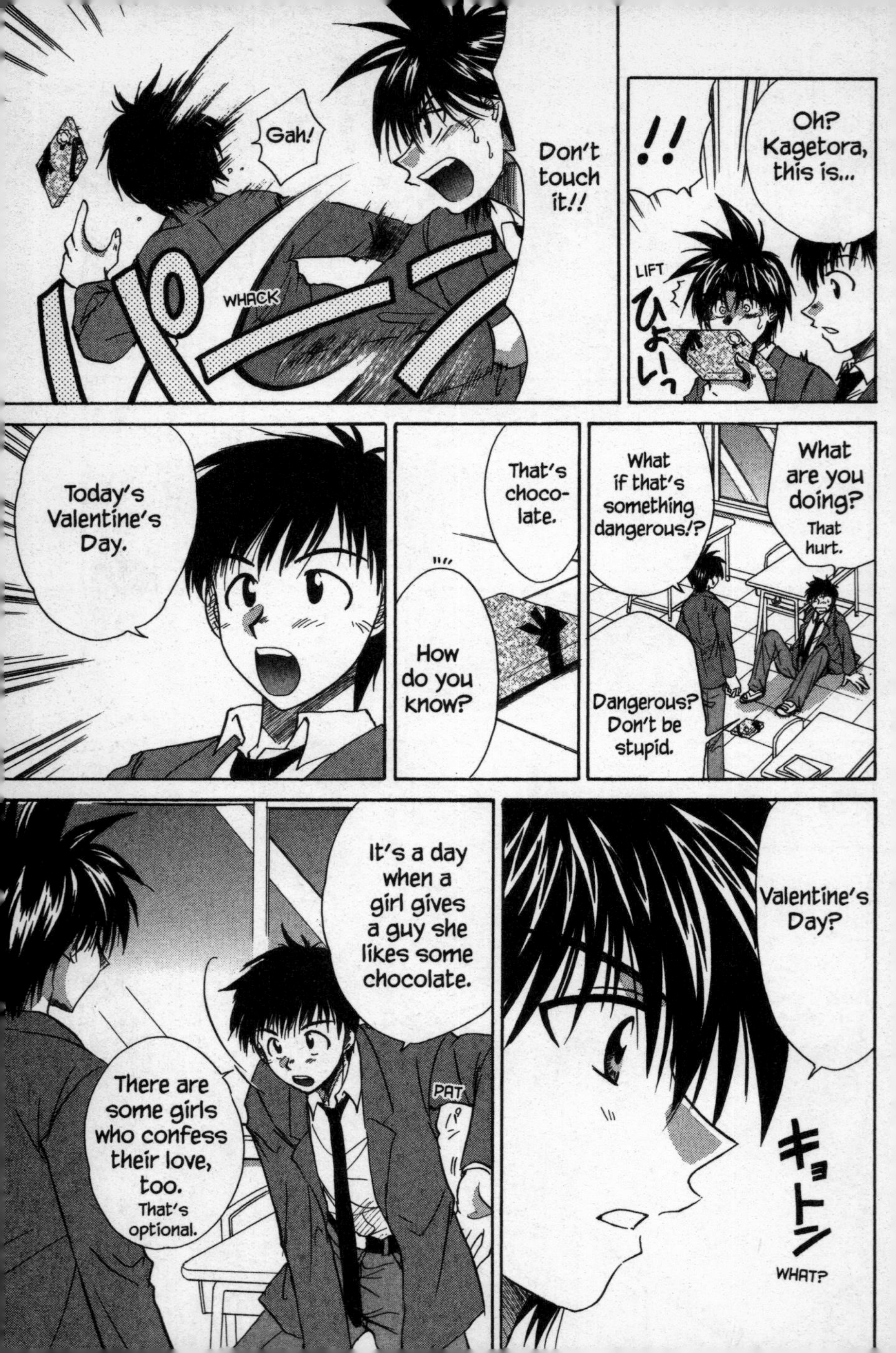

Oh? Kagetora, this is...
!!
LIFT
ひょーいっ
Don't touch it!!
Gah!
WHACK
What are you doing? That hurt.
What if that's something dangerous!?
Dangerous? Don't be stupid.
That's choco-late.
How do you know?
Today's Valentine's Day.
Valentine's Day?
キョトン
WHAT?
It's a day when a girl gives a guy she likes some chocolate.
There are some girls who confess their love, too. That's optional.
PAT
パ

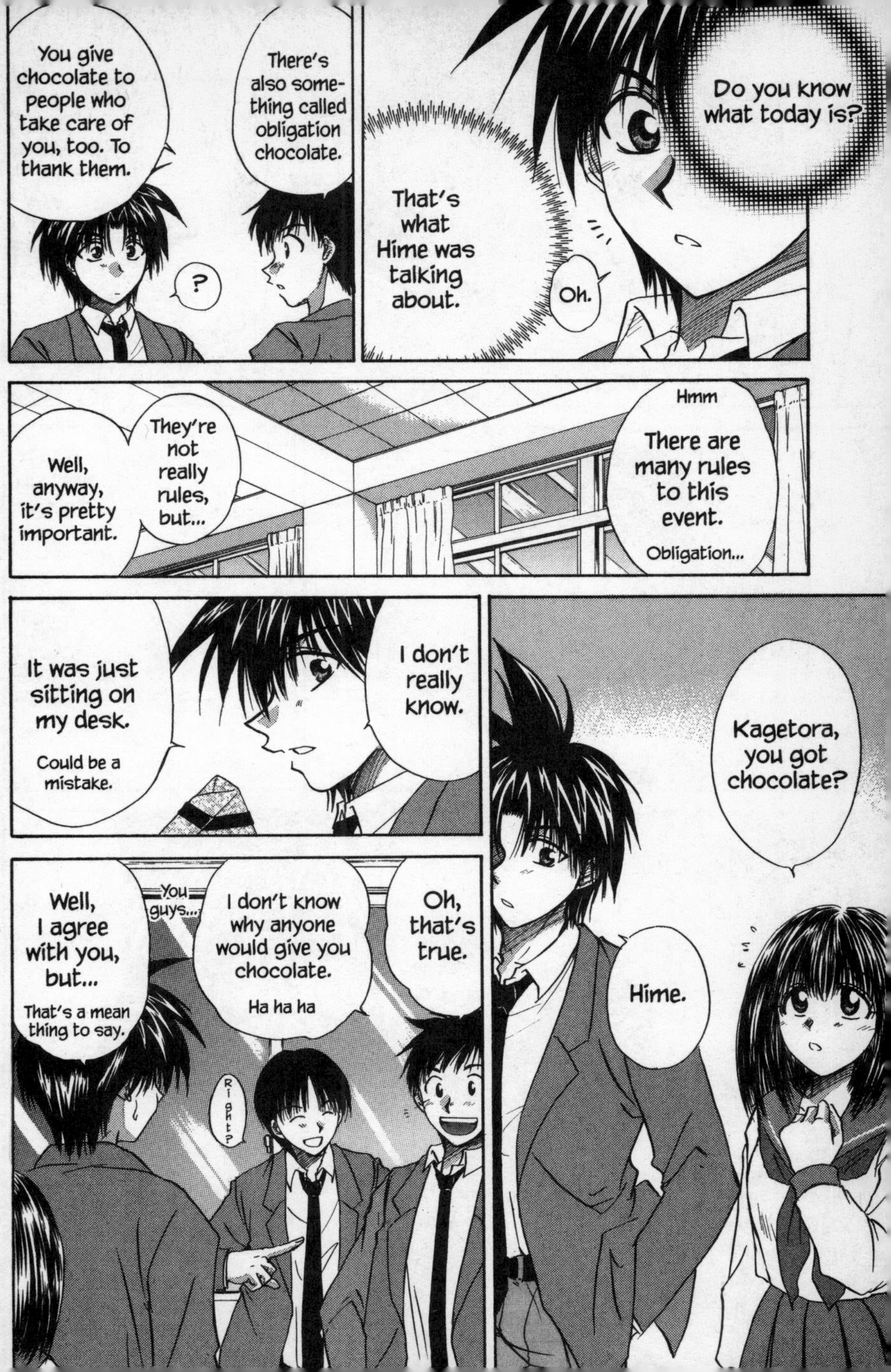
Do you know what today is?
Oh.
That's what Hime was talking about.
There's also something called obligation chocolate.
You give chocolate to people who take care of you, too. To thank them.
?
Hmm
There are many rules to this event.
Obligation...
They're not really rules, but...
Well, anyway, it's pretty important.
Kagetora, you got chocolate?
Hime.
I don't really know.
It was just sitting on my desk.
Could be a mistake.
Oh, that's true.
I don't know why anyone would give you chocolate.
Ha ha ha
Right?
You guys...
Well, I agree with you, but...
That's a mean thing to say.

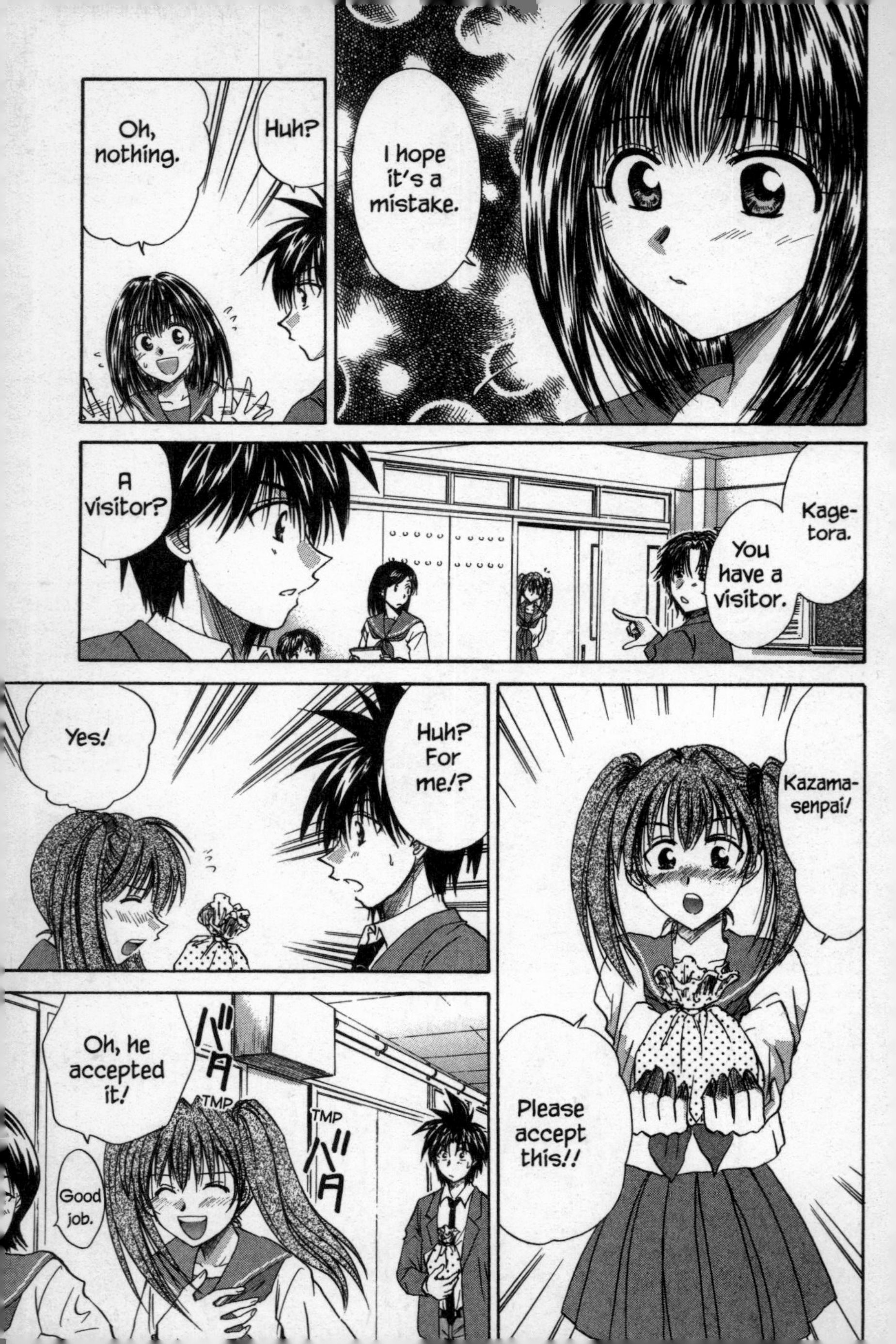

I hope it's a mistake.
Huh?
Oh, nothing.
Kage-tora.
You have a visitor.
A visitor?
Kazama-senpai!
Please accept this!!
Huh? For me!?
Yes!
バタ
TMP
バタ
TMP
Oh, he accepted it!
Good job.

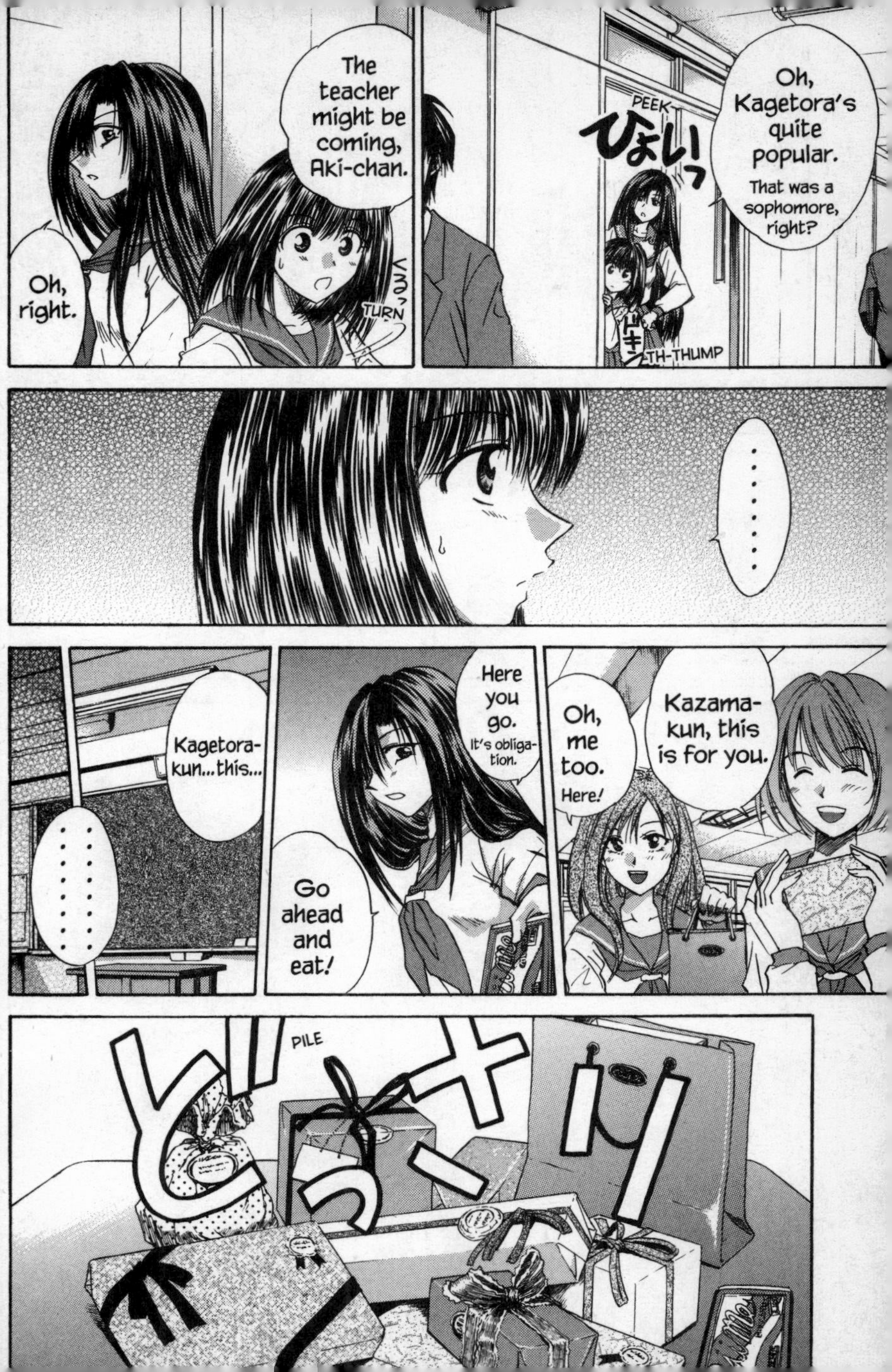
Oh, Kagetora's quite popular.
That was a sophomore, right?
ひょいっ
PEEK
ドキン
TH-THUMP
The teacher might be coming, Aki-chan.
TURN
Oh, right.
......
Kazama-kun, this is for you.
Oh, me too.
Here!
Here you go.
It's obligation.
Go ahead and eat!
Kagetora-kun...this...
......
PILE

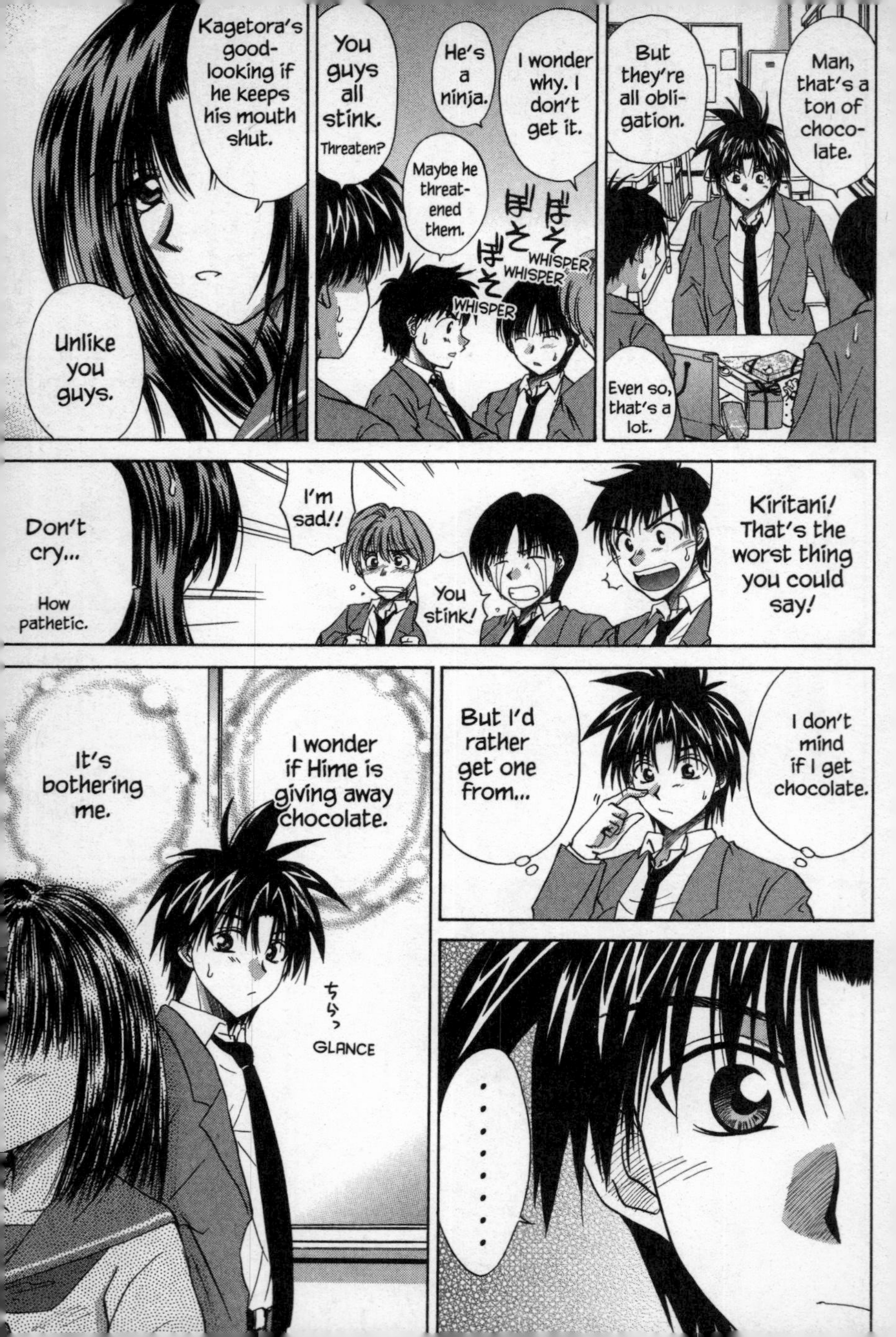

Man, that's a ton of chocolate.
But they're all obligation.
Even so, that's a lot.
I wonder why. I don't get it.
He's a ninja.
Maybe he threatened them.
ぼそ ぼそ ぼそ
WHISPER WHISPER WHISPER
You guys all stink.
Threaten?
Kagetora's good-looking if he keeps his mouth shut.
Unlike you guys.
Kiritani! That's the worst thing you could say!
I'm sad!!
You stink!
Don't cry...
How pathetic.
I don't mind if I get chocolate.
But I'd rather get one from...
I wonder if Hime is giving away chocolate.
It's bothering me.
ちらっ
GLANCE
....

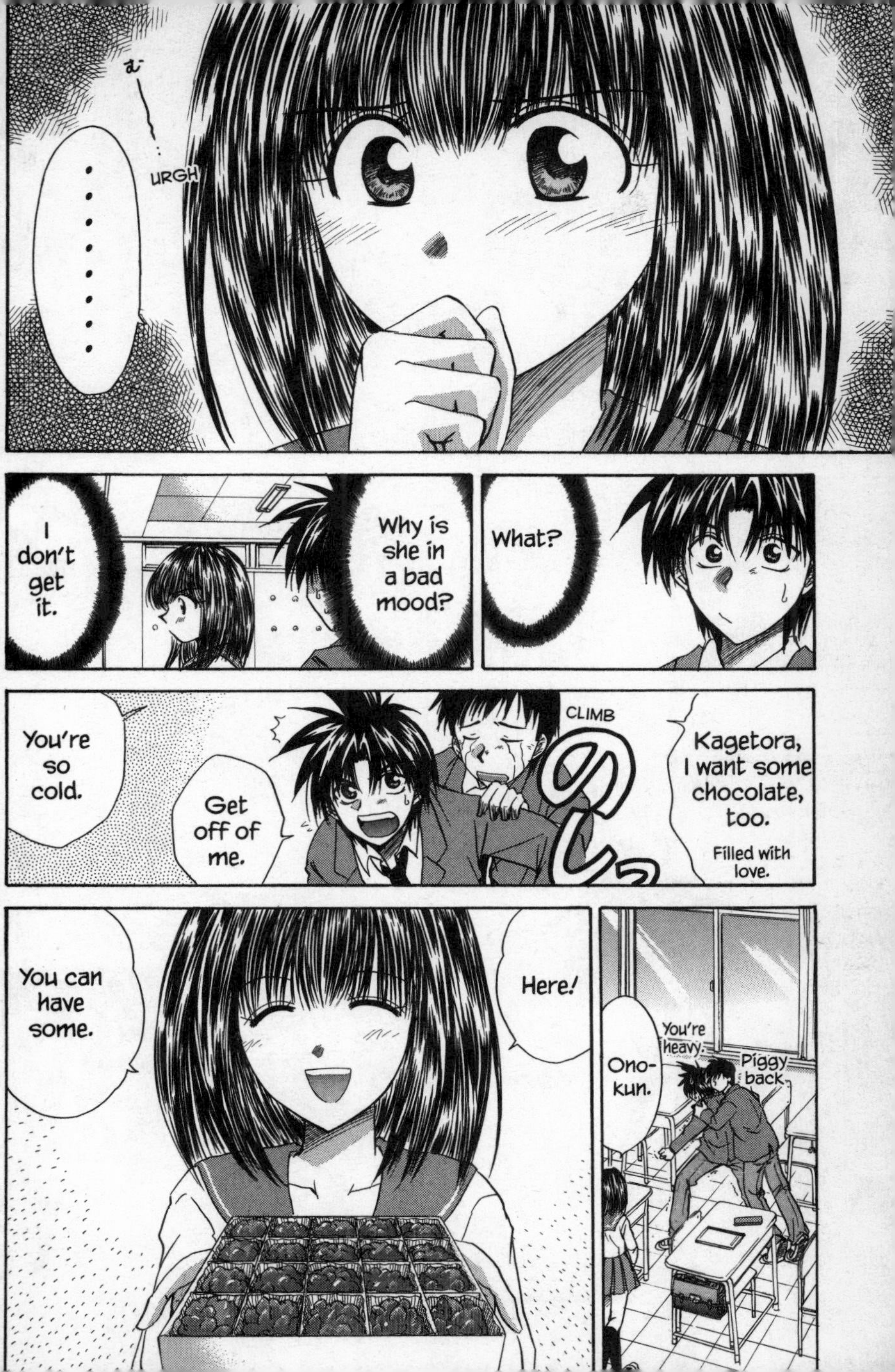

URGH
....
What?
Why is she in a bad mood?
I don't get it.
Kagetora, I want some chocolate, too.
Filled with love.
CLIMB
Get off of me.
You're so cold.
Piggy back
You're heavy.
Ono-kun.
Here!
You can have some.

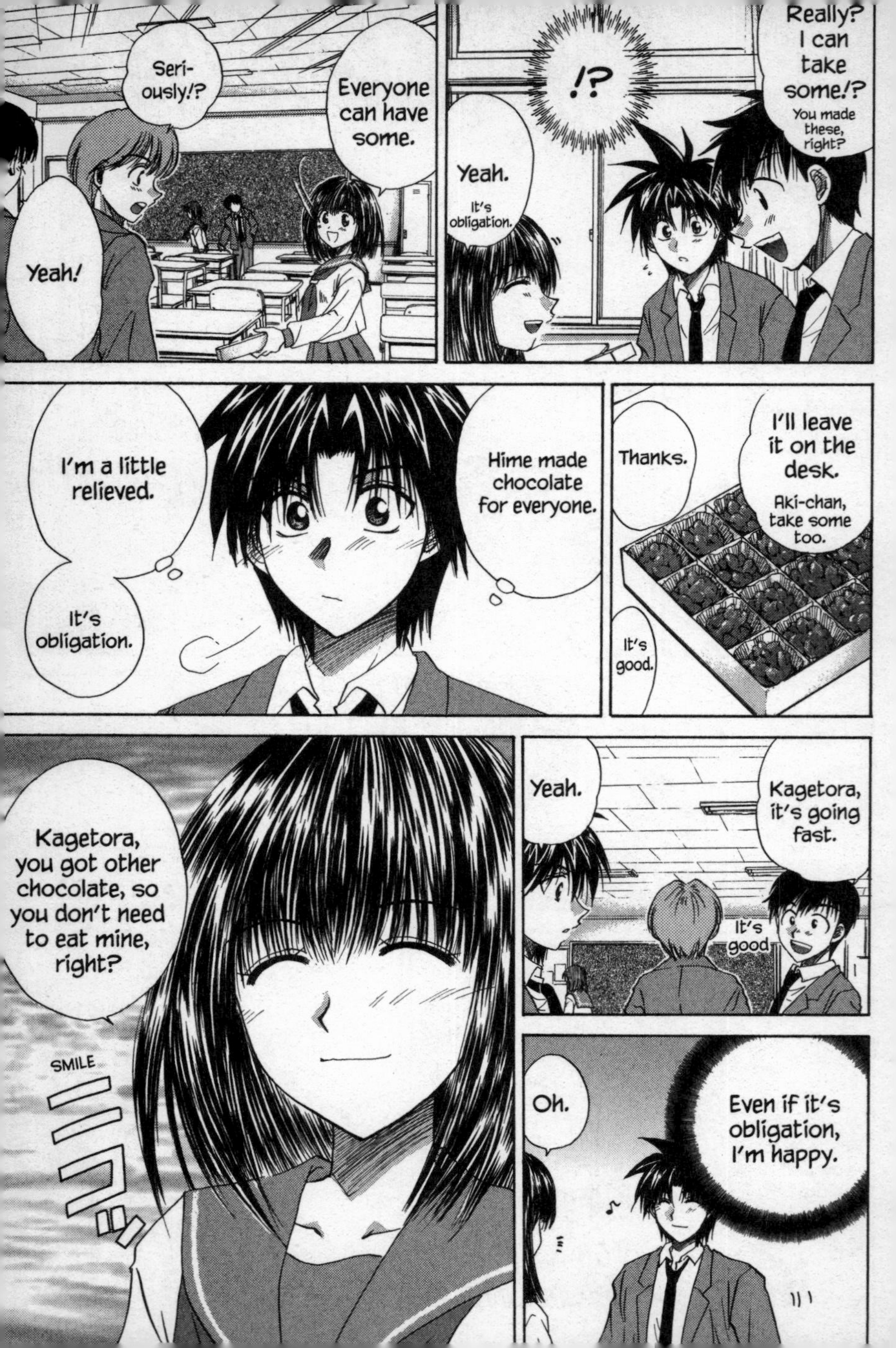

Really? I can take some!?
You made these, right?
!?
Yeah.
It's obligation.
Everyone can have some.
Seri-ously!?
Yeah!
I'll leave it on the desk.
Aki-chan, take some too.
Thanks.
It's good.
Hime made chocolate for everyone.
I'm a little relieved.
It's obligation.
Kagetora, it's going fast.
Yeah.
It's good
Even if it's obligation, I'm happy.
Oh.
Kagetora, you got other chocolate, so you don't need to eat mine, right?
SMILE

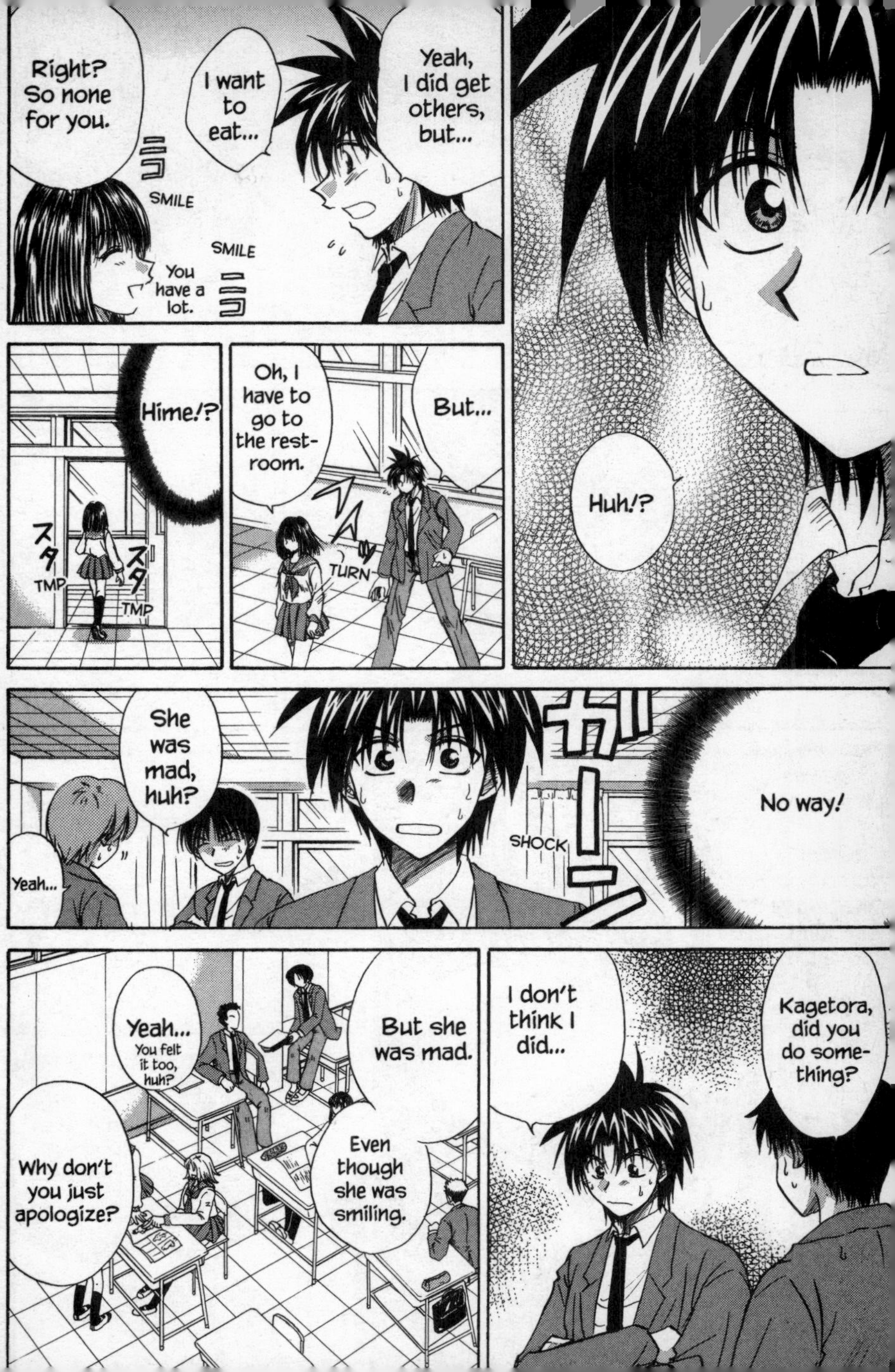
Huh!?
Yeah, I did get others, but...
I want to eat...
Right? So none for you.
ニコ
SMILE
SMILE
ニコ
You have a lot.
But...
Oh, I have to go to the rest-room.
TURN
Hime!?
スタ
TMP
スタ
TMP
No way!
SHOCK
She was mad, huh?
Yeah...
Kagetora, did you do some-thing?
I don't think I did...
But she was mad.
Even though she was smiling.
Yeah... You felt it too, huh?
Why don't you just apologize?

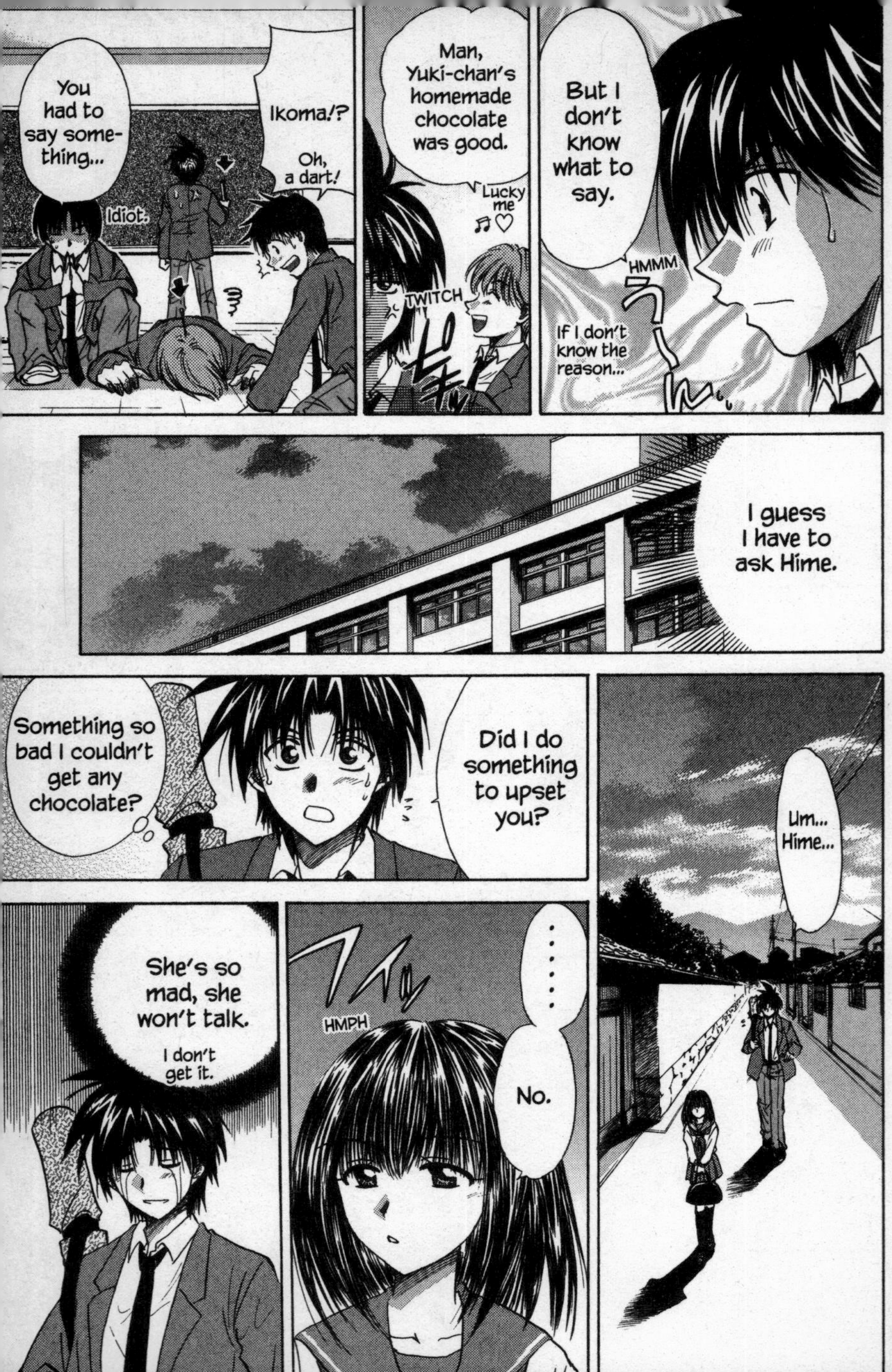

But I don't know what to say.
HMMM
If I don't know the reason...
Man, Yuki-chan's homemade chocolate was good.
Lucky me ♫♡
TWITCH
Ikoma!?
Oh, a dart!
You had to say something...
Idiot.
I guess I have to ask Hime.
Um... Hime...
Did I do something to upset you?
Something so bad I couldn't get any chocolate?
......
No.
HMPH
She's so mad, she won't talk.
I don't get it.

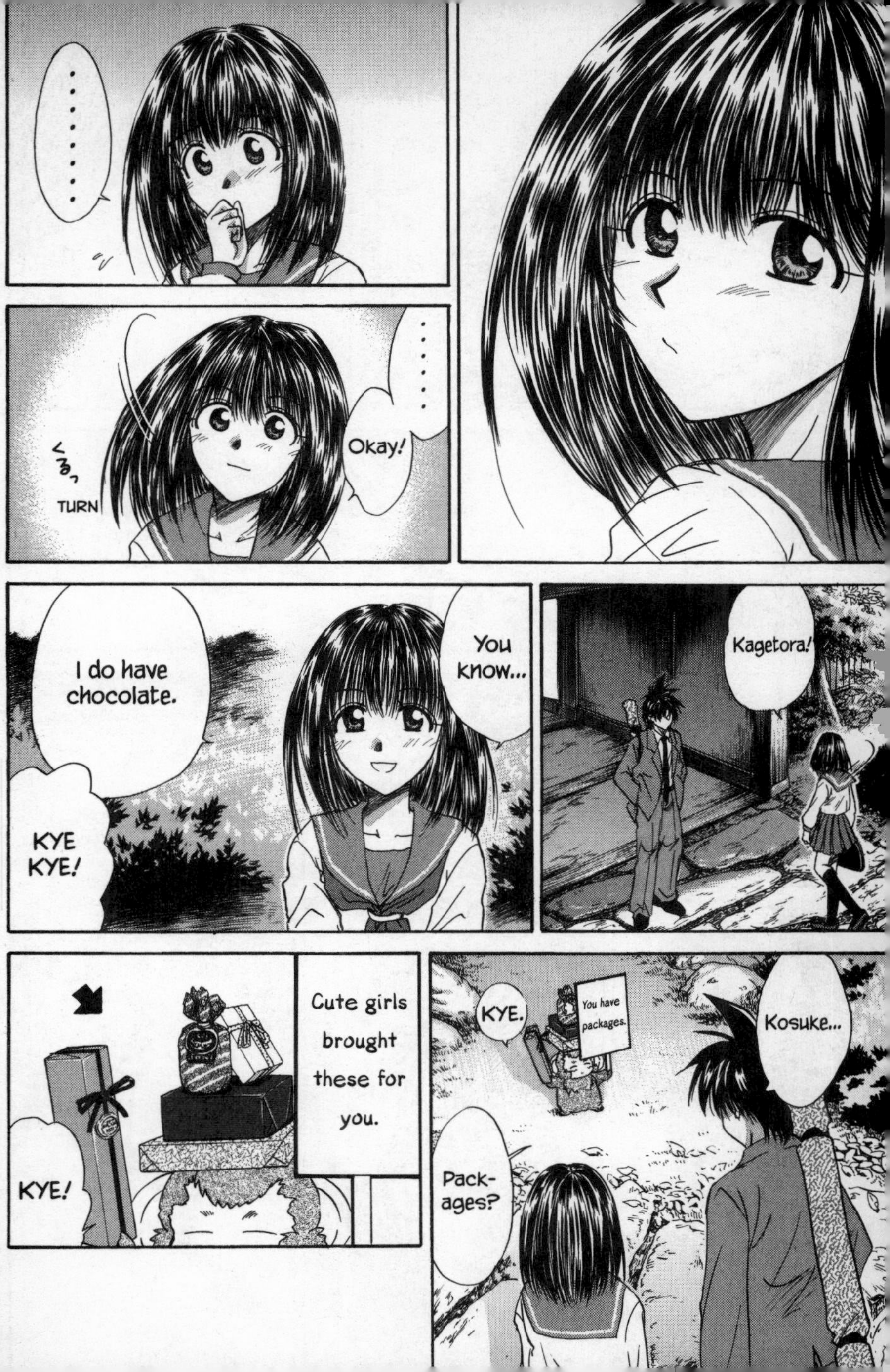
......
......
Okay!
くるっ
TURN
Kagetora!
You know...
I do have chocolate.
KYE KYE!
Kosuke...
You have packages.
KYE.
Pack-ages?
Cute girls brought these for you.
KYE!

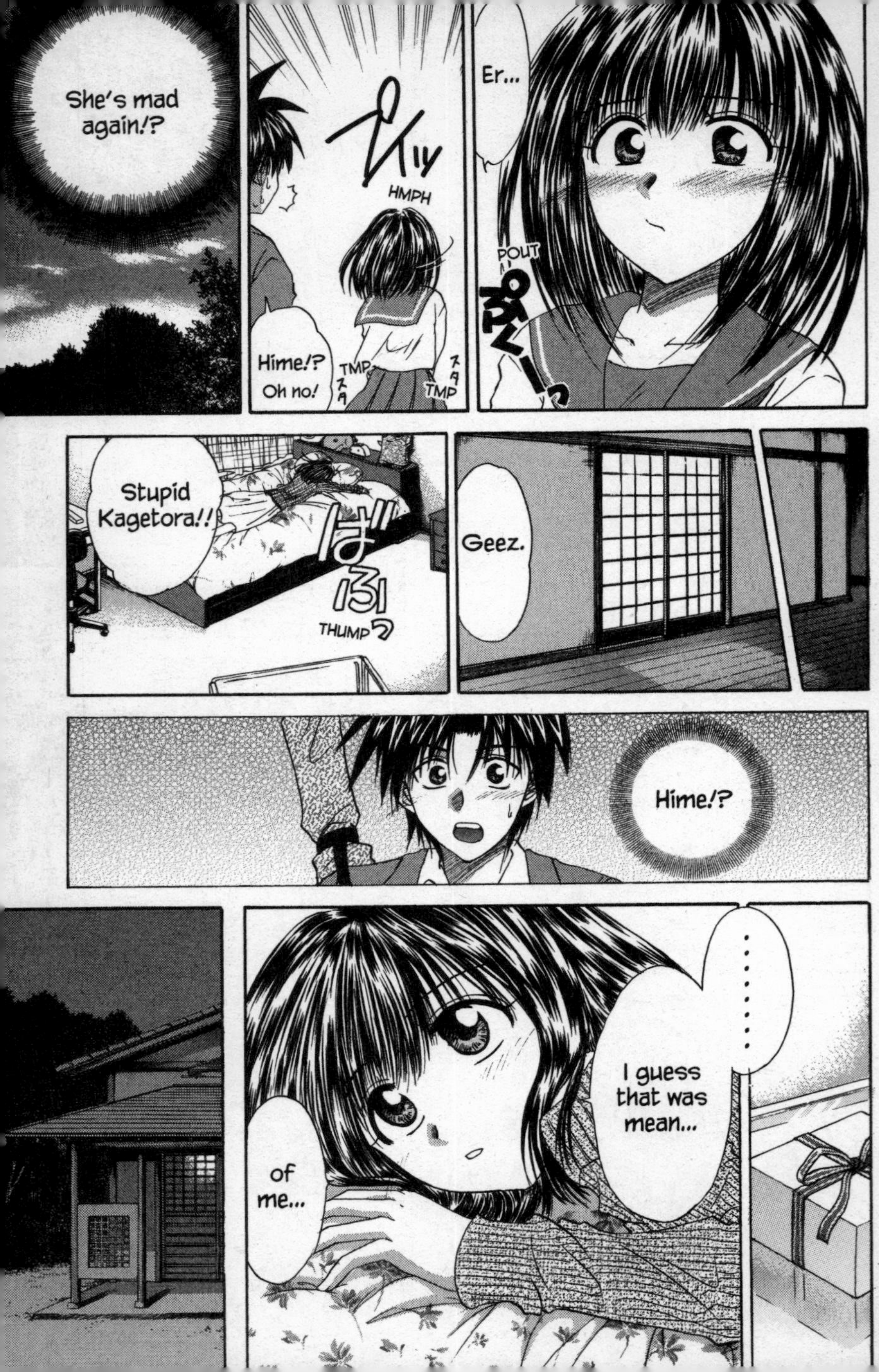
Er...
POUT
HMPH
Hime!?
Oh no!
TMP
TMP
She's mad again!?
Geez.
Stupid Kagetora!!
THUMP
Hime!?
......
I guess that was mean...
of me...

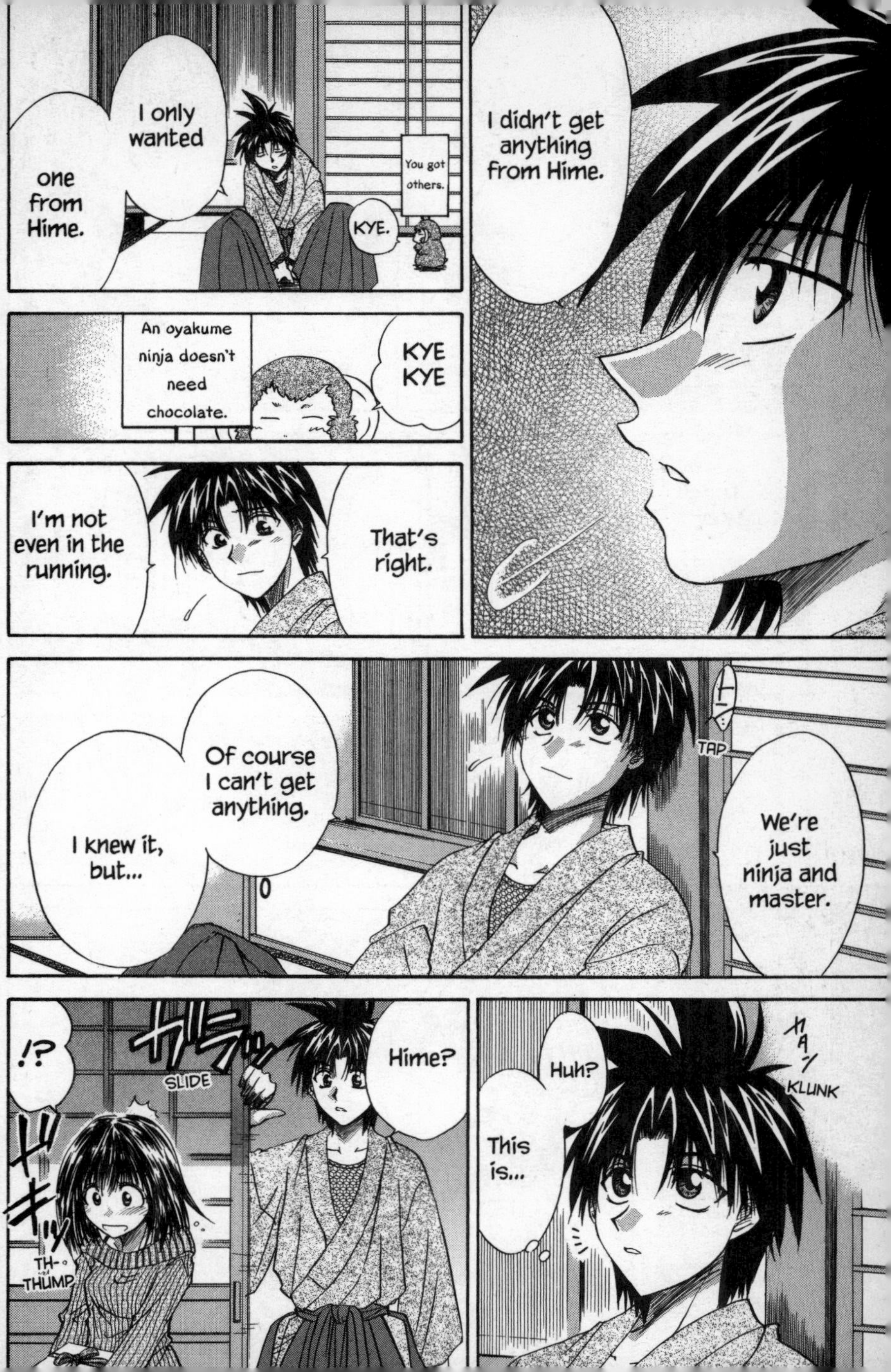

I didn't get anything from Hime.
I only wanted one from Hime.
You got others.
KYE.
An oyakume ninja doesn't need chocolate.
KYE KYE
That's right.
I'm not even in the running.
TAP
We're just ninja and master.
Of course I can't get anything.
I knew it, but...
KLUNK
Huh?
This is...
Hime?
SLIDE
!?
TH-THUMP

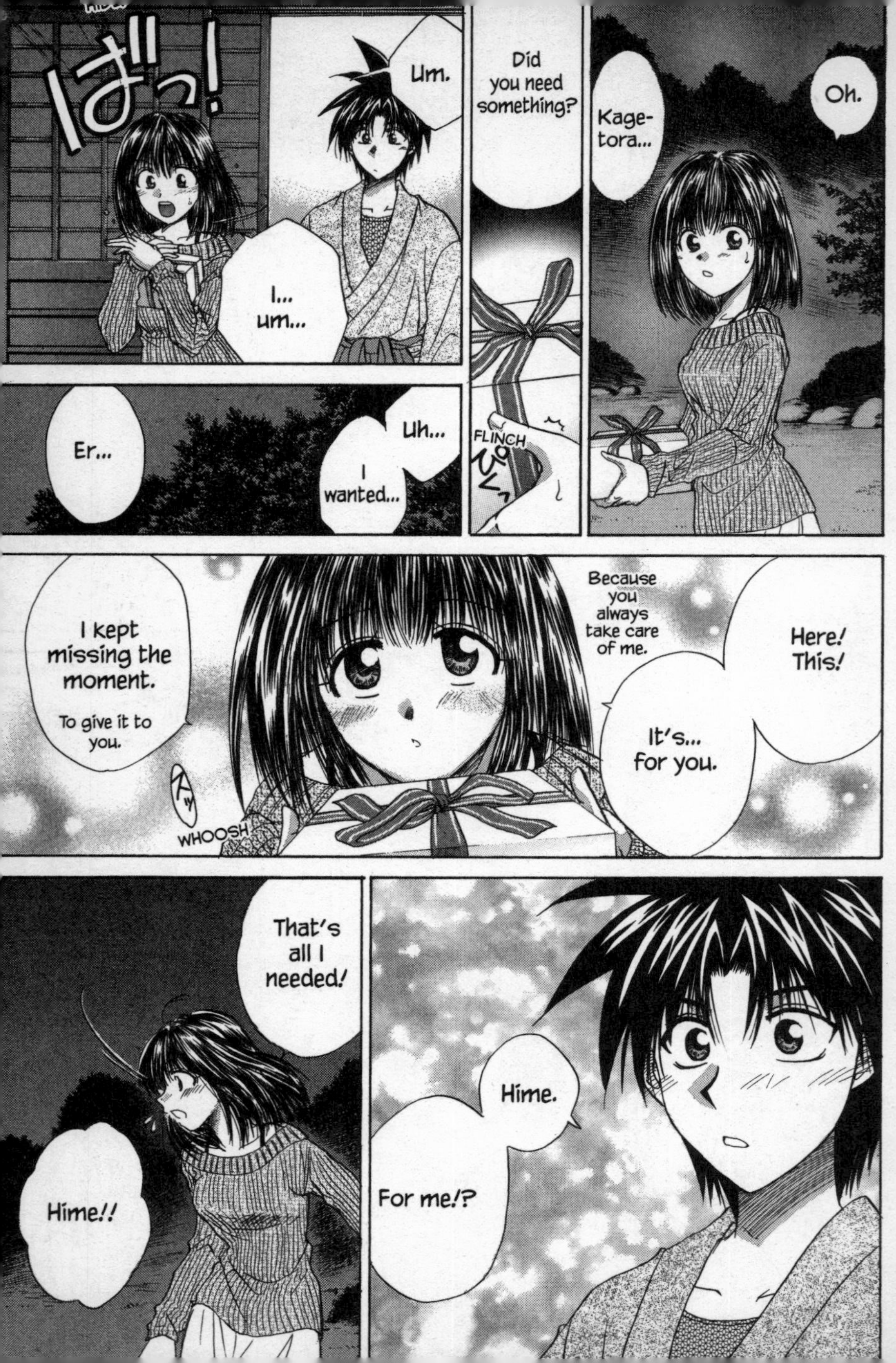
Oh.
Kage-tora...
Did you need something?
FLINCH
Um.
I... um...
Uh...
I wanted...
Er...
Here! This!
Because you always take care of me.
It's... for you.
I kept missing the moment.
To give it to you.
WHOOSH
Hime.
For me!?
That's all I needed!
Hime!!

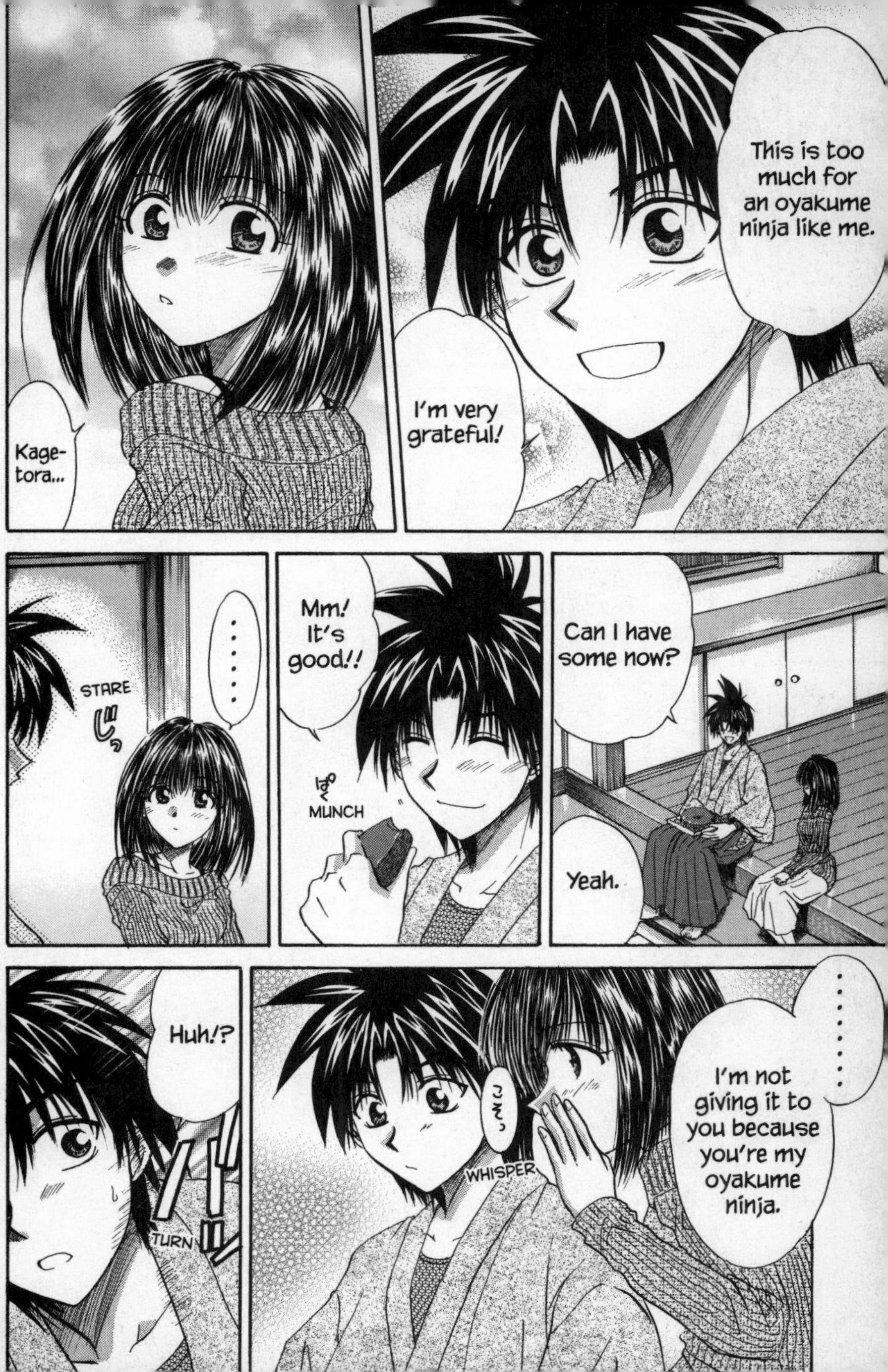
This is too much for an oyakume ninja like me.
I'm very grateful!
Kage-tora...
Can I have some now?
Yeah.
Mm! It's good!!
MUNCH
......
STARE
......
I'm not giving it to you because you're my oyakume ninja.
WHISPER
Huh!?
TURN

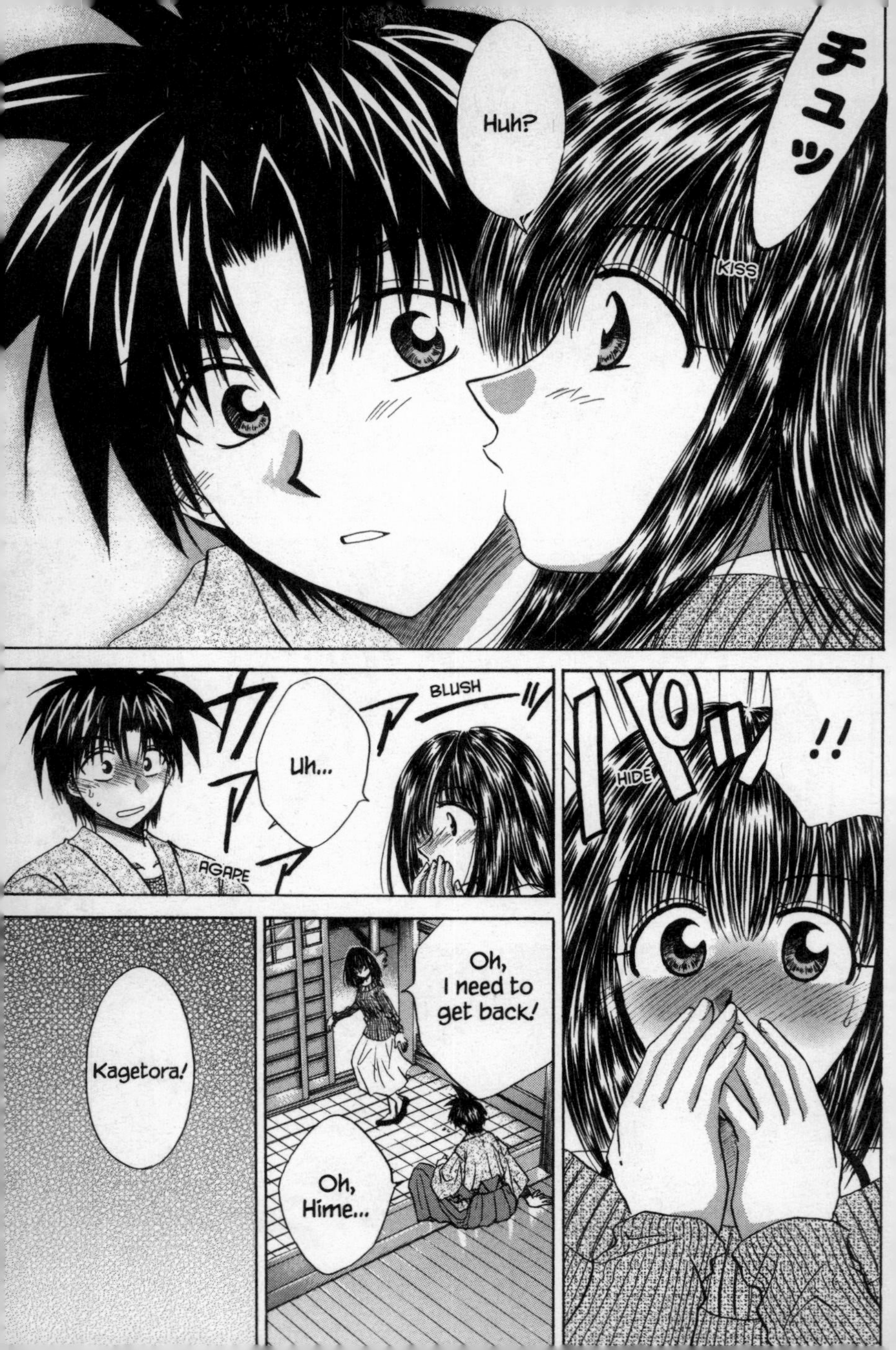
チュッ
KISS
Huh?
パッ
HIDE
!!
カァァァ
BLUSH
Uh...
AGAPE
Oh, I need to get back!
Oh, Hime...
Kagetora!

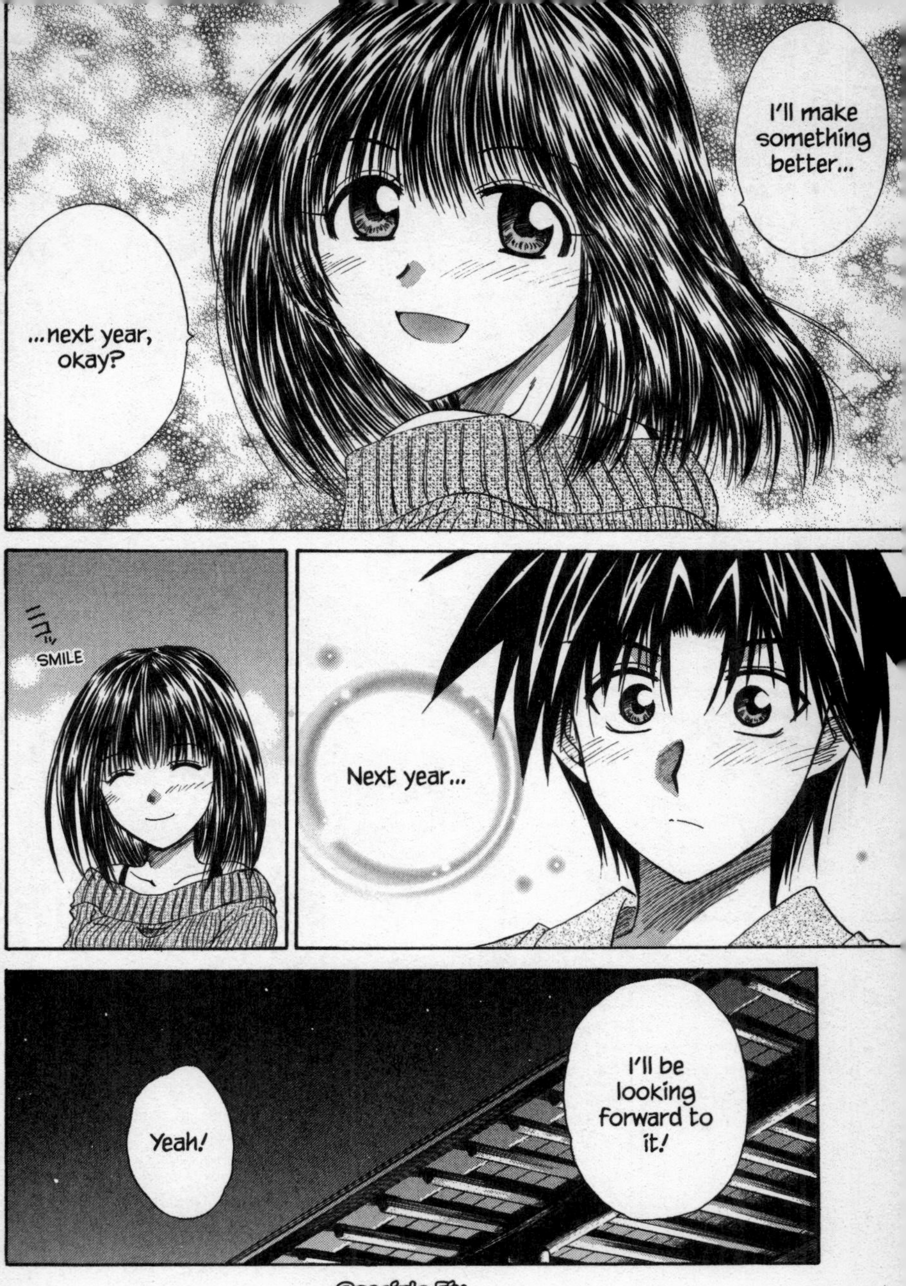
I'll make something better...
...next year, okay?
Next year...
SMILE
I'll be looking forward to it!
Yeah!

Specials Fin

Bonus Page

This is Segami. We're already in volume 8 and I'm pretty surprised I got this far. It's still going to continue, so please stay with me and enjoy. (laugh)

About Ninjas, Part 8

I've started to take lessons in ninja skills. (laugh) It's quite fun! It's just that I'm so out of shape, my body is creaking every lesson. It's different from karate and stuff because after you throw your opponent, you actually go and "kill" the opponent. Yeah, I guess ninjas would kill their opponent…

If this were real life, I don't know how many times I would've been killed…

The road to becoming a ninja is a long one…

About Traveling

I haven't gone just for pleasure. (cry) I've been to places only if I have stuff to do. I'd like to go somewhere and have it be 100% pleasure and 0% work!!

About Weapons

I get many questions on where I get my weapons, but I get them mostly from a gift shop in Kamakura. They do have ninja weapons at ninja-related facilities all over Japan. So good luck finding them!

Thank you

Thank you for all your letters! I hope by the time this volume is out, I'll have written back…I will continue working hard to write back. ♪

I'll see you again.

He appeared a lot this time. (laugh)

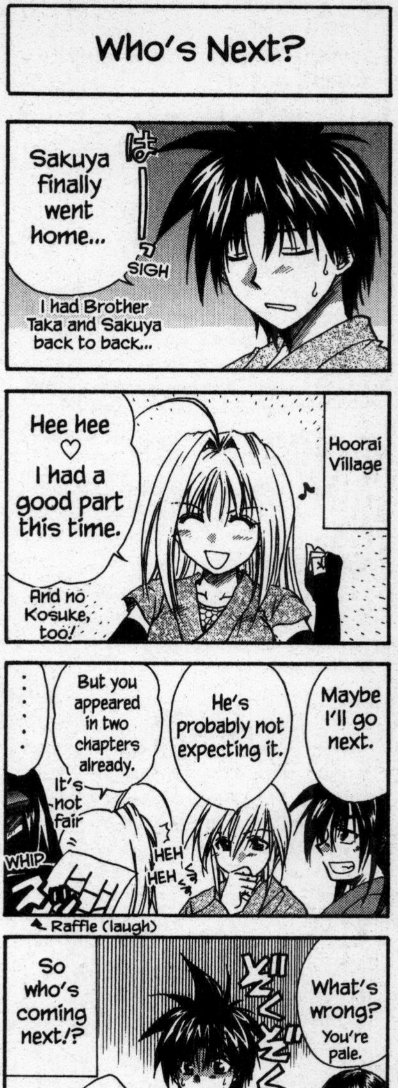
Who's Next?
はーっ
SIGH
Sakuya finally went home...
I had Brother Taka and Sakuya back to back...
Hoorai Village
Hee hee ♡ I had a good part this time.
And no Kosuke, too!
Maybe I'll go next.
He's probably not expecting it.
HEH HEH
But you appeared in two chapters already.
......
It's not fair
WHIP
Raffle (laugh)
What's wrong? You're pale.
SHIVER
So who's coming next!?
I don't know.

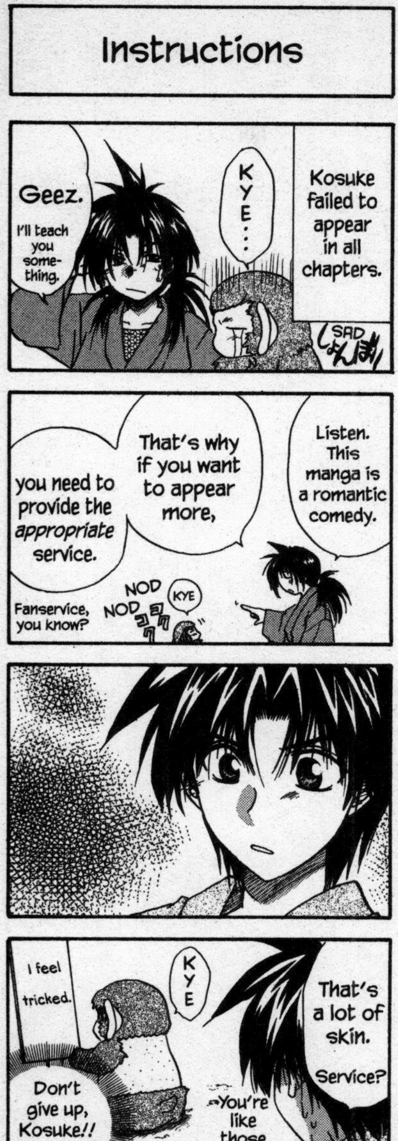
Instructions
Kosuke failed to appear in all chapters.
SAD しょんぼり
KYE...
Geez.
I'll teach you something.
Listen. This manga is a romantic comedy.
That's why if you want to appear more,
you need to provide the *appropriate* service.
KYE
NOD NOD
Fanservice, you know?
That's a lot of skin.
Service?
KYE
You're like those poodles.
I feel tricked.
Don't give up, Kosuke!!
You'll be the main character one day!!

Haircut done by Shiroumaru.

My Loving Car

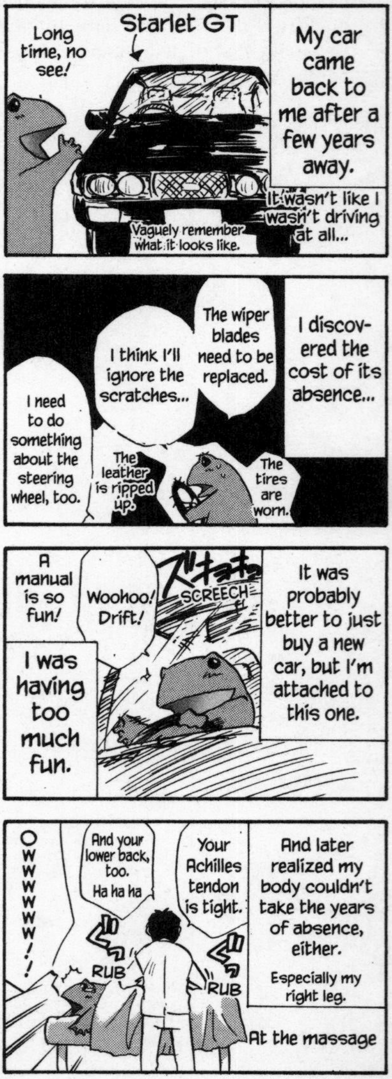

My car came back to me after a few years away.
It wasn't like I wasn't driving at all...
Starlet GT
Long time, no see!
Vaguely remember what it looks like.
I discovered the cost of its absence...
The wiper blades need to be replaced.
I think I'll ignore the scratches...
The tires are worn.
The leather is ripped up.
I need to do something about the steering wheel, too.
It was probably better to just buy a new car, but I'm attached to this one.
SCREECH
Woohoo! Drift!
A manual is so fun!
I was having too much fun.
And later realized my body couldn't take the years of absence, either.
Especially my right leg.
At the massage
Your Achilles tendon is tight.
RUB
And your lower back, too. Ha ha ha
RUB
OWWWWWW!!

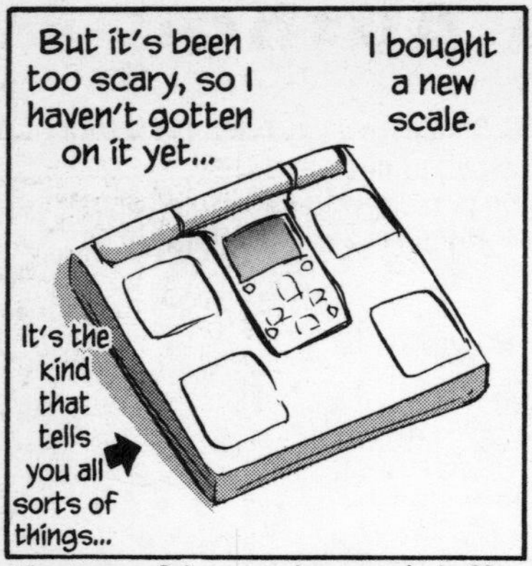

I bought a new scale.
But it's been too scary, so I haven't gotten on it yet...
It's the kind that tells you all sorts of things...

You know, fat percentage and stuff...

Special Thanks!

Assistant:	Tanaka-kun, Oshima-chan
Helper:	Keisui Takaeda-sama
Editor:	Mr. Morita
Comics Editor:	Houdo-san
All my readers	

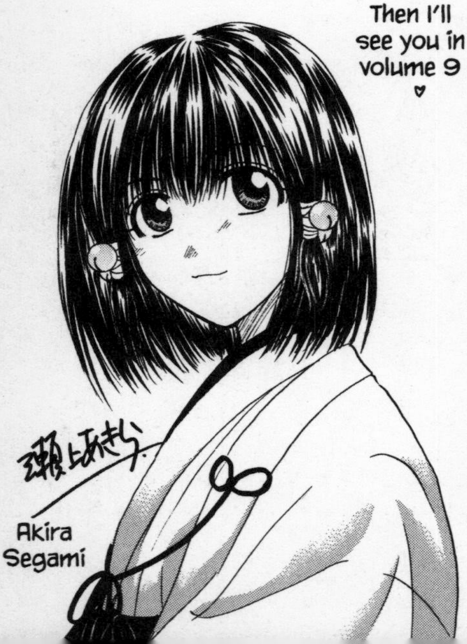

Then I'll see you in volume 9 ♡
Akira Segami

About the Author

Akira Segami's first manga was published by Shogakukan in 1996. He went on to do a few other small projects, including two short stories entitled "Kagetora" in 2001 and 2002. The character proved to be popular with fans, so Segami began his first ongoing series, Kagetora, with Kodansha in 2003. The series continues to run today.

Translation Notes

Japanese is a tricky language for most Westerners, and translation is often more art than science. For your edification and reading pleasure, here are notes on some of the places where we could have gone in a different direction in our translation of the work, or where a Japanese cultural reference is used.

Basho, page iv

Basho refers to Matsuo Basho, one of the greatest haiku (a poem on the subject of nature that uses 5-7-5 syllables) poets in Japanese history. The author is referring to a journey that Basho took that resulted in the poet's most famous journal, "The Narrow Road to the Deep North."

***Ohagi*, page 69**

Ohagi is a Japanese sweet dish made with sweet rice and covered with red beans. It is also known as *botamochi*, but the Japanese only call it *botamochi* when they eat it in the spring. *Ohagi* is the name for this dish when it is eaten in autumn.

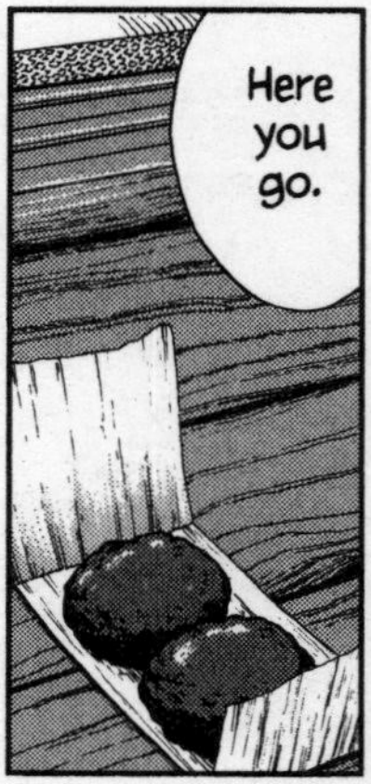
Here you go.

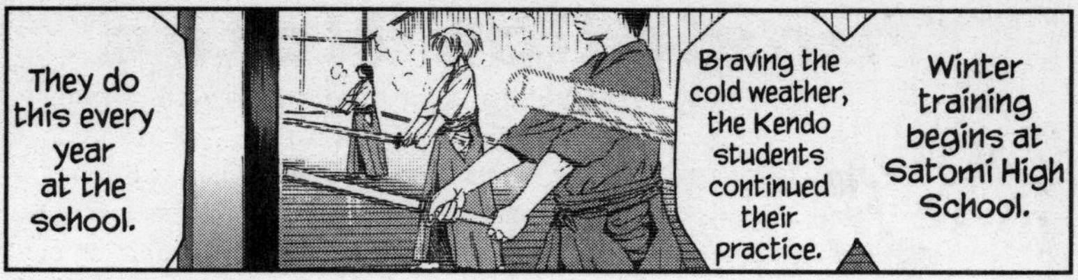
Winter training begins at Satomi High School.
Braving the cold weather, the Kendo students continued their practice.
They do this every year at the school.

Kendo, page 121

A sport/martial art similar to fencing. People use bamboo swords and fight wearing special protective gear.

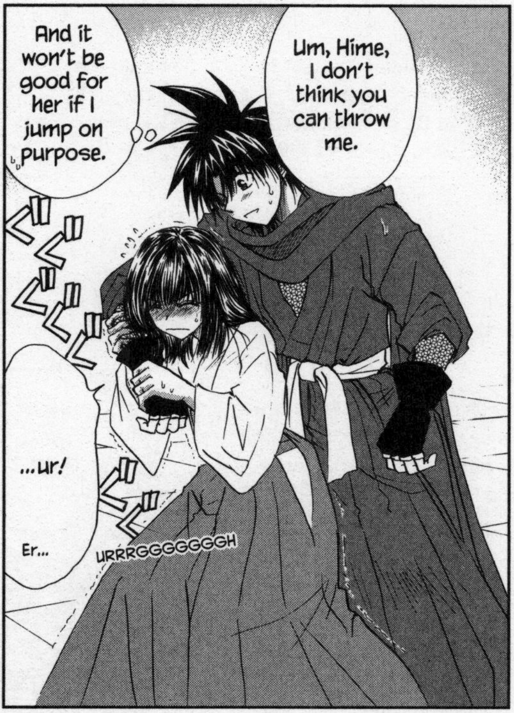
Um, Hime, I don't think you can throw me.
And it won't be good for her if I jump on purpose.
...ur!
Er...
URRRGGGGGGGH

Jujitsu, page 126

Jujitsu is a Japanese martial art, in which artists use the attacker's force and redirect it against them.

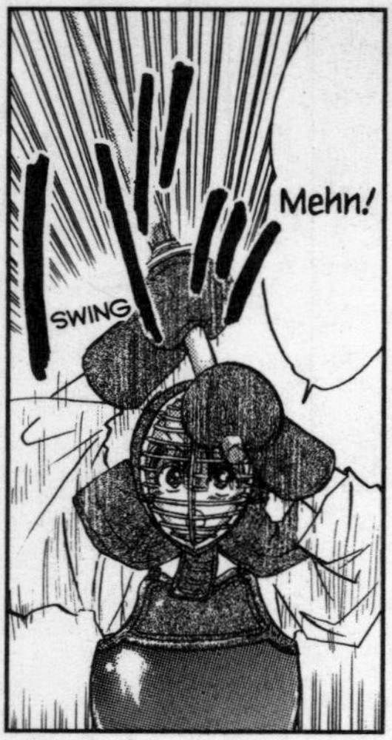
SWING
Mehn!

***Mehn*, page 127**

Mehn is a shout used in Kendo. It mean's "mask," and it refers to a move in kendo when the person shouting is aiming for the head.

***Naginata*, page 130**

A *naginata* is a long-handled sword. It looks like a spear with a short sword at the tip of it. In modern Japan, it is usually used in martial arts for women.

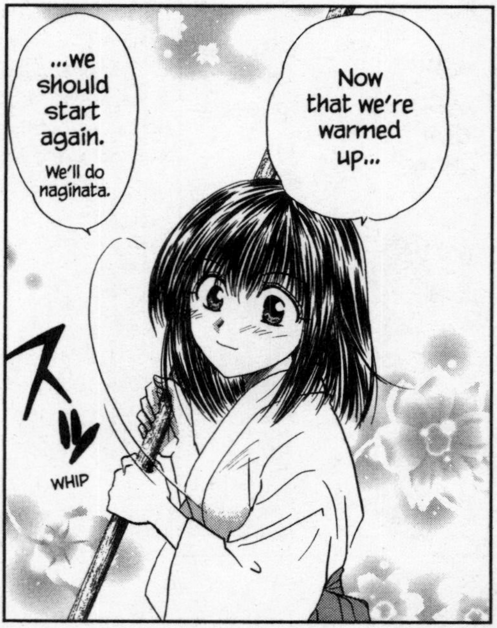
Now that we're warmed up...
...we should start again.
We'll do naginata.
スッ
WHIP

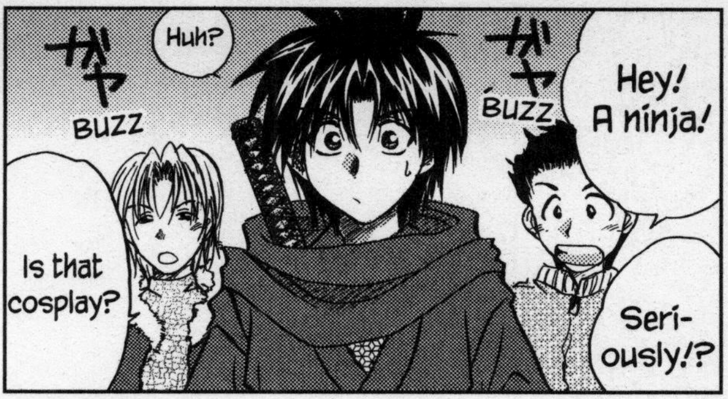
Hey! A ninja!
ガヤ BUZZ
Huh?
ガヤ BUZZ
Seri-ously!?
Is that cosplay?

Cosplay, page 150

Cosplay is a term invented in Japan, joining the two words "costume" and "play." It usually refers to a person who dresses up as a character from an anime or game.

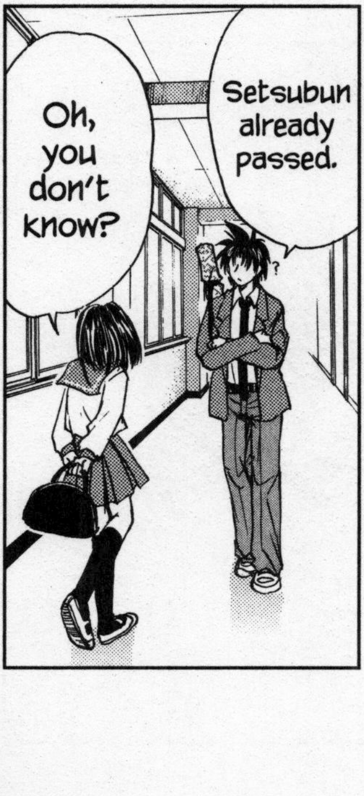
Setsubun already passed.
?
Oh, you don't know?

***Setsubun*, page 187**

Setsubun is the day before a new season begins. It usually refers to the beginning of spring, and is celebrated on February 3. Japanese people celebrate by throwing soybeans out the door, chanting "demons outside! Good fortune stay in!"

Kamakura, page 205

Kamakura is a city located in Kanagawa prefecture, which is southwest of Tokyo. It is a popular tourist spot because of all the temples and shrines and its beautiful beach.

School Rumble

BY JIN KOBAYASHI

SUBTLETY IS FOR WIMPS!

She . . . is a second-year high school student with a single all-consuming question: Will the boy she likes ever really notice her?

He . . . is the school's most notorious juvenile delinquent, and he's suddenly come to a shocking realization: He's got a huge crush, and now he must tell her how he feels.

Life-changing obsessions, colossal foul-ups, grand schemes, deep-seated anxieties, and raging hormones—School Rumble portrays high school as it really is: over-the-top comedy!

Ages: 16 +

Special extras in each volume! Read them all!

DRAGON EYE

BY KAIRI FUJIYAMA

HUMANITY'S SECRET WEAPON

Dracules—bloodthirsty, infectious monsters—have hunted human beings to the brink of extinction. Only the elite warriors of the VIUS Squad stand as humanity's last best hope.

Young Leila Mikami is one of the squad's most promising recruits, but she's not only training to battle the Dracules, she's determined to find the magical Dragon Eye, a weapon that will make her the most powerful warrior in the world.

Special extras in each volume! Read them all!

MANGA BY TORU ZEKU
ART BY YUNA TAKANAGI

DEFENDING THE NATURAL ORDER OF THE UNIVERSE!

The *shiki tsukai* are "Keepers of the Seasons"—magical warriors pledged to defend the planet's natural order against those who would threaten it.

When 14-year-old Akira Kizuki joins the *shiki tsukai*, he knows that it'll be a difficult life. But with his new friends and mentors, he's up to the challenge!

Special extras in each volume! Read them all!

TOMARE!

[STOP!]

You are going the wrong way!

Manga is a completely different
type of reading experience.

To start at the *beginning*, go to the *end!*

That's right! Authentic manga is read the traditional Japanese
way—from right to left. Exactly the *opposite* of how American
books are read. It's easy to follow: Just go to the other end of
the book, and read each page—and each panel—from right side
to left side, starting at the top right. Now you're experiencing
manga as it was meant to be.